NO ONE CAN STOP THE RAIN

NO ONE CAN STOP THE RAIN

Glimpses of Africa's Liberation Struggle

George M. Houser

Foreword by Julius K. Nyerere

The Pilgrim Press
NEW YORK

Printed in the United States of America

Photographs were taken by the author unless otherwise indicated.
Artwork is by James Dickerson.
Map on p. xxii is from *History of African Civilization* by E. Jefferson Murphy. Copyright © 1972 by E. Jefferson Murphy. Reprinted by permission of Harper & Row, Publishers, Inc.
Map on p. xxiii is from *Africa News* 29, no. 1 (January 1988). Used by permission.

Library of Congress Cataloging-in-Publication Data

Houser, George M.
   No one can stop the rain: glimpses of Africa's liberation struggle / by George M. Houser.
   Foreword by Julius K. Nyerere

   Includes index.
   ISBN 0-8298-0795-0
   1. Africa—Politics and government—1960–   .   2. National liberation movements—Africa.   3. Nationalism—Africa.   I. Title.
DT30.5.H68   1988
960'.32—dc19   88-19496
                                                         CIP

The Pilgrim Press, 132 West 31st Street, New York, N.Y. 10001

Here in prison
rage contained in my breast
I patiently wait
for the clouds to gather
blown by the wind of history.

No one
can stop the rain.

—Agostinho Neto,
Luanda prison,
July 1960

Contents

Contents

PART 3 YEARS OF TURMOIL 133

Foreword

I **have known** George Houser for a long time, and through him the American Committee on Africa. We first met in the 1950s, when I went to the United Nations as a "Petitioner" seeking support for the independence struggle of my country, which was then the United Nations Trust Territory of Tanganyika administered by the United Kingdom.

On my first visit to the United Nations the U.S. government gave me a peculiar visa, which was of very short duration and limited me to a specified radius from the United Nations Headquarters! It was George Houser who introduced me to people who supported the African anti-colonial struggle. Through him I learned that not all American people acquiesced in decisions of the American government, which seemed to us to be backing up Tanganyika's government at that time—that is, the British colonial power. Indeed, through him and his colleagues in the ACOA, I was able to make contact with many sympathetic Americans, including politicians. I got a practical insight into American democracy at work and its openness.

To George Houser and his colleagues I must in the 1950s have been just one among many African leaders from the different colonial territories of Africa. But each of us was received with friendship and respect—a not unimportant matter, especially in those days when racial discrimination was a common experience in the colonial countries. All of us who came to the United Nations or the United States during our campaigning for independence received help and encouragement from the ACOA.

As far as I know, the committee had no money to give us nationalist leaders, but that was not what we wanted, either for ourselves or our parties. What it gave us was a knowledge that we were not alone in the world, that on the contrary our demand for independence had sympathy and support in a very powerful country. With ACOA members and friends we could sometimes talk over political problems arising during the struggle and gain a new perspective on them. And from them we could rely upon a continuing educational process within the United States itself—about colonialism, about Africa, and about the independence movement. They were a small group, without resources to break into the news media. But they went quietly forward, and they did gather political support for our cause.

This work has continued. Since the 1950s I have met George Houser many times, usually in Africa. From my colleagues in other countries—those who are now leaders of their nations and many others who played an honourable part in the independence struggles—I know that George and the committee have continued to be active and supportive. He has a fascinating story to tell.

This story is one that should be told, because it is unfinished. Namibia is not yet free. South Africa is still suffering under the oppression of apartheid. The peoples of both countries are fighting for freedom with ever increased intensity despite South Africa's state terrorism and the constant threat or actuality of imprisonment, torture, and death. The need for continued (and indeed intensified) moral, political, and material support from friends in America and Europe as well as Africa has never been greater.

There are now many other very active antiapartheid organizations in America and Europe, which are doing a very good job. But the foundations for their work were laid by those people who were active on these issues in the 1940s, 1950s, and early 1960s—people like George Houser.

There is another reason why George's story should be told. The independent countries of Africa are now almost all in deep economic trouble; some still have serious internal political problems that have resulted in violent conflict or dictatorships. An understanding of the political problems faced during the independence struggles, and of the personalities of those days, can help to make these current problems more comprehensible to people who get from their newspapers and television screens only stories of bad news from Africa, often laced with contempt for the leaders and peoples of our continent.

It is a pleasure to me to have this opportunity to say thank you to George Houser and his colleagues in the American Committee for Africa. This is a book written by George, without any input from me or—as far as I know—from anyone else in Africa. So it is an American story and an American view of some political events in Africa during the last few decades. But it is also the view as perceived by a human being who respects other human beings and believes that it is the duty of all of us to work—in our own way and our own context and within our own limitations—for the promotion of justice and human dignity and respect everywhere. It is a story written by someone who tried to carry out that duty—and none of us can do more.

Most of Africa is now independent—politically. There is very much that remains to be done, in very many spheres, to convert that political independence into the reality of freedom and dignity for all Africa's people. As we in our part of the world have learned to say—*a luta continua*. The struggle continues.

MWALIMU JULIUS K. NYERERE

Preface

I **have written** this volume from the perspective of one who has spent more than 30 years of his life concerned with developments in Africa. I find, in retrospect, that my experience falls into four phases, each one corresponding roughly to a phase of recent African history. So I have divided my writing about Africa into four parts.

The first, "The Gathering Rain Clouds," reflects Africa under colonial domination and my introduction to it.

The second, "The Winds of Change," deals with the relatively uncomplicated period of Africa's progress toward independence and with the growth of anticolonial movements. There was an aura of excitement and optimism during this phase and recognition that something special was being born.

The third part, "Years of Turmoil," deals with the traumatic period that began in mid-1960 with the independence of the Congo. The major international powers became involved. Guerrilla warfare was adopted as a necessity by those engaged in the liberation struggle. Division among African movements and leaders foretold conflicts destined to continue long after the colonial powers had left.

The fourth part, "The Final Conflict," begins with the military coup in Portugal in 1974, which overthrew the dictatorial regime established by Salazar. It opened the way for the independence of Portuguese colonies and quickened the struggle for independence in Zimbabwe. Conflict developed in Western Sahara as Spain relinquished its control. The superpowers were increasingly drawn into a contest on the African continent, focusing on Angola and South Africa.

The final chapter, "You've Got to Take the Long View," forms a conclusion.

It is not that these four phases differ totally from one another; yet they show enough contrast to provide a convenient framework for looking at historical events, corresponding changes in U.S. policy, and the changing character of my own experiences. I hope that this approach may add to an understanding of events in Africa, as well as of the context within which U.S. policy has developed and been carried out.

Obviously this book does not pretend to be a history, nor does it consistently trace developments in any given country, even within the time span of my own activity. Rather, as its subtitle suggests, it attempts to give glimpses into the struggle for independence in Africa based on my own experiences and observations.

GEORGE M. HOUSER

Acknowledgments

A couple of years before I retired from the American Committee on Africa (ACOA), I had lunch with Dr. Howard Spragg, a Union Theological Seminary classmate, who was then executive vice president of the Board for Homeland Ministries of the United Church of Christ. We talked about our plans for the future. I said I would like to spend some time writing about my experiences with organizations and individuals in Africa's struggle for independence. Howard was very interested and suggested that I be in touch with him when the time came.

When I was ready, Howard gave me an essential boost with a grant for initial research. Subsequently came the arrangement with the Pilgrim Press, associated with the Board for Homeland Ministries, to publish my manuscript. I am deeply grateful to Howard and the board for their assistance.

I also want to express my gratitude to others who have helped me along the way. A grant from the Ford Foundation made it possible for me to spend several months plodding through the mass of files of the ACOA and the Africa Fund to put them in minimal order for use in research. In early 1982 the files were deposited with the Amistad Research Center in New Orleans, where they could receive professional attention. I am grateful to Dr. Clifton Johnson, director of Amistad, for making all the facilities of the center available to me.

Peter and Cora Weiss helped enormously through the Fund for Tomorrow, which provided a grant to cover incidental travel and typing costs. I was also given a grant for research through Dr. George Shepherd of the Graduate School of International Studies of the University of Denver.

I owe a debt of gratitude to my colleagues at the ACOA for giving freely of their time in discussion and checking facts and for permission to use the title of a pamphlet on Angola, which I co-authored in 1975, as the title for this book.

I have had a happy relationship with the Pilgrim Press during the writing of this book. Discussions with Larry E. Kalp, editor-in-chief, have been most helpful. Susan C. Winslow, the consultant with whom I worked, has won my admiration for the meticulous care with which she has edited and tightened my manuscript without changing my meaning.

On the whole I was not able to do what I would have liked to—submit the manuscript to many of my friends and co-workers, authorities on African affairs, for suggestions and corrections. A few friends did look at limited sections of the manuscript—Prof. John Marcum of the University of California, Santa Cruz; Rev. Larry Henderson, for more than 20 years a missionary in Angola; Mrs. Janet Mondlane of Mozambique; Gil Fernandes, first ambassador of Guinea-Bissau to the United States; and Ambassador Mohammed Sahnoun of Algeria. I am grateful for their suggestions.

In addition, I wish to thank my friend and neighbor James Dickerson, whose artistry was of great help in preparing symbolic line drawings and the cover. I know that he gave generously of his time and talent because of his support for the liberation struggle in Africa.

Two individuals have been most critical to this writing and to them I am especially indebted. The first is Karen Rothmyer, assistant professor at the Columbia University School of Journalism. For two years she was one of my co-workers at the ACOA and the Africa Fund. She more than anyone else gave me editorial advice. She read the manuscript in bits and pieces and finally the whole. Her knowledge of African affairs and her writing skills were invaluable as she gave me sound advice on where my emphases should lie.

The other person is my wife, Jean. She not only typed the manuscript in its various phases, becoming something of an expert on the computer in the process, but gave essential advice on content, structure, and grammar as well. She also kept me going when I occasionally weakened in my resolve to finish the work.

Finally I owe eternal thanks to my host of African friends, many of whose names appear in the pages of this book. I am especially indebted to Mwalimu Julius K. Nyerere, who honors me by his foreword to this book. I hope my many references to him in these pages properly reflect the fact that there is no African leader for whom I have more admiration.

Parties, Movements, and Organizations

AFRICAN COUNTRIES

ALGERIA (1962)*

ALN	National Liberation Army (Armée de Liberation Nationale)
CRUA	Revolutionary Committee of Unity and Action (Comité Revolutionnaire d'Unité et d'Action)
FLN	National Liberation Front (Front de Liberation Nationale)
GPRA	Provisional Government of the Algerian Republic (Gouvernement Provisoire de la République Algerienne)
MTLD	Movement for the Triumph of Democratic Liberties (Mouvement pour le Triomphe des Libertés Démocratiques)
PPA	Party of the Algerian People (Parti du Peuple Algérien)

ANGOLA (1975)

ALIAZO	Zombo People's Alliance (Alliance des Ressortissants de Zombo)
ERA	Emergency Relief to Angola (ACOA project)
FNLA	National Front for the Liberation of Angola (Frente Nacional de Libertação de Angola)
GRAE	Revolutionary Government of Angola in Exile (Govêrno Revolucionário de Angola no Exilio)
MFA	Armed Forces Movement (Movimento das Forças Armadas, in Portugal)
MPLA	Popular Movement for the Liberation of Angola (Movimento Popular de Libertação de Angola)
PDA	Democratic Party of Angola (Partido Democrático de Angola)
SARA	Service for the Assistance of Angolan Refugees (Serviço de Assistência aos Refugiados de Angola)
UNITA	National Union for the Total Independence of Angola (União Nacional para a Independência Total de Angola)
UPA	Union of the Peoples of Angola (União das Populações de Angola)
UPNA	Union of the Peoples of Northern Angola (União das Populações do Norte de Angola)

*Dates indicate year of independence.

CAMEROONS (1960; *formerly* FRENCH CAMEROONS)

UPC   Union of the Peoples of the Cameroons (Union des
               Populations Camerounaises)

GHANA (1957; *formerly* GOLD COAST)

CPP   Convention People's Party
MAP   Moslem Association Party
NPP   Northern People's Party
UGCC   United Gold Coast Convention

GUINEA-BISSAU (1974; *formerly* PORTUGUESE GUINEA)

FARP   People's Revolutionary Armed Forces (Forces Armées
               Révolutionnaires du Peuple)
PAIGC   African Party for the Independence of Guinea and Cape
               Verde (Partido Africano de Independéncia de Guiné e
               Cabo Verde)

KENYA (1963)

AEMO   African Elected Members' Organization
KAU   Kenya African Union
LEGCO   Legislative Council
NPCP   Nairobi People's Convention Party

MALAWI (1964; *formerly* NYASALAND)

NAC   Nyasaland African Congress

MOZAMBIQUE (1975)

COREMO   Revolutionary Committee of Mozambique (Comité
               Révolucionário de Moçambique)
FRELIMO   Mozambique Liberation Front (Frente de Libertação
               Moçambique)
MANU   Mozambique African National Union
MNR or   Mozambique National Resistence (Resistência Nacional de
  RENAMO   Moçambique)
UDENAMO   National Democratic Union of Mozambique (União
               Democrática Nacional de Moçambique)

UNAMI   African National Union of Independent Mozambique
(União Nacional Africana de Moçambique Independente)

NAMIBIA (*called* SOUTHWEST AFRICA *before 1968*)

CANU	Caprivi African National Union
DTA	Democratic Turnhalle Alliance
ONC	Ovambo National Congress
OPO	Ovamboland People's Organization
SWANLA	South West African Native Labor Association
SWANU	South West African National Union
SWAPO	South West Africa People's Organization
UNTAG	UN Transitional Assistance Group

NIGERIA (1960)

AG	Action Group
NCNC	National Council of Nigeria and the Cameroons
NPC	Northern People's Congress

SENEGAL (1960)

RDA	African Democratic Rally (Rassemblement Démocratique Africain)

SOUTH AFRICA (1910)

ANC	African National Congress
BPC	Black Peoples' Convention
NUSAS	National Union of South African Students
PAC	Pan Africanist Congress
SAIC	South African Indian Congress
SANROC	South African Non-Racial Olympic Committee
SASA	South African Students' Association
SASO	South African Students' Organization
SSRC	Soweto Students' Representative Council
UDF	United Democratic Front

UNITED REPUBLIC OF TANZANIA (1961; *formerly* TANGANYIKA)

TANU	Tanganyika African National Union

WESTERN SAHARA (*called* SPANISH SAHARA *before* 1976)

POLISARIO	Popular Front for the Liberation of Saguia el Hamra and Rio de Oro (Frente Popular para la Liberación de Saguia el Hamra y Rio de Oro)
SADR	Saharan Arab Democratic Republic (La République Arabe Sahraouie Démocratique)

ZAIRE (1965; *formerly* BELGIAN CONGO, *then* DEMOCRATIC REPUBLIC OF THE CONGO)

ABAKO	Association for the Preservation of Culture and Interests of the Bakongo (Association des Bakongo)
BALUBAKAT	Katanga Baluba Association
CONAKAT	Confederation of Tribal Association of Katanga (Conféderátion des Associations Tribales du Katanga)
MNC	National Congolese Movement (Mouvement Nationale Congolais)

ZAMBIA (1964; *formerly* NORTHERN RHODESIA)

NRANC	Northern Rhodesia African National Congress
UNIP	United National Independence Party
ZANC	Zambia African National Congress

ZIMBABWE (1980; *formerly* SOUTHERN RHODESIA)

ANC	African National Congress (see SRANC)
ANC	African National Council (later the UANC, United African National Council)
FROLIZI	Front for the Liberation of Zimbabwe
NDP	National Democratic Party
PCC	People's Caretaker Council
PF	Patriotic Front
SRANC	Southern Rhodesia African National Congress
UANC	(see ANC)
ZANLA	Zimbabwe African National Liberation Army
ZANU	Zimbabwe African National Union
ZAPU	Zimbabwe African People's Union
ZIPRA	Zimbabwe People's Revolutionary Army

ALL-AFRICAN BODIES

AAPC	All African People's Conference
AATUF	All African Trade Union Federation
CONCP	Conference of Nationalist Organizations of Portuguese

Colonies (Conferência das Organizações Nacionalistas das Colónias Portuguêsas)

OAU	Organization of African Unity
PAFMECA	Pan African Freedom Movement of East and Central Africa (later PAFMECSA with the addition of southern Africa)
SADCC	Southern African Development Coordination Conference

UNITED STATES

AASF	African American Students' Foundation
ACOA	American Committee on Africa
AFL-CIO	American Federation of Labor-Congress of Industrial Organizations
AFSAR	Americans for South African Resistance
ASA	African Studies Association
CIA	Central Intelligence Agency
COBLSA	Campaign to Oppose Bank Loans to South Africa (ACOA project)
CORE	Congress of Racial Equality
FOR	Fellowship of Reconciliation
ILGWU	International Ladies' Garment Workers Union
NAACP	National Association for the Advancement of Colored People
NCCJ	National Council of Christians and Jews
UAW	United Auto Workers

INTERNATIONAL BODIES

AAPSO	Afro-Asian Peoples' Solidarity Organization
EEC	European Economic Community
ICFTU	International Confederation of Free Trade Unions
ICJ	International Court of Justice (World Court)
IOC	International Olympic Committee
NATO	North Atlantic Treaty Organization
WFTU	World Federation of Trade Unions

MOROCCO
(FR.)

TUNISIA (FR.)

ALGERIA
(FR.)

LIBYA
(ITAL.)

EGYPT

SPANISH SAHARA

MAURITANIA

SOUDAN

NIGER

FRENCH WEST AFRICA

CHAD

ANGLO-EGYPTIAN
SUDAN

ERITREA (ITAL.)

FRENCH
SOMALILAND

BRITISH
SOMALILAND

GAMBIA
(BR.)

SENEGAL

GUINEA

UPPER VOLTA

NIGERIA
(BR.)

FRENCH EQUATORIAL AFRICA

ETHIOPIA

ITALIAN SOMALILAND

PORTUGUESE
GUINEA

IVORY
COAST

GOLD COAST (BR.)

TOGO

DAHOMEY

CENTRAL AFRICAN
REPUBLIC

SIERRA
LEONE
(BR.)

LIBERIA

BR. TOGO

BR. CAMEROUNS

SPANISH GUINEA

CAMEROUN

UGANDA
(BR.)

KENYA
(BR.)

GABON

CONGO

RUANDA-URUNDI
(BELG.)

BELGIAN CONGO
(BELG.)

TANGANYIKA
(BR.)

ZANZIBAR (BR.)

CABINDA
(PORT.)

ANGOLA
(PORT.)

NORTHERN
RHODESIA
(BR.)

MOZAMBIQUE (PORT.)

NYASALAND
(BR.)

MADAGASCAR
(FR.)

Broken lines indicate borders appearing after
1945 or in existence as administrative units.

SOUTH-WEST
AFRICA
(S. AFR.)

BECHUANALAND
(BR.)

SOUTHERN
RHODESIA
(BR.)

SWAZILAND
(BR.)

UNION OF
SOUTH AFRICA

BASUTOLAND
(BR.)

Africa 1945

Africa 1987

THE GATHERING
RAIN CLOUDS

It was still dark at 4:30 A.M. when I was awakened by someone softly calling my name. "George, George, it's almost time to leave." It had been a short night. I had arrived only the evening before at the small Sahara town of Tindouf in western Algeria as the guest of POLISARIO (Popular Front for the Liberation of Saguia el Hamra and Rio de Oro, the two parts of Western Sahara). In the low-lying reception center, my companions and I were shielded from the whistling wind and blowing sand. Although it was cool outside, I was quite comfortable lying fully clothed on blankets on the concrete flour. It was Sunday, November 4, 1979.

A quick splash of water on my face at a nearby well, a cursory brushing of teeth, and I was ready for the ride into Western Sahara with the POLISARIO guerrillas. They had been involved in a desert war against the occupying forces of Morocco in Western Sahara ever since Spain gave up control of the area in early 1976. Three weeks before I arrived, their forces had won an important battle and driven Moroccan forces out of Mahbes, until then the easternmost Saharan town still occupied by Morocco. Our objective was to visit Mahbes.

After hastily eating some bread and drinking some highly sweetened tea, 12 of us took our places in two Spanish Santanas for the three-hour trip. The POLISARIO men carried rifles. The only other non-Saharan was a Spanish journalist. Day was just breaking as we headed west, following only tracks in the sand. There were no roads. As we sped along at amazing speed, I could not help briefly wondering about a possible Moroccan attack. The evening before I had signed a waiver of responsibility for the Algerian government in case of any sort of "accident." Five months earlier I had spent almost two weeks with POLISARIO and only seen Moroccan planes flying very high. So this time I felt like something of a veteran.

By the time we reached Mahbes, the sun was bright and warm. There had been no road signs for Mahbes. Our Santanas just went over the brink of a barren hill and there, all of a sudden, a few hundred yards distant was what had once been a desert town, marked by an abandoned water tower, low buildings, and a walled area that was formerly a Spanish military post.

The place was absolutely deserted except for a few scrawny dogs. On the side of a building, written in Arabic, was the Moroccan slogan "For God, King, and Country." But the basic impression was of destruction. Trucks were turned over and burnt. Coke cases clearly marked "Casablanca," damaged helmets, spent bullets, and empty ammunition boxes were strewn around. In poorly constructed bunkers were the Moroccan soldiers' personal effects—books, papers, and letters postmarked Morocco.

After wandering around for a while, we piled into one of the vehicles and drove a few hundred yards to what must have been the center of the fighting on the perimeter of the town. Here there were trenches and, what I was not really prepared for, bodies. Who knows how many had died in the battle for Mahbes? I counted perhaps 50 Moroccans lying as they had fallen three weeks before, in various stages of decomposition from sun, wind, and sand. The POLISARIO dead had been buried, but the Moroccans had fled in tanks in disarray. When I asked, I was told the Moroccan dead would be buried as a humanitarian act, but I do not know that they were.

I had been on African battle sites before, but this was the first time I had actually seen the dead on the field. It was different from seeing refugees or wounded in hospitals. It was a shock to me, who had never shot anything more powerful than the BB gun my father gave me when I was 10 and who had gone to prison in 1940 protesting the peacetime conscription before U.S. involvement in World War II.

Later, as we were returning across the desert toward Algeria, I asked myself how I came to be at that spot on that day. Why wasn't I preaching a sermon on this Christian Sabbath somewhere in Colorado, where I was an ordained minister in the United Methodist Church, instead of being in the company of devout Muslims fighting for the independence of their country?

CHAPTER ONE

Becoming Involved in Africa

Although I have been involved in African affairs since 1952, I was not trained for that field either academically or professionally. At that time, I was a Methodist minister attached to the Rocky Mountain Annual Conference and a member of the national staff of the Fellowship of Reconciliation (FOR), a religious pacifist organization. No one asked me to take on an African concern. No one paid me to become involved. I took up the cause because I was morally committed to the struggle of people for freedom. Since I have a religious approach to life, I look upon my concern with Africa as a matter of divine guidance and a valid extension of my vows as a Christian minister.

During the 30 years of my activities related to Africa, the early 1950s to the 1980s, my focus has always been on the liberation struggle. In my many trips to Africa I have tried to experience the dynamics of that struggle by becoming acquainted with African liberation movements and their leaders and by going to places where things were happening. In the United States I have worked through organizational channels to try to influence the policy of the government toward Africa.

My purpose in writing this book is not to relate an autobiography but to describe the struggle for independence. I approach it from a personal perspective not because I think my actions have played a determining role but because a certain uniqueness of my experience as both an observer and a participant may illuminate the story of that struggle.

How did I become involved in Africa? A word about my background may help the reader understand the step-by-step process, unwitting at first, by which I became the head of an American organization devoted to African affairs.

EARLY YEARS

I come from a ministerial family. In their youth my parents were Methodist missionaries in the Philippines. My earliest childhood memories are of Manila and of Filipinos, who were constantly in our home. Although I was very young, I must have been influenced subliminally by the fact that some of my parents' closest friends were of another country and race. Our family never stayed long in one spot. After Ohio, where I was born, and the Philippines, we lived in New York State, California, and Colorado, in all of which my father pastored churches.

While a student at the College of the Pacific in Stockton, California (now the University of the Pacific), I spent the year 1935–1936 as a scholarship exchange student at Lingnan University in Canton, China. My parents encouraged me in this enterprise, despite the extra expense not covered by the grant, because they realized that the year in China would expose me to new, wider influences. I know that association with a Chinese roommate, other Chinese students, and my fellow American exchange students was a high point in my life. Because of the China experience— visits to villages, contact with other religions, the observation of events in another country at a time when Chiang Kai Shek's control was being challenged by Mao Zedong's rising Communist movement and the Japanese were about to invade—I could no longer see the world in quite the same way.

When I returned to the United States, my parents had moved to Denver, so I transferred to the University of Denver, where I graduated. During my college years I became actively involved in world affairs. As a member of the Student Christian Movement, I participated in activities for peace, racial justice, and economic equality. Through the National Council of Methodist Youth, I attended many national meetings, which not only deepened my religious commitment but gave me an outlet for action on political and social issues.

Influenced by my parents, my experience in China, and my association with student Christian activities, I decided to enter the ministry. I was attracted to Union Theological Seminary in New York by outstanding professors such as Reinhold Niebuhr and Harry Ward, men who had achieved national reputations and combined Christian ethics with political action. That was what I wanted.

I was a product of the 1930s. The Social Gospel, putting the Christian ethic into practice on the social scene, was the credo that moved me. I was a pacifist as well as a supporter of organized labor and all efforts to challenge racial discrimination and segregation. I joined the Young People's Socialist League, affiliated with the Socialist party, headed by Norman Thomas. As a seminarian I participated in my first picket line in support of A. Philip Randolph's Brotherhood of Sleeping Car Porters.

I moved out of the seminary dormitory on the upper West Side to a slum area on the lower East Side of New York. I specifically chose a part-time job at the Church of All Nations helping transform street gangs into clubs rather than accept a job as youth pastor in a suburban church. I felt that living in an underprivileged community was one way of learning more about the struggle against poverty. In an old tenement on First Street where I lived with five other young men, I saw something of slum conditions—no heat in winter and bedbugs in summer.

PRISON

In the fall of 1940, more than a year before the United States entered World War II, the government enacted the first peace-time conscription law in U.S. history. Eight of us seminarians decided to disobey the law, which required every young American male to register, in spite of the fact that as theological students we would automatically be exempted from military service. We felt that the most effective resistance was registering "our refusal to comply in any way with the Selective Service and Training Act." We optimistically wrote to the Draft Board on October 16, 1940. "We do not expect to stem the war forces today; but we are helping to build the movement that will conquer in the future."

Our act of civil disobedience was major headline news. Our group was besieged by the press and newsreel agencies, and our action was played up in news shorts in movie theaters. We were applauded by friends and sympathizers and blasted by those who opposed us. And we were threatened by Selective Service officials not just with the legal five years prison and $10,000 penalties but with 20 years on a conspiracy charge. It was a sobering experience.

Perhaps the most meaningful worship experience of my life took place in the chapel of the seminary on the eve of our sentencing, when the entire seminary community, in spite of great differences on the issue, was drawn together. James Russell Lowell's great hymn "Once to Every Man and Nation Comes the Moment to Decide" took on special significance on that occasion.

On November 14 we were sentenced to a year and a day at the federal prison in Danbury, Connecticut. That was a year of learning for me— about prison life, about our fellow inmates, about resistance activities in prison by striking to protest racial discrimination and poor food. We were thrown together with men of many backgrounds and races. The harsh reality of prison life, the ache of separation from the outside world and loved ones, still could not dampen a feeling of satisfaction in being able to help some of our inmate friends by writing letters for them, informal counseling, teaching classes, and participating in the sports activities. I always felt proud that I was number one ping pong player on the prison team.

As our prison term drew toward the end, most of our group of eight wanted to return to Union Seminary. But because the seminary imposed certain conditions that we felt would limit our freedom of action, five of us chose to go to Chicago Theological Seminary.

THE FELLOWSHIP OF RECONCILIATION

I found it very difficult to take my academic work seriously that final year of seminary (1941–1942). The prison experience was too fresh in my memory. The United States was about to enter the war. I was recruited by A.J. Muste, head of the Fellowship of Reconciliation, to work in the Chicago area. Muste was a Presbyterian clergyman, a pacifist, a former Trotskyist, and a social and political radical. I greatly admired him. I always felt he was in the tradition of the Old Testament prophets.

I was to be on the staff of the FOR for 13 years. I had been ordained an elder in the Methodist Church in Colorado in 1943, and I assumed that after a temporary period of organizing in the area of peace and race relations, I would settle into a church somewhere. But this was not to be. I became deeply involved in the struggle against racism when, in 1942, we founded the first Committee of Racial Equality (CORE) in Chicago. A year later this became a national effort under the name of the Congress of Racial Equality and I became executive secretary. I was able to combine this work with my FOR work because one of my FOR responsibilities was to adapt the nonviolent methods of Mohandas K. Gandhi, who influenced me greatly, to the struggle for racial justice. One of my two closest associates was James Farmer, who became the first president of CORE and later in the 1960s its executive director. The other was Bayard Rustin, who led a stimulating one-man crusade challenging Jim Crow nonviolently.

Although I organized many projects for FOR, my main activity was challenging racism. After two years in Chicago and another two in Cleveland, I moved to FOR national headquarters in New York in 1946. CORE was the primary vehicle for action on racial issues. Our theme was nonviolent direct action in resisting segregation. We organized interracial housing establishments in segregated areas; sit-ins at discriminatory restaurants; and interracial waiting lines at the box offices of theaters, roller rinks, and other public places, effectively blocking the entrances unless all were admitted.

We organized the first "freedom ride" into the South in April 1947, which challenged Jim Crow laws in interstate travel following the 1946 decision of the Supreme Court to revoke them. Rustin and I collaborated with others on a song that we would sing at public gatherings to the tune of the spiritual "No Hidin' Place Down Here." The first verse went

> You don't have to ride Jim Crow.
> You don't have to ride Jim Crow.
> On June the 3rd
> The High Court said
>   When you ride interstate
> Jim Crow is dead,
> You don't have to ride Jim Crow.

Our activities in CORE were a little in advance of the major civil rights campaign of the later 1950s and 1960s, when Martin Luther King and the Southern Christian Leadership Conference rose to prominence and CORE became a much larger national movement. But the tactics we inaugurated were the same as those popularized on a larger scale a few years later.

During all these years I participated in innumerable picket lines and protest poster walks. I was chased by threatening gangs of irate whites who opposed our actions against discrimination, and on a few occasions I was arrested and locked up.

Although I was not serving the church directly, I felt committed to the Christian gospel of love. I made no easy assumption that I was ushering in the kingdom of God, but I felt I was attempting to fulfill the demand of discipleship. My family—my wife, Jean, and the children, Martha, David, and later Steven and Tom—maintained an active relationship with our local church, and I preached on Sunday as occasion demanded.

Until the end of the 1940s my knowledge and concern about Africa was miniscule. Yet in retrospect, it was as easy and natural for me to develop an active concern about South Africa as it had been to organize a committee to support India's struggle for freedom during the years I was in Chicago. All that was needed was an event, an issue, something to highlight the South African problem. This came with a civil disobedience campaign against the system of racism known as apartheid.

CHAPTER TWO

Nonviolent Fighters for Freedom

My introduction to the African liberation struggle began with the "Campaign to Defy Unjust Laws," sponsored by the African National Congress of South Africa (ANC). The year was 1952. Word about plans for a forthcoming, massive, nonviolent Defiance Campaign in South Africa to resist the apartheid laws came to me from my friend and coworker Bill Sutherland. He was excited about the campaign, which he had learned about from a South African editor whom he had met in London. Sutherland and I were both pacifists and had worked together on numerous projects to combat segregation in the United States by non-violent methods. His opinions meant a lot to me.

Nevertheless, my first reaction to Sutherland's enthusiastic reports and urging us to active support was hesitant. A lot was going on right here at home. I felt overwhelmed with existing commitments and was not eager to take on new ones. Sutherland's persistence had its effect, however. Somewhat protestingly at first, I began to reach out for more information, and together he and I, along with Bayard Rustin, began to plan a program.

INITIAL CONTACTS

As executive secretary of CORE, I began to correspond with leaders of the South African campaign—Walter M. Sisulu, the secretary general of the ANC, and Yusuf A. Cachalia, secretary general of the South African Indian Congress (SAIC). The Defiance Campaign was a coalition effort, primarily of Africans and Indians, with some participation from the Coloured community through the Franchise Action Council. Sisulu wrote me (March 26, 1952), "Your letter of the 17th of March has been a source of great inspiration to me. I am very delighted to learn that your organization [CORE] has taken such a great interest in the struggle for fundamental human rights by my organization."

Up to this time I had only rudimentary knowledge about South Africa. I had read Alan Paton's *Cry, the Beloved Country.* I was acquainted with Mohandas K. Gandhi's work in South Africa (1893–1914) and his experiments with nonviolent tactics in combatting discrimination against the Indian minority there. I knew that the Indians, who had come in 1868 as indentured workers in the sugar cane fields, numbered only a few hundred thousand out of a population of less than 15 million. I learned that in 1952 the Afrikaners were to celebrate the 300th anniversary of the coming of their Dutch forebears to South Africa. The Union of South Africa* was an amalgam of two Afrikaner republics (Transvaal and the Orange Free State) and two British colonies (Natal and the Cape of Good Hope, where the British arrived about 1820). It was created in 1910 as an aftermath of the Boer War, in which the British defeated the Afrikaners. The Coloured population, numbering about a million, came from miscegenation despite the racism of the whites. Black Africans, about 70 percent of the population, had been subjugated by the expanding white population much as the American Indians had been conquered by white settlers moving west across the United States. They did not have the vote. I quickly learned the importance of the election victory of the National Party of the Afrikaners under D.F. Malan in 1948. They instituted their program of apartheid, meaning "aparthood" in Afrikaans.

Through correspondence with Sisulu and Cachalia and memoranda from their movement, I saw the plan for the campaign develop. The sponsoring organizations committed themselves to "declare war" on apartheid laws. They concentrated on the pass laws, which restricted the free movement of Africans around the country, and the Group Areas Act, which established clearly designated areas where various racial groups could live.

The ANC had written to Prime Minister Malan in January demanding the repeal of these laws by February 29, failing which, mass action would begin. Cachalia sent me copies of the correspondence. Malan threatened "to quell any disturbances" and made the statement, often quoted since, which reflects the essence of the white supremacist position: "It is self-contradictory to claim as the inherent right of the Bantu, who differ in many ways from Europeans, that they should be regarded as not different, especially when it is borne in mind that these differences are permanent and not man-made."[1]

The kickoff for the campaign was originally scheduled for April 6, 1952, Van Riebeck Day, the 300th anniversary of the coming of the white man to South Africa. The European community planned large demonstrations and celebrations. It was a natural time for black opposition demonstrations too. But the Joint Action Committee apparently did not feel quite ready for a full effort. Sisulu wrote to me (March 26, 1952) that "on the 6th of April we shall only have meetings and demonstrations and a pledge shall be taken. Thereafter the Executive will fix the date for the Defiance of Unjust Laws." He also said, "We need money for propaganda, to assist some of the needy families, those people who are going to court and imprisonment."

We in New York were enthusiastic supporters of the plan to keep the campaign nonviolent. Sisulu had written me (March 26) that he had just returned from a provincial tour and was satisfied with the response of the

---

*South Africa became a republic in 1961.

people. "We have made emphasis on a nonviolent approach, having judged my people from the strike of 1950, they will certainly behave well."

In the meantime I had begun a correspondence with Professor Z.K. Matthews, president of the Cape Province branch of the ANC and head of African studies at the only university-level school for Africans in South Africa, the University College of Fort Hare.

Referring to the tactic of nonviolence in the campaign, he wrote me (March 13, 1952), "We take great comfort from the fact that Gandhism was born on South African soil. Through these same means India was able to achieve a tremendous upsurge of consciousness of destiny among the people of India."

At about this time I also began a correspondence with Manilal Gandhi, a son of Mohandas K. Gandhi, who was still editing the publication *Indian Opinion*, started by his father. My friend Donald Harrington, minister of the Community Church in New York, who had known Manilal, wrote to me (February 25, 1952), "As you perhaps know, Manilal Gandhi spent a good deal of time with us here at Community Church while he was in New York and we were deeply impressed with his immense spirituality and saintly qualities. He is very much like his father, more so than any of the other sons."

Gandhi wrote me (March 10, 1952) that he was a "bit doubtful to what extent our struggle is going to remain nonviolent, as those who hold the reins are far from believers in the principles of nonviolence. . . . That is why I have not aligned myself with their movement and am fighting my own battle." At that time he was 3 days into a 21-day fast, but he advised us that we "should certainly give [our] sympathy and moral support to the cause and watch how things go."

AMERICANS FOR SOUTH AFRICAN RESISTANCE

In New York we felt we had enough information about the Defiance Campaign to make a decision on what to do. We decided to set up an ad hoc support group for the campaign and adopted the name Americans for South African Resistance (AFSAR). Donald Harrington and Charles Y. Trigg, minister of the Salem Methodist Church of Harlem, were chosen as cochairmen. I was secretary. The Executive Committee included Roger Baldwin, Norman Thomas, Bayard Rustin, A. Philip Randolph, and Conrad Lynn. Our task, as we conceived it, was to be a vehicle for information about the campaign and to raise funds. The National Action Committee in South Africa was calling for 1 million shillings (about $150,000) by the end of March.

Three questions about the ANC came up. First was the question of the bona fide militancy of the organization. My friend Bill Worthy, a black American journalist who had been active in antiwar and antisegregation causes, wrote from Copenhagen in April, questioning whether CORE money should go to the ANC. He had heard that it was opportunistic and compromising. For example, the ANC had supported the "fake" Native Representative Council, a body made up of Africans with government approval but no power.

What Worthy did not know and we discovered later was that the ANC's sponsorship of the Defiance Campaign represented a new militancy. The ANC had been organized in 1912 as the South Africa Native National Congress. Its program for years was purely reformist—petitioning the government for change, sending delegations to London and later to the United Nations, essentially working among the more educated Africans to induce some change from within. But in 1944 the ANC Youth League, committed to a more radical and militant program, was formed. In 1949 the youth in effect took control of the organization with new leaders such as Nelson Mandela, Oliver Tambo, and Walter Sisulu. The Defiance Campaign was the first major effort of these new leaders.

The second question related to nonviolence. Could the ANC maintain such a discipline among the mass of participants in a civil disobedience effort? Gandhi was skeptical. He advocated postponing the campaign on the grounds that the people were not prepared to act nonviolently. We realized that he was not really a leader of the campaign and had only limited influence on policy.

G.M. Pitje, former president of the ANC Youth League, wrote me (April 14, 1952), "It is difficult to see how a campaign of nonviolence can succeed in a country like ours. All white South Africans agree fundamentally on the discriminatory policies. . . . where they differ is in their methods of implementing such a policy." He pointed out that the present leadership of the ANC was revolutionary. At their December 1951 ANC conference, Manilal Gandhi spoke at length on nonviolence and "the reaction of the audience was unfavorable to him." Our feeling in New York, however, was that the official policy of nonviolence would have an effect and that we should support the civil disobedience tactic as a practical measure that would at least minimize violence.

The third question about the ANC was the influence of Communism. We were living in the midst of the Joseph McCarthy "red scare" in 1952. Although all our supporters were unalterably opposed to McCarthyism, we were not interested in joining forces with the Communists in a united front. Although we were not well acquainted with the details of ANC organization, we did not easily accept the charge of Communist control made by advocates of racism. We knew that the Suppression of Communism Act in South Africa, adopted in 1950, had outlawed the Communist party there, but the main function of the law was to quell all opposition to the system of apartheid. We knew that in our own country the red label was sometimes put on our own activities in CORE simply because we actively opposed racism.

Yet we were not unconcerned about reports of significant Communist leadership in the ANC. A longtime coworker in peace and race relations activities, Homer Jack, on returning from South Africa in 1952, wrote me (September 12, 1952) "I am dismayed at the communist strength in the campaign." He said of Dr. Yusuf Dadoo, president of the South African Indian Congress and known openly to have been a member before the Communist party was banned, "He is a devoted man, albeit an unabashed Communist. . . . if I were in South Africa I would definitely participate in the campaign and work overtime to oust the commies from control." Others with whom we were in touch acknowledged the strong influence of Communist leadership but denied its domination in the ANC and the campaign. Among these were Manilal Gandhi; Arthur Blaxall, secretary of the South African Christian Council; and Patrick Duncan, son of a former governor general and the first white man to be arrested in the campaign.

Our group satisfied itself that the campaign had a good chance of being effective, nonviolent, and democratic, and we were anxious to support it. Our first public activity was a mass meeting on April 6 in solidarity with the ANC and the SAIC. Through mailings and mass distribution of leaflets in the American idiom, we called on people to join us "to support the drive against Jim Crow in South Africa," "use Palm Sunday to help Africans get freedom," and "show the world we oppose Jim Crow abroad as well as at home."

About 800 people attended our meeting at Abyssinia Baptist Church in Harlem, where Adam Clayton Powell was minister. Subsequently I wrote to Sisulu about it and sent our first check (about $300) collected at the meeting to support the campaign.

The Harlem meeting plus my correspondence with campaign leaders helped establish us as serious supporters of the effort. On June 18, only a few days before the Defiance Campaign was to begin, Sisulu asked me to assist "in publicizing our statements, bulletins, photographs and other propaganda material. . . . in this way you will at the same time save us a large amount of expenditure." We were honored to be accepted in this collaborative manner and eagerly took on the responsibility.

BEGINNING OF THE DEFIANCE CAMPAIGN

The Defiance Campaign began on June 26. A group of 52 were arrested at the Boksburg "native" location (the then-current term for an urban African township) 20 miles from Johannesburg. They had broken the law by trying to enter the location without a pass. A second group were arrested in Johannesburg at 11:30 P.M. for defying the curfew. The leader, Flag Boshielo of the ANC, said to the police, "We are nonviolent fighters for freedom. We are going to defy regulations that have kept our fathers in bondage."[2] Bulletin No. 2 of the National Action Committee for the Defiance Campaign, which I received soon afterward, reported that volunteers broke apartheid laws in six different centers in the Union. Nelson Mandela, who was volunteer-in-chief for the campaign, Sisulu, and Cachalia were all arrested on June 26.

Those arrested at Boksburg were held in jail nearly four weeks until their trial. They all pled guilty and were given seven days in jail or a £1 fine, which only one paid. Other leaders were given four to six months in jail under the Suppression of Communism Act. In sentencing them the magistrate said, "It is common knowledge that one of the aims of communism is to break down race barriers and strive for equal rights for all sections of the people. . . . The Union of South Africa with its peculiar problems created by a population overwhelmingly non-European is fertile ground for the dissemination of communist propaganda. This would endanger the survival of Europeans."[3] It was this kind of mentality that made us discount the charge of Communist influence in the movement. Opposition to apartheid and the support of Communism were made synonymous. By this definition we were all Communists.

Our sources of information about the campaign were several—bulletins from South Africa, continued correspondence, press reports in American papers, and, most important, Professor Z.K. Matthews. He arrived in New York in late June 1952 to serve for a year as the Henry Luce Visiting Professor of World Christianity at Union Theological Seminary.

We met frequently, and he shared the stream of information coming to him from South Africa, especially letters from his son Joe. Joe was a lawyer in Port Elizabeth, an active campaign center, and a leader of both the Youth League and the ANC. With this kind of inside information we began to issue bulletins about the campaign at least once a month. Our mailing list grew modestly but steadily.

Joe Matthews wrote to his father (September 3, 1952) that in Grahamstown in Cape Province the people forced the City Council to close down the beer hall in the African location. "For days the people stood in front of the beer hall praying and singing the African National Anthem until the place was shut up. It was built at a cost of £8,000 and brought the Municipal Council a revenue of £240 a week. That is one of the good by-products of the campaign; it has dealt a death blow to hooliganism and drunkenness."

This same letter reported that the biggest demonstration of the campaign took place on August 26 in Johannesburg against the arrest of leaders. The courts were jammed with 2,000 people, and thousands more gathered in the open square outside at a rally that lasted until dark. At an unprecedented request by the prosecutor, the court adjourned for 15 minutes to allow Dr. James Moroka (president of ANC and himself on trial) to address the people. Amid shouts of "Afrika," he stood on a chair and asked the people to leave the building quietly so that the case could continue. They left immediately in perfect silence. Subsequently Moroka and 19 others were found guilty under the Suppression of Communism Act and were sentenced to nine months in prison at compulsory labor, suspended for two years. By September 4,000 protestors had been arrested.

A letter from Sisulu (September 16, 1952) urged us to send money. "We need plenty of funds as you can see. Our budget is becoming bigger every month." We were severely limited in what we could do. We were certainly not professional fund raisers. American interest in South Africa was

Walter Sisulu, secretary general of the ANC of
South Africa, at his house in Orlando location,
South Africa, 1954.

growing but among a pretty select group. Nevertheless, some local and
national church bodies put the issue on their agendas. Bostonians Allied
for South African Resistance (BAFSAR) formally affiliated with us. They
sponsored public meetings, distributed literature, mostly supplied by the
AFSAR New York office, and raised some funds.

AFSAR sent about $5,000 to South Africa during the campaign, much
of it through Matthews. We were excited about the support we received.
Contributions came from all parts of the United States and from Canada
and India. A woman in Arizona sent us her diamond ring, saying she could
not conscientiously wear it knowing that it represented slave labor. We sold
it and sent the proceeds to South Africa. A family in Ohio contributed
$100 at Christmastime and said it represented funds they had saved for
family gifts. Some seminarians sent funds saved by eating sacrificial meals,
and a person who refused to pay federal tax for military purposes sent
$100.

Z.K. MATTHEWS AND THE UNITED NATIONS

Spurred by the Defiance Campaign, in October 1952 India took the lead in
calling on the UN General Assembly for an agenda item that for the first

time would deal with the whole racial conflict in South Africa. Previously South African issues were concerned only with the treatment of people of Indian and Pakistani origin and the question of South West Africa (now Namibia). A cross section of Asian countries supported India. The item was assigned to the Ad Hoc Political Committee. African and Asian delegates wanted Z.K. Matthews to give expert testimony before it, an unusual procedure at that time. No one could have spoken with greater authority.

AFSAR helped organize a letter-writing campaign to the UN and the U.S. Mission to the UN seeking approval for Matthews's appearance. Among the distinguished Americans who wrote on his behalf was Harry Emerson Fosdick, minister of the prestigious Riverside Church in New York. A reply from the U.S. Mission explained diplomatically that to allow petitioners to appear before the UN "would involve radical changes in the structures and procedures of the U.N."[4] The function of the UN, Fosdick was told, was to reconcile judgments and policies of governments, not to function as fact-finding agencies. The United States made clear it would vote against Matthews's appearance.

I recall a visit about this time to Matthews's apartment at Union Seminary. As I entered, two men were leaving. After they departed, Matthews explained, "They were from the U.S. State Department and came here to urge me not to insist on speaking at the UN. If I did, the United States would have to vote against me." The UN, dominated at that time by the United States, did not approve Matthews's request.

RIOTS IN SOUTH AFRICA

The Defiance Campaign faced a crisis in October and November 1952 when riots broke out in the eastern Cape Province, especially in Port Elizabeth and East London. AFSAR had word from Manilal Gandhi and others that the riots were quite separate from the campaign, although the government tried to associate them.

Matthews told me that the crisis arose in East London when armed police interfered with an open-air religious service in the African location, for which permission had been given. The preacher was reading from the Bible about the oppression of the Israelites when two vehicles loaded with police drove up and ordered the crowd to disperse within five minutes. Yet in less than two minutes the police ordered a baton charge. Before the crowd could leave the square, shots were fired and a man was killed. The police then drove through the streets of the location, firing at random. One man was killed while sitting in his kitchen reading a newspaper. The rioting started after this, first with stone throwing and later with setting fire to buildings. Altogether 13 people were killed and at least 50 injured.

Other riots took place in the New Brighton Location at Port Elizabeth where 11 Africans were killed and at least 27 injured; at the Denver Hostel in Johannesburg, where 3 Africans were killed and 5 injured; and at No. 2

Location at Kimberley, where 13 Africans were killed and at least 28 injured. Although these were widely separated places, the incidents were triggered by police violence in each instance, and the Africans were killed by gunfire. Two Europeans were killed in East London, a Catholic nun and an insurance representative. Three Europeans were killed in New Brighton.

As a result of the riots, the government cracked down on all organized protests. Quintin Whyte, head of the South African Institute of Race Relations, wrote to me (November 14, 1952), "While we must distinguish between the campaign and the riots, nevertheless the state of tension is very high. There has been a marked hardening against liberals in the country." The institute was a nonpolitical body that confined itself to carefully researched studies on the state of race relations in the country. It was generally liberal and opposed to apartheid, as its own interracial staff and constituency would indicate. But it was careful not to take action other than through its literature and reports.

Whyte's letter was an important assessment of the campaign. He said that it was "training heroes and martyrs as well leaders for future work." He spoke of the "remarkable self-control of the resisters" and summarized that the effect of the campaign was "to unite non-Europeans to give expression to African nationalism; to train for the future; to demonstrate the power of Africans; to make Europeans question themselves; to make the government more adamant; to make liberal Europeans more unpopular; and in the long run to gain concessions."

BROADENING CAMPAIGN—GOVERNMENT REACTION

The discipline of the volunteers in the Defiance Campaign began to win new adherents and to gain the sympathy of some skeptics about the practice of nonviolence. On December 8, international publicity was given to the arrest of Patrick Duncan and Manilal Gandhi as part of a group that violated the law by entering the Germiston location near Johannesburg without passes. Duncan's arrest attracted special attention not only because of his father's rank but also because he was on crutches as a result of a motor accident. He was sentenced to 100 days in jail or a $280 fine. Gandhi was given a 50-day sentence or a $140 fine. Both chose to serve their sentences.

Up to December 16, 1952, the total number arrested in the campaign was 8,057. In response to the growing impact of the campaign, the government passed the Public Safety Act and the Criminal Laws Amendment Act. Dr. R.T. Bokwe, brother-in-law of Matthews, wrote me on December 30 saying that no meetings of more than 10 people were allowed in African locations or in reserves (now rural homelands). Practically all African leaders, including himself, had been served letters from the minister of justice forbidding them to attend gatherings. He could not even attend a church service.

A so-called Whipping Post Law was passed, under which anyone who received funds for any organized resistance to laws of the Union was punishable by five years' imprisonment, a £500 fine, and 15 lashes with the cane. In early 1953 Blaxall wrote me (May 9, 1953), "Actually I think at this time that Congress would find it extremely difficult to get volunteers now that the punishment is almost certain to be flogging, which is no joke." He thought the ANC would lie low for the next six months to see what would happen in parliament.

In light of these developments, we in New York were hesitant to send more funds. I wrote to Bokwe (April 24, 1953), who had received a good portion of the several thousand dollars we had sent to South Africa, "We have not wanted to send any further money until we knew whether you or any others might be placed in jeopardy. Do you have any advice for us in this regard?" Previous letters from Bokwe had informed us that our donations had paid fines for some resisters who had become ill in jail and had helped families whose breadwinners were temporarily out of circulation.

The fact is that after the government passed this new legislation, the Defiance Campaign came to a halt, and the work of AFSAR had to change. We explained in our April 1953 bulletin that we had not sent any funds recently "because we are awaiting clarification of the Whipping Post Law." Bokwe wrote me (March 22, 1953), saying that he had received our last contribution and then added, "We have good reason to believe that mail is subjected to scrutiny. One is thus unable to write you as freely as one should have liked to."

By this time I had developed a keen interest in South Africa. I had initiated a correspondence with Chief Albert J. Lutuli, who was elected president of the ANC in December 1952. He had been the elected chief of the Groutville Mission Reserve for 17 years. When he was told by the South African government that he would have to choose between his chieftancy and his work with the ANC, he unhesitatingly chose the ANC, and the government deposed him. The elders of Groutville were so incensed at the government action that they never chose another chief.

Lutuli was a devout Christian. He had toured the United States in 1949 under the auspices of the United Church of Christ and had been a member of the Executive Committee of the South African Christian Council. At the time of his deposition, he wrote a statement that testified to his own faith: "Laws and conditions that tend to debase human personality must be relentlessly opposed in the spirit of defiance shown by St. Peter when he said to the rulers of his day, 'Shall we obey God or man?'"[5]

AFTERMATH

Activities of AFSAR apparently attracted some attention in South African government circles. In a South African newspaper, Eric Louw, then minister of economic affairs, called attention to support that AFSAR was giving to the campaign and the relief of those arrested.

On April 15, 1953, elections (for whites) were held in South Africa, the first since the Nationalists came to power in 1948. They strengthened their hold on the government by increasing their majority in parliament. Apartheid was extended, and the Population Registration Act was passed, requiring all people in South Africa to register with the government by race. Plans were laid for eliminating Sophiatown, an area of Johannesburg where Africans could own land, and creating the area now called Soweto.

Toward the end of the academic year 1952–1953, during which he had spoken all over the country, Z.K. Matthews ran into some difficulties. He had been told when he tried to testify at the UN that his job at Fort Hare was in jeopardy. He had planned to stay in New York until June and then sail to South Africa, at about half the cost of flying. His problem was that his South African passport expired at the end of May, and the government adamantly refused to grant an extension. This meant that he had either to leave Union Seminary before the end of the term or undertake the expense of plane tickets. With the help of friends the extra money for the airfare was raised.

Matthews had been apprehensive about the treatment he would receive when he returned home. He sent a cable on May 20 saying, "Arrived safely. Survived close police scrutiny. Some documents seized." He wrote me on July 9, 1953, detailing his harrassment: "Any day now I am expecting to be raided the same way other leaders of the ANC have been. I understand the purpose of the raids is to find, if possible, evidence of treason or sedition or contravention of the Suppression of Communism Act. Altogether we are living in a state of uncertainty about what is going to happen next." The government was laying the foundation for the infamous treason arrests of 1956.

Since the Defiance Campaign had come to an end, we in AFSAR had a series of meetings to decide whether we should disband, set up a more permanent organization dealing with South Africa, or establish something even broader. We decided on the third course. Thus AFSAR was transformed into an organization that would relate to the whole anticolonial struggle in Africa. I, of course, was now most eager to visit South Africa as well as other parts of the continent. I wrote to Bill Sutherland, who was in London waiting to go to the Gold Coast, that the National Council of FOR had voted that I should try to visit South Africa sometime in 1954. "I am extremely skeptical that there is any chance of getting in, but I am going to give it a try."

CHAPTER THREE

Journey to Africa

Z. **K. Matthews** frequently impressed on me the importance of traveling to Africa, especially to South Africa. The last time I saw him in New York, he said, "I expect to see you at Fort Hare soon." But for me a trip was not that simple. The chief problem was whether I could get a visa from the South African government. They certainly could not have been happy about my association with Americans for South African Resistance. Also I had misgivings about leaving my family for an extended time. I wasn't even sure what countries I would be visiting. By my departure date I had received a Portuguese visa to visit Angola, a British visa for the Gold Coast (now Ghana) and Nigeria but not for their colonies in East and Central Africa, a French visa for colonies in West and Equatorial Africa, and a Belgian visa for the Belgian Congo (now Zaire). That was it. I had decided that my best chance for a visa to South Africa would be to apply from some place in Africa, such as the Belgian Congo, where I was not known.

I had letters of introduction from well-connected friends, a press card from NBC radio to enable me to get stories and taped interviews, and a press card from the Afro-American Newspaper chain. Armed with these documents, in May 1954 I boarded the *Queen Mary* for London, on the first leg of my journey to Africa, feeling heady with the romance of sailing into adventure in the unknown.

LONDON

My planned week in London expanded to three weeks, partly because of the futile wait for word on the British visas and partly because I wanted to take advantage of the presence in London of personalities and organizations that could help orient me to the African scene.

At this time I knew nothing about the designation "prohibited immigrant," a phrase that was to become much more familiar over the years. This was my initiation. I had hoped to visit Uganda, Kenya, and Tanganyika in East Africa and Nyasaland and Northern and Southern Rhodesia, which together formed the Central African Federation, with British colonial ties, but this was not to be. I saw scores of people for help—members of Parliament, church missionary leaders, the U.S. ambassador to Britain, Winthrop Aldrich, with whom my senator from New York, Jacob Javits, interceded on my behalf. Aldrich replied (June 1, 1954), "It seems possible that Mr. Houser may have been refused visas because the

British affiliate of the organization he represents, the Fellowship of Reconciliation, has had certain connections with individuals in the territories in question regarded as agitators."

Three Labour MPs, including Fenner Brockway, had identical letters from Oliver Lyttleton, the colonial secretary, saying (June 1954), "the governors of Nyasaland, Northern Rhodesia, Kenya and Tanganyika have confirmed that Mr. Houser has been declared a prohibited immigrant. Their decisions were reached after very careful consideration and I regret that I am unable to intervene in this case." Brockway had been particularly helpful. He was chairman of the Movement for Colonial Freedom, an organization I was to work closely with over the years.

Finding out exactly why I was declared a prohibited immigrant became a matter of guesswork, but weeks later at a sherry party at the home of the British governor of the Gold Coast, Sir Charles Arden-Clarke, I was introduced by the governor to Michael Ensore of the Gold Coast Department of External Affairs. Ensore inquired, "Is your first name George?" When I affirmed it, he thought for a moment and said, "I have read about you some place." Then he continued, "Oh yes, I received a report from the British office in New York giving me your background in race relations work." This report was undoubtedly responsible for my prohibited status. The British authorities certainly did not want a visitor who had been active against racism in the United States in East Africa during the Mau Mau crisis.

My London weeks were put to good advantage. I met the leaders of organizations I would be working with for years to come. John Hatch, the Africa expert of the Labour party, took me to the home of Seretse Khama, who later became the first president of Botswana. Khama was the chief of the Bamangwato tribe of colonial Bechuanaland, who had been deposed by the British Labour government in 1951 because he had married a white British woman. Khama felt that pressure from Prime Minister D.F. Malan of South Africa was responsible. I had a fascinating evening with him and his attractive blond wife, Ruth. She kidded him about his royal blood and he joined in. They had two children. Khama laughingly told me about meeting some American army personnel, who called him "Your Highness" and were constantly bowing.

I was introduced to the Kenya situation through extensive discussion with two exiles—Joe Murumbi, later vice president and foreign minister of Kenya, and Mbyiu Koinange, later minister of state in Kenya and an adviser to Kenyan president Jomo Kenyatta. Murumbi was trying without success to get a U.S. visa to undertake a speaking tour for the American Friends Service Committee. We had a fellow feeling because of our mutual visa problems. Koinange, a Kikuyu leader, was suspected of being tied in with the Mau Mau. He had organized a network of 127 Kikuyu schools, which the colonial government banned. Kenyatta, of course, was already in detention for suspected leadership of the Mau Mau rebellion.

One of my most important London contacts was George Padmore. Born in Trinidad, he had studied in the United States and moved to

London. He was closely identified with the world Pan-African movement and was probably the closest associate of Kwame Nkrumah, the charismatic nationalist leader in the Gold Coast. They had been secretaries of the Fifth Pan-African Conference, held in Manchester, England, in 1945. During several visits in his home, he gave me a framework for understanding the struggle against colonial domination in various parts of Africa— from the Gold Coast and Nigeria, where the struggle was very active, to the Belgian Congo and Angola, where virtually no stirrings were discernible.

Padmore gave me a letter of introduction to Nkrumah. I also had a letter from Fenner Brockway. No two letters could have been more important for me in opening the door to Nkrumah a short time later when I visited his country.

DAKAR, SENEGAL

I was enthralled by Dakar, my first glimpse of Africa. The city was the capital of French West Africa, a federation of eight territories: Senegal, Mauritania, French Sudan (now Mali), French Guinea, the Ivory Coast, Upper Volta (now Burkina Fasso), Niger, and Dahomey (now Benin). The population of the huge area was, at the time, only about 17 million. French colonial policy was to integrate the area into France. The French tried to frenchify the individual African, both educationally and politically. Only French was used in the schools after African children learned the language. Africans were well integrated into the political structure. The legislative body, the Grand Council, had 40 members, 5 from each territory. It sent 20 representatives to the Assembly in Paris. Thirty-two of the council members were African. The president of the council was Coloured (of mixed blood). The mayor of Dakar was African.

I was particularly interested in race relations and the African view of French colonial policy. The population of Dakar was about 300,000, of which 10 percent were French. I discovered that virtually all taxis were driven by Africans, practically all hotel personnel were African with the usual exception of a European manager, and the only out-and-out segregated place in Dakar was the Yachting Club, as I was told by a Frenchman. Yet there was very little mixing of the races on the streets or in stores or restaurants. Cultural, educational, and economic differences were responsible. Illiteracy among Africans was high. A skilled African worker was paid about $25 a month, compared to $200 to $350 for a European.

About half the population lived in the Medina section, which I visited with Simon Sambou, an African employee of a French firm. I was absolutely amazed to see the conditions under which people could live. The small, dingy huts were made of all kinds of material—old wood, tin, and mud and sticks—with thatched roofs. Everyone went barefoot because the streets were of loose sand. Every few blocks there was a water faucet, which was turned on at certain times of day. There were few public toilets, but there was an open drainage ditch, where much of the waste was only too obvious to eye and nose.

Sambou also took me to the island of Gorée, just a 15-minute launch ride from the mainland. Originally settled by the Portuguese, it had a fort, and it changed hands with each conquering European power—Dutch, English, and finally French. As with many other forts along the west coast of Africa during the slave trading era, slaves were imprisoned there before being shipped across the ocean. The dungeons I saw were a bitter reminder of days gone by.

In Dakar I felt no vivid stirring of an African nationalism. Sambou thought of himself as a Frenchman and was in fact a citizen of France. I talked with the African mayor of Dakar, Lamine Gueye, a Socialist, who was not unhappy with the idea of independence in a French union. I also met Boissier Palun, president of the Grand Council of French West Africa, who reflected similar indeas. At Radio Dakar I met Doudou Gueye, who had been active in the Rassemblement Democratique Africain (RDA), which was strongly nationalist. At the height of its popularity the RDA had 9 out of 20 seats reserved for French West Africa in the Paris Assembly and 7 out of 40 in the Dakar Grand Council. But by 1954 it was in eclipse. Gueye had in fact served nine months in jail for his activities.

I gathered that the African people really wanted independence but would not have objected to having it within the French Union. They wanted complete economic equality. They wanted to see African officials in high positions. And they wanted these changes more rapidly than the French would grant them. The people thought of themselves as black Frenchmen to some extent. This lesson was drummed into them in school. Still there was an African nationalism not satisfied. They saw the difference in economic standards and where the real power was.

LIBERIA

What a contrast Liberia was to Senegal! After leaving Dakar, I spent most of a week in and around the capital, Monrovia. Instead of having a French atmosphere, it was American. I had a momentarily embarrassing experience when I changed money in a bank. When I handed the teller U.S. currency and asked for Liberian money, he gave me a blank stare and then very kindly informed me that it was the same currency. I felt my face turn red under my sunburn.

The Constitution of Liberia is patterned after the U.S. Constitution. English is the official language. The flag is similar to the American flag except that it has 1 star and 11 stripes, which stand for the 11 signers of their Declaration of Independence of 1847. The economy was dominated by two U.S. companies, Firestone Rubber and Republic Steel. The capital is named for the American President James Monroe.

The settlers who came to Liberia were ex-slaves sponsored by the

American Colonization Society. When they arrived in 1821, they were met by suspicious and sometimes hostile natives, who resisted their efforts to establish themselves on the mainland. So the first group of about 80 so-called Americo-Liberians (a term that was in disrepute) lived for a time on a small piece of land in the Mesurado River (now Providence Island). In a sense these settlers carried on a conquest of Liberia except that they did not have the backing of a powerful nation.

Liberia had two built-in problems. One was the relationship between the indigenous people and the descendants of the American ex-slaves. In 1954 the population of Liberia was estimated at between 1 and 2 million. The Liberians of American ancestry, who numbered about 40,000, dominated the country, holding virtually all the government jobs. Theoretically government policy was to play down the differences and encourage assimilation. However, this involved tribal people coming out of the bush, receiving education, and becoming part of the modern world—a long, slow process. They resented their role as seeming second-class Liberians. The bloody coup of 1979, which unseated the Americo-Liberians from power, could be foreseen long before it happened.

The other major problem was economic. The country was very poor. In 1947 the government budget was $700,000. Seven years later, when I was there, it was about $12 million. There was very little capital for the government to tap. In 1954 there was a hut tax of $1.00 a year in the villages and a small income tax. Agriculture was the basis of the economy, consisting mostly of fruit, cocoa, coffee, and rubber. The only way for the government to develop the country was through attracting outside capital.

Liberia's poverty struck me from the moment of my arrival at Robert's Field, 50 miles from Monrovia. There were no waiting taxis or buses. A visitor without transportation would have been stuck. I was met by David Howell, an American executive of the YMCA. We drove to Monrovia over a dirt road marred with water-filled potholes because it was the rainy season. For almost half the distance we went through a forest of rubber trees owned by Firestone.

Firestone came to Liberia in 1927 with a 99-year lease on 1 million acres. At that time it employed about 15,000 tree tappers at a basic wage of 30 cents a day. The government received 25 percent of Firestone's profits. Liberian wages were very low, the minimum being 4 cents an hour. Even senators received only $4,800, and good government jobs paid about $3,500.

There was only one political party, the True Whig party, dominated by the president, William Tubman, and the elite. Because the possibilities for making a living were so limited in Liberia and government jobs offered the greatest security, there was a tendency for the better-educated people and those with the greatest leadership potential to gravitate into civil service or politics. But once in the system there was the fear of losing the job. This led to conformity. One government official whom I interviewed asked a stenographer to take notes. I was told by others later that probably a transcript of our discussion was on its way to President Tubman. Not all of this hush-hush atmosphere was a result of a one-party system. Part of it was due to the fact that Monrovia is a relatively small community with only 25,000 people. Gossip was free. Political opposition would almost amount to a palace revolution.

I noted that the national budget had grown and more funds were going into health and education. The government felt strong enough to bargain more effectively with Firestone. Optimistically I felt that one should see the stormy past of Liberia in order to appreciate where it is now, but clearly trouble lay ahead.

THE GOLD COAST

I arrived in Accra, capital of the British colony of the Gold Coast (now Ghana), on June 15. There could not have been a more opportune time to arrive in this most exciting country of black Africa. On that day elections took place to choose an All-African Assembly for the first time. The Assembly would have the responsibility of bringing independence to this colony, the first one south of the Sahara to achieve it.

I was met at 1:00 A.M. by Bill Sutherland, who had been living in the Gold Coast for several months and had recently married Efua, later one of the outstanding women of the country. During my three-week visit, he was unusually helpful in taking me around and introducing me to many leaders of the Gold Coast revolution.

ABOUT NKRUMAH

I had keenly anticipated meeting Kwame Nkrumah, who had been described by John Gunther as "one of the most remarkable personalities in Africa. . . . as leader of the Gold Coast revolution he personifies the hopes of black nationalism everywhere on the continent. . . . He has been called the 'African Nehru'."[1] Nkrumah was the great leader of one of the most united and exciting mass movements in the world at that time.

Nkrumah had had his early schooling in the Gold Coast. He had spent 10 years in the United States and had graduated from Lincoln University in Pennsylvania in 1939. In London from 1945 to 1947, he attended the London School of Economics and, most importantly, played a leading role in West African politics and the Pan-African movememt.

Nkrumah was recalled to the Gold Coast by the United Gold Coast Convention (UGCC), the most important political organization at that time, to assume the post of general secretary. Two years later he split with the UGCC and formed the Convention Peoples Party (CPP) because he felt that the UGCC was going too slowly. Nkrumah coined the slogan "self-government now" in contrast to the UGCC's "self-government in the shortest possible time." While he was imprisoned for political agitation, he was elected to the British-dominated National Assembly in 1951. In a flurry of publicity, accompanied by mass adulation, he was released with his term still unfinished to become "leader of government business," as the CPP took the majority of elected seats in the Assembly. His title was soon changed to prime minister. Independence was still years away. The elections on the day I arrived took place almost three years before independence and represented a test of the popularity of Nkrumah and the CPP.

ELECTIONS IN ACCRA

The atmosphere of Accra was utterly dynamic. Sutherland had made arrangements for me to stay with Walter and Maisie Birmingham near the University College of the Gold Coast, at Achimota, near Accra. Walter, a British Quaker, was a professor of economics. More important to me, he was supervisor for two election polling stations in villages 20 to 30 miles outside Accra. After only three hours of sleep, we headed off to see the voting process in a country that was 90 percent illiterate.

I was enthralled by the long lines of people, some of whom had walked more than five miles to the polling station. One group of voters was delayed because the canoe in which they had to cross a river had sprung a leak and repairs had taken most of the day. What a colorful picture they made, men and women in brightly colored tunics and dresses typical of the Gold Coast, waiting patiently but with excited expectation.

The voting procedure made maximum use of symbols rather than words. Each party had a symbol: a red cockerel for the CPP, a blue elephant for the Ghana Congress party, a star and crescent for the Moslem Association party. Each voter was given a ballot to be placed in a ballot box

Political party symbols
in Gold Coast election
1954

marked with the party symbol of his choice. Of course, the area near Accra was strongly CPP oriented.

That evening Sutherland and I went to the Polo Ground in Accra to watch the election returns. Perhaps 20,000 people were gathered. Young people had formed long lines of jubilant snake dancers, chanting "Nkrumah, Nkrumah" as they wove in and out of the crowd. A band was playing the unique swing music of the Gold Coast called "high life." On the strength of my NBC press card, we were able to get into the small area of the stands constructed for officials and cameramen. The excited crowd sang, danced, and cheered from early evening until about 3:00 A.M. At one end of the field, election results were put on a large temporary score board. The climax came in the early hours of the morning when Nkrumah appeared to make a brief statement. The final results were not known for two days.

The CPP won an overwhelming victory, with 71 out of 104 seats in the Assembly. The next-highest number of seats, 16, was won by the so-called CPP rebels, previous party members who ran independently. Fewer than a million cast votes, and in the popular vote the CPP won slightly less than 55 percent of the ballots cast. This indicated a potential but not a well-organized opposition to Nkrumah and the CPP. But in the euphoria of the moment, this was not of great concern. The British governor, Sir Charles Arden-Clarke, called Nkrumah to organize a government. For the first time, all the government ministers were African and members of the CPP.

MEETING NKRUMAH

On the morning of June 17 I learned that there was to be an Nkrumah press conference. With my press credentials I gained easy admission with the other 20-odd correspondents. Nkrumah entered the crowded room wearing brilliant kente cloth. Impressive in answering questions decisively, he presented a mildly socialist program and said he thought of the CPP as much like the Labour party in Britain. I asked the final question of the conference, which dealt with the Gold Coast's role on the international scene, particularly in light of the competition between the United States and the USSR. Nkrumah replied that the Gold Coast would pursue an independent line much like that of India under Jawaharlal Nehru. I saw him ask an aide who this fellow was. Afterward I introduced myself and gave him the letters of introduction from Brockway and Padmore. After reading them, he greeted me warmly and enthusiastically arranged an appointment.

The CPP as an organization also impressed me. At its headquarters I met Tawiah Adamafio, the acting secretary. He told me that it had 87 sound trucks, for spreading its message around the country. It claimed 1,750,000 members. The party had a flag, a symbol, and special songs and used "Freedom" as its word of greeting. I went for a ride through the streets of Accra in one of the CPP sound trucks in the postelection jubilation. As we rolled by, it was exciting to see the great numbers of people, including many children, who raised their arms in a salute and lustily yelled, "Freedom," accenting the last syllable.

A victory parade was organized through the heart of Accra. Nkrumah and other party leaders stood in the back of jeeps. Nkrumah's jeep was preceded by CPP youth on bicycles and followed by lorries with drumming and music. Thousands gathered at a small stadium, the Arena, for a victory rally. Each speaker began by shouting, "The CPP," and the crowd responded, "Ever great." The climax of the rally was an appearance by Nkrumah.

I met with Nkrumah several times and was deeply impressed. In a newsletter I sent home I wrote, "There is no doubt that he is the leader of the movement, and its inspiration. He is a man of the masses. He is the kind of leader about whom myths and legends begin to be told. He has his bitter opponents around the country, but in the places where I circulated among the common people he was greatly admired. He went to jail for his commitment to freedom. He was the leader of the movement which hastened the day of self-government. He has the reputation of a man with simple tastes. He and other African ministers refused to move into the special ministerial homes the British had built for them on the grounds that they wanted to stay near the people. Also Nkrumah has the reputation of being accessible to the people. Anyone can go to his home and see him if he is there and is not occupied with a matter of pressing importance. He has a most engaging and disarming smile."

The first time I met Nkrumah alone was at his home. For half an hour in the midst of his hectic schedule he gave me his undivided attention. We talked briefly about nonviolence, then a special concern of mine. The CPP had risen to power on the strength of a program of nonviolent "positive action," which Nkrumah said was critical to their success. We spent considerably more time talking about Pan-Africanism. Fenner Brockway had just proposed that Nkrumah set up a Pan-African movement headquarters in Accra. The Pan-African impulse was strong in Nkrumah and he wanted to move ahead with this project as rapidly as possible. He indicated plans for a West African federation, beginning with Nigeria, Gambia, Sierra Leone, and Liberia. The French-speaking areas would be brought in later.

We also talked about the attitude of the people of the Gold Coast toward Americans. This subject interested Nkrumah, of course, because of his own 10 years in the United States. I had been surprised by the friendliness of people toward Americans from the moment of my arrival in Accra. People on the street, recognizing perhaps my American haircut or clothes, went out of their way to be helpful. They seemed quite unaware of racial discrimination and segregation in the United States but were more hostile toward the British, as a result of the colonial experience. They had a vague familiarity with the U.S. Constitution and, of course, with the American struggle for freedom from British colonialism. They had also had a good experience with both white and black American military personnel in West Africa during World War II.

I had a dramatic experience at a CPP rally in Kumasi, capital of the Ashanti region, some 100 miles north of Accra. Several thousand people were gathered on a hillside on that Sunday afternoon, and speakers were using a CPP sound truck. I roamed the outskirts of the crowd, recording some of the proceedings and taking pictures. I spotted seven or eight small children wending their way past the crowd, balancing goods from a nearby market on their heads without using their hands. Fascinated, I ran over and asked if I could take a picture. They were happy to cooperate. As I was leaving them, two angry-looking young men approached and wanted to know why I was taking pictures of children who were not too well dressed. Was I going back to the United Kingdom to show the British that the Gold Coast was not ready for independence? I quickly explained that I was not going to Britain, that I was American. Their attitude immediately changed completely. They smiled, shook my hand, and said, "That's different. You people in America are in favor of independence for the Gold Coast."

Whether Americans deserved such an expression of confidence and friendship is debatable. This attitude was in sharp contrast to those that developed later both in Ghana and elsewhere in Africa. But at this time, Nkrumah also expressed sympathetic feelings toward the United States. There was no anti-American propaganda in evidence.

On a second meeting with Nkrumah at his home he was hurried. He had to go to a piano recital by a visiting British artist. So, on the spur of the moment, he asked me to go with him. My substantive discussion with him took place seated beside him in his newly acquired Cadillac en route to the recital and during the intermission at the concert. I rationalized the Cadillac as a necessity for one in Nkrumah's position but was disappointed to see what I felt would be an inevitable process of growing privilege for the leader of government. At the concert I was seated in the front row between Nkrumah and K.A. Gbedemah, later finance minister of Ghana and the person credited with holding the CPP together while Nkrumah was in jail.

In snatches of conversation with Nkrumah, I asked his opinion of the Moral Rearmament movement, which was active in Africa at the time. He indicated complete distaste for the MRA. In fact he called the members fascists and said he did not want them in the Gold Coast. He pointed to their activity in South Africa and asked, "Have they done anything to get rid of apartheid?" We also discussed the Moslem Association party. He thought it should be banned. "There is no room for a party based on religion," he said. "We don't want another Pakistan in West Africa."

MEETING THE GOVERNOR-GENERAL

I had a letter of introduction to Governor-General Sir Charles Arden-Clarke from Patrick Duncan of South Africa, who had described him as an enlightened colonial administrator. I spent perhaps 45 minutes with him at historic Christianborg Castle. He seemed unusually open in discussing his relationship with Nkrumah, which was good, as Nkrumah also said. The governor had certain reserve powers during this transition period, which would give him authority to take control, if, as he put it, "the government starts running off the tracks." But if he had to use them, he said, "the experiment will have failed." He felt that full independence should come by 1956. "This will keep the Gold Coast ahead of Nigeria and this is important from the point of view of keeping face in the Gold Coast." The governor was not concerned about the degree of socialism in Nkrumah's planning. He said cocoa was already under government control, as were roads. He did not discuss the role of the United Africa Company (UAC), controlled mostly by British interests, which accounted for 60 percent of the exports and 40 percent of the imports of the country. He felt that if there was no hitch in the government, the relationship between an independent Ghana and Britain would be good, but he realized that the people resented imperialist Britain at present. One of Nkrumah's right-hand men, Kofi Baako, whom I interviewed on tape, gave credit to the governor for playing an important role in leading the Gold Coast to the brink of independence.

TRAVELS IN THE GOLD COAST

As I traveled to other parts of the country (the Northern Territories, Ashanti, Trans-Volta, and Togo), I got some idea of the problems ahead. Economically the Gold Coast was dependent on one crop—cocoa. Most people were subsistence farmers. Although the country had mineral resources of bauxite, industrial diamonds, manganese, and some gold, as well as rich resources of timber, about 60 percent of total exports were in cocoa. All the cocoa was sold to the government-controlled Cocoa Marketing Board, which shipped it to London, where it was sold on the world market by the Cocoa Marketing Company, not to be confused with the Board. The world price at that time was £515 a ton; the farmer was paid only £135 a ton. The difference made for dissatisfaction in Ashanti, where most of the cocoa farms were. The country was too dependent on one export.

I found from my discussions in Ashanti, the Northern Territories, and the Togo-Trans-Volta areas that there was spirited opposition to Nkrumah. The editor of the *Ashanti-Pioneer* in Kumasi looked upon him as something of a dictator and likened him to Mussolini, who basked in the adoration of the people. In the town of Tolon in the Northern Territories I met one of the most prominent chiefs, the Tolon-Naa. He had won one of the 12 seats of the Northern People's party, having defeated the CPP by 10 votes. He represented the traditionalists, whom Nkrumah wanted to consign to constitutional positions with no power. In Trans-Volta I met Antor, leader of the Togo Congress party, who won the only seat his party captured. He represented the Ewe tribal nationalists, who were more interested in ethnic unity than in Gold Coast national unity.

Despite these tendencies toward disunity, my overwhelming impression of the Gold Coast was one of a dynamic, anticolonial area with an inspiring leader and a massive popular movement, which represented a hopeful sign for the future.

NIGERIA

The Nigeria of 1954 was politically very much alive but otherwise quite different from the Gold Coast. Nigeria was large, with a population of 30 million (about 120 million in the 1980s), which made it the most populous country in Africa. There was no one dominant political movement or one universally accepted political leader. The country was ethnically, politically, and culturally divided into three distinct regions—the West, the East, and the North. I spent two and half weeks in the West and East but did not visit the North, the largest in area and population, until some years later.

EXPLORING LAGOS AND IBADAN

I did a lot of walking through the busy streets of Lagos, the capital and a major seaport. The home of the Anglican archbishop of West Africa, which fronted on the marina, served as a hostel, and I was fortunate to be able to stay there. With my tape recorder I often interviewed people on the street or picked up sidewalk music. Quite a group would gather when I stopped to talk to someone. As in the Gold Coast, people for the most part "liked Americans too much," as they put it. I was surprised once, when I asked, "Do you want self-government soon?" A fierce argument broke out in the crowd of onlookers. Practically everyone vociferously expressed the desire for independence now, and for the British to get out, except one from the North, who bravely said, "No, we do not want independence now. It will mean we in the North will be dominated by the South." That conveyed something of the emotion that underlay the issue of self-government among the common people of Nigeria. I was eager to find the reason for this difference in attitude.

Nigeria was ruled by a British governor-general with a cabinet of Nigerians and Britons. He retained power in the areas of finance, police, foreign affairs, and defence. In all the country there were only about 10,000 whites, mostly British, and more than half of them were in Lagos in government, business, or professional jobs. Business was dominated by such companies as the West Africa Company, G.B. Ollivant, and Kingsway Department Store. There were a number of French companies too. The port was operated by European firms. The casual observer was more impressed, however, by African activity. Unlike Africans farther south on the west coast, the Africans of Nigeria were small entrepreneurs and traders. The streets of Lagos and Ibadan (capital of the West) were lined with shops of all kinds. Yoruba women, dressed in traditional blue blouses and wrap-around skirts and casually wound turbans sat along the streets in little stalls, selling flashlights, key rings, cloth, cigarettes, and various kinds of food. In other parts of West Africa one comes across the Hausa people of northern Nigeria carrying their wares—ebony and ivory objects, crocodile skin bags—always ready to bargain.

I was pleased that the Nigerians, at least those in petty bureaucratic positions, did not stand in awe of a white man. I learned quickly that being called "master" by some Nigerians meant no more than being called "mister." Getting my tape recorder out of the Lagos airport was a case in point. It took three trips to the airport (about 12 miles each way) and a deposit of £15 to accomplish the deed. My white skin was irrelevant.

YORUBA AND IBO—THE ACTION GROUP AND THE NCNC

I was particularly fascinated by the very active political life. The Eastern and Western regions both had major political movements. Although there was an attempt to rise above ethnic background, on the whole the Action Group, founded in 1951 and headed by Obafemi Awolowo, was dominant in the West, where the Yoruba people were the strongest. In the East, where the Ibo people were the overwhelming majority, the National Council of Nigeria and the Cameroons (NCNC), founded in 1944 and headed by Nnamdi Azikiwe, was the dominant political force. In the North, where the Hausa and Fulani people were strongest, the major political party was the Northern People's Congress led by the Sardauna of Sokoto.

Both the Action Group and the NCNC had adopted the slogan "Self-government by 1956." My impression after talking with many leaders was that they did not really expect independence in two years, but that they did expect to have the equivalent of what the Gold Coast had, a Nigerian prime minister. Nigeria, of course, became independent in 1960. The real problem seemed to be whether Nigeria could become "one nation indivisible" with a federal government when regionalism was so strong.

My knowledge of Nigerian politics was gleaned from many interviews—in Lagos, Ibadan, and Enugu (capital of the East). I met Awolowo, leader of the Action Group, at his home in Ibadan. He welcomed me warmly and was quite informal, nonauthoritarian, polite, and quiet in our discussion. He emphatically desired a strong federal government.

I flew from Lagos to Enugu in the same plane with Azikiwe, prime minister of the East, who was just returning from a trip overseas. He had studied at Lincoln University and we had corresponded. Both "Zik," as he was called, and Awolowo were fiercely competitive, and each hoped to be the first prime minister of an independent Nigeria.

At NCNC headquarters I had a long talk with Kolawole Balogun, who, although a Yoruba, was national secretary of the NCNC. He told me that the struggle in Nigeria had not had a direct-action phase, such as in India or the Gold Coast, but worked along political and constitutional lines.

Ayotunde Rosiji, a lawyer and secretary of the Action Group, gave me some feeling of anti-Ibo feeling among the Yoruba leaders. "The Ibo are pushers," he said. He gave them credit for being good propagandists. My sense of Yoruba dislike of the Ibo was further reinforced when I visited Enugu. I was met at the airport by a magistrate, B.F. Adesola. He was exceedingly helpful in introducing me to many people and in giving me a tour of the area, but he also let me know that he did not like the East. He was Yoruba and eager to get home to the West. So many people generalized about the personality traits of the Ibo that it made an impression on me. The Ibo are supposed to be blunt and tactless as well as aggressive. Most of the Westerners wanted to go back to the West. They saw the seat of Nigerian culture as being in the West.

In Enugu I spent considerable time talking with Mazi Mbone Ojike, minister of works in the East and vice-president of the NCNC. He had studied at the University of Chicago and had written a couple of books on Africa, which were widely read in the United States. He tried to dispel any question in my mind about the universal appeal of and support for the NCNC in Nigeria. He pointed out that its founder was Herbert MacAulay, a Yoruba, and that Zik, an Ibo, was his protégé. Each of the regions had two representatives on the National Executive Council of the NCNC.

I gained the impression that the NCNC was more committed than the Action Group to developing a socialist government and economy; that it was committed to a strong federal government rather than strengthening the regions; and that at least in its printed and spoken record, it deemphasized tribal divisions.

The Action Group was very conscious of its base in the culturally developed West. Yoruba areas of Nigeria were divided traditionally into 16 kingdoms. Village chiefs owed allegiance to the 16 hereditary kings. In the Ibo East, no kingdoms existed. Chiefs simply ruled over their own families or clans in limited geographical areas.

Both these movements, united in their desire for self-government, regarded the North as less developed. There were no university graduates from the North in 1954, I was told. Western-style education was almost unknown in that heavily Muslim area. Yet it was the largest area and was bound to be the dominant political force in the future.

Before the discovery of oil, more than a decade later, Nigeria was almost exclusively agricultural. Aside from the coal mines around Enugu in the East (which employed 7,000 workers) and a small cigarette factory in Ibadan in the West, the economy was based on cotton and palm products, peanuts, and cocoa.

I had a particular interest in the role of Christian missions in Africa. I concluded that their main contribution toward change in Nigeria was indirect, through schools and hospitals. This was the almost universal attitude I ran into among Nigerians. The Nigerian minister of the large Anglican church in Lagos told me that missions were responsible for 75 percent of the schools in the West and 90 percent in the East. The North lagged behind educationally, he said, because Christian missions were restricted from operating in a predominantly Muslim area.

THE CAMEROONS

After the dynamism of the Gold Coast and Nigeria, I felt a letdown in the Cameroons. This French area had been a German colony before World War I and after the defeat of Germany had been put under the League of Nations mandate system. After World War II, it became a UN trust territory divided between a large French-governed area and smaller British one. In Douala, the largest city and chief seaport of the French Cameroons, where I spent only three days, French attitudes dominated. Africans wore Western clothing. Of the 3.5 million population, about 10,000 were French, the majority living in Douala, which then had about 100,000 people.

I had a brief and instructive encounter with one anticolonial, nationalist movement, the Union of the Peoples of the Cameroons (UPC). Its leader, Ruben Um Nyobe, went regularly to New York to petition the UN Trusteeship Council for a target date for independence. Although he was not then in Douala, I was able to meet on short notice members of the UPC Executive Committee.

This group had a political sophistication I had not yet met on my journey. Not knowing me, its members were understandably suspicious. They asked me to submit a list of questions I wanted to discuss. I did so, asking about the country, government policy, and their activities for independence. They in turn raised a series of politically loaded questions for me as an American—what about McCarthyism, the Korean War and U.S. participation in it, the Indo-China War (Dienbienphue fell about that time), and racism in the States? They reflected no easy, pro-American attitude such as I had encountered earlier. They had the suspicions of the United States that later became very common among liberation movements in Africa. The UPC's objective was independence from France, and they opposed anything, such as the U.S. alliance with France, that stood in the way. I agreed with their objective and tried from the first to explain the difference between U.S. government policy and actions of individual Americans. It wasn't easy.

Meeting the UPC was a valuable learning experience for me. In contrast to leaders of the Gold Coast and Nigeria, who felt they were on the road to self-government and were cooperating with the British colonial government, the UPC was a minority movement at odds with the French government and destined to remain so. Even after independence it continued its struggle against a government it thought was too friendly to France. Its futile guerrilla efforts led subsequently to the violent death of Nyobe.

I witnessed a shocking incident on the streets of Douala. It was triggered by a minor accident involving a small truck driven by an African and a passenger car driven by a white man. I didn't know who caused the car's dented fender. The white man emerged from his car enraged and immediately started striking and then kicking the youthful African, who made absolutely no response by word or gesture. This incident was in such stark contrast to the rebelliousness of the UPC leaders that I was taken aback. How could this happen? I asked myself. The Frenchman apparently thought he could get away with this physical attack with impunity. The African felt he was helpless. This incident somewhat prepared me for experiences lying ahead.

GABON AND LAMBARÉNÉ

I had decided in New York that if possible, I would take a side trip to visit Dr. Albert Schweitzer's hospital at Lambaréné in Gabon, part of French Equatorial Africa (now divided into Chad, Gabon, Republic of the Congo, and Central African Republic). En route I spent a few days in Port Gentil and Libreville, where I was struck by the climatic change. I had left Douala in a heavy downpour, for it was the rainy season in West Africa. Yet only a few hundred miles to the south just below the equator, there had been no rain for months. It was dry and relatively cool. In the mornings and evenings of August a sweater felt good, and a blanket was comfortable at night.

Both cities were small and were dominated by a busy lumber industry. I visited a plywood factory in Port Gentil built with U.S. Marshall Aid funds after World War II. Twelve Europeans and several hundred Africans were employed there. In the small hotel I talked at length to a Swedish-born lumber man from South Africa while I waited almost two days for the occasional plane flying across the vast tropical forests to Lambaréné. As a stereotype of a racist South African, his opinions both fascinated and repelled me. He saw the African as a threat and was strongly opposed to any racial mixing. He believed that a strong alliance of Western Europe, the United States, and South Africa would be the salvation of the white man. Our arguments were heated but civil. I felt no political stirrings in Gabon to challenge the views held by this white businessman.

I felt a certain awe of Dr. Schweitzer based on his reputation as a musician, theologian, and medical missionary. I had heard and read so much about him that I was eager to visit his hospital. Unfortunately I was not to meet *le Grand Docteur* himself because he was then in Europe. However, I developed new feelings about Schweitzer, even in his absence, because the force of his personality dominated the hospital.

The hospital lies on the Oguwe River in a captivating tropical setting of tall trees and thick foliage, just what a jungle is supposed to be like. The town of Lambaréné is two or three miles from the hospital grounds, and the only means of transportation was by canoe, paddled by several Africans chanting in fascinating rhythm. When I arrived at the hospital, I felt as though I were in a small village. There must have been a thousand or so people there, half of whom were patients and the other half their families. There were about 250 in a separate leper village. Not all patients were confined to bed, and their families were kept busy at various tasks essential to the life of the community. Family groups lived together in small rooms and prepared their own food.

The place was also something like a barnyard. An animal was cared for as diligently as a human being, it seemed. A two-week-old baby gorilla, whose mother had been shot, had just been brought in. A chimpanzee, a recent arrival, had been paralyzed but was recovering nicely. Other animals included wild pigs that came from the surrounding forest for feedings, a pelican, some antelope, goats, sheep, guinea pigs, chickens, ducks, and geese.

Central to the community was the medical care. A great deal of surgery was performed. People suffering from all kinds of tropical diseases came in. At almost any time of the day or night patients were brought in from river canoes on stretchers. Their ailments were diagnosed and treatment given as quickly as possible.

In spite of the valuable service the hospital rendered, I had serious reservations based on my observations and discussions with quite a few of the staff. I felt decidedly critical of the paternalistic staff attitude toward Africans. They were invariably called "natives" and were treated like irresponsible children. There was a separation of whites and blacks in just about everything.

I also felt that the hospital was really a one-man show. It was clear that Schweitzer, a man of fixed opinions, was in charge, and there was no apparent concept of partnership. There were no staff meetings. The finances were solely Schweitzer's responsibility. I was given an old-type sun helmet to wear even in the shade of those huge trees because, as it was explained to me, Europeans should be an example to Africans, it was healthy to be shielded from the sun, and Africans would learn from the European practice.

My most serious criticism, however, was that there was no concept at all of helping to prepare the people for eventual freedom from colonialism. There was not even a serious effort to train African nurses, let alone African supervisors. Thus I felt that despite the real importance of its medical care, the enterprise was irrelevant to the age of independence that lay just ahead.

THE BELGIAN CONGO

Shortly after my arrival in the Belgian Congo (now Zaire) I asked a Belgian colonial administrator if the Congo would be independent some day. He replied in a completely unconcerned manner, "Oh yes, some day, perhaps in twenty-five to fifty years." His nonchalance spoke clearly—the idea of Congo independence was not to be taken seriously, not in our lifetime. I saw no serious steps being taken by the Belgians to give Africans responsibility or to prepare them for an independent future. And there was no obvious African movement to challenge Belgian power. The scene was politically quiescent.

BELGIAN COLONIALISM

The Belgian Congo was one of the richest countries in Africa in the 1950s. Probably 80 percent of the people lived off the land. About 50 percent of the economy was agricultural, the chief products being rubber, cotton, palm products, cocoa, and coffee. About 50 percent was industrial, producing copper, industrial diamonds, tin, cobalt, and uranium. Belgium was, of course, the chief invester and trading partner. The United States was second, accounting for about 25 percent of the imports and 13 percent of the exports.

I was introduced to Belgian colonialism in Leopoldville (now Kinshasa), the capital. I also spent time in Kasai Province near Luluabourg (now Kananga), and in Elizabethville (now Lubumbashi) in the heart of mineral-rich Katanga Province. Leopoldville was different from anything I had previously seen. Tall buildings and well-manicured boulevards advertised the country's wealth. Large American cars were plentiful in the streets. The downtown shops, hotels, and restaurants were owned and operated mostly by Belgians, yet Europeans numbered only about 90,000 out of a Congolese population of some 12 million.

My plane from Gabon had landed at Brazzaville, capital of French Equatorial Africa, on the north bank of the Congo River at one of its widest spots, the Stanley Pool. Gen. Charles de Gaulle had made it the center of his Free French government during the Nazi occupation of France in World War II. I went by bus to the launch that crosses the river from Brazza to Leo (as the two cities are abbreviated). I was surprised to find what amounted to segregation of passengers on the boat—whites in the bow and Africans in the stern. I was subsequently told that the signs designating separate areas had only recently been taken down, primarily because of French pressure on the Belgians, but that in practice segregation lingered on. The designations now were First and Second Class.

I stayed at the Union Mission House. Accommodations were simple with two or three persons in a room and meals served family style. The cost was minimal. I was not entranced by the missionaries I met there. Maybe it was only I, but they seemed stuffy and had no particular interest in the development of the country from the African viewpoint. They considered all Africans just servants and referred to them only as "natives" and "boys."

The Union Mission House was conveniently located; I could walk downtown in about 20 minutes. I was amazed at how empty the streets were after dark. Then I learned that there was a curfew. No African could be in the European section of the city after 9:00 P.M. without a permit. The only Africans I saw were night watchmen outside buildings or homes, frequently with a small fire burning to keep warm. There was no music, no babble of voices. What a contrast with Accra and Lagos! And yet there were more than 300,000 Africans in the city and only 17,000 Europeans.

I had two interviews with the press attaché of the Belgian governor-general, named M. La Brique. We discussed Belgian colonial philosophy and policy and the differences with British and French policies. He said Belgain policy was somewhere between the British and the French. The British, on the one hand, working on the assumption of eventual independence, maintained a kind of indirect rule. African leadership was accepted in middle and lower positions of government. Chiefs were not replaced unless they were troublesome. The British, of course, maintained final control. The French, on the other hand, worked on the assumption of assimilation—make the African into a good Frenchman, integrate French Africa into France.

The Belgian approach was more elitist. La Brique explained that the Belgians tried to achieve African assimilation into full partnership with the Belgians on a high plane. That is, as soon as an African achieved advanced education and lived economically and culturally on a European level, the differences were wiped out. The Congolese became an *evolué*, or "evolved one." He no longer had to observe the curfew, for example. However he must carry a card identifying himself as an *evolué*.

La Brique contrasted the Belgian system with the apartheid of South Africa. Racial segregation there is based on a racist legal structure, he explained. In the Congo the system was based on educational, cultural, and economic standards. For example, an African could stay at a downtown hotel if he was well behaved and had the funds. Furthermore the Belgian government was trying to preserve the country for the Africans, he told me. White immigration was severely limited. No poor whites were allowed to come in. Any white settler must place on deposit with the government the equivalent of $1,000 each for himself, his wife, and any dependents over 21. Minors must have $500 on deposit. If the settler's enterprise did not work out, funds were thus available to send him back where he came from. La Brique seemed genuinely to feel that this kind of approach would eliminate any racial animosity.

Governmentally the Belgians exercised direct control over the Congo. They had first arrived there in 1881 and for 28 years the territory was the private domain of King Leopold. It became a Belgian colony in 1909. The king of Belgium appointed the governor-general and the governors of the six Congo provinces. The Belgians believed they were gradually moving toward giving the people a voice in government by establishing a system of councils. When I was there the governor-general established an Advisory Council consisting of about 30 whites and 5 blacks. It had no power. It was hand-picked and supposedly represented various interests in the territory—business, agriculture, industry, religion. A system of city councils was also just beginning to function in the six major cities. White council members were chosen by white voters; the Africans were chosen by a show of hands at public meetings. This whole system was not being challenged by the African people.

How unreal this Belgian approach seemed. In New York I had been given the name of Dr. John Karefa-Smart, who was working with the World Health Organization in Brazzaville. At the first opportunity, I crossed the river to Brazza and met him. Born in Sierra Leone, he had attended Otterbein College in Ohio and received an M.D. from McGill University in Montreal. Years later, after his stint with WHO, he was foreign minister of independent Sierra Leone but was removed in a military coup.

I spent considerable time with Karefa-Smart, who had a great distaste for Leopoldville. Invariably, he told me, there would be a racial incident. One took place about the time I was there. When he entered the Palace Hotel to visit an American, he was challenged because of his race and threatened with being bodily thrown out until others intervened. In Brazzaville no such incident had ever occurred.

When I was in Luluabourg, chief city of Kasai, with 50,000 Africans and 2,300 Europeans, I went into the post office to buy a stamp. I joined the line of 15 or 20 Congolese at the stamp window. Soon a European woman entered and went to the front of the line, where she received immediate service. Other Europeans did the same. It seemed to be the accepted practice. Curious eyes settled on me for not following suit.

The brand new railroad station at Luluabourg had what in the United States would have been called a Jim Crow entrance and window labeled "indigènes," where the "natives" went. In Elizabethville, one evening I went to a large carnival with a young white American missionary. I was surprised to see no Africans there. When I asked why, I was told that the next evening was for Africans; they went on different nights.

Whatever the rationale for Belgian policy may have been, the fact was that the Congo was not only a colony but also suffered under racist laws and customs. Some African police carried side arms but no bullets. Africans could not move around without a pass on the theory that no African should be allowed in an urban area unless he had a job. Evening meetings of Africans were prohibited without a special permit. As a missionary explained to me, this helped to keep down subversive ideas.

VISITING MISSIONARIES

I spent a little more than a week in Kasai Province, the breadbasket of the Congo. I stayed at the American Presbyterian Congo Mission at Mutoto, outside Luluabourg. It was run by Southern Presbyterians from the United States. The 16 missionary families were most kind and generous to me. From them I learned a lot about rural mission work and the country. I thought the missionaries a strange combination. They didn't seem to have much political insight. They weren't too well acquainted with the African scene nor were they politically analytical. Yet they realized that changes were bound to take place. They had a paternalistic attitude toward the Africans, speaking of them usually as "natives." One of the women said she doubted the mission would be there more than 10 or 15 years. They were trying to train the Congolese to take over.

One of my most interesting experiences was "itinerating" with one of the younger missionaries, Bill Washburn. In two or three days we probably traveled 200 miles. This was Benelulua country, where the language was Tschiluba, which Washburn spoke well. The narrow dirt roads were lined with villages built by the government so that they would be accessible. Each village had several hundred people living in mud and stick huts thatched with palm leaves. Water had to be fetched from a spring or stream some distance away in receptacles balanced on the head. Each village had its chief. I was introduced to patriarchal and matriarchal family systems, the dowry system, the custom of determining age by some long-ago event rather than by the year, and the compulsory-crop system—cotton and peanuts in this area.

The Africans seemed to stand in awe of the Europeans, or perhaps of the missionaries. As we drove along the road, people walking along the side would raise their hats as we approached. When we were engaged in a large village discussion, Bill would draw a line in the dirt as an indication that Africans should stand outside that line, and they would do so.

The mission operated schools, hospitals, and clinics. People sought advice on many subjects. In one village an angry dispute was in progress. Some boys had been playing hookey from school. In order to put pressure on the families to make their children attend classes, a couple of the African teachers had taken chickens as "hostages," to be returned if the children turned up in class. In one case a teacher had eaten a "hostage." Washburn was asked to adjudicate. I watched as the discussion, in Tschiluba, went on at length. Finally Washburn ruled that the chickens should be returned and the one that had been eaten should be paid for. There was no further wrangling.

MY VISIT TO ELIZABETHVILLE AND MY SOUTH AFRICAN VISA

I spent several days in Elizabethville. Segregation was a fact of life there as in Leopoldville and Luluabourg. The "native" city was a distance away from the European area. Schools were separate, the railroad station had windows for "indigènes" and "Européens," and there was a curfew.

The city was the center for the Union Minière du Haut Katanga, a Belgian mining company. The company had about 18,000 employees at an average wage of about $22 a month plus food. A rather complete welfare system was designed to keep them happy. The workers and their families lived in neat, company-built and company-owned houses. The company operated a hospital for them and paid for their care. It also issued clothing. Yet when I toured a mine with a Belgian guide, who explained all these amenities, he referred to the Africans only as "niggers."

All during my trip down the west coast of Africa I had given thought to my plan for visiting South Africa. By the time I reached the Congo I knew what I was going to do. I had a round-trip air ticket from New York to Johannesburg. At a travel agency in Leo I asked to exchange my return air ticket for a boat ticket from Cape Town to Southampton, England. That was no problem. Then I went to the South African consulate to see if I could get a transit visa from Johannesburg to Cape Town to catch my ship. I hoped my anxiety did not show as I talked with the young vice-consul. He thought it could be arranged and asked me to return in a couple of days. With great misgivings I returned at the appointed time, and he gave me my passport with the transit visa stamped in, saying that in a case like this he didn't even have to contact Pretoria. I was exultant.

ANGOLA

I had my first contacts with Angolans while I was in Leopoldville. My friend Homer Jack had given me the post office box number of Manuel Barros Necaca. I had written Necaca from New York telling him when and where I would be in Leo and expressing the hope that we might meet, but I had no idea how to reach him.

The day before my departure for Luanda, capital of Angola, on August 9, I was eating my dessert at the evening meal at the Mission House when I heard a knock at the back door. In a moment a missionary came to me to say that three "natives" were asking for me. He indicated that he knew them. They were from Angola and he suggested that it wasn't very important for me to talk with them. But I was delighted to see Necaca, a tall, impressive man, and his companions. One of them, who worked at the Portuguese consulate in Leo, gave me somewhat unsettling news. He had gleaned information from in-coming cables that the Portuguese had been following my movements in Africa. They were undecided whether to let me board the Sabena plane for Luanda the next day because I was regarded as a propagandist who had mistakenly been given a visa to Angola in New York. My Angolan visitors hoped for the best for me and looked forward to talking with me when I returned from Angola in two weeks.

Necaca, who was of the Bakongo people, had learned English by working as a nurse with a British Baptist mission near São Salvador in northern Angola. Before he departed he introduced me to the third Angolan, his nephew, who up to this time had not said a word. His name was Holden Roberto, and he was later to be the most important of them all.

AN OPPRESSIVE ATMOSPHERE

In Angola I learned what a police state is. I was met at the airport of Luanda, by American missionary friends, who took me to the Methodist headquarters, Missão Evangelica. Here my orientation to Angola began. I felt quite comfortable with these missionaries, not just because we were Americans and Methodists but also because I could relate to their attitudes toward Africa and Africans. They were in the process of turning over leadership of the church to Angolans. They never spoke of "natives" but only of Africans or Angolans. They were obviously not happy with Portuguese colonial policy, but, in spite of their cordiality, they were clearly concerned about my being there. I soon understood why.

Weeks before my arrival in Luanda, Portuguese officials had begun calling the missionaries. When is Houser arriving? they wanted to know. "As soon as he arrives he must be brought to police headquarters to fill in papers and receive his *guia* ["permit to travel"] before he goes elsewhere in Angola." There was no mistaking that the authorities were apprehensive about my visit. That made the missionaries nervous because they felt their own work could be threatened by something I might do or say. So my first briefing was on Portuguese pressures on the missionaries.

I was told about a young missionary from South Dakota who had written his mother about the contract labor system in Angola. His mother thought his fascinating letter should be given wider circulation, and so excerpts appeared in his college newspaper. The town newspaper picked up the item, and from there it came to the attention of the Portuguese. In short order the young missionary was on his way home by demand of the Portuguese authorities.

In another incident all church members who attended a reception for a visiting black American bishop (Matthew W. Clair) were detained for questioning after the bishop left the country because he had criticized the contract labor system at the reception.

The missionaries had developed a policy for response to Portuguese pressures. They accommodated, maintaining a correct, if not cordial, relationship with the police and authorities. They did not make provocative statements or write anything politically controversial in their letters or reports back home, and they were careful when on home leave not to make public statements that could be used to damage the mission work. By inference, politely but clearly, they hoped I would adopt this policy also. That put a lot of pressure on me, for I wanted to do anything I could to expose the viciousness of Portuguese rule in Angola.

After this briefing, I was taken to police headquarters. One of the missionaries acted as interpreter. I answered simple questions about my trip so far in Africa, what I thought about Luanda, how long I planned to stay, where I wanted to visit. I was given permission to visit Malange, 150 miles inland, where there was a large Methodist station at Quessua, and to travel to Lobito, 300 miles to the south. Then my passport was taken, to be picked up the next day.

When I returned for my passport, I was told the right official was not there to handle it. When I went back a second time, other excuses were given. It was clear that I would be traveling around Angola without a passport.

COLONIALISM PORTUGUESE STYLE

I spent a lot of time walking around Luanda and was occasionally driven to the outskirts of the city. Luanda was beautiful. It is situated on a bay forming a well-protected harbor, beyond which lies the Atlantic Ocean. Because Angola is south of the equator, August is relatively cool. The city seemed more Portuguese than African. The buildings were quite tall, of Mediterranean-style architecture.

Officially Angola was an overseas province of Portugal. From the Portuguese point of view, it was not a colony but a part of Portugal. The governor-general was appointed from Lisbon, as were the governors of the five provinces. Unlike the French colonies, there were no elections and no legislature. The country was administered through the 5 provinces, 16 councillor districts, 70 subareas headed by administrators, and 290 administrative posts headed by *chefes do posto*. The population was 4.5 million, composed of about 2 percent white, 0.07 percent mestico, and almost 98 percent African.

The population of Luanda was about 100,000 in 1954. Most of the Africans lived in an outlying area called the *musseques*, meaning "sand." It was not unlike the Medina section of Dakar. The huts were made of odds and ends, and the "streets" were simply sand. I did not see any running water. I did see young boys wheeling barrels of water, purchased at a shop, through the sand toward their homes. There was no public sanitation.

I was surprised that there seemed to be less obvious racism than in the Congo or even in the French colonial areas. I saw some black and white youngsters in the same schools. They were even playing together. I saw some few Africans in restaurants eating with whites. On the train to Malange there were two or three blacks in a coach with whites. Africans went to the cinema. Thus, there seemed to be no legally enforced segregation policy.

The Portuguese had a policy of integrating educated Angolans into Portuguese society. Those Africans who wore European clothing, spoke Portuguese, and outwardly were culturally European could win the status of *assimilados*, "assimilated ones." Perhaps 1 percent of the Africans were so designated, but this did not really mean the end of racism, nor did it lessen the bitterness of Africans.

One African pastor, who was an *assimilado,* told me how his son had been arrested and held in jail for not having his ID card. The pastor went to the police to get his son out but was laughed at and told that his son was "only a black boy." The son was rather roughly interrogated for another day before being released.

Although relationships between the races seemed freer in Luanda than in either French or Belgian areas, there was no welfare system such as the Belgians had nor any policy to protect Africans from an influx of poor Portuguese. The official policy of Portugal was to encourage immigration.

With Portugal the poorest country in Europe, it was inevitable that low-income Portuguese would come to Angola, and they did, competing with Angolans for menial and low-paid jobs. Luanda was the only place I had visited where there were no African taxi drivers. They were all Portuguese.

On my flight to Lobito I sat beside a man from Sweden. After many years in the Cameroons, he had come to Angola, where he had a large, successful farm. He told me how much he liked Angola, which he called the last "unspoiled" part of Africa. He referred to Africans as "niggers" and said the African knew his place. Education only "spoils" the African, he said. He had a wife and four children and two mestico children, by mestico women, whom he also took care of.

I gained renewed respect for what the missionaries were doing, particularly in education. They were in the business of "spoiling" Africans through their schools. In effect, the Protestant schools were all private, receiving no subsidy from the state. Since Portugal is a Catholic country, the Catholic schools were state schools completely subsidized by the government. There were 40 Methodist schools in the Luanda district with about 2,000 pupils. There were only two high schools in all of Angola. The illiteracy rate was more than 95 percent. Yet a study of Protestant churches in Lobito indicated that almost 75 percent of the members were literate. Obviously the mission education program was having an effect.

CONTRACT LABOR

One of my objectives in Angola was to find out about the so-called contract labor system. Although I had discussions with many people in Luanda about how the system worked, it became much clearer on my trip to the Quessua mission station, outside Malange. I traveled all day by diesel train to Malange. We rode through forested areas where much coffee, sisal, cotton, and tropical fruit were grown. Malange is 3,500 feet above sea level on the plateau on high rolling grassland that runs down the center of the continent. The climate is cool.

I was met at the station by Ted Cooper of the Methodist mission. After I had settled in at his home, he said we must go without delay to the office of the district administrator, which for several weeks had been pressing him to let them know when I would arrive. We spent from 7:00 to 9:30 P.M. in the office with Cooper translating. After routine questions about my observations on Angola, I was asked if I had any questions. I asked about contract labor. The administrator explained that Africans were lazy and didn't want to work. The contract labor system was designed to force them to do essential work. He carefully explained that only the unemployed were picked for such labor. They were paid a wage and provided with clothing, food, and a place to live. I did not argue, although his statements did not correspond with other facts I had been given.

Afterward, back at Cooper's house, my host said that the administrator was completely incorrect in saying that only unemployed were taken. Some of Cooper's own workers had been taken by the police at night and sent off for the labor force.

The Quessua mission, where I stayed with an agriculturalist, Lloyd Schaad, had been founded in the late 19th century. It covered several square miles and included nine small villages. Of the 12 missionaries, only 2 were ordained. They served as teachers in the schools, professors in the Bible school, agriculturists, and doctors and nurses.

The villagers all experienced the contract labor system either directly or indirectly. From my observations and discussions I gleaned that any male over 16 was legally liable for this labor, and the authorities were not too scrupulous about taking even younger boys. The term of service could be as short as three months or extend to a year or so. The place of work could be either private or government sponsored, and it could be in the sugar cane fields, coffee plantations, harbor, roads, mines—wherever labor was needed. Frequently labor was procured by night raids on villages. The police would go from hut to hut looking at identification papers, take the number of workers needed, put them in the local jail for the remainder of the night, and then ship them off to their workplace. The local *chefe do posto*, a Portuguese, told Schaad that he had to produce a quota of 25 workers a month. He in turn would tell the chief of a village how many he must produce. If more were needed to fill out the quota, night raids were made. Bribery was an endemic part of the system. A family with any money could often buy off the chief or the Portuguese *chefe do posto* to release their son, husband, or father from forced labor.

Contract laborers repairing a road near Malange, Angola, 1954.

Schaad said that frequently villagers working on the farms near Quessua would disappear. One morning a few days previously, four men working with him did not show up. Suspecting that they might have been picked up during the night, he hurried to the police station. He discovered that two of the men had already been shipped out, but the other two were still being held. They were released when Schaad said that they were employed by him.

One worker at Quessua with whom I talked had just returned from a year and a half at a sugar factory, most of it under the contract labor system. He received $15 at the end of his term, tax deducted.

On a walk in the countryside Schaad and I came across some teenage boys on contract labor, pounding rocks with huge hammers. They had built their own grass huts near by. I carefully snapped pictures, taking seriously Schaad's warning that my camera might be confiscated if anyone in authority saw me.

Not much farther on we came to a dirt road where 20 people—men, women, and boys—were repairing potholes. They broke up large anthills close by, carried the earth in baskets to the holes, and filled them in. I was told that the village was responsible for giving one week a month to road repair. The work was being done at a leisurely pace. I could well understand why. It wasn't they who had cars to drive on the roads.

On a Sunday I accompanied a carload of African and American pastors to several villages where services were held. We traveled perhaps a hundred miles on dusty roads and stopped in half a dozen villages. Dust from the wheels filled the car and burned my nostrils. It was so heavy that it made the Africans look almost white.

In each village I asked about contract labor. Mpolo was typical, with a population of about 150, mostly young boys and girls, women, and older men. One hundred attended the service, all but 15 of them women. All the men over 16 had been taken for contract labor or had gone to a city to avoid being picked up.

LOBITO

I returned to Luanda briefly before taking off for the beautiful port city of Lobito to the south. Here I stayed with the Rev. Larry Henderson, a United Church of Christ missionary, and his wife, Ki. Lobito then had a population of about 25,000, 20 percent of whom were white. The city lies on a natural harbor protected from the ocean by a long, narrow reach of land. Most of the Europeans lived on this lovely strip between the ocean and the bay. The Africans lived in a separate section. There were only two schools, one Catholic and one UCC, each of which had about 200 pupils. The rest of the children received no education.

After the mandatory visit to the police and a call-back, we traveled to many places in the area, including Benguela about 20 miles south, which was a port and a center of the sugar cane industry. The big Catumbela sugar plantation had about 5,000 workers, many of them on contract labor. We met the pastor in Lobito, the Rev. Jesse Chipenda. In later years I met his two sons, Daniel, who was an important political figure in the Popular Movement for the Liberation of Angola (MPLA) and then a dissident, and José, who was on the executive staff of the World Council of Churches in Geneva.

Chipenda's home was on a hill. To reach it on foot we went through the African section. There were no sanitary facilities and the stench was overpowering when the wind blew the wrong way. But the pastor's house had a commanding view of the city, looking out over the African section and the salt flats, where sea water is evaporated to obtain salt.

There were about 500 members in Chipenda's church, but he told me that of the 200 that came from rural areas, only 50 had families with them. This was typical because so many men came to the urban area to avoid contract labor.

We went to a mid-week meeting at the church. About a hundred people discussed two things in Portuguese—keeping homes clean and the evil of alcohol. I was asked to meet with 15 or 20 leaders, who asked about my trip and my impressions of Angola. Inevitably we got into a discussion of independence. I suggested the necessity of struggle for freedom. The response was that if Angola were to achieve independence, the Portuguese in Angola would have to lead the struggle and that would not put the Africans in any better position than they were then. The pastor suggested an analogy: Sometimes when an African catches a grasshopper he pulls off its wings so it can't fly away. "The African is like the grasshopper who has had his wings pulled off and doesn't know how to fly any more."

The next day while I was walking around the residential area of Lobito, I was startled when a young African boy dashed suddenly from behind a bush, thrust some papers into my hands, and disappeared as quickly as he had come. I glanced at the three sheets, written in Portuguese, and put them in my pocket. After I left Angola I had the anonymous letter translated. The writer had been at the meeting the night before. His message was a frustrated cry for help: "We cannot win the struggle by ourselves. Help us." I felt rather impotent.

My last day in Lobito I went with Henderson to a garage where his car was being repaired. When we returned home, he told me that we were being tailed by two plainsclothesmen, whom he recognized from having seen them before in uniform. One had been in the garage. One was stationed outside the house, his motocycle close by. To test the information, I went out for a walk. They followed me around.

When I left by taxi the next day, I did not see the plainclothesmen at the house, but they were waiting at the airport. One of them boarded the plane to Luanda. Whether I was followed there I do not know, but I felt tremendously uneasy and rather dragged out by the whole Angola situation. I was caught between the government on the one hand and the missionaries on the other with no movement to appeal to. I wondered what effect this would have on me over the long pull. I thought Angola was one place in Africa I didn't want to work, not because it wouldn't be challenging, but because I doubted if I could last. As it was, I was not sure what to say about the situation when I was in the United States. The missionaries wanted me to say as little as possible.

My passport was returned to me at the last moment as I boarded the plane.

SOUTH AFRICA

It was about a five-hour flight from Elizabethville to Johannesburg. As we flew over Southern Rhodesia, I looked down on the farms with a haunting regret that I could not visit there on this trip. However, my thoughts were essentially about arriving in South Africa. I was expectant and nervous. My apprehension deepened when immigration forms were passed around. One question was "Have you ever been convicted of a crime in any country? If so, give details." I debated with myself on how to handle this. My convictions in the United States involved nonregistration under the Selective Service Act and various arrests for opposing racial segregation. I surely could not give details on these and hope to get into the country. On the other hand, I didn't want to tell an outright lie. So I compromised. I left this space blank, hoping the immigration office would overlook it.

It was already dark when we landed in the early evening. As I walked up the ramp to the airport building, I spotted Arthur Blaxall, with his white hair and distinctive goatee, whom I recognized from photographs. He was the only person I had written to about coming to South Africa. Then I waited in line. The immigration officer was pleasant. He came to the space I had left blank, looked at me, and then without a word wrote no. Maybe my passport identification as a clergyman helped. As I went through customs I breathed a sigh of relief. Exhilarated, I passed the barrier and met my host and his wife, Florence. I was in South Africa at last!

We drove in the Blaxalls' car through part of Johannesburg and then some 20 miles to Roodeport. It was a clear, cool spring evening. The elevation in Johannesburg is about 6,000 feet. Even in the semidarkness, things I had read about began to come to life. We passed African locations and mine compounds. I could see the slag heaps against the sky.

Roodeport is one of the cities on the ridge that runs down the middle of Africa. The Afrikaners settled there after their great trek from the Cape in the early 1800s because of the favorable climate and the spring water. In the morning I could see the beauty of springtime more clearly—blossoms on the fruit trees, flowers and vines in bloom, the veld brown like California in summer.

My visa gave me only a few days in South Africa to be in transit from Johannesburg to Cape Town. Blaxall and I decided that I should go to government headquarters in Pretoria, about 50 miles from Johannesburg, and ask for an extension. I first made a reservation on a ship leaving Cape Town on September 24 (which would give me three weeks in South Africa) and then drove to Pretoria where, without any difficulty, my visa was extended.

I was struck by how similar Johannesburg seemed to American cities— bustling traffic, large buildings, many stores and businesses. It was strange after being in Africa for several months to see a city really lighted up at night, in contrast to most cities in Africa, which were rather dimly lit. The fact that blacks outnumbered whites almost five to one was not obvious because of the government policy of keeping Africans in clearly defined areas on the outskirts of the city. Inspite of their disproportionate numbers, dark-skinned people seemed unobtrusive. The Africans were on the whole dressed in Western clothing, making them seem no more numerous than blacks in many parts of the United States.

A CLIMATE OF PROTEST

My visit to South Africa (the only one, as it has turned out) did not alter my basic analysis of the situation there. I had some familiarity with it as a result of our work in support of the Defiance Campaign. What the trip did was to make the individuals I had corresponded with or read about become real, and I myself had some experience with apartheid, learned the meaning of banning, and saw the police in action.

Circumstances were clearly building to revolution. Two opposing forces were lined up—one side trying to preserve privilege, white dominance, black subservience, apartheid; the other side demanding equality, a decent standard of living, the advantages of education free from segregation. At this time the struggle was focused more on the necessity of political revolution than on a basic change in the economic order. South Africa was unique in that exploitation of the blacks was not by a conquering white colonial power from outside the country but by South African-born whites.

The pattern of segregation as I observed it, kept the black African "in his place" so effectively that the average white person just could not become well acquainted with an African without tremendous effort. The social pressure on a white person to accept the pattern was intense. The status quo was very comfortable even if there was an underlying feeling of insecurity. I was in many European homes. Not one was without servants. Servants to do the cooking and housework were cheap. This arrangement left the whites free for other activities. When I visited on the servant's day off, the helpless floundering to prepare a meal was obvious and amusing.

Seeing conditions firsthand modified a couple of my preconceptions. I was not so appalled by bad housing conditions in the African locations as I had expected to be, perhaps because I had seen as bad or worse conditions in the Medina section of Dakar, the musseques of Luanda, and the cité of Leopoldville. Conditions were certainly deplorable in Moroka and Pimville near Johannesburg, Eastwood and Bantule near Pretoria, Cato Manor near Durban, and Windermere near Cape Town. Two or three families were living together in ramshackle huts constructed of old lumber and odd pieces of tin and paying as much as $8.50 rent a month, about half a monthly wage. But in other locations (Orlando, Attridgeville, Langa) at least some of the houses, constructed under the municipal councils, were quite neat, though overcrowded and often without electricity or running water.

I was impressed by public criticism of the government in the press. A residue of liberalism led to the expression of diverse opinions in newspapers, to criticism of the government by opposition white political parties, and to occasional demonstrations by organizations such as the Torch Commando. In contrast to Angola and the Congo, there was ferment in South Africa; it was by no means politically dead. The mutual animosity of the Afrikaans- and English-speaking elements, which had a long history behind it, undoubtedly contributed to expression of opposition. A little of this rubbed off in relations with the black population.

As I passed a gold mine in Johannesburg, my attention was focused on a relic of the Defiance Campaign. Printed in large red letters on a wall, very visible from the road, was a sign saying "Defy Unjust Laws." In contrast to this, at almost the same spot there was a road sign, so reminiscent of cattle and deer crossing signs on American highways, that read, "Drive slowly. Natives crossing ahead."

There was something different about the behavior of Africans in South Africa compared with Africans I had seen in Angola and the Congo. One of the first Africans I met was wearing an African National Congress pin in his lapel. He said he wore it wherever he went as an indication of his rejection of apartheid. At a small nonpolitical gathering I met a quite ordinary African youth who told me he had been arrested twice during the Defiance Campaign.

A sign near the gold mines, Johannesburg, South Africa, 1954.

I was fascinated by an incident in downtown Johannesburg. A white man driving a car around a corner swerved suddenly and caused an African to jump back. It didn't look like too narrow an escape for the African, and it seemed obviously unintentional on the part of the driver. When the car slowed down, the African went to the side of the car and shook his finger vigorously, admonishing the driver to watch where he was going. When I saw this—a black man telling a white man off—I knew I was in a different situation.

An Indian leader in the Defiance Campaign told me of an unusual experience he had had. He was attacked one night in an African location by a group of tough, lawless youngsters called *tsotsis*. While he was being roughed up, he had the presence of mind to raise his thumb in the salute of the Congress movement and shout "Afrika," in the manner popularized during the Defiance Campaign. Immediately the ruffians stopped, and he heard one of them say as they hurried away, "We made a mistake."

IMPRESSIVE LEADERSHIP

My awareness of political ferment was deepened by the leaders I met. I visited Chief Albert J. Lutuli in the town of Stanger, some miles from Durban in Natal Province. He was serving his second banning order at that time. The first had been imposed in 1952 for his support of the Defiance Campaign and was reimposed in 1954. Two laws were involved— the Riotous Assemblies Act and the Criminal Laws Amendment Act. Under the ban he was confined to his immediate geographical area. He was permitted to preside over the ANC Executive Committee as long as it met in his area, but he could not participate in a public meeting. He was not restricted, as were others, under the Suppression of Communism Act, which prohibited the proscribed person from being in "gatherings," defined as meetings of more than two people.

Lutuli was an impressive man. He had a deep, resonant voice, an excellent sense of humor, and unshakable convictions. He believed in struggle but wanted it to be nonviolent. I interviewed him on tape, later broadcast on NBC radio when I returned home. He said, "I have become a man who has embraced nonviolence. I don't see any other method we can employ. The right goal of any people is freedom. Our success depends on how successful we can be in arousing and educating our people. We must imbue in them the spirit of nonviolence. I think therein lies our hope."

I illegally called on Walter Sisulu at his home in Orlando, an African location near Johannesburg. Any white person going into a location was required to have a special permit, which I did not seek. Blaxall drove me to Sisulu's small house and left me there to talk for several hours. Sisulu was under ban and was charged with violating it by having met with six people. He was prohibited for two years from being in a gathering and was barred indefinitely from membership in the ANC, of which he had been secretary general since 1949.

We talked about the history of the ANC going back to 1912 and about

Chief Albert J. Lutuli, president of the ANC,
1954.

resistance campaigns in South Africa, specifically the Defiance Campaign.
He felt that the political consciousness of the masses had been raised by
the 1952 effort. He was looking forward to plans for the Congress of the
People, to be held in 1955, and to the adoption of the Freedom Charter, on
which work was already in progress. In summarizing his position in a
taped interview with me he said, "The oppressed people of South Africa
are determined as never before. They are not prepared to budge an inch."

Blaxall introduced me to Oliver Tambo, who struck me as a warm and
gentle person. He was then a young attorney, who shared an office with
Nelson Mandela. Both of them were leaders in the ANC. After the death
of Lutuli and the life imprisonment of Mandela and Sisulu, Tambo was
president of the ANC even while in exile.

I was eager to record some African music and was told about the
dancing and singing on Sunday afternoons at the Crown Mines. This
seemed to be a tourist attraction and was probably looked upon as good
public relations by the mining company. Tambo offered to take me.
Segregation was not observed in the arena, but I did not see other Africans
in the audience. We were watching the beginning of the program when
Tambo suddenly said to me, "I almost forgot. This is a gathering. I am
under ban. I will wait for you outside." He left and in a few minutes I too
left and joined him outside.

I met with Manilal Gandhi at the Phoenix Settlement near Durban,
founded by his father in 1904. The first civil disobedience campaign
against racial restrictions on Indians was planned there. About a thousand
shared the life of the community before Gandhi left in 1914 to return to
India. Manilal returned to the settlement in 1916 as a young man to carry
on some of his father's work, such as editing *Indian Opinion*. He was rather
slow of speech, but was obviously deeply committed. He felt that the

Mr. and Mrs. Manilal Gandhi at Phoenix Settlement, Natal, South Africa, 1954.

Defiance Campaign had a tremendous effect because it made the govern-ment take notice of the injustices being perpetrated. Through the day and night I spent with Manilal, I felt a closeness to the mystique of the great Mahatma, for whom I had an unusual reverence.

I was able to renew my relationship with Z.K. Matthews at his home in Alice in Cape Province. Matthews was looked upon as an elder statesman in the ANC. He gave solidity and respectability to the organization. He felt that a continuation of the Defiance Campaign was not in the immediate offing, and that the only real opposition to the Afrikaner Nationalist government had to come from Africans with the ANC as the spearhead. At that moment, he said, people were taking a deep breath waiting for the next step forward. Although Matthews was not under ban when I saw him, he had not recovered his passport, which had been confiscated on his return from the United States. He expected his real problems would come at the University College, where he was on the government payroll. He was not wrong.

Patrick Duncan drove from Maseru in Basutoland (now Lesotho) to spend the day with me at Matthews's home. Duncan had been a colonial civil servant in Basutoland. He developed a strong antipathy toward apartheid, became convinced of the Gandhian path of nonviolence, and resigned his position in Basutoland, thus setting the stage for his participa-tion in the Defiance Campaign. He was making a meager living by farming and selling secondhand books.

Duncan was a charming person with the manner and bearing befitting one of good family, but he had strong convictions, upon which he acted.

He was also an individualist who could not really fit within anyone's organized movement for long. Although deeply opposed to apartheid, he belonged to no organization and felt he could make his best contribution by writing.

POLICE STATE ATMOSPHERE

In all my discussions the injustices of South African racism were clearly delineated. In 1954 the population was about 12 million (it more than doubled by the 1980s). There were 1 million Coloureds and less than half a million Asians, mostly Indians. Only the Europeans had real voting rights, although the Coloureds in Cape Province could vote for Europeans. Africans, in a separate election, could vote for three Europeans to represent them in the lower house of Parliament and four in the upper house. Basic to the idea of apartheid was the principle that Africans belong in a tribal setting in the specially designated rural reserve areas (today called Homelands), which occupied about 12.5 percent of the country. Even there Africans could not own land without special permit. In the Western Areas of Johannesburg a few Africans owned land, but the government, under the Native Resettlement Act, was moving all Africans from these sections to set up the area now called Soweto (South West Townships).

The pass laws controlled the movement of Africans around the country. The whites needed black labor. Therefore the "privilege," rather than the right, of an African to go to a city or to a European-owned farm depended on obtaining a pass. The philosophy behind the system was that the city is the white man's domain. No African migration to Cape Town, for example, had been permitted since 1949.

I visited the court in the location of Langa near Cape Town to hear some of the cases. Practically all of them had to do with pass-law violations. The magistrate was not a judge but the commissioner of native affairs for the area. One woman being tried had been in the Cape Town area for five years with her husband and family without a pass. She was given a suspended sentence of 30 days hard labor on condition that she be out of the area in a month. Where was she to go? Back to the reserves, leaving her family?

In the urban areas there was a curfew usually at 9:00 P.M. Under the Reservation of Separate Amenities Act any public place could refuse service to a nonwhite person. Under the Group Areas Act whole communities could be moved from one place to another if the area had been designated for whites only.

These laws and many others completely encompassed the life of the African in a police state atmosphere. I had some experience of this myself. When Matthews saw me off on the night train to Port Elizabeth, he whispered, "There are two police following us." I asked him if they were following him or me. He responded, "They follow me everywhere." As I waved farewell I thought, "Well, they may have been following Z.K., but they are now following me." I had a sinking feeling as I realized I would be under surveillance during the remainder of my stay in South Africa.

When I arrived in Port Elizabeth there was not another person in the world, outside of Matthews, who knew where I was, or so I thought. I went to the hotel he had recommended. I had hardly set my bags down in my room before the telephone rang. I picked up the receiver and heard the telephone click down on the other end. "Aha," I thought. "Now the police know I am here."

Later in the day I called Joe Matthews, the lawyer son of Z.K., who had sent us the reports during the Defiance Campaign. We agreed to meet that evening on the street outside the hotel. I spent the day wandering around the city. After dark I met Joe Matthews and Dr. J.L. Njongwe, his uncle and the treasurer of the Cape ANC. They decided that the safest place to talk was in the car while driving. We headed out of town along the unlighted road bordering the Indian Ocean. We had driven about five miles when quite suddenly two cars converged on us; one stopped in front of us and one behind. I was startled. The others seemed to take it in stride. A plainclothes policeman whom my companions knew thrust his head in an open window and said, "I strongly suspect you are guilty of violating the ban by being in a gathering." Both Matthews and Njongwe were under banning order.

We were taken back to police headquarters. It was about 11:00 P.M. I was interrogated for about an hour and a half by a police lieutenant who had obviously been roused from bed. I was told that I was not under arrest but was asked all kinds of questions—whom did I know in South Africa, what organizations was I a member of, what was my purpose in South Africa? I gave only the obvious answers and gave no names other than Z.K. Matthews, whom I had, of course, met in New York.

I was dismissed, had a short night's sleep, and left the next day for Cape Town, only three days before my ship was to sail. I spotted the plainclothes police, who I expected would be in the Cape Town Airport. They were standing behind open newspapers, Hollywood style, keeping an eye on me. The same two were in the lobby of the Mt. Nelson Hotel, which I went to, again half hidden behind their newspapers. They followed me wherever I went. I took down the license number of their car, which turned up unfailingly wherever I happened to be. My main concern was for my tape recordings and notes. Somewhat amateurishly I tried to hide them in the hotel room because I felt it might be raided in my absence. Then I decided I should leave them some place else, where they would be safe. I went to the office of the South African Institute of Race Relations and talked with the young woman in charge, who agreed to keep the material for me.

I definitely felt under wraps because of the police surveillance. As far as I could tell, there were three detectives, two white and one black, tailing me at various times. I gave them the slip on my second day in Cape Town because I was walking and they were riding. I cut through parks with no roads and for one day they did not know where I was.

That was the day I contacted I.B. Tabata, the leader and socialist theoretician for the Unity Movement. We had corresponded in connection with the Defiance Campaign, which he criticized as he did the ANC. I found him a stimulating thinker, although his movement was not destined to be a major political factor.

Tabata introduced me to others of his movement and took me to the African location and to the Coloured areas of the city.

While Tabata was driving me through Cape Town, I saw the unmarked police car that had been following me approach from the opposite direction. I ducked under the dashboard. Later in the day the woman at the South African Institute of Race Relations called to tell me she had had a strange telephone call. Someone had called her saying that he was a friend of mine. I had not shown up for a lunch date, and he wondered how to reach me. I had, of course, made no such date. She answered that she didn't know anyone by my name. That evening when I was back in the hotel, the police were on hand again.

For the rest of my time in Cape Town I acted like a tourist. What a beautiful city it is, looking out on the confluence of the Atlantic and the Indian oceans with spectacular Table Mountain and its shroud of clouds as a backdrop! I visited the university and the court in Langa; on a bus trip in to the country, I saw vineyards and fruit trees blossoming in the spring.

I wrote to Catharine Raymond, my coworker at the FOR office in New York (September 23, 1954), "Don't believe anything you read in the *New York Times* that indicates any softening of the apartheid policy. There is recognition that certain things are impractical, not because of the welfare of the African, but because of the white man's interests. This little piece of the Earth's surface is in for very stormy days. The only fundamental question here is the color question. It runs through everything. There must be a dozen items in any newspaper every day based on this issue. The situation is revolutionary. The tragedy is that even the liberal whites who can see this cannot extricate themselves enough from their comforts to do anything effective. This place will have a whole series of blow-ups for years to come." I could write almost the same things today, more than 30 years later.

My last day in Cape Town I picked up my tapes and notes from the institute and stuffed them in the pockets of the raincoat I was carrying. With some trepidation, I went through to board the ship. To my joyful surprise, my bags were not even opened, and yet only a few yards away the same police that had been following me were still watching. I was grateful for the noninterference without understanding it.

The next morning I went up on deck as the ship slowly slipped away from the dock. I looked down and spotted the black policeman still on duty watching me. Rather impishly, I waved to him. He did not respond.

THE WINDS OF CHANGE

In the 1950s Africa was not a controversial continent. It was just not an issue. To most people, even those who were internationally aware, it was a vague area of the world that might have some potential but was not of concern.

The more than 50 component countries of Africa were dominated by Western European powers—Britain, France, Belgium, Portugal, Spain, and Italy. Only Egypt, Liberia, Ethiopia, and Libya were independent—barely so. But strivings for self-determination were accelerated by the end of World War II. Former colonies in Asia were largely independent by the end of the 1940s. The Bandung Conference in Indonesia in 1955 was newly independent Asia's announcement to the world that it intended to exercise its influence on international affairs. Asian achievements were certainly going to speed up demands for independence and equality in Africa.

Africa was not then an arena for a conflict between the superpowers. The United States had very little presence on the continent and was satisfied to work through its allies in Western Europe and their colonial governments. The Soviet Union had no presence at all because the colonial powers resisted any of its attempts to establish one. There were virtually no indigenous Communist parties in Africa, except for South Africa, which outlawed the party in 1950.

The United Nations was essentially a Western club during the 1950s. When it was founded in 1946, there were only 54 members, including 14 Afro-Asian states. An Afro-Asian group was formed at the UN in 1955, after the Bandung Conference.

For the most part, African nationalist movements were just getting organized in the 1950s. Except for the war in Algeria and the Mau Mau rebellion in Kenya, the struggle proceeded nonviolently and constitutionally. In the more repressive colonies such as those under Portuguese domination, it proceeded virtually not at all. Pan-Africanism, as a continentwide expression of nationalism, was born in its modern phase with the All African People's Conference in 1958. Eight independent states formed an African group in the UN. The people of the United States under Dwight D. Eisenhower were generally anticolonial but had little incentive to press for a vigorous government policy to implement their sentiments. Not until 1958 was a Bureau of African Affairs organized in the U.S. State Department. Virtually no organizations gave real time and attention to the struggle against colonialism and racism internationally, and there were only limited efforts within the black community.

In retrospect the 1950s seemed like an era of innocence, which nurtured an optimistic hope that the struggle for independence would be simple and that its achievement would be a panacea. Catching the spirit of the era, Prime Minister Harold Macmillan of Britain said in a famous speech in Cape Town in February 1960, "The wind of change is blowing through this continent, and whether we like it or not, this growth of national consciousness is a political fact. We must accept it as a fact, and our national policies must take account of it."

Two overwhelming events signaled the end of that era and the beginning of another. One was the Sharpeville Massacre in South Africa, after which the main liberation movements were banned by the government and the method of struggle began to move toward violence. The second was the independence of the Congo and the beginning of the involvement of the big powers in African affairs. As the era ended in 1960, 17 countries became independent.

In the United States, John F. Kennedy defeated Richard M. Nixon in the presidential campaign of 1960, "passing the torch to a new generation." The UN General Assembly passed overwhelmingly Resolution No. 1514, whose aim was to speed the end of colonialism. The United States abstained, one of the last acts of the Eisenhower administration. A saving grace was a dramatic public act by Mrs. Zelma George, a black member of the U.S. delegation, who stood up in the General Assembly, signifying her opposition to her government's position.

It was in this setting that the American Committee on Africa came into being.

CHAPTER FOUR

Bridging the
American–African Gap

A handful of us gathered around a table for a breakfast session at Hotel Ten Park Avenue in May 1953. The single agenda item was how to launch a new American organization that would relate to the dynamic events unfolding in Africa. Agreement on a name was the easy part. We chose the American Committee on Africa. How to raise a budget, find a staff, and develop a program was much more complex.

We authorized a survey of the organizational scene and later agreed with its conclusion that "there is no overall organization concerned with the whole continent of Africa" and thus there was a place for our committee.

We drafted a prospectus for the infant organization proclaiming that "One of the world's continents is missing from America's conscience. . . . In America individuals and organizations are being compelled by the march of events to pay heed for the first time to a vast new portion of the world. . . . The ACOA is being organized to help bridge this gap between Africans and Americans."

We filed a certificate of incorporation in September, hoping for an eventual tax-exempt status. Our planning group was transformed into a Executive Committee, which included Norman Thomas, the Socialist leader; Roger Baldwin, for years director of the American Civil Liberties Union; A.J. Muste, the pacifist leader; George Carpenter, Africa secretary of the National Council of Churches; Rayford Logan of Howard University; Conrad Lynn, a civil rights lawyer; Donald Harrington, minister of the Community Church; James Farmer, a founder and later director of CORE; Peter Weiss, a lawyer and director of the International Development Placement Association; and Walter Offutt of the national staff of the National Association for the Advancement of Colored People (NAACP).

A VOCATIONAL DECISION

The question was, how after this largely academic process, could an organization be brought into reality? No one seemed to be available to raise the funds to hire a staff to breathe life into the structure. Harrington was the chairman and I was the secretary, but we each had other commitments. The idea that I would take on a full-time responsibility in the field of African affairs had never entered my mind. Furthermore, I was just preparing for a long trip to Africa and could not think beyond that.

We were saved from a stalemate by the return of George Shepherd (later a professor at the University of Denver) from a two-year stint in Uganda as an adviser to the Federation of Uganda African Farmers. There he had been outspoken on behalf of African independence and had visited Jomo Kenyatta in Kenya about the time of the Mau Mau rising. His plans to return to Uganda were sabotaged when the State Department withdrew his passport. No amount of protest changed the policy; the era of McCarthyism was having its effect.

Shepherd was eager to continue to work in African affairs. Fortunately, a research grant allowed him to give some time to the ACOA. He gathered a group of volunteers. Free office space on East 35th Street was given by the Community Church of New York. The committee's publication *Africa Today* was launched in mimeographed form, edited by Keith Irvine, who had lived in the Gold Coast.

Just after I left for Africa in April 1954, the ACOA's first public conference was held in New York on the theme "Is Colonialism Dying in Africa?" Professor Rayford Logan of Howard University, an outstanding scholar on Africa, was the principal speaker. The *Christian Science Monitor* (May 10, 1954) commented, "Not until the American Committee on Africa was formed have American liberals had an outlet for expressing their views on African policies of the State Department."

From April to October 1954 I traveled in Africa, as related in part 1. Returning to New York, I was excited by my experiences and wanted to continue my African involvement. However, I was committed to a long, nationwide speaking tour for FOR, which had sponsored my trip. The thought that I might work full-time in African Affairs through the ACOA first struck me when I was riding the train across Idaho to speak in Seattle. Although my commitment to nonviolence was still firm, I felt the need for a change from FOR and therefore decided to leave its staff.

Of several interesting possibilities, none was so challenging as working with the ACOA. I talked extensively with Shepherd and Peter Weiss, both of whom encouraged me, and with others on the Executive Committee. Although no one felt absolutely confident about funds, they thought it was important to give it a try. I finally decided to do so. I wrote to Roger Baldwin, my one close adviser who thought the committee could not make a go of it (August 2, 1955): "I considered various other possibilities which were open to me, and I decided in full knowledge of the risks involved that I would take this chance, at least for a short time."

The ACOA embarked on its full-time program with a staff of two. Lydia Zemba left Doubleday to join me. Six months later Catharine Raymond, my long-time coworker at FOR and CORE, joined me and helped to hold the organization together for 10 years.

GETTING DOWN TO WORK

Shortly after my duties began, I had an urgent letter (March 23, 1955) from Father Trevor Huddleston, an Anglican priest in Johannesburg. "We are in need of roughly £3,000 to keep our school open until the end of next year." The background to this appeal was the enactment in 1953 of one of the most far-reaching pieces of apartheid legislation, the Bantu Education Act. Under this law the government took control of education and mandated a curriculum designed to fit its racial theories about the innate differences between the races. Henrik Verwoerd, then minister of native affairs and later prime minister, said in defense of the act that "There is no place for the African in the European community above the level of certain forms of labor." Heretofore the government had subsidized private schools, mostly under church or mission auspices, but now any such financial assistance was dependent on the acceptance of the government-endorsed curriculum with its apartheid assumptions. Many church groups spoke out against the act, but they also recognized that without financial support from government circles, they would not be able to operate for long.

The most highly publicized case of refusal to accept government aid under the Bantu Education Act was St. Peter's School in Johannesburg, which was sponsored by the parish of Huddleston, a staunch opponent of the government's racial policies.

I had been immensely impressed by the tall, slender, graying Huddleston when I met him in South Africa in September 1954. He had identified himself with the struggle of the Africans, and no white person was more accepted or respected among Africans than he. He was 41 in 1954 and had been in South Africa for 11 years. Later, when he left South Africa, the *New York Times* (May 14, 1955) commented, "Huddleston was literally driven from South Africa because he publicly condemned at every opportunity the Nationalist Party policy of apartheid as immoral and un-Christian."

When Huddleston visited New York in March 1956, the ACOA arranged a public meeting for him. His opening words to the large audience were: "I am a completely prejudiced person. Although I am a South African citizen and have a South African passport, at present, and do very greatly and deeply love South Africa—I do not love the government of South Africa or its policies, or the general racial attitude of white South Africa today. In the eyes of the government that constitutes treason. And so you have before you a traitor to his country. I am sorry, but there it is."

Although the ACOA was just starting and had no financial resources to call upon, we felt it imperative to respond to Huddleston's appeal. So we launched the Project Fund primarily to support St. Peter's School and others that rejected government control of education and consequently were faced with closure. Our first brochure was to facilitate a fund-raising drive.

The response was good. The *Christian Century* (July 20, 1955) ran a lead editorial with the headline "Raise Fund for Free African Schools." "It is good news to learn that the American Committee on Africa has started a modest fund." The magazine urged contributions to the Project Fund, and other magazines and organizations supported the appeal. By mid-year 1956 the fund had raised almost $10,000, most of which was sent directly to South Africa. Huddleston wrote to me (December 22, 1955), "I can't tell you how tremendously moved and grateful we are for this magnificent gift."

Inevitably I spent a considerable amount of time in the halls of the UN. Here I met many outstanding African leaders. Among the most memorable was Julius Nyerere, with whom I would have contact over many years. A teacher, he was president of the newly formed Tanganyika African National Union (TANU) and later was for more than 20 years president of the United Republic of Tanzania. He came to New York as a petitioner from what was then the Trust Territory of Tanganyika. What an unforgettable personality he was—slight of build, a high forehead, small black toothbrush moustache, quiet-spoken but with an easy laugh and a delightful sense of humor. The U.S. government, following the advice of the British, restricted his movements to within a few blocks of the UN. Nyerere, characteristically, made light of it. He looked young, more like a graduate student than a teacher and certainly not like a man soon to be cast in the role of father of his country. On later visits we arranged meetings where Nyerere spoke, reflecting a strong anticolonial bias, yet without rancor, and always with a pragmatic message.

I also met Sylvanus Olympio, later the first president of the Republic of Togo. He came as a petitioner from the Trust Territory of French Togoland. Suave, always impeccably dressed, he spoke perfect French and English. Later his leadership of an independent Togo was cut short by a coup in which he tragically lost his life. He was the first of many African leaders I knew who died in acts of violence.

Among the issues debated at the UN in which we were involved were the racial situation in South Africa, the Algerian question, and the status of South West Africa.

For several years the ACOA published the *Africa-U.N. Bulletin,* periodically reporting on UN issues and commenting on U.S. policy. It was edited by Elizabeth Landis, a lawyer and a vice-president of the ACOA, who became an expert on Namibia.

At the end of one year we took stock. Our mailing list had expanded significantly. We had raised enough funds to sustain a two-person staff. Our program expanded satisfactorily as we built our Project Fund into a going concern. We had organized a series of meetings featuring speakers such as Father Huddleston and the South African authors Peter Abrahams and Alan Paton. We held a reception for Dr. Nnamdi Azikiwe, premier of the Eastern Region of Nigeria, and organized a series of four public meetings on "Africa and the Arts" and a series of five on "Forces Making for Social Change in Africa," which attracted about 2,000 people. We published the magazine *Africa Today* and inaugurated a literature service that came to have more than 50 titles.

CHAPTER FIVE

Nkrumah, Ghana, and Pan-Africanism

One person and one country more than any other symbolized the "winds of change" period in Africa. The person was Kwame Nkrumah, the country Ghana. Ghana achieved independence essentially without violence and with the understanding and good will of Britain. Nkrumah received almost universal acclaim. A.M. Rosenthal of the *New York Times* wrote of him: "He has a way of making people who never believed in their importance seem worthy of respect in their own eyes. He has made himself the symbol of Ghanaian independence."[1]

GHANAIAN INDEPENDENCE

March 6, 1957, was Independence Day. Bill Sutherland, who was still living in Ghana, wrote me a month before that it looked as if the event would go off peacefully. This had not been assured because Nkrumah had opposition. Although in the last elections before independence, the Convention Peoples Party (CPP) had taken almost three fourths of the seats in Parliament, the opposition National Liberation Movement had won 12 seats to the CPP's 8 in Ashanti. On the eve of independence, however, the king of the Ashanti had said to Nkrumah, "Let's be friends."

The independence celebration was dramatic, culminating in the lowering of the Union Jack at midnight and the raising of the new flag of Ghana. Vice President Richard M. Nixon, who headed the official U.S. delegation, reported to President Dwight D. Eisenhower: "The continent of Africa is emerging as one of the great forces in the world today. . . . There is no area in the world today in which the prestige of the U.S. . . . is more uniformly high than in [Ghana]. . . . It can truly be said that the welcome mat is out for investment of foreign private capital in Africa."[2] He noted that Communist leaders considered Africa as important now as they had China 25 years before, but that "communist domination in the states of the area [West Africa] is not a present danger."

Among individual guests Nkrumah invited to the independence celebration were prominent Afro-Americans, including Martin Luther King, Ralphe Bunche, A. Philip Randolph, and Congressman Adam Clayton Powell. Homer Jack was the ACOA's representative. We had set up a Gold Coast Celebration Committee, co-chaired by Eleanor Roosevelt and Channing Tobias. More than 500 people responded to the invitation to sign a greeting from the American people, which was presented to Nkrumah by Jack.

In New York the ACOA chose Ghana's independence as the occasion for organizing their first large public gathering. Town Hall was filled to overflowing. At least 50 percent of the close to 2,000 people were black. In a taped message Nkrumah stressed that "Our attainment of freedom may be considered a unique achievement because there has been a relative absence of violence, because we have chosen to effect our revolution through parliamentary channels." The crowd responded with tremendous enthusiasm when the new flag of Ghana was presented by the official representative of Ghana.

Under Nkrumah, Ghana became the mecca for African nationalists from all over the continent. Nkrumah nurtured this role for his country with himself as the leader. The first conference of African independent states was held in Accra in April 1958. It proclaimed "the right of the African people to independence and self-determination and to take appropriate steps to hasten the realization of this right." Only eight months later the first All African People's Conference (AAPC) representing liberation movements from all over the continent, met in Accra.

Nkrumah was ambitious. His goal was the establishment of some form of West African federation, and he undoubtedly saw himself at its head. He talked of a Ghana-Guinea union shortly after Guinea's overnight independence in September 1958. He attempted to form a joint union with Mali and asked nine African states to establish a joint army. George Padmore became the adviser to the prime minister on African affairs until his death in 1959, and Nkrumah then set up a Bureau of African Affairs to advise the government on dealing with the nationalist movements in Africa. The Kwame Nkrumah Institute was set up in 1960 as a political training ground for the representatives of liberation movements, both in the theory of Pan-African socialism and in positive action.

In July 1958 Nkrumah made his first trip back to the United States in more than 10 years. He had a session with President Eisenhower, addressed the Washington Press Club, and was introduced by Vice President Nixon to the Senate while garbed in the colorful kente cloth traditionally worn by Ashanti chiefs. He even shook hands with dyed-in-the-wool segregationists such as Senators Russell Long and Allen Ellender. He was a guest on NBC's "Meet the Press," led a parade through Harlem, and spoke at a street-corner rally at 125th Street arranged by Hope Stevens, vice president of the ACOA.

From the ACOA's perspective, a most important part of Nkrumah's visit was a dinner in his honor that we sponsored at the Waldorf Astoria Hotel. The NAACP and the Urban League accepted our invitation to co-sponsor the event, and the Grand Ballroom was filled to capacity. Nkrumah's speech was a major statement of policy. He reiterated one of his principal themes: "The independence of Ghana itself cannot be regarded as complete so long as large parts of Africa remain under colonial rule and so long as the people of our continent are separated by artificial barriers imposed by the colonial powers."

THE ALL AFRICAN PEOPLE'S CONFERENCE

The euphoria of optimism that characterized the struggle for independence in the 1950s was reflected more perhaps in the All African People's Conference held in Accra in December 1958 than in any other event of the decade. Inspired by Nkrumah and Padmore, it took place a little more than a year after the independence of Ghana. It was an exhilarating prospect, and I was determined to be there. Through my contacts with Padmore and Nkrumah, ACOA representatives were given fraternal-delegate status. In addition to myself the delegates included my long-time colleague Homer Jack; Frank Montero, an ACOA board member, who was with the National Urban League; William X. Scheinman, also a board member; and John Marcum, a political scientist at Lincoln University.

When we arrived in Accra, excitement was building. Ghana had prepared well. At the front of the Community Center hall was a huge map of Africa and the words, "People of Africa, unite. We have nothing to lose but our chains. We have a continent to regain. We have freedom and human dignity to attain." The road leading to the building was lined with Ghanaians holding posters aloft with such slogans as "Hands Off Africa," "Africa Must Be Free," "Down With Imperialism and Colonialism," and "We prefer independence with danger to servitude in tranquility," a favorite Nkrumah saying.

There were some 300 delegates representing 65 organizations and parties. Among the delegates were many who later became prominent leaders in their own countries and in Africa at large. Of the nine independent African countries, only Sudan was absent because of a recent coup. Repre-

ACOA delegation with Kwame Nkrumah, prime minister of Ghana, at the AAPC in Accra, Ghana, December 1958. Left to right, John Marcum, Homer Jack, George Houser, Nkrumah, Frank Montero, William Scheinman.

sentation came from the parties rather than the governments since the AAPC was nongovernmental.

Patrice Lumumba, then an unknown representing the recently formed National Congolese Movement, headed a Congo delegation. I was waiting at Nkrumah's headquarters when someone asked if the photographer was present. Apparently he was not, but I had my camera on my shoulder and offered to take the picture that Nkrumah wanted with himself and Lumumba. This was how I first met Lumumba and took the first photograph of him and Nkrumah together.

Among other leaders present were Kenneth Kaunda, Joshua Nkomo, and Hastings K. Banda from the Rhodesias and Nyasaland. The South African government would not permit either the ANC or the SAIC representatives to leave the country. The South African delegation, therefore, consisted of Patrick Duncan and Jordan Ngubane of the Liberal party; Michael Scott from Britain, representing Chief Hosea Kutako of South West Africa; an American, Mary Louise Hooper, because she had worked closely with Chief Albert Lutuli; Alfred Hutchison, a treason-trial defendant who had escaped the country; and Ezekiel Mphahlele, a teacher who later became a prominent writer. Strong delegations came from the National Liberation Front (FLN) in Algeria, Egypt, Kenya, Nigeria, and of course Ghana. From French Africa, Togo, the Cameroons, and Senegal were the best represented. Holden Roberto, who participated under the name Rui Ventura, represented Angola.

The Soviet Union, through its chapter of the Afro-Asian Peoples' Solidarity Organization (AAPSO), had eight observers. The specialist was Professor I.I. Potekhin, deputy director of the Academy of Science of the USSR. This was my first of several meetings with this fascinating man, who had been studying Africa for 30 years. He told me of the difficulties Soviets confronted in trying to visit Africa. I could understand this from my own prohibited-immigrant experiences. He pointed out that Soviet interest in Africa was very new but very much alive and that the Soviet Afro-Asian Council was among the most active in AAPSO. At no point in the meetings did the Soviet delegation attempt to gain the limelight.

Observers from the People's Republic of China kept a low profile except for one issue. Among the flags flying in front of the Community Center was that of Nationalist China. The Chinese protested, and by the next day, the flag had been removed.

Messages from many world leaders came to the conference. It was a sign of ineptness, some of us felt, that there was no official greeting from the United States. Charles Diggs, a first-term black congressman who was at the conference as an observer, and a few others were greatly disturbed. Mostly as a result of Diggs's intervention, a personal but uninspired message finally came from Vice President Nixon on the last day: "I have been following with great interest the proceedings of the All African

Patrick Duncan (left) and Alfred Hutchinson (right), South African delegates to the AAPC in Accra, Ghana, December 1958.

People's Conference now taking place in Accra. I take pleasure in extending my personal best wishes for its successful conclusion." Most Americans at the conference were relieved that such a lukewarm greeting was not even read to the assemblage.

There were 25 or so representatives of American nongovernmental organizations at the AAPC. In addition to the ACOA they included the American Federation of Labor-Congress of Industrial Organizations (AFL-CIO), African-American Institute, American Society of African Culture, Harlem-based United African Nationalist Movement, American Friends Service Committee, Associated Negro Press, and African academic specialists.

Nkrumah was the guiding light of the conference. He made the opening speech and was greeted with overwhelming applause when he said, "Africa is not an extension of Europe." He had picked Tom Mboya, the young leader of the Kenya Federation of Labor, as conference chairman, Mboya did not know he had been so honored until he arrived at the airport from London. He soon became a dominating figure. Kennett Love reported for the *New York Times* (December 9, 1958) that Mboya put aside his prepared address and "made a speech during which one could have heard a pin drop in the pauses between the bursts of cheering and clapping."

We of the ACOA knew Mboya better than most because he had traveled and spoken under our auspices in the United States for two months in 1956. He was a clever and captivating speaker. At one point he said, "Whereas 72 years ago the scramble for Africa started, from Accra we announce that those same powers must be told in a clear, firm and definite voice, Scram from Africa."3

There were two emotional high points of the conference. One was the tremendous response to the statement of the FLN, which was then deeply immersed in its war for independence from France. The other was the demonstration for the release of Jomo Kenyatta, who had been imprisoned since 1953. While Gikonyo Kiano was speaking for Kenya and the Pan-African Freedom Movement of East and Central Africa (PAFMECA), Kenyan delegates and others in the hall raised placards and shouted, "Free Jomo Kenyatta," "Hands off Kenya." It seemed like an American political convention.

In these early days of Pan-Africanism, competition for leadership was just taking shape. In Accra the most obvious rivals were Egypt and Ghana, personified respectively by Gamal Abdel Nasser and Nkrumah. Nasser did not attend the AAPC, but there was a strong delegation from the Egyptian-dominated AAPSO.

AAPSO had been set up about a year before the AAPC at a conference held in Cairo. The Cairo Council of AAPSO sent 13 delegates to Accra. One of the leaders told me that they were apprehensive about the competitive relationship with Accra. In fact he said they had brought a large supply of literature to the conference, which they were not even distributing for fear that it would be misunderstood as a move toward exerting undue influence.

Nkrumah was reportedly unhappy that invitations had been sent to AAPSO. One of his phrases that lent itself to great speculation was, "Do not let us forget that colonialism and imperialism may come to us in a different guise, not necessarily from Europe." This was usually interpreted as a reference to Nasser's designs.

One of the motives of Nkrumah and Padmore in initiating the conference in Accra was to establish a rallying point for nationalist forces south of the Sahara free from the influence of the great powers. This was a theme of Padmore's book *Pan Africanism or Communism* (1956). The underlying theme of the Accra conference was definitely international neutrality. Mboya put it succinctly: "We are not inclined to the East or the West. . . . Africa must be friendly but always maintaining and safeguarding her independence."

An underlying policy question at the conference dealt with methodology. The call to the conference had stated that the struggle for freedom in Africa would be conducted along nonviolent lines. Nkrumah enunciated this principle in his opening speech. The Algerian delegates felt this was a slightly veiled criticism of their war for independence and attacked the nonviolence principle. The leader said, "Nonviolence is out of date."

At this moment in history, with the exception of the FLN in Algeria and the Mau Mau in Kenya, virtually all the movements, even in South Africa, were working along nonviolent lines or within a constitutional framework established by the colonial powers. Mboya formulated a statement, which was accepted by the conference: "We believe in nonviolence and positive action, but the attitude and approach of the colonialists will determine the tactics we use."

While the conference was in session, Ghana's parliament approved the Ghana-Guinea Union. It was announced that Ghana was making available to Guinea $28 million in credits. A joint commission was set up to study economic, communications, and constitutional questions. Whether this move was more than an Nkrumah gesture was not clear. Guinea was French-speaking and in the franc zone, whereas Ghana was English-speaking and in the British Commonwealth. Nevertheless, the announcement during the conference disturbed the Nigerians. Since the combined population of Ghana and Guinea was only about 7 million while Nigeria had more than 35 million, the Nigerian delegation expressed some exasperation at Ghana's pretensions to leadership.

Movements from East and Central Africa were already established as a regional pressure group before the AAPC was held. PAFMECA* was organized at a conference held in Mwanza, Tanganyika, in September

*In 1962 it became PAFMECSA, as southern Africa was added to the area it covered.

1958. Its constitution and resolutions committed it to nonviolence, to Pan-Africanism, to establishing a headquarters in Dar es Salaam, and to setting up a Freedom Fund and accepting all people as citizens, regardless of their place of origin. PAFMECA maintained a united front at Accra and continued to exist as a separate entity after the AAPC had finished its work.

In spite of competitive relationships, the AAPC struck a strong note of unity in its recommendations. It specifically endorsed the broad objective of creating an African commonwealth. It denounced the imperialist powers for creating artificial boundaries to divide the peoples of Africa. The independent states were called upon to "form a legion of volunteers who would be ready to protect the freedom of the African peoples." In his closing address, Nkrumah said that the conference had "laid the foundations for the African community. From here we shall go forth with renewed strength and determination to join all our forces, having created a climate for unity between the independent states and those of us in Africa who still have freedom to attain." A permanent secretariat was established in Accra to implement decisions of the AAPC.

The South African delegation was pleased that the conference called for an international boycott of South African goods. Chief Lutuli in South Africa commented, "It heartened us to see that a boycott made sense to liberatory forces outside our own country . . . in Africa small Ghana shines."

A little more than a year later, in January 1960, the second AAPC was held in Tunis. Again an ACOA delegation was given fraternal-delegate status. Peter Weiss, Professor John Murra of Vassar College, and I were the observers.

The atmosphere in Tunisia was different from that in Accra. This was the Arab, Muslim world. Tunisia had been independent almost four years. A major focus of the conference was the war for independence raging in Algeria just next door. While we were meeting in Tunis, several other conferences were in session that affected Africa—a round table discussion in Brussels on Congo independence, constitutional discussions on Kenya in London, a conference on Mali in Paris, and an economic planning conference in Tangiers.

Two issues made the Tunis conference memorable. One was the Algerian war for independence. Ahmed Boumendjel, leader of the FLN delegation, received a rousing response when he called for volunteers from African countries for the FLN struggle. He invited freedom fighters to come not only to support the FLN but to learn techniques for fighting their own battles. Unlike Accra, in Tunis nonviolence was just not an issue. President Habib Bourguiba of Tunisia set a moderate tone in his opening speech: "Many methods of struggle are as respectable as the other. The man speaking to you has used them all. Personally I am always inclined to use pacific means . . . which has not prevented me from picking up arms." The tone of the conference was much more openly critical of the United States than had been true in Accra, primarily because of American support of France in Algeria.

The wildest demonstration took place following the announcement of the Brussels agreement that the Congo would become independent on June 30. The shouting and applause were genuine and spontaneous. The fact that Belgium would give up its rich colony was seen as a signal that all Africa would soon be free. Among the warnings against neocolonialism was Bourguiba's statement that "Colonialism often appears in new and more subtle forms." He reaffirmed the nonaligned position of Accra in his statement, "We are willing to accept aid from wherever it comes, providing it does not attack our independence. . . . We have adopted nonalignment because we want to preserve our freedom of choice and enlarge our circle of friends."

Another high point of the conference was a mass rally of more than 200,000 Tunisians with participation by the AAPC to protest French atomic tests in the Sahara, then a sore point in the relations between France and Africa.

Neither Nkrumah nor Mboya attended this conference. Mboya was at the Kenya discussions in London. Nevertheless, there was a struggle between them, symbolized by a difference on international trade union alignments. Mboya and the Kenya Federation of Labor were affiliated with the Western-oriented International Confederation of Free Trade Unions, while Nkrumah was backing a newly formed All African Trade Union Federation, with which the Ghana Trade Union Congress was affiliated. This caused a falling out between these two African leaders that never healed.

I had the feeling after the Tunis conference that the AAPC had done its job. Initiative was already passing to the independent states, and the nongovernmental liberation movements would have to find another vehicle for their work.

I ended my trip to Africa in February in Ghana, where I had a long meeting with Nkrumah. He enthusiastically expressed the hope that the next AAPC could be held in the Congo. He talked about the Volta River project and the need for funds. He said that if the West and the World Bank did not respond to appeals, he would turn to the East, meaning the Soviet Union. He claimed at that time that he did not want to get involved with the East but was strongly neutralist and therefore supported the AAPC.

CHAPTER SIX

Birth of an Angolan Movement

How innocently some political organizations have their beginnings. So it was with an Angolan movement that evolved into the Union of the Peoples of Angola (UPA). I saw and felt, in an unusual way, the evolution of this movement from an unsophisticated, tribally based organization to one that attracted international attention. Later I was in touch with other Angolan movements, but my meeting with Manuel Barros Necaca in Leopoldville in 1954 was my first contact with one that was hoping to challenge Portuguese power through organized channels.

MANUEL BARROS NECACA

When I first met Necaca, his incipient movement seemed to have no name. Some time in 1957 they adopted the name Union of the Peoples of Northern Angola (UPNA). My meetings with Necaca were fleeting, but in between them we carried on a substantive correspondence. In his early letters, the movement seemed to be anti-Portuguese but ethnocentric rather than nationalist. Between 1956 and 1958, Necaca tried to explain to me again and again that his movement was not of Angola but represented the Ancient Kingdom of the Kongo, a portion of northern Angola with headquarters at São Salvador. The people were Bakongo, the same ethnic and linguistic group that was dominant in the western Belgian Congo and the southernmost part of French Equatorial Africa. This was simply one example of the division of Africa by European powers, which had indiscriminately severed tribal groups.

Necaca's argument was legalistic. "It was not legal the fact of calling the Ancient Kingdom of the Kongo as Angola because we are not from Angola, but from the Kongo Kingdom territory," he wrote February 5, 1957. He explained to me that in 1884 the king of the Kongo, Dom Pedro V, was deceived into signing an agreement that acknowledged the king of Portugal as his liege lord. He quoted Dom Pedro: "My brother, the King of Portugal, sent me this chair and I sent him a letter thanking him for his gift and that is the only letter I ever signed my mark to or ordered to be sent." This deception was the legal basis for Portugal's seizing control of the Kongo Kingdom, which was then integrated into Portuguese Angola. The rejection of this act provided the basis for the position Necaca and his group were taking.

Necaca was particularly eager for facts about his country to be brought to the attention of the UN. He wrote about forced labor on the coffee plantations of northern Angola. In June 1957 he sent me a copy of a six-page petition directed to the secretary general of the UN. It came from São Salvador do Congo, in Angola, rather than from Leopoldville, and detailed grievances of the people. In a note he explained that "as a security measure, we have not published the names of the petitioners."

Shortly after this (November 23, 1957) Necaca wrote saying they would like to send a delegation to the UN and wanted me to ask the delegations of Ghana, Liberia, and India to give assistance. "If you arrange with one of the governments and agreement is reached," he wrote, "please inform them that we shall delegate two members of our Union to meet them at any place they choose reasonable for an interview (home town or New York)."

I wrote back candidly about the problems they faced (January 25, 1958). One was their political aim of reconstituting the Ancient Kingdom of the Kongo. This could probably not be done, I said, and violated the new sense of nationalism in Africa. A second was a lack of organization and activity in Angola. I expressed my opinion that international attention tended to be attracted to an area where something was happening that made it impossible to overlook the problem. "I mention these things to you not to discourage you, but rather to express my own deep concern for what you are trying to do."

A transformation began to take place in UPNA. Necaca wrote (February 9, 1958), "It is of course very difficult to think of a restoration of the Ancient Kingdom of the Kongo since Africa is not yet independent. The support of several nations at the U.N. seems to be impossible at the moment. For the time being, the thing which matters the most to us is the changing of the conditions now prevailing in Angola. The question of the restoration of the Ancient Kingdom of the Kongo will be considered later on when better circumstances will allow it." He also indicated that he and his group were beginning to make contact with leaders in Luanda.

I informed UPNA about the All African People's Conference. Necaca wrote me that his colleagues wanted to participate. However, they wanted to send someone who could stay longer, would have mobility, and would not suffer under Belgian restraints. He wrote his first letter to George Padmore May 10, 1958, giving me as a reference.

Necaca sent me Padmore's almost immediate response (May 14, 1958). "I am delighted to know that you are associated with Mr. George Houser of the ACOA. Mr. Houser is well known to us and is being a helpful colleague. We in this part of Africa get very little information about what is happening in either the Belgian Congo or Portuguese territories. . . . We shall look forward to a close collaboration between us." Padmore then invited UPNA to attend the AAPC and said he would "take the liberty of including the name of your organization in the list of sponsors."

Necaca replied to Padmore (June 20, 1958) that they would send someone and then added, "For security's sake, please do not mention the name of our organization in the agenda that you are going to draft. No publicity should be made about our participation."

Initially Necaca had planned to attend the AAPC himself. But subsequently it became clear that he could not do so. He had five children and could not take the risks of the long and dangerous trip to Accra without travel documents or of being long away from Leopoldville. Furthermore, because of his responsible job with the Nogueira Company, a Portuguese firm, his presence would be missed, and investigations of his whereabouts could lead to undesirable results.

HOLDEN ROBERTO

UPNA had assurances from Padmore that a delegate would be welcomed, and taken care of and could stay on after the conference to give information about Angola and the Congo. Necaca's nephew, Holden Roberto, was chosen for the assignment. Born in 1923, Roberto was the son of Necaca's older sister and was nine years younger than his uncle. He was named after the British Baptist missionary Robert Holden Carson Graham, who baptised him. His father, Garcia Roberto, had worked at the Baptist mission in São Salvador.

I had met Holden Roberto briefly in Leopoldville. He spoke excellent French and good Portuguese and was rapidly improving his English. He struck me as an intense and serious person, not given to small talk or easy humor. He was of medium height and wore glasses, which gave him a scholarly look. Later he almost always wore dark glasses. I was told his eyes were very sensitive to light even in darkened rooms. Some said he wanted to convey a sense of mystery. He was ambitious. In his earlier days he was eager to learn and took advice, but he ceased doing that as time went on.

As he was growing up, Roberto was a protégé of his uncle. Although born in São Salvador, Angola, he was taken to Leopoldville at the age of two and educated in the British Baptist school. He returned to São Salvador for two more years of schooling in 1940 with Necaca's help. Back in the Belgian Congo, he worked as an accountant for the colonial government and became acquainted with Patrice Lumumba in Stanleyville. He was drawn into political activity by Necaca, who also got him a job with the Nogueira Company. Although married, Roberto had no responsibilities that would stand in the way of an extended absence. Furthermore, he held no prominent position in the European world that would make his disappearance arouse suspicion or lead to investigation.

Roberto left on his nearly three-month journey to Accra in August. Later he recounted his sometimes harrowing travel experience to me. The only documents he carried were a vaccination certificate and a permit to cross the Congo River to Brazzaville. Once in the French Congo, he went to the port of Point Noire, where friends helped him to board a coastal steamer for Douala in the Cameroons. There he was permitted ashore on a fabricated excuse of a need to visit a (nonexistent) ailing sister. He narrowly escaped detection by French military patrols near the border of the British Cameroons. Once across the border, he walked, hitchhiked, and bussed to Lagos, where he waited for Padmore to return to Accra from a trip abroad before receiving his permission to enter Ghana. He traveled from Lagos to Accra by ship.

On October 20, 1958, he wrote from Accra. "Dear Mr. Houser, I beg to inform you that I am sent by União das Populações do Norte de Angola [UPNA] led by Mssrs. Eduardo J. Pinock and Manuel Barros Necaca, to attend the Conference of all African Peoples and to continue to United States as you know yourself. I think you remember when we met at Union Mission House in Leopoldville. . . . I gave you at that time my name and my address." He asked me to write to Padmore on his behalf, and indicated he felt it very important to come to the UN as soon as possible. He signed the letter "Haldane" Roberto, one of the names he used at this time.

Roberto kept a low profile in Accra. He wrote an occasional article for the Ghana *Times* under the name of Rui Ventura. His name did not appear on any list or any document of the AAPC. He wrote a paper, distributed at the conference, entitled "The Angola Drama." In it he spoke of the political independence of Angola as the choice of the more than 4 million Angolans. This document was written in the name of the Union of the People of Angola (UPA), "Northern" having been eliminated from the name. He did refer to UPNA but as having exceeded the limits of its constitution, thus leading to the formation of UPA in 1958.

Roberto also wrote a speech, which, to preserve his anonymity, was read for him by Tom Mboya of Kenya, chairman of the conference. It began: "For the first time a voice from Angola is heard today. This means that the iron curtain around Angola is burst open."

Roberto remained in Accra for almost a year. He wrote articles for the press and corresponded with African leaders. In a long letter to Nkrumah (January 13, 1959) he outlined the Angolan situation. He presented a long report to an African conference in Monrovia, Liberia, as "the itinererant Secretary-General of the UPA." He wrote me particularly about helping to arrange a trip to the UN in New York. On November 24, 1958 he wrote me that he expected to receive financial aid from his organization in Leopoldville. "I cannot say how long I shall be in the U.S. because I do not think there is any point in my returning to the Belgian Congo or Angola as long as conditions remain as they are. I think I can serve my country's cause better abroad than by keeping within the clutches of the colonialists."

I wrote to Padmore suggesting that perhaps Roberto could be attached to the Ghana delegation to the UN, which would be taking minimum risk. The ACOA agreed to provide official sponsorship, if needed, for obtaining a U.S. visa and guaranteeing that he would not become a public charge.

Roberto finally came to the UN attached to the delegation of Guinea, not Ghana, in the fall of 1959. His travel document had the name Jose Gilmore. He worked anonymously as much as possible. No publicity was given to his presence. He used our office virtually as his headquarters. We introduced him not only to key UN secretariat personnel but to many

African delegates. Subsequently Homer Jack took him to Washington to meet people in Congress and the State Department, as, of course, we did for many petitioners to the UN.

In our office we mimeographed UPA's statement, which Roberto wrote, and circulated it at the General Assembly. It asked simply that the General Assembly demand that Portugal make annual reports to the UN on conditions in Angola under Article 73E of Chapter 11 of the charter. "Our goal," the statement read, "is of course the self-determination of the people of Angola." Roberto left New York in January, 1960.

Roberto's activities abroad called considerable international attention to Angola. UPA's stature increased in the Congo too. On November 7, 1959 an article in *Presence Congolais* called the UPA "a vast Angolan political movement." Also, to the despair of Portuguese authorities, it continued, "The UPA has managed to cover the whole of Angola from the north to the south with tracts, placards, posters, calling for immediate independence."

The next time I saw Roberto was at the second AAPC in Tunis in February 1960. He was elected to the Executive Committee and his movement began to receive considerable support. During an intermission at the conference he beckoned me to sit beside him, opened his briefcase, and invited me to look. It was filled with paper money—French francs. He told me it had just been given to him by the Algerians. However much the gift amounted to, it looked impressive.

Following the conference, I went to Leopoldville and spent considerable time with Necaca. Congo independence having been formally agreed to in Brussels in January, restraints on political activity were somewhat relaxed. UPA had an office with its name over the entrance in large letters. Still headed by Necaca, it now had 17 offices around the lower Congo and three vehicles. Roberto was a member of the council, not the leader.

Discussions were taking place at this time for a united front between UPA and two other Angolan movements, the MPLA, especially strong in Luanda, the capital, and the Zombo People's Alliance (ALIAZO), which had its main following among a subgroup of the Bakongo, who originated near Maquela do Zombo in northern Angola. Necaca felt UPA was growing inside Angola but was not yet able to issue membership cards because of the risk to the members. It had more than a hundred organizers around the country, a clear indication of its growth.

In the light of repressive Portuguese policy in Angola, it was shocking for President Eisenhower to visit Portugal in May of that year and say to Salazar that the United States and Portugal "have worked together without a single difference of opinion." The Portuguese leader expressed gratitude that the president comprehended "Portugal's civilizing mission in Africa."

CHAPTER SEVEN

Tom Mboya and the Kenya Emergency

In August 1956, the day before his 26th birthday, Tom Mboya passed customs and walked into the lobby of Idlewild (now Kennedy) International Airport in New York. Keith Irvine and I of the ACOA were waiting to greet him. We had invited him to come on a two-month speaking tour. The wide, thin-lipped smile on his very black, round, almost moonlike face immediately made a fine impression. Although of only average height, Mboya carried himself with such assurance that he attracted attention almost everywhere. He said simply with outgoing friendliness, "Hello, it's good to be here."

I had first heard of Mboya in a letter from Michael Scott of the Africa Bureau in London. Mboya, at Ruskin College, Oxford, in 1956–1957 on leave from his duties as general secretary of the Kenya Federation of Labor, had told Scott that he would like to visit the United States, particularly to make contact with the trade union movement. The ACOA was approached about sponsoring his visit.

It was difficult to give a quick response. Mboya was unknown in the United States. His visit would have come in August and September, notoriously a poor time for speaking tours, and we had no funds to cover the cost. Nevertheless, we decided to take a chance in the hope of interesting some of the major American unions in this young African labor leader. From August 14 to October 6, as I traveled with Mboya and had him in my home, my admiration for his outstanding abilities increased.

EARLY LIFE

Mboya told me about his early years.* He was born August 15, 1930, on a sisal plantation in Kenya's white highlands, north of Nairobi, where his father worked as a laborer and later as an overseer. His family was of the Luo tribe, the second largest in Kenya after the Kikuyu. The Luo ancestral homeland is on Rusinga Island in Lake Victoria, in western Kenya.

Mboya's education began in a Catholic mission school, where lacking books and slates, the children learned to write by tracing letters in the sand. In 1942 he went to a Catholic boarding school and subsequently to a Catholic high school, where he received his certificate in 1947.

*A more extensive account is in his own book *Freedom and After* (1963). See also a biography by David Goldsworth, *Tom Mboya, the Man Kenya Wanted to Forget* (1982).

Mboya trained as a sanitary inspector at the Royal Sanitary Institute Medical Training School in Nairobi. Elected president of the student council, he began to learn organizational skills. He qualified in 1950 and worked on the staff of the Nairobi City Council. After being elected president of the African Staff Association, he transformed it into a trade union. In 1953 he founded the Kenya Local Government Workers Union, registered it as a trade union, and was elected national general secretary without pay. Showing its displeasure, the Nairobi City Council dismissed him from his job. The government workers' union then affiliated with the newly formed Kenya Federation of Labor, and Mboya was chosen general secretary.

The emergency against the Mau Mau was declared by the Kenya colonial government in 1952. Mboya joined the Kenya Africa Union, of which Jomo Kenyatta was general secretary, in 1953, not long before it was banned, and became director of its Information Service. During the years of the emergency, no political organizations were permitted. Lacking a direct political instrument, the Kenya Federation of Labor increasingly became a center for complaints by the people, and Mboya gradually rose to political prominence. In 1954 his horizons broadened as he traveled to Geneva, Brussels, and London. In Brussels he impressed leaders of the International Confederation of Free Trade Unions (ICFTU) and established a lifelong relationship. Later in the year he visited India and Pakistan.

Mboya's leadership in settling a strike of dock workers in Mombasa in 1955 catapulted him into a position of first-rate importance in Kenya. Not only did the strikers win a 33.3 percent wage increase, but major violence was avoided by his skillful negotiations.

FIRST U.S. VISIT

When Mboya arrived in New York in August 1956, his star was just rising. He was not yet firmly established, nor was he the controversial figure he later became. The qualities that led to his rapid rise were very recognizable. He was young, dynamic, and unusually articulate. His brilliance as a speaker seemed all the more remarkable because of his limited formal education. A disciplined person, he could work long hours without seeming to tire. He had the unusual quality of following through organizationally, and he kept up a remarkable correspondence. I have scores of letters from him, both on organizational details and substantive analysis of events. Adding to his attractiveness was the fact that he came from a country engaged in a struggle, both colonial and racial, that captured international attention.

The ACOA held a public meeting for Mboya in New York at which the *Herald Tribune* gave him good coverage. He pointed out that in Kenya the Legislative Council (LEGCO) had 14 white elected members representing

45,000 European Kenyans and 6 government-appointed (not elected) Africans representing 6 million Africans. The best land in the highlands north of Nairobi was owned by Europeans. In Operation Anvil in 1954 aimed at stamping out subversion, 35,000 workers were arrested in Nairobi in one day. He pointed to the loss of thousands of lives, the expenditure of millions of pounds, and the 40,000 Africans in detention. In his speeches he constantly demanded more effective representation for Africans in the Legislative Council. He did not yet ask for majority rule.

Mboya's summer and early fall speaking tour was heavily geared to meetings with trade unions. Union leaders were very receptive. The ACOA's work to establish connections with the unions was beneficial to us too. Meetings were arranged with such leaders as George Meany, president of the AFL-CIO; Walter Reuther, president of the United Auto Workers (UAW); A. Philip Randolph, president of the Brotherhood of Sleeping Car Porters; David Dubinsky of the International Ladies' Garment Workers' Union (ILGWU); Philip Murray of the United Steelworkers; Sidney Hillman of the Amalgamated Clothing Workers; and Ralph Helstein of the United Packinghouse Workers. The tour took him to New York, Boston, Pittsburgh, Chicago, Cleveland, Detroit, Los Angeles, Atlanta, and Washington. In addition, he spent about 10 days in Canada.

As always, Mboya had a clear idea of what he wanted to achieve through the trip. First, he wanted to interpret events in Kenya to the American people. He did this not only through numerous meetings but by a host of radio and television appearances. Second, he wanted union support not only for scholarships to help train Kenyan labor leaders but also for funds to build a union headquarters in Kenya. Third, he wanted to lay the foundation for a scholarship program to bring Kenyan students to U.S. universities. He realized all these objectives.

On December 20, 1956, soon after he returned home, he excitedly wrote me about the decision of the AFL-CIO to grant the Kenya Federation of Labor $35,000 towards the erection of a trade union center. "Thus," he wrote, "at least one important aspect of my trip has been fulfilled. . . . For this the ACOA must take some credit since but for your initiative to me it would never have been achieved."

Most helpful at the beginning of Mboya's scholarship program was William X. Scheinman, president of a small company that manufactured airplane parts. He generously contributed to causes he believed in, and he believed in Tom Mboya. He himself paid the plane fare for a number of Kenyan students to come to the United States for study and then set up a foundation to help finance travel for about 50 students in the next two years.

RETURN TO AFRICA

On his return to Nairobi after more than a year away, Mboya was greeted by a throng of exuberant followers, the press, and 40 police. His baggage was ransacked for "seditious literature." He wrote in his *Freedom and After,* "I felt at that moment I was fully back in the Kenya I remembered."

The Kenyan political situation underwent a change in 1957. For the first time, on a small scale to be sure, Africans were to participate in electoral politics. As a prohibited immigrant, I was not able to visit Kenya but followed events through correspondence with Mboya and through the press. Under the so-called Lyttleton Constitution, 8 Africans were to be elected to the Legislative Council along with 14 Europeans, 6 Asians, and 2 Arabs, each group by a separate roll of voters, i.e., Africans voting only for Africans and so on.

Mboya was urged by his trade union colleagues to be a candidate. On December 13, 1956, he wrote to me that he was 1 of 37 candidates for the eight seats. There were only 126,000 registered African voters. The election date was March 1957. Mboya had three opponents in his constituency, Nairobi. His slogan was "Democratic equality for all peoples regardless of race or color." When he told me he needed funds for his campaign, we raised about $2,000 from individuals and some unions. After three months of spirited campaigning, Mboya won, but not overwhelmingly.

The eight Africans elected took their seats in LEGCO on March 26. They were now in a position within the government to exert pressure toward majority rule, leading inevitably (more than six years later) to independence.

Mboya played a key role in the next few years. He wrote me (November 20, 1957), "We [the elected members] have already met on our own and decided to form ourselves into a political party." It was called the African Elected Members Organization (AEMO). In spite of competition among the African leaders, they maintained a united front on most main points. Their first decision, Mboya wrote, was to reject the Lyttleton Constitution. "Thus none of us will accept a ministerial or parliamentary undersecretaryship. This is aimed at bringing the government to a definite standstill until they negotiate a better constitution with us." The elected members accepted positions in the legislature, where they could voice positions, but not in the administration, where they would have had to exercise responsibility for carrying out decisions under the colonial government. They refused two ministerial posts and demanded 15 more seats in Parliament, which would have given them a single vote majority in LEGCO.

The AEMO decided to send two delegates, Mboya and Ronald Ngala, to London to campaign against the Lyttleton Constitution and for an increase in African representation. Since I happened to be London in July 1957 at this same time, returning from my trip to Africa, I met with Mboya and Ngala. They made an impact on the British public through their press conferences, public meetings, and sessions with members of Parliament.

The position of the AEMO was effective enough that several liberal European and Asian members of the Kenyan LEGCO resigned, and the

Lyttleton Constitution was abandoned. In its place the Lennox-Boyd Plan came into effect, named for its author, the new colonial secretary. Under this plan, African representation in LEGCO was increased by 6. In addition, there were to be 12 "specially selected" members—4 Europeans, 4 Asians, and 4 Africans—chosen by LEGCO itself. The 8 African members were prepared to accept the 6 new elected African members but not the 4 to be chosen by LEGCO, for that body was still dominated by Europeans and thus the 4 "specially selected" members would be beholden to the Europeans. Nevertheless, 8 Africans offered themselves for these 4 seats. All but one of the African-elected members (who was absent at the time) adopted a strong public statement condemning these potential candidates as "stooges, Quislings and black Europeans," who by their action were identifying "themselves with those who seek the perpetual domination and suppression of the African people and consequently must be treated as traitors to the African cause." The signers, in addition to Mboya, included Daniel arap Moi, now president of Kenya; Ronald Ngala; and Oginga Odinga, later vice president and a leading Luo politician.

The Kenyan government was quick to react to this flouting of the Lennox-Boyd Plan. The African legislators were faced with two serious charges. One was conspiracy to violate the election law by putting undue pressure on the African candidates. The second was criminal libel for publishing defamatory material against the candidates. During this period in the spring of 1958 Mboya wrote me many letters. On April 12 he wrote that two days previously, "Police visited my office armed with a search warrant. . . . They took away my office typewriter as an exhibit." On April 16, "If conviction is secured it does not only mean several years in jail and/or heavy fines, but probably being debarred from LEGCO and voting for at least five years." His supporters planned to bring in an outstanding defense lawyer from Britain, who was expected to cost at least £5,000. "I cannot refrain from approaching ACOA and other friends for help since on our own we are completely helpless."

The ACOA responded by converting our Defense Fund geared to cases in South Africa to a more general Africa Defense and Aid Fund. Our concern was for the struggle against racism and colonialism in all of Africa, and we were beginning to receive urgent appeals for assistance from several countries. We immediately sent $2,000 in reply to Mboya's appeal. The case was finally decided in July 1958. The first charge of conspiracy was dropped, but the defendants were found guilty on the second charge and fined $200 each, which they paid.

Mboya was invited to the first anniversary of Ghana's independence as Nkrumah's personal guest. The two men established a mutually satisfying relationship at that time. Mboya wrote to me after his return to Kenya on April 1, 1958, "All the talk about dictatorship, tribal conflict, etc. is nonsense. The Nkrumah government is conscious of its responsibilities and also its place as the first experiment which must not fail." Referring to the competing relationship of Nkrumah and Gamal Abdel Nasser, he said, "I can tell you that Nasser has no chance with Africa south of the Sahara. Nkrumah is well established and all of us look to Ghana rather than Egypt." The influence of Nkrumah on Mboya was apparent. He established the Nairobi Peoples Convention Party, patterned after the Convention Peoples Party of Ghana, and became its president.

In 1958 and 1959 Mboya's prestige was at its height. In July he was elected chairman of the ICFTU Eastern, Central, and Southern African Region. In October he was invited to Ethiopia as a guest of Emperor Haile Selassie. In November he went to London to make public the sworn affidavit of Rossen Macharia, declaring that he had given false evidence at the trial of Jomo Kenyatta in 1953 that Kenyatta was the leader of the Mau Mau. When he arrived in Accra in early December for the AAPC, he was informed at the airport that he had been chosen chairman. "This was my biggest moment," he wrote me (November 13, 1959).

SECOND U.S. VISIT

It was at this time that the ACOA invited Mboya to make another speaking tour in the United States to coincide with our observance of the first Africa Freedom Day, April 15, a date established by the nine independent African states. No time could have been more propitious. Euphoria for freedom in Africa was at its zenith. Mboya's personal popularity was at an all-time high. Only Nkrumah's reputation or Kenyatta's could have eclipsed it. Mboya was young, had a strong trade union base in his own country and internationally as well, and had the prestige of having chaired the AAPC. *Life* magazine (February 2, 1959) said, "Tom Mboya is not only the outstanding political personality in Kenya but [is] among the most important in all Africa."

Up until the last moment the ACOA could not be sure Mboya would be able to keep his commitment to the U.S. tour. The Kenyan political situation was tense. On March 6, 1959, European police raided his home at 4:00 A.M. with a search warrant to look for "proscribed and subversive literature and documents concerning terrorist activities." At the time Julius Nyerere was a guest in his very small home. Later in the day his office at the Nairobi Peoples Convention Party and the headquarters of the party newspaper, *Uhuru*, were also raided. The editor and the party secretary were convicted under the emergency regulations. In New York we were fearful right up until departure time that Mboya would also be detained, making useless our preparatory work. I wrote on March 12, "In case you should be detained . . . I want to let you know that there will be quite a big protest here. We will be able to turn the meeting in Carnegie Hall, where we will have several thousand people gathered on April 15, into some kind of protest rally. I hope this will not be necessary." Fortunately it was not.

Mboya arrived in New York on April 8. I wrote an article in *Africa*

Tom Mboya, president of the
Kenya Federation of Labor, on
a speaking tour in the United
States, 1959.

Today (May–June 1959) about this visit. "Thirty-five days and about 100
speeches later he returned home. He had criss-crossed the U.S. giving as
many as six addresses a day from New York City to San Francisco, from
Boston to Miami Beach." Almost every one of Mboya's meetings was
packed beyond expectations. Twenty-seven hundred people paid to hear
him speak at Carnegie Hall in New York, and hundreds were turned away.
One thousand were turned away at Rackham Auditorium in Detroit. On a
warm Friday afternoon at the University of Michigan, 800 students delayed their weekend to hear him. At Northwestern University, the auditorium was changed at the last minute when 900 students turned up at a
hall that could hold only 200.

Mboya also addressed presitigious and influential groups from the
Senate Foreign Relations Committee Subcommittee on Africa and various
city Councils on Foreign Relations to the conventions of the ILGWU and
Americans for Democratic Action. He met privately with national leaders,
including John F. Kennedy, Hubert Humphrey, Adlai Stevenson, Martin
Luther King, Jr., and Roy Wilkins and with union leaders. David Rocke-
feller arranged a dinner in his honor. The demand to meet Mboya came
from almost every quarter of the American public.

I accompanied him on much of his schedule. Particularly interesting
was his 11:00 A.M. meeting with Vice President Richard Nixon. Bill
Scheinman and I thought the discussion would last about half an hour,

leaving time for his speech at Howard University at noon. During our far-reaching but not innovative conversation, we lost track of time. At 12:00 I interrupted to tell Nixon we were late and had no ready transportation to Howard University. Quickly Nixon assessed the situation and said, "That's all right. I am late for appointment too. I'll drive you to Howard." And so we were driven in the vice president's waiting black limousine to the university, where throngs of students, faculty, and some community people, almost all black, were waiting. In preparation for the election campaign the next year, a picture of Nixon accompanying the young African leader appeared in many journals. Nixon may very well have had the potential black vote in mind as he deposited Mboya at the university.

Mboya made a hit around the country. I was constantly amazed at the way he held his audiences and never had a note in front of him. His phrasing was good, such as "We prefer to govern or misgovern ourselves" or "The Western world must match the internationalism of Communism with the internationalism of democracy." Asked at the University of Michigan what he thought of the future of South Africa, he replied with meaning and humor, "Black."

Probably the most concrete result of Mboya's 1959 tour was the establishment of the airlift of Kenyan and East African students to U.S. colleges and universities. On every campus where he spoke, he talked with the president or other officials about scholarships for African students. By the end of the tour he had promises of more than 40 scholarships. If any of the university administrators thought that talk about scholarships was idle chatter, they did not know Mboya. Immediately upon his return to Kenya he set machinery in motion to receive applications, screen them, and raise funds. In the United States Bill Scheinman had already set up the African American Students Foundation (AASF) with Frank Montero and myself as vice presidents, to provide transportation for the students.

The fund appeal—initially to raise $39,000 to charter a flight to bring 81 Kenyan students to the United States—was led by Jackie Robinson, Harry Belafonte, and Sidney Poitier, and it had amazing results. On September 9, 61 men and 20 women arrived at Idlewild Airport and were met by a contingent led by Robinson, who himself had contributed $4,000. He wrote: "I have had few more rewarding experiences in my entire life." He said of the students, "As they talked in the same quiet, calm, self-assured way with which Tom Mboya made such a hit on his recent tour here, I couldn't help but feel that here undoubtedly was a whole group of potential Tom Mboyas, Kwame Nkrumahs and Nnamdi Azikiwes."[1]

The next year, 1960, three planes were chartered to bring 222 students from East and Central Africa. This was an election year. Mboya had met and impressed both Nixon and Kennedy. The AASF needed $100,000 to finance the airlift, and it was decided to approach both candidates. Robinson, a Republican, asked Nixon to seek a grant through the State Department. Nixon did but was initially turned down. Then Mboya came from Kenya and went to Hyannisport, with Scheinman and Montero, to request a grant from the Kennedy Foundation.

Nixon, hearing of the request to Kennedy, put muscle into his approach to the State Department, which agreed to a grant of $100,000. In the meantime, the Kennedy Foundation also appropriated $100,000. The AASF was overwhelmed—$200,000! What could political competition not lead to? But the two grants were not to be. *Time* magazine (August 29, 1960) ran a story on the behind-the-scenes machinations. Hugh Scott, the majority leader in the Senate, had announced the grant to the upper house, but when he learned that the Kennedy Foundation had come through, he furiously denounced the Kennedys for trying to take the project away from the government. Kennedy in the Senate denounced Scott for the "most unfair, distorted and malignant attack I have heard in 14 years in politics." Of course the grant from the State Department never came through.

STRAINED RELATIONS

The path of a political leader is complicated, and so it was for Mboya. For example, not long after the All African People's Conference, Mboya's relations with Nkrumah became strained over trade unionism. The neutrality of the AAPC between the Communist and non-Communist worlds applied to trade unions as well. Consequently many Pan-Africanists, including Nkrumah and the Ghana Trade Union Congress, supported a neutralist All African Trade Union Federation (AATUF), thus avoiding making a choice between the non-Communist ICFTU and the World Federation of Trade Unions based in Eastern Europe. Mboya was the ICFTU representative in East and Central Africa. Because he refused to shift his loyalty, his relations with Nkrumah cooled markedly.

As Mboya rose to great prominence in Kenya, he became controversial. The right-wing white politicians looked upon him as an extreme nationalist because of his leadership in efforts to increase African representation in LEGCO, his union base, and his efforts to limit the power of the white minority. But the attitude of his political peers was mixed. He had a mass following in Nairobi even among the Kikuyu, but other political leaders, including elected Africans in LEGCO, viewed him with attitudes ranging from respect to dislike. John Marcum, an American specialist on Africa, wrote to me (May 12, 1959), just after Mboya's triumphal U.S. tour, "Quite frankly and confidentially I find that Mboya has antagonized many of the moderate nationalists, largely because of his go-it-alone tendencies. By issuing statements in the name of the elected representatives without consulting them, he seems to have seriously impaired his claims to speak for Kenya nationalists. I am not attempting to belittle his significance but I do think caution should be exercised in appraising his domestic strength."

Mboya was indeed a complex personality. He was politically ambitious, competitive, and arrogant toward some. He was resented for his tendency to seek the limelight. Yet his colleagues needed his skill as a negotiator, debater, and drafter of statements. He never tried to compete with Ken-

Tom Mboya (left) Jomo Kenyatta (center), later prime minister of Kenya, and Joseph Murumbi, at Kenyatta's home, on Self-government Day, 1 June 1963.

yatta, however. He recognized that when Kenyatta was released from detention, he would be the leader. Mboya told me in November 1960 in Lagos, Nigeria, at the inauguration of Nnamdi Azikiwe as head of state, that he would like to be foreign minister some day, since Kenyatta was sure to be prime minister. But all this lay far ahead.

POSTSCRIPT

I was quite unprepared for the shocking news that reached me late on Saturday, July 5, 1969, that Tom Mboya had been assassinated. Early in the afternoon as Mboya emerged from a pharmacy in downtown Nairobi, a lone gunman fired two bullets, one of which entered his heart. The riddle of who instigated Mboya's murder has never been satisfactorily settled. That it was not just a private vendetta of the man who pulled the trigger is clear, although he was later executed for the crime. Most believe that it was a political murder involving prominent Kenyan politicians.

Thus ended the life of one of the most brilliant and capable African leaders to emerge from the liberation struggle. Who knows what role Mboya might have played in the development of Kenya and indeed in the wider African scene, had he lived? I personally felt as if with Tom's death I had lost a member of my family.

CHAPTER EIGHT

Algeria and the National Liberation Front

The **Algerian** revolution was the major anticolonial conflict of the 1950s. Indeed, it was a war in which the army of the FLN used guerrilla tactics against a French army that was 16 times its size during the height of the fighting. The methodology of the struggle and the contrasting sizes of the contending forces made the Algerian conflict unique. Not only this, but the struggle was internationalized through the UN debates and by Tunisian and Moroccan support for the FLN, especially after their independence in 1956. Further, the Algerian issue became important in U.S. foreign policy, especially toward the French.

CONFLICTING VIEWS

Initially the ACOA was not as intimately involved in North Africa as it was south of the Sahara. When I first visited Libya and Tunisia in late 1958, the Algerian liberation struggle was in full swing and I had some acquaintance with the FLN through work at the UN and contacts made at the AAPC in Accra.

Part of my initial hesitancy about the FLN came out of my pacifist background. It was one thing to support movements using nonviolent methods; it was another to support a movement engaged in a violent revolution. I fully supported the right of Algerians to independence from French domination. Yet the conflict was violent. There was no movement in Algeria advocating nonviolent resistance. There was no Gandhi or Lutuli giving a nonviolent message; the FLN represented the only effective opposition to French rule.

Another part of my dilemma was the fact that I represented the ACOA, which was not pacifist and supported the FLN. Of course, I could remain aloof from the Algerian struggle, but then, could I be relevant to any struggle for freedom that was not clearly nonviolent? For the first time, I found myself facing a conflict situation in which nonviolence was not a practical alternative.

Not prepared to accept a position of irrelevancy in this struggle against colonialism, I worked my way through this inner conflict. I accepted the justice of the FLN cause. I recognized that the ACOA's function was to interpret that cause to the American people and attempt to influence U.S. policy, not to condone violence or give military aid. Thus, somewhat uneasily, I found it possible to rationalize my support for the Algerian revolution.

REPESENTATIVES OF THE FLN IN NEW YORK

Through Moroccan and Tunisian friends the ACOA met the FLN representative, M'Hammed Yazid, when he came to New York in 1956 to lobby at the UN for the Algerian cause. He and Abdelkader Chanderli, who joined him later, were talented, mature diplomats, who were an effective team. Yazid was French educated and had attended university in Paris. He became secretary general of the Association of Muslim students in France. A convinced Algerian nationalist, he joined the FLN shortly after its formation in 1954. As part of the FLN's external mission, he attended the Bandung Conference in 1955, where he was instrumental in gaining international recognition for the Algerian cause. Subsequently he became a minister in the first Provisional Government of the Algerian Revolution (GPRA) when it was organized in 1958 at a critical stage in the fighting with France.

Chanderli had fought with the Free French forces during World War II and worked with UNESCO in Uruguay. When the revolution started in 1954, he went to the external mission of the FLN in Cairo, which assigned him to join Yazid in New York. Through Yazid and Chanderli at the FLN office the ACOA was able to keep in touch with events in Algeria.

Both men were responsible for making the Algerian issue a major one at the UN. They constantly moved around the country, speaking before student, church, and labor audiences, participating in radio and TV programs, and seeking ways to meet members of Congress. The ACOA facilitated their contacts in many ways. Unlike liberation movements south of the Sahara, they operated without as severe financial limitations and never once approached us for funds. They also had support from the Arab world. Already experienced men, they put out their own public relations material and maintained effective press contacts. Further, they had allies at the UN, particularly the group of countries that had organized the Bandung Conference.

THE ALGERIAN BACKGROUND

As I did my homework on Algeria, my sympathy for the objectives of the revolution deepened. I learned about the Berbers, who occupied the land as far back as recorded history, and the Carthaginians, Romans, and Arabs, who conquered the area in turn. Today the Berbers and Arabs, virtually all Muslim, are almost indistinguishable. The Berber language is spoken in a few isolated areas, but Arabic is the official language. French is spoken among the well educated.

The French invaded the region in 1830 and dominated it until independence. The French settlers, or *colons*, in the 1950s numbered about 1 million, close to 10 percent of the population. Official French policy was to integrate Algeria into the French republic. In fact, however, the *colons*, who greatly influenced French policy in Algeria, as the white minority did British policy in Southern Rhodesia, discriminated economically and politically against the mass of the people. Two percent of the population (mostly *colons*) controlled one third of the farm land. Forty-three percent of the population (Arab Algerians) eked out an existence on the worst land. Although the Algerians could vote, there were separate voter rolls. The French elected one deputy for every 80,000 French voters, while the Algerians had one deputy for every 700,000 Algerians. The code of 1881 denied Arab Algerians trial by jury and excluded them from many civil administrative posts. Eighty percent of the civil servants were Europeans.

Resistance to French occupation began in the 1830s, led by the renowned Abdel Kader, who was not subdued until 1847. He wrote with some disdain to the French king, Charles X, "Have you seen the wave made when a gull brushes the sea with its wing? This is the image of your passing over Africa." The green and white standard of Abdel Kader became the banner of the FLN and ultimately the flag of Algeria.

Modern Algerian nationalism began in the 1920s and 1930s under the leadership of Ahmed Messali Hadj and Ferhat Abbas. When Messali Hadj's nationalist organization, the Star of North Africa, was banned in 1937, it immediately reformed as the Party of the Algerian People (PPA). Abbas promoted a Manifesto of the Algerian People in 1943, signed by 56 nationalists, calling for agrarian reform, equality between the Arabic and French languages, the establishment of civil liberties, and the release of political prisoners. Subsequently this group became a moderate nationalist organization.

The conflict between Algerian nationalists and France was exacerbated in 1945 when troops were called in to quell a demonstration in Setif, which began as a celebration of the Allied victory in Europe but was transformed into a rally for independence and equality. Thousands of Muslims and 103 Europeans were killed in the rioting. Abbas and 4,000 others were arrested.

A succession of ever more-militant organizations formed, such as the Movement for the Triumph of Democratic Liberties (MTLD) and the Revolutionary Committee of Unity and Action (CRUA). Within these organizations young leaders arose, such as Ahmed Ben Bella and Hocine Ait Ahmed, who were prepared for armed insurrection if political methods proved fruitless. They were two of the "historic nine" leaders, who, despite their differences and later in-fighting, are still honored as the fathers of the Algerian revolution.

Planning for an armed revolt began in earnest. It was decided to call for an uprising on November 1, 1954. The Algerian people were appealed to dissolve other organizations and join in the National Liberation Front.

The FLN was nonideological. It accepted Communists only if they renounced their association with the Communist party. Labor unions, women's groups, students, and professional associations joined the FLN. Its position was stated in August 1956: "Ours is a national struggle to destroy an archaic colonial regime—it is not a religious war. It represents a march to the historical path of human progress—it is not a return to feudalism. Lastly, it is a struggle for the rebirth of the Algerian state in the form of a democratic republic."

By August 1956 the FLN had established itself as the leader of the Algerian revolution. By 1957, its fighting force, called the Army of National Liberation (ALN), was a well-disciplined fighting unit approaching 40,000. The fighting inside Algeria was borne by 6,000 or so guerrillas. The rest were stationed in Tunisia and Morocco, where they infiltrated Algeria to replace fighting units there. Traditional guerrilla hit-and-run tactics were used. Attacks were made on *colon* farms, police posts, army patrols, and transportation and communication facilities; then the attackers would melt into the population.

A confrontation between the French and the FLN took place in the so-called Battle of Algiers in early 1957. The FLN called a general strike to coincide with the debate on Algeria at the UN. Almost 100 percent of the Algerian personnel struck in the railways and in the postal and telegraph services in Algiers. The French military responded by assaulting FLN positions in the casbah. In retaliation, FLN terrorists bombed restaurants and parks. The French destroyed suspected FLN strongholds and arrested and tortured suspects. It was a dismal period of the war, which left the FLN infrastructure in Algiers severely damaged.

THE ALGERIAN CAUSE AT THE UN

The Algerian issue came up for the first time at the UN General Assembly in 1955, included on the agenda by the narrow vote of 28 to 27. The French delegation strenuously objected and walked out. The issue was postponed for a year, by which time Yazid had arrived.

On October 6, 1956, Yazid and a colleague, Hocine Ait Ahmed, who had come from Cairo, paid me what diplomats call a "courtesy call" to get acquainted. Like most of the other "historic nine," Hocine was fairly young, about 35, when I met him. He had already been playing a leading role for 10 years. He had founded the Special Organization within the MTLD that had planned the armed struggle and the organization of the FLN. His responsibility was the overall work at the UN.

Six days after this first meeting, startling news came over the wires. Five top Algerian leaders were on a plane that was hijacked by a French pilot, who landed in Algiers, where the French authorities arrested them. The five had been guests of the sultan of Morocco. They had been in a Moroccan plane with a French crew flying well out over the Mediterranean to avoid Algerian territory when the pilot received an order from the French military authorities to land in Algiers, which he obeyed. The five leaders spent the rest of the war in French prisons. Hocine was one of the five, as was Ahmed Ben Bella, who became the first president of Algeria.

The ACOA sent a letter to President Eisenhower asking the United States to protest the arrest. U.S. policy was clearly stated in the reply by the director of the Office of Western European Affairs, "I must point out that the Algerian nationalist leaders are French citizens and that there is accordingly no legal basis for any U.S. government intervention with the French authorities on their behalf."[1] The United States backed the French position that Algeria was an integral part of France and accordingly had opposed placing the Algerian item on the UN agenda on the grounds that it was a domestic issue.

Yazid and Chanderli engineered a vigorous campaign at the UN. In 1957 two strong resolutions called for the right of Algerian self-determination and for negotiations between Algeria and France. The United States opposed both. Very few prominent American voices were raised in criticism of French policy in Algeria and of U.S. support for it. One exception was John F. Kennedy, then chairman of the Senate Foreign Relations Subcommittee on Africa. On July 2, 1957, he called on the administration to stop supporting France's Algerian war and to start working for Algerian independence. Secretary of State John Foster Dulles commented that if the senator wanted to tilt against colonialism, he ought to concentrate on the Communist variety rather than the French.

Kennedy's speech, as reported in the press, was a topic of conversation with many African nationalists with whom I talked during my travels at that time. On my return, I wrote Kennedy (August 14, 1957), "I thought you'd be interested to know that the many Africans with whom I talked were overjoyed at the fact that finally an important public official in the U.S. was speaking out on this question." The ACOA did what it could to publicize the speech. In Africa it was never forgotten, for it took political courage to make such a speech in the light of the U.S. alliance with France.

GROWING SYMPATHY FOR THE ALGERIAN CAUSE

The French bombing of Sakiet-Sidi-Yousef, a Tunisian village near the Algerian border, on February 8, 1958, raised a wave of sympathy for the Algerian cause. The raid was in reprisal for Tunisia's giving sanctuary to FLN troops. A surprise attack was launched by 25 French bombers and fighter planes on a traditional market day. An estimated 8,000 civilians were clustered in open areas without any protection. At least 68 Tunisians, all civilians, including 28 women and children, were killed, and 90 others were severely wounded. Seventeen of the planes were U.S. built. The reaction to this French indiscriminate bombing was almost universally condemnatory.

The Algerian War aroused mass opposition in France to the government's policy, not dissimilar to the outcry in the United States against the

Vietnam War many years later. French authorities admitted that approximately 600 Algerians were killed every week. The torture of prisoners was common practice.

The French newspaper *Le Monde* (March 26, 1957) carried a letter from a French professor, René Capitant, to the minister of national education, resigning his post teaching law at the University of Paris in reaction to the suicide of a student from the University of Algiers who had been imprisoned and tortured. This student, Ali Boumendjel, was not an anonymous person to me because he was the brother of Ahmed Boumendjel, who had led the FLN delegations to the AAPC in Accra and Tunis. Ali had jumped to his death from a prison in Algiers rather than submit to further torture.

In March 1958, after meetings with concerned organizational representatives in New York, the ACOA decided to write an open letter to the French people. Norman Thomas was helpful in formulating a first draft. "Do not, we beg you, straightway dismiss this as an unasked, unwarranted interference in your affairs. We, the signers of this letter, are only too conscious of our own country's failings. We are writing because our nation and yours have lived together through so many of the crises of man's struggle for freedom and peace, and are now so closely united by the will to preserve them." The letter indicated to how great an extent the Algerian war involved the United States, as, for example, France's use of American planes to bomb the Tunisian village. The letter urged France to begin negotiating with the recognized representative of the Algerian people. We had a good list of signers, including Thomas, Roger Baldwin, Eleanor Roosevelt, and Arthur Schlesinger, Jr.

After all our careful work, however, the letter was never sent or publicized. We had second thoughts on the timing. Reinhold Niebuhr wrote me (April 23, 1958), "I agree with every word in the letter, but I don't agree with the advisability of publishing it in France or here." A long letter from a French friend, Mrs. Anne Marie Stokes, who had done volunteer work with the ACOA and was sympathetic to the FLN, was even more decisive. She spoke of the depth of feeling in France on the Algerian crisis, the way it was splitting the country, and the bravery of some French people who were speaking out against the war. She said (April 1958), "Only by sticking out your own neck, by risking something from your own country, will you persuade them. Are you ready for that? . . . Have you ever thought what it means at this present time not to kill or torture; it means perhaps to become a martyr. This is a lot to ask of people."

At this particular juncture a number of professors in France were speaking out bravely and jeopardizing their own positions by opposing the war. On January 12, 1958, a group of 150 high-ranking professors met in Paris in response to the kidnapping by paratroopers in Algeria and subsequent torture and death of a colleague, Maurice Audin. A leader of this "university revolt" was Laurent Schwartz, professor of mathematics at the Sorbonne. He referred to the Algerian conflict as "a slow rotting process

Algerian refugees in Tunisia, 1958.

. . . and as this rotting is in itself comfortable, one settles into it and it leads to decadence. It is time to stop this process of decadence. The Audin affair will have been one moment of the awakening of public opinion faced with the dangers of the disappearance of democracy in France. We can, alas, doubtless not save Audin, but in a sense we can be saved by him."[2]

This meeting of professors was followed by at least three other conferences, ending with their call for negotiations and eventual Algerian independence. "If France refuses this solution, . . . Algeria will sooner or later be torn from her . . . [and France will] become a diminished, morose, wounded and ineffective nation."[3]

The U.S. government continued to support France, its North Atlantic Treaty Organization (NATO) ally, and never seriously protested the use of U.S. and NATO military equipment or the use of French NATO forces in Algeria. We watched while an army insurrection took place in Algiers on May 13, 1958, and a military administration was set up headed by General Raoul Salan under the slogan "Algérie française." The resulting political crisis brought Charles de Gaulle to power in France on June 1 and a return to civilian rule in Algeria. De Gaulle committed himself to a French Algeria, and the military insurrection ended.

THE POLICY OF DE GAULLE

De Gaulle ushered in the Fifth French Republic. The FLN countered by setting up the GPRA, headquartered in Tunis, with Ferhat Abbas as president. As fighting continued, and opposition inside France from Socialist, labor, and church groups, led by Jean Paul Sartre and Simone de Beauvoir, mounted, De Gaulle's policy shifted. He said, "I deem it necessary that recourse to self-determination be here and now declared in the name of France."

De Gaulle offered Algeria a choice among integration, autonomy with the French community, or independence. The problem was that it was not clear what "self-determination" meant. He declared that the Sahara oil would remain in French hands and that the free choice of the Algerian people must be endorsed by the French. Nevertheless, the GPRA declared itself ready to enter into pourparlers with France to discuss the conditions and guarantees for the application of self-determination. The five men chosen to take part included Ahmed ben Bella and Hocine Ait Ahmed, both of whom were in prison. However, France took no step for a cease fire, and the war continued unabated. The two sides agreed on only one point—self-determination.

In 1959 the ACOA published two public statements on Algeria, which received some attention. One, signed by 16 members of Congress, was the first such statement by U.S. legislators. The second, "A Call for Peace in Algeria," was signed by 46 prominent Americans and released as debate on Algeria began in the UN. Both statements spoke with hope for the future in the light of the agreement of De Gaulle and the FLN on the principle of self-determination.

In Algeria, however, the *colons* and the ultras (extreme rightists) revolted. They accused De Gaulle of betraying them, crying, "De Gaulle to the gallows." The January 1960 attempt at an armed insurrection was short-lived as the army came to De Gaulle's support. By June 1960 De Gaulle was speaking of an Algerian Algeria. "To pretend that the Algerians are French or want to become such is a frightful joke." On the anniversary of the beginning of the war, November 1, De Gaulle spoke to the French people about the plan he was following. "This course leads not to an Algeria governed by metropolitan France, but to an Algerian Algeria. This means an emancipated Algeria, an Algeria in which the Algerians themselves will decide their destiny."[4]

Independence was still more than a year and a half away. In New York Chanderli was in charge of the office, for Yazid, as a minister in the GPRA, was needed in Tunis and elsewhere. We helped Chanderli arrange meetings with the first three senators he met, Frank Church of Idaho, Frank Moss of Utah, and Gale McGee of Wyoming, who, in 1960, had jointly made a trip to Africa. At our Africa Freedom Day observance in April 1960, the Algerian flag was presented publicly for the first time in New York. Chanderli wrote to me after one of the meetings we had arranged for him (June 22, 1961), "Thanks to your constant desire to develop better understanding of the Algerian situation, I was able to explain the latest developments to a very fine audience."

CHAPTER NINE

The Central African Federation: An Ill-fated Partnership

I n 1921, after a trip to Africa, Winston Churchill, then colonial secretary in the British cabinet, wrote: "It will be an ill day for the native races when their fortunes are removed from the Imperial and august administration of the Crown and abandoned to the fierce self-interest of a small population of white settlers."[1] The British Crown may not have been as beneficent as Churchill suggested, but he was certainly correct in pointing to the danger of allowing white settlers to formulate and execute policy in the multiracial colonial areas of British East, Central, and Southern Africa.

The formation of the Central African Federation in 1953 represented one of the major attempts of white settlers to maintain and extend their domination in that part of Africa. The federation consisted of Northern Rhodesia (now Zambia), Southern Rhodesia (now Zimbabwe), and Nyasaland (now Malawi). It lasted only 10 years.

Most important among my early contacts with men who were later leaders in this part of Africa were Kenneth Kaunda (now president of Zambia), Hastings K. Banda (president of Malawi), Joshua Nkomo (a major nationalist figure in Zimbabwe), and Kanyama Chiume (the first foreign minister of Malawi). We met initially in Africa but became better acquainted when each of them came to the United States on speaking tours, which I arranged and promoted through the ACOA.

AFRICAN LEADERS ON TOUR IN THE UNITED STATES

The year 1959 was crucial for the Central African Federation, then only six years old. On the whole, the white minority of the three territories favored it, while the African populations were militantly opposed. The African political organizations were engaged in two struggles—to oppose the hated federation and to win independence and majority rule for their separate countries. Their protest campaign reached a climax between February 26 and March 11, when the colonial authorities banned the three territorial congresses, rounded up suspects, and jailed their leaders.

Nkomo, president of the African National Congress in Southern Rhodesia (SRANC) was outside the country at the time. He decided that rather than return and be arrested he would travel widely to try to win support for his people's struggle. Chiume, a major leader of the Nyasaland African Congress (NAC) and one of five Africans elected to the Nyasaland Legislative Council, was returning to Africa from Britain. He too decided not to go home. Nkomo and Chiume joined forces in their international campaigning and both went to the United States.

Banda and Kaunda, who were at home when the government cracked down, were both arrested and imprisoned, Banda for almost 13 months and Kaunda for 10. Directly after Kaunda's release in January 1960 and Banda's in April, I cabled each man, inviting him to speak at the ACOA's second observance of Africa Freedom Day and to make an extended speaking tour. We were overjoyed when both men accepted. Thus these four outstanding leaders from the same area of Africa were in the United States within a few months of one another. Although their messages were similar, their individual styles differed greatly.

BACKGROUND TO CONFLICT

After my own lengthy discussions with these four African leaders, I realized that the struggle for independence in Southern Rhodesia was likely to be more protracted than those in Nyasaland and Northern Rhodesia mainly because the white population was larger in proportion to the black population in Southern Rhodesia (5 percent) than in Northern Rhodesia (2 percent) and Nyasaland (1 percent). There was also a technical difference in political status: the northern two territories were British protectorates and Southern Rhodesia was a so-called self-governing colony. The principle of British "guidance" and "guardianship" was pater-nalistically supposed to operate in the protectorates, whereas white domi-nation, virtually unrestricted by British influence, prevailed in the south. The principle of "the paramountcy of native interest," enunciated in the Devonshire Declaration of 1923, applied in the north but not in Southern Rhodesia. The constitution of Southern Rhodesia, adopted in 1923, put effective power into the hands of the white settlers. Britain retained the legal right to intervene in protection of African rights but chose not to use this power.

The patterns of discrimination in the three territories were not unlike Jim Crow practices in the U.S. South before the civil rights struggle of the 1960s—separate entrances and seating arrangements in shops and public places. Even most churches were segregated. Only a handful of Africans had the franchise. To be on the regular roll of voters, Africans had to meet high standards of income, property ownership, and education, which eliminated them from any significant political power. In Southern Rho-desia they were controlled even more extensively through legislation that allocated one third of the best land to Europeans, limited trade unions and the right to strike, abolished communal land ownership, and restricted the number of cattle on the land.

The federation was a means of extending the power of the white minority and, from an African perspective, was a barrier to realization of majority rule. The federation was dominated by Southern Rhodesia. The white minority in the protectorates knew their position would be strengthened against both British interference and African pressure by the political, economic, and military power that Southern Rhodesian Europeans represented. Sir Roy Welensky, then the prime minister of Southern Rhodesia, undoubtedly spoke for most whites when he made his notorious "Red Indian" speech in 1952 threatening Africans: "I say to the Africans . . . if they do not come with us, they will meet the same fate which came to Red Indians in the U.S.A.: they disappeared."[2]

African nationalist organizations arose in protest against white control. The Nyasaland African Congress was formed in 1944, although it was ten years before it became a dynamic instrument for change. The Northern Rhodesia African National Congress (NRANC) was organized in 1948 out of a federation of African welfare societies. It likewise became a militant instrument of protest after Harry Nkumbula became president in 1952 and Kenneth Kaunda secretary general a couple of years later. The SRANC was not organized as an effective national instrument until 1957.

Acts of civil disobedience, nonviolent for the most part, were increasingly encouraged by the various congresses. In Southern Rhodesia young militants deeply offended white government officials by entering office buildings by the main entrances rather than those designated for Africans, refusing to doff their hats or stand at attention when Europeans entered the room, and encouraging boycotts of discriminatory facilities. In Northern Rhodesia the NRANC initiated a boycott of butcher shops because of their particularly insulting treatment of African patrons. Such actions were reformist rather than revolutionary, demanding an equal place for Africans within the system. But the tone of the protests took on a political implication. Nkomo said: "What we are asking for immediately is therefore direct participation in the territorial legislature and Government. And we ask not as suppliants but as people who know that their rights cannot indefinitely be withheld from them."[3]

The language of the protests against the federation became strong and determined. Banda in a speech in 1958 said: "To hell with Federation. . . . They can send me to prison. They can kill me. I will never give up my fight for freedom."[4] At the annual meeting of the NRANC, all delegates took the pledge, "I promise to Almighty God that because the proposed federal plan is a wicked plan, I shall continue to fight against it." Kaunda later commented, "The only good thing about federation was the unity it brought amongst us."[5]

The white protagonists of the federation popularized the word partnership to define the desired relationship between black and white. A kind of limited interracialism came into vogue, particularly in Southern Rhodesia, exemplified by the Capricorn Africa Society, which wanted to abolish all racial discrimination, and the Interracial Association, consisting of a few genuinely liberal whites and a handful of elite blacks. But on the whole, these efforts were short-lived and looked upon skeptically and even cynically by Africans. The phrase "tea-time partnership" was coined. On the whole, Cecil Rhodes's phrase "equal rights for all civilized men" was the accepted principle for whites. Roy Welensky said, "We will give the African equality when he has shown himself fit for it."[6] Godfrey Huggins (later Lord Malvern), the first prime minister of the federation, said of partnership, "It is the same that exists between the rider and his horse. They don't eat or sleep together but there is a working understanding between them."[7]

Any hope that partnership in the federation might have worked was dashed by the declaration of a state of emergency, the banning of the congresses, and the arrest of the leaders in early 1959. From the perspective of the federation government, the crisis was triggered by the report of the Nyasaland government that they had uncovered a sensational plot. According to a friend of mine on the scene, the plot called for "concerted violence and disruption leading up to the massacre of 8,000 whites in the protectorate [Nyasaland], plus loyal Africans."[8] The signal was to have been the beating of a drum located near Banda's home. Chiume was supposed to have been one of the architects of this gruesome plot. When he heard of it, he remarked, "How could I have master-minded such a plot after a long absence from home and from several thousand miles away?" Welensky (who had become prime minister of the federation) sent federal troops from Southern Rhodesia into Nyasaland. The prime minister of Southern Rhodesia, Sir Edgar Whitehead, arrested the ANC leadership, outlawed the organization, declared a curfew, banned meetings of more than three people, and forbade the distribution of literature so that there could be no diversionary action while the troops stationed in Southern Rhodesia were in Nyasaland.

I wrote a letter of protest to Welensky. His two-page response (April 15, 1959) clearly outlined his views. He said Europeans were responsible "for all the real development that is taking place. . . . Although we are quite content to share fully the political and economic life of this country with the Africans as they progress, we as Europeans have no intention of being swamped, massacred or pushed out." He spoke of African nationalists as "Congress thugs" and then said "pressure from the outside which attempts to insure that solution on the lines of Ghana is imposed on this country can do nothing except cause bloodshed."

When the emergency was ended, Nkomo, Chiume, Kaunda, and Banda, touring the United States, had already laid the groundwork for a new round of action. In Southern Rhodesia the National Democratic Party (NDP) was set up in place of the banned SRANC. In a few months time, Nkomo became president.

In Nyasaland, even before Banda was released from prison, the Malawi Congress party had been set up, and he was chosen, uncontested, as president. The founding conference of the new United National Independence Party of Northern Rhodesia (UNIP) was held shortly before Kaunda's arrival in the United States, and he was elected president.

NKOMO AND CHIUME

I had met both Nkomo and Chiume at the AAPC in Accra in 1958. Nkomo was not easily forgotten partly because of his huge size. He was tall and heavy, even at 42, yet he carried his weight with great ease. He walked with a rhythmic sway, almost like a glide. He had a kind of mischievous smile and soft laugh that gave him an appearance of good humor and jollity, although he could be very stern.

Nkomo was the son of a peasant who later became an evangelist and teacher. He was born in Matabeleland (the southwestern portion of Southern Rhodesia where the Ndebele people predominate) on June 7, 1917. He was 19 before he completed his elementary education at a government school. Thereafter he worked for five years in odd jobs such as those of carpenter and lorry driver before earning enough money to continue his secondary education and postgraduate studies in South Africa. In 1947 he returned to Southern Rhodesia and became the organizing secretary of the Rhodesian African Railway Workers Union. In the meantime he continued his studies by correspondence with the University of South Africa and finally won his B.A. degree in 1951. His railway union became one of the most powerful African organizations in the country and by 1952 had 22 branches. From that base he went on to become a prominent African political leader.

Chiume, in contrast to Nkomo, was small, slim, wiry, and intense. He struck me as quieter than Nkomo, but he was more fiery and easily gave vent to his feelings. He was born on the shores of beautiful Lake Nyasa on November 24, 1929. When he was eight, he moved to Tanganyika to live with his uncle after his mother's death. He had his basic education in Tanganyika, partly in a government school in Dar es Salaam. After a two-year course at Makerere University in Uganda, he received a diploma in education. While at Makerere he became active in politics, joined the NAC, and became president of the student political society. He taught for a year in a mission school. In 1956, back in his home country, he was elected to the Legislative Council from the Northern Province and was recognized as one of the outstanding nationalist leaders.

At a joint press conference in New York, Nkomo and Chiume talked about the imposition of a federation dominated by 300,000 Europeans on 7 million Africans. They spoke of the report of the Devlin Commission, set up by the British government, that Nyasaland was police state and that the NAC had been suppressed although it was a genuine movement of the people. They referred to the suppression of the SRANC because of its stand against federation, to the mass detention of SRANC members, and to the enactment of the Preventive Detention Act. They called for an end to federation, the lifting of the ban on the congresses, and the release of political prisoners. They announced that one of their aims while in New York was to campaign for the question of Central Africa to be put on the agenda of the UN General Assembly, an aim that was easily realized.

Nkomo's and Chiume's tour took them to all parts of the United States,

Joshua Nkomo (left), president
of the ANC of Southern
Rhodesia, and Kanyama
Chiume (right), a leader of the
Nyasaland African Congress, on
a speaking tour in the United
States, 1959.

where they spoke to college audiences, trade unionists, and church groups
and met with legislators and officials in Washington and with delegates at
the UN. Sometimes they traveled and spoke together, at other times
separately.

Nkomo gave an impressive, statesmanlike speech and charmed those he
met privately. A professor at the University of the State of New York at
New Paltz, after reporting that Nkomo "had made a tremendous impression on everyone here,"[9] told me about his being in a snack bar with some
students when he let drop the fact that he loved apples. A couple of the
girls immediately dashed out to one of the orchards near the campus,
raided the trees, and brought back a sackful of apples. Then the juke box
came on with a rock-and-roll record, which Nkomo remarked he liked
very much. This seemed to be a signal for other students to go to a nearby
record shop to buy it for him. My professor friend wrote, "You should
have seen the big smile when they presented Nkomo with the record and
the apples in the auditorium before he spoke next."[10]

Chiume spoke dramatically and with a wit that he himself seemed to
enjoy. His first child was named Kwacha Michael (after Michael Scott)
Chiume. "Kwacha," meaning "dawn," had become a rallying cry of the
congress movement in Nyasaland, like "Freedom" in Ghana and "Uhuru"
in Kenya. The publication of the NAC had also been called *Kwacha*. With
the banning of the NAC, the public use of the word was likewise forbidden. In his underplayed humorous way, Chiume reported to American
audiences that his son was named Kwacha so that he would have a legal
excuse for using the banned word. If authorities questioned him, he would
say, "I am just calling my son."

Nkomo had an extracurricular experience of American racial discrimination right on the ACOA's doorstep. Needing a haircut, he entered a shop on the ground floor of our office building, only to be told that he could not be served. We were surprised. We immediately protested to CORE and the New York State Commission Against Discrimination. A few days later the barbershop was tested again and service was given. This incident was reported in the *Washington Post* (November 5, 1960) because Nkomo mentioned it in a speech at Howard University, in what he called "pinpricks" of racial incidents in the United States. Referring to his and Chiume's speaking tour, Nkomo said, "We are here to encourage Americans to make changes fast."

BANDA AND KAUNDA

In a way it was a problem for the ACOA to have two outstanding African leaders such as Banda and Kaunda under our auspices at the same time. Nkomo and Chiume traveled together as colleagues, and it was clear that Nkomo was the senior both in years and rank. But the relationship between Banda and Kaunda was an unknown quantity. Although I had met them previously, they did not know each other well. Their first real get-acquainted meeting was in my office. They had both just been released from prison and were presidents of their respective organizations. How well would they hit it off? Who would get top billing?

Our concern was short-lived. Banda behaved like a prima donna. Kaunda did not. Furthermore, Banda was in the country for only one week, Kaunda a month. They appeared on the same program only twice, at a press conference in our office and on the stage at Town Hall for the Africa Freedom Day celebration. On those occasions Kaunda never attempted to upstage Banda. The traditional African respect for age must have contributed to the ease of relationship, as the younger man always expected the older man to be first.

Banda was about 20 years older than Kaunda, being in his mid-50s in 1960. He was short and somewhat stocky. He was serious and not given to cracking jokes or laughing easily but was a fiery speaker with a straightforward message: "Down with the Federation." He called himself the "extremist of extremists" on this issue and lived up to this description. He was quiet in personal conversation but on the public platform became emotional and shouted vigorously like an orating preacher. In one of his speeches in Africa he exhorted the crowd, "Go to your prisons in your millions singing hallelujah, kwacha, ufulu. . . . We must fill the prisons. This is the only way to get freedom. To hell with Federation!"[11] He couldn't ask a New York audience to take the same sort of action, but his language was stimulating and aroused people with his emotional appeal.

Banda was born in Nyasaland in 1903. He was only 13 when he left his home on foot and purportedly walked all the way to Johannesburg, the better part of a thousand miles, where he worked in a gold mine. He saved his money and bought passage to the United States, where he lived for 12 years. He obtained a degree from the University of Chicago and an M.D.

from Meharry Medical College in Nashville. (One of the things he told me he wanted to do in the United States was to visit Chicago and call on the landlady of the house where he had lived. This he did in 1960.) After leaving the United States in 1938, he took an advanced degree at the University of Edinburgh and then set up a medical practice just outside London with a large clientele, mostly white, by 1952. A year later he returned to Africa, to Kumasi in the Gold Coast. I first met him there in 1954. He developed a good relationship with Kwame Nkrumah, whom he had known in London.

Although Banda was in voluntary exile for more than 40 years, he kept in touch with events. In London he had known George Padmore and the future African leaders around him. He had published a pamphlet against the Central African Federation in 1949. He returned to Africa to be closer to events unfolding in the 1950s. He was invited back to Nyasaland in 1958 by the young leaders of the NAC there, who felt he would provide mature leadership in the crucial period of their struggle. He returned on July 6, the date on which six years later Malawi became independent.

Time magazine (July 21, 1958) described his return. "As he got off the plane, he uttered the one word 'Kwacha.' The crowd roared in response and Banda was draped in a ceremonial leopard skin and carried on their shoulders to a car to the beat of tomtoms. He drove off escorted by red robed young freedom fighters on motor cycles." Banda became the idolized leader of the people. He was called affectionately by his African name, Kamuzu (meaning "Little Root"), or the Great Kamuzu. The title of Ngwazi was later bestowed on him, meaning "the greatest of the great."

I had a cordial relationship with Banda as a result of our two meetings and occasional correspondence even before he came for Africa Freedom Day. In a letter from London (June 25, 1958), just before his return home, he said that he would like to visit the United States and would accept an invitation to make a tour under our auspices. His letter sobered me, for he certainly suppressed any innate sense of modesty he might have had. "At present I alone can speak with authority from and for the Nyasaland African Congress." He wrote me again from Nyasaland (July 24, 1958), "The welcome I am receiving from my people has to be seen to be believed. Even I, myself, did not realize to what extent I am held in esteem by my people here . . . literally it is within my power now to set Nyasaland on fire or at peace. The people will do almost anything I say." This undoubtedly was true.

The campaign under Banda's leadership did shake the empire. He was arrested on March 3, 1959, and detained not in Nyasaland but in Southern Rhodesian jails. When he was released, he was flown back home for talks with the Nyasaland governor, Sir Robert Armitage, and the British colonial secretary, Iain MacLeod, opening up the next stage in Nyasaland's progress toward independence. Immediately after this Banda came to New York.

Kaunda was a vivid contrast to Banda. He was about six feet tall and very dark with penetrating brown eyes. He combed his hair straight up, giving the impression of its being windblown. He was rather retiring, reserved, and polite and was a good listener. He was not always easy to understand, and at times I had to listen carefully to decipher his words, which seemed to trip over one another. I discovered later that in his youth he had had to wrestle with a stammer. By slowing down his speech and concentrating on enunciating clearly, he had improved his speech enormously. I always felt a quiet strength in Kaunda. His leadership quality sprang from his personal discipline and conviction, not from any flamboyance. Modesty and a kind of shyness marked the man at least in his younger days, and yet he was very personable. It was easy to begin to call him "Kenneth" almost immediately. Banda, by contrast, did not encourage familiarity and was called "Dr. Banda" even by his close colleagues.

Kaunda was born in 1924 in the Northern Province of Northern Rhodesia. His father was a teacher and headmaster of a school at Lubwa and later an ordained minister and evangelist in the Church of the Livingstonia Mission of Nyasaland. Although his father died when Kenneth was only eight, the boy was greatly influenced by him. Religious observance, prayers, and hymn singing were an important part of their family life. Although he is not a church member, religion has continued to be an important part of his personal discipline.

Kaunda went to primary school and teacher's training school at home but had two years of secondary school in Lusaka. He taught for four years in Lubwa, traveled in Tanganyika and Southern Rhodesia, and taught at Mufulira on the copper belt, where he became active in the NRANC. He returned home to the Northern Province in 1949, intending to farm, but he was increasingly drawn into politics. In 1952 he was chosen organizing secretary of the NRANC in his province and in 1953 secretary general of

Kenneth Kaunda, president of UNIP, on a speaking tour in the United States, April 1960. *ACOA files.*

the national organization, necessitating a move to the capital, Lusaka. Working closely with Nkumbula, president of the NRANC, he became a national figure.

In 1953 a campaign of nonviolent positive action was initiated by the NRANC, especially on the copperbelt. NRANC members invaded shops and post offices, ignoring the posted segregation notices. When some of the leaders were arrested, the NRANC responded with boycotts, which led to the ending of many petty apartheid practices. Kaunda and Nkumbula suffered their first jail experiences in 1955 for possessing banned literature.

At the invitation of the Labour party, Kaunda spent several months in England in 1957, campaigning both for constitutional changes in Northern Rhodesia and against the federation. I first met him at the Africa Bureau in London, although we had been corresponding for three years. He was invited to India in 1958, where his admiration for Gandhi was deepened and his belief in nonviolent action was strengthened.

During 1957 and 1958, Kaunda and other NRANC leaders were increasingly disillusioned with Nkumbula as his commitment became blunted by too much drink. On October 24, 1958, just two months before the AAPC, to which both Nkumbula and Kaunda came, the movement split, and the Zambia African National Congress (ZANC), under Kaunda's leadership, was set up. It lasted only five months before it was banned, although Nkumbula's NRANC was not. Kaunda was imprisoned and the stage was set for the next phase in the struggle for independence.

Several things stand out about Kaunda. First is his personal discipline. At the time of the boycott of the butcher shops, he became a vegetarian. He does not eat meat to this day. Second is his private religious practices. He is a praying man and has told me prayer strengthens him in his task. Third is his belief in nonviolence, influenced both by his religious convictions and by his admiration for Gandhi. His convictions have been tested and modified by his years as president. He is a man without bitterness. After his imprisonment he commented, "A man who gathers honey expects to be stung. I am therefore not embittered. I have come out with a clear conscience."[12] Finally there is his hesitancy to assume leadership. His associates had to push him to agree to break with Nkumbula. One of his white associates commented, "How can a man with as gentle a nature . . . continue to ride the tiger of African politics?"[13]

The second Africa Freedom Day, for which Banda and Kaunda came to the United States, was a great success, with at least 1,500 filling Town Hall. The honorary co-chairpersons were Eleanor Roosevelt, Martin Luther King, George Meany, A. Philip Randolph, Walter Reuther, Jackie Robinson, and Harry Belafonte.

Both Kaunda and Banda made spirited speeches. Kaunda started his with what he called the "freedom shout," explaining that this was how political meetings began in Northern Rhodesia. The leader shouts, "Freedom Africa," and the crowd responds, "Now, now, now!" A few days later

Kaunda led the crowd in this same shout at a street-corner rally at Seventh Avenue and 125th Street in Harlem.

Banda's schedule took him to Washington and Chicago in addition to giving interviews and making radio and TV appearances in New York. Kaunda spoke widely in all sections of the country. In a press conference in New York he reaffirmed his dedication to nonviolence, in spite of reports of violence in Northern Rhodesia. "No circumstances can be so trying as to justify violence. . . . Nonviolence is a dynamic and not a dormant force as you all know."[14] It seemed to me that his experiences in political leadership were sure to temper these convictions.*

*A book by Kaunda, *The Riddle of Violence* (1980), dealt with the theme of nonviolence from a political and a theological perspective. Although retaining great respect for nonviolence, he had changed his position owing to his governmental responsibilities and the pressure of events, particularly the conflict in Southern Rhodesia. He believed Britain should have used force against the move toward a unilateral declaration of independence by the white minority in 1965. The violence would have been much less than that of the guerrilla struggle, he thought. He also said, "I ended up supporting armed struggle in Zimbabwe because I no longer believe that *anything* is preferable to the use of force."

CHAPTER TEN

South Africa's "Colony"

My first knowledge about the former German colony called South West Africa came principally from an Englishman. I had a long talk with Michael Scott, an Anglican priest, when he came to New York in 1947 to present a petition to the newly established United Nations on behalf of the Herero people of South West Africa. He described his participation in the nonviolent campaigns against apartheid in South Africa and his imprisonment the year before. He had been called upon to help the people of South West Africa (now Namibia)* by the old Herero chief, Hosea Kutako, who needed a voice at the UN.

From Scott I learned some essentials about South West Africa. The land is rich in mineral resources—diamonds, copper, uranium—but much of the area is desert. In fact, the name Namibia derives from the Namib desert, which stretches the length of the country along the Atlantic coast to some 50 to 70 miles inland. The word means "shield" or "enclosure" in the Nama language. This inhospitable expanse helps explain why the European invasion of the territory (it became a German colony in 1894) came late.

In 1947 the area had roughly a million people, with perhaps 10 percent being European—mainly Afrikaner, German, and British. The rest of the population was (and is) made up of four major tribal groups, of which the Herero are one. In their war against imperial Germany in 1904, 60,000 had been killed, leaving a population of 15,000.

Germany lost South West Africa, as it did all its African colonies, after its defeat in World War I. Administration of the area was assigned to South Africa, under the League of Nations mandate system. When the UN was set up after World War II, all the former mandated territories were placed under the UN trusteeship system, with the exception of South West Africa. South Africa refused to accept this decision and continued to administer the area as a mandate, in effect as a colony. Thus the international controversy over the status of the country began. Jan Christian Smuts, as prime minister of South Africa, tried to incorporate South West Africa into the Union of South Africa, but that was not allowed by the UN. The Chief's Council of the Herero decided to send a delegation to the UN to present their grievances, but South Africa forbade them to leave the country, so they asked Michael Scott to make the journey on their behalf.

---

*The UN officially adopted Namibia as the country's name on June 12, 1968 (Resolution No. 2372). South Africa still likes to cling to South West Africa but compromises by calling the country South West Africa/Namibia. Black nationalists from the area called themselves Namibians even before 1968.

SCOTT AND KERINA AT THE UNITED NATIONS

Scott was not permitted to make a verbal statement to the UN for two years, however, because up until 1949 no nongovernmental representative had been allowed to speak on behalf of a subject people. His presentation, even more dramatic as coming from someone white and English, and the succeeding debate led to the passage of two resolutions. One asked South Africa to make annual reports to the UN on conditions in the country. The second referred the question of the legal status of South West Africa to the International Court of Justice (ICJ) for an advisory opinion.

I never met a more dedicated person than Michael Scott. Our paths were to cross frequently over the years—at the UN, where he went almost every autumn for the debate on South West Africa, in London, and in Africa. Ill health had caused him to go to South Africa in the early 1940s. There he established the Campaign for Right and Justice. He was imprisoned in Durban for joining the nonviolent civil disobedience campaign against the Asiatic Land Tenure and Indian Representation Act. He stood up against angry white farmers in the Transvaal when he exposed the horrible conditions of African contract labor. It was the publicity about this sort of action that led Africans to invite him to represent Chief Kutako at the UN. The South African government expelled him in 1950. Shortly thereafter he founded the Africa Bureau in London in order to pursue his campaign for justice, especially in South West Africa.

Scott was unforgettable. He seemed almost ascetic in his personal discipline. He never spent much time thinking about where he would stay or what he would eat or wear. His clothes were unpressed, whether he wore his clerical garb or a business suit. He was the kind of person who attracted sympathetic support because he was so completely immersed in his cause that he was unmindful of mundane distractions. Yet he needed someone of a practical mind to take care of the essentials of daily living. Luckily, there were a host of such devoted friends wherever he went.

Scott was not, however, otherworldly. His concern was for the welfare of people. He was not usually inspiring to listen to because he seemed shy and was very soft spoken. His speeches at the UN were frequently too long and rambling and at times boring, although they were filled with important facts. Their strength came from the integrity and single-minded commitment of the speaker and the known fact that he had put his own life on the line for the people for whom he spoke. How ridiculous it seemed to those who knew him that the U.S. government placed restrictions on him in New York. During most of the more than 30 years that he came to the UN he was not permitted to travel north of Columbus Circle or south of 21st Street, a distance of perhaps two miles. The reason was that he refused to answer questions put by U.S. immigration officials about organizations he was connected with. Instead, he referred them to his autobiography, *A Time to Speak* (1958), in which he described his political and religious philosophy and dealt extensively with his differences with Marxism.

In the mid-1950s a Namibian petitioner joined Scott at the UN. He was Mburumba Kerina, born in Tsumeb, the first of his countrymen to go to the United States to study. He arrived in 1953, attended Lincoln University on scholarship, and graduated in 1957. When I met him he was called Eric Getzen according to his passport, which was valid only in South Africa and the United States. He explained at the UN that he had had to change his name to Getzen and his Herero identification to that of Cape Mulatto, in order to obtain the document.

Kerina was an ambitious young man. As the only Namibian around the UN for about six years, he attracted attention. But at first he had no organizational status. In early 1955 he wrote to the UN asking to be heard as a petitioner, but he was not approved for more than a year. In December 1956 he and Scott made oral presentations to the Fourth Committee of the General Assembly, which dealt with agenda items related to colonialism.

The UN was still in its infancy as far as Africa was concerned, and it was not clear how petitioners should be handled. Scott was interrupted five times by the chairman on the ground that he had gone beyond his subject, and he was ruled out of order. The portion of his testimony that mentioned the treason trial, then in progress in South Africa, was ordered omitted from the record. This kind of interference was later abandoned.

OTHER PETITIONERS AT THE UNITED NATIONS

It was only at the UN that any attention was paid to South West Africa. Very little protest occurred in the territory itself. The UN concern was essentially legalistic. In 1957 the UN created a Good Offices Committee on South West Africa "to discuss with the government of South Africa a basis for an agreement which would continue to accord to the territory . . . an international status." What could be more dull or less threatening to South Africa in its continued exercise of authority and extension of apartheid to the area?

Three extraordinary events led to interesting discussions at the UN. One event involved the ACOA office. On September 24, 1958, I received a letter and a package from Cape Town. I opened the package first. It mystified me because it contained a copy of Robert Louis Stevenson's *Treasure Island*. On turning the pages, I quickly discovered that a tape was embedded in the center of the book. Its presence was explained by the letter from a person with a familiar name, Herman Toivo Ja Toivo, president of the Ovamboland National Congress, a new organization of Namibians working in Cape Town. Toivo had written, "I have posted a book to you which I would like you to please do me a favor and hand it over to Mr. Kerina." Music filled most of the tape, but in the middle was a ten-minute message from Toivo to the Fourth Committee calling on the UN to displace South Africa and set up its own administration in South West Africa.

After long debate at the UN, it was decided that the tape could be used only in an informal gathering of the Fourth Committee. It said nothing essentially new, but it introduced Toivo, one of the most renowned Namibian nationalists, and set a precedent about hearing taped material.

A second extraordinary event was the arrival in New York in early 1959 of Jariretundu Kozonguizi. I had heard from a friend in South Africa that Kozo, as he was called, was a student "of more than average ability" at Fort Hare University College. His scholarship had been withdrawn, it was suspected, because he had written letters of protest to the UN on behalf of a Namibian student organization that he headed. He had been the subject of periodic inquiries by the Special Branch of the police, and he and Kerina, whose friend he was, were "marked men as far as the administration of South West Africa was concerned."

After graduation in 1956, Kozo had worked with Toivo in Cape Town, been politically active in Windhoek, and was added to the Chief's Council as a youth member. When Scott urged Kutako to send someone fresh from the territory to the UN debates, the chief designated Kozonguizi. He left South West Africa without seeking permission and made his way via Bechuanaland (Botswana), Northern Rhodesia, and Tanganyika, to New York, arriving in February 1959. The ACOA organized a schedule for Kozo. I accompanied him on a two-day trip to Washington to meet congressmen, labor leaders, and State Department officials. Kozo did a creditable job of interpreting the South West African situation.

A third unusual event contributing to UN discussions was a presentation by Allard Lowenstein and colleagues of their trip to South West Africa. Lowenstein, a former leader in the U.S. National Student Association and later a member of Congress, had a fertile mind and active nature that attracted others to his cause. He became intensely interested in Africa, met Kerina and Scott, and at Scott's urging gradually developed a plan for a journey to South Africa and South West Africa in order to gather up-to-date information. He was joined by two other young men, Sherman Bull and Emory Bundy. His fascinating book *Brutal Mandate* (1962) detailed his surreptitious meetings with Namibian leaders such as Chief Kutako often in the dead of night in areas that he had no permission to visit. The climax was his successful engineering of the escape of Johannes Beukes, a Coloured Namibian whom the South African authorities were seeking, across the border from South Africa to Bechuanaland by hiding him in the rear of a small Volkswagen.

The four men—Lowenstein, Bull, Bundy, and Beukus—told their story at the UN. Nevertheless, despite their testimony, that of Kozonguizi, Scott, and Kerina, and up-dated information on the abuses wrought by South Africa's policy of apartheid in South West Africa, the UN did not challenge South Africa's control.

These days in the late 1950s were heady for the young Namibians at the UN. Both Kerina and Kozonguizi were politically ambitious. Without making any serious analysis of the facts, many optimistically assumed that the problem of Namibian independence could be solved peacefully by negotiation or by the International Court. Events in New York were headlined in South West Africa and the two young Namibian petitioners were acclaimed. Kerina sent me a clipping from the *Windhoek Advertiser* (November 16, 1959) headed, "Getzen as premier UNO lobby talk." A key sentence went on: "The name of South West African-born Mburumba Kerina, as the veteran of the petitioners has been mentioned as a likely candidate for premiership." How ridiculously premature this was. But a young man could not help being influenced by the promise of political rewards. In a very nice way, Kutako wrote to Kerina May 10, 1960 (sending a copy to me), telling him to curb his actions designed to build up his own image and reminding him that Michael Scott was still regarded as chief spokesman.

The fact was, of course, that independence was a long way off. The UN did not have the will or the power to challenge South Africa's unshaken insistence on control, and the struggle by Namibian nationalists would have to grow immeasurably before a fundamental change in the status of the territory could be realized.

NAMIBIAN POLITICAL GROUPINGS

During the 1950s and early 1960s, political organizations, although dreadfully weak, were taking form within the country to challenge South Africa. The oldest political groupings were essentially traditional and ethnic. The Namas, Damaras, and Hereros each had tribal organizations, but that of the Hereros was the most prominent. The Herero Chief's Council, composed of two dozen elected members, antedated the coming of the Germans to their homeland. Hosea Kutako was an officer in the Herero military when the Herero revolted in 1904. He was wounded and taken prisoner in the bloodiest battle of the war. Upon his release he taught school, but with his official recognition as the traditional leader of the Herero in 1925, he gave full attention to his new responsibility.

Another political grouping was built around the students, the intellectual elite. It was also basically Herero and centered in Windhoek. Kozonguizi had been president of the South West African Student Body, an organization formed in June 1952 at a conference at Windhoek of about 35 students. He had explained to me that the Student Body grew out of the impatience of the younger generation with the discussions at the UN. They were greatly influenced by the wave of nationalism sweeping South Africa under the leadership of the ANC and especially by the Defiance Campaign. They hoped to launch an organization to break down tribal barriers and infuse a national consciousness. When the students graduated from secondary school, the Student Body folded and was succeeded in 1955 by the broader South West Africa Progressive Association.

The methods of the students were different from those of the Herero traditionalists and inevitably resulted in tension. The Chief's Council, although committed to self-government, hoped for intervention by the

UN, and their tactics consisted of petitions, deputations, and conferences. The students wanted a national organization and used more militant methods.

A third political grouping, ultimately the most effective, began in Cape Town among the Ovambos, the largest tribal group in South West Africa. They were (and are) almost half the population. They came from Ovamboland in the north, an area that had not been occupied by the Germans. The Ovambos had been introduced into occupied South West Africa primarily as workers in mines, factories, and European-owned farms, frequently recruited by the South West African Native Labor Association (SWANLA). Fifty to 75 percent of the black employees of South West Africa were migratory workers, overwhelmingly Ovambos. They also worked in South Africa, some on contract and others finding jobs on their own.

Herman Toivo Ja Toivo was central to the organizing effort of Ovambos in Cape Town. He and his friend Jacob Kuhangua were recruited in 1951 by SWANLA to work in the mines in Johannesburg. Finding working and living conditions at the mines impossible, after only a week, they deserted their jobs. Eventually they made their way to Cape Town, where they found work and lived in an African township.

Soon Toivo and Kuhangua became the center of a discussion group that led to the formation of the Ovamboland People's Organization (OPO) in 1958 with a constitution based on Nkrumah's CPP in Ghana. Toivo was expelled from South Africa shortly afterward as punishment for having sent me the taped message for the UN. Accompanied by Kozonguizi, he made stops along his journey home to Ovamboland to meet Nama leaders and won their agreement to establish a new national organization to represent the country as a whole. He also met with Clement Kapuuo, deputy chief of the Herero, and seemingly won his support. At the mining center of Tsumeb he was arrested for entering the mining compound without a permit. He spent Christmas 1958 in jail and was then placed under house arrest in his home village. In the meantime, the OPO was established in Windhoek and by April 1959 was functioning with Sam Nujoma as president.

In September 1959 a new organization, the South West African National Union (SWANU), was formed at a conference of 2,000 in Windhoek. For some, SWANU was meant to be the national front representing all groups. Kozonguizi, then in New York, was elected president. The treasurer was affiliated with OPO, and Nujoma and other Ovambos were on the Executive Committee. The Namas and Damaras were also represented. Despite this breadth, however, SWANU essentially represented the Herero student elite.

By the end of 1959, three main political bodies were active in South West Africa: the traditionalist Herero Chief's Council; OPO, consisting principally of Ovambo contract laborers in Windhoek; and SWANU, aspiring to represent the whole country. Each was anticolonialist. There was some overlapping but each had its separate identity.

December 10, 1959, was a turning point in the struggle for liberation.

In Windhoek, police and African nationalists clashed, leaving 13 Africans dead and 44 wounded. I was informed almost immediately by Jane Kerina, the American wife of Mburumba Kerina, that according to a message from South West Africa, "The situation is critical. We are in a state of great fear." The clash had not been unexpected. The petitioners, particularly Kozonguizi, had warned the UN that such a confrontation would take place.

Under apartheid law, all "native" locations had to be at least 500 yards from any European-inhabited area, separated by a permanent buffer zone. The so-called Old Location at Windhoek violated this law because the European area had expanded. The authorities decided that all 16,000 inhabitants of the Old Location must therefore move to a new place called Katatura (meaning "We have no place of our own" in Herero) some three and a half miles from Windhoek. The people, who of course had not been consulted, were opposed to the move as being farther from their work, more expensive to rent, and unattractive. They protested by petitions, marches, and finally boycotts of all government-sponsored facilities. Protests culminated in a nonviolent demonstration on December 10, when several thousand people gathered. Police ordered them to disburse. When that did not happen quickly enough, they began to shoot, resulting in deaths and injuries.

OPO, SWANU, and the Chief's Council had worked effectively together to oppose the forced removal. Perhaps this was the moment of their greatest unity. Whether it could have been strengthened after the December 10 demonstration is speculative. The authorities, however, acted to make this impossible. Some leaders were arrested immediately, others were deported, and more than a hundred were sent to their home areas. Nujoma, president of OPO, was banished to Ovamboland, Kuhangua also was placed under house arrest in the north. Restricted in their freedom to organize, many leaders fled the country. Many went to New York and the UN, where Nujoma and Kuhangua arrived in 1960. Others obtained scholarships for study in Britain or Scandinavia and continued their political activities from exile.

Meanwhile, OPO was converted from a tribal base to a national base. Renamed the South West Africa People's Organization (SWAPO), it was open to all Namibians. By June 1960, SWAPO was officially established with Nujoma as president. The former OPO representatives on the SWANU executive committee resigned, and the two organizations went their separate ways.

CHAPTER ELEVEN

From Treason to Massacre in South Africa

On December 10, 1956, Frieda Matthews, wife of Z.K. Matthews, wrote to me, "You have heard the news. My husband and son [Joe] are both in gaol and likely to be there for some time. No bail has been allowed as yet. The charge is of course a fantastic one I think—high treason. Just because they have tried to fight for our rights."

TREASON TRIALS

Indeed I *had* heard the news. Just five days before, South Africa had again been front-page news, the first time since the Defiance Campaign. One hundred fifty-six leaders of the struggle against apartheid had been arrested in the early morning hours of December 5. They were charged with high treason, which was defined as disturbing, impairing, or endangering "the existence or security of the [government] by committing hostile acts . . . and [conspiring] to overthrow the existing government by use of extraparliamentary, unconstitutional, illegal, and violents means."[1] If found guilty, the accused could be given the death penalty. The case was to be a major issue in South Africa for some years.

It was fortuitous that Mary Louise Hooper, an American friend who later worked with the ACOA, happened to be in South Africa at the time and could see at close hand what was happening. While on a group tour of South Africa in 1956, she had met Chief Albert Lutuli and other leaders of the ANC and had become deeply committed to the antiapartheid cause. She decided to return to South Africa and was working with Lutuli when the arrests took place. She wrote detailed letters and sent press clippings frequently, cautiously using the name S.H. Norris or S.H.N. and never mentioning Lutuli by name but only as her "boss." She was rightly suspicious as to whether all her letters came through; indeed some did not. In her first letter (December 23, 1956) she wrote, "My boss was taken too at 4:30 A.M. on the first day of the arrests. Most of the people were taken on those first simultaneous raids before dawn all over the Union. Just like Nazi tactics—the heavy knock on the door in the wee hours, the secret spiriting away by military planes before anyone knew where they were being taken."

THE CONGRESS OF THE PEOPLE

The arrests were not unexpected. Five months earlier Lutuli had written, "We are awaiting a dramatic arrest of leaders of our liberatory movement."

For well over a year the government had been laying the groundwork. In September and October 1955 the police had raided almost one thousand homes and offices in search of evidence of sedition. These raids came on the heels of an historic conference called the "Congress of the People," which met to draw up a "Freedom Charter." This charter is still the basic program of the ANC. It opens: "We the people of South Africa, declare for all our country and the world to know: that South Africa belongs to all who live in it, black and white, and that no government can justly claim authority unless it is based on the will of all the people."

Z.K. Matthews has been credited as a principal architect of the Freedom Charter. The year he was in New York, he had discussed with me his idea for a document that could be adopted by a large representative gathering. Shortly after he returned to South Africa, he said at a large meeting in the Cape Province (August 3, 1953), "I wonder if the time has not come for convening a national congress to draw up a democratic constitution for the future." The idea caught on. The ANC and the other groups that formed the so-called Congress Alliance (the Congress of Democrats, the Coloured People's Organization, and the Indian Congress), which had sponsored the Defiance Campaign, needed some new initiative when the Defiance Campaign was called off.

A vast amount of local work was done in preparation for the gathering. Since no hall was available, a friendly Indian merchant at Kliptown, about 12 miles west of Johannesburg, offered his extensive yard. A platform was constructed and heavy planks were used for seats. A camp kitchen was set up, and a low fence was built with only one entrance, where credentials of delegates could be checked.

Arthur Blaxall attended the gathering on Saturday, June 25, and wrote me about it in detail. He reported (July 13, 1955) that the 2,858 delegates to the Congress of the People included 2,196 Africans, 320 Indians, 230 Coloureds, and 112 whites. The main business was the reading, discussion, and adoption of the Freedom Charter.

On Sunday afternoon, 25 police stormed the place, carrying search warrants to look for treasonable material. They announced that papers would be examined and names and addresses taken. "The great sea of people rose," he wrote, "and raised their right fists with upstretched thumbs," in the Congress salute. This went on for a full 10 minutes until the chairman quieted the crowd and the police went about their business. It took four hours. "It speaks volumes for the controlled spirit of the vast crowd," Blaxall wrote (June 27, 1955), "that there were no incidents and only a few arrests were made for secondary offenses such as irregular passes. . . . I was frankly surprised at the success [of the event] both with regard to size and general arrangements . . . June 25–26 will rank high in the annals of the struggle to establish a nation in which all discrimination, hatred and injustice will vanish away."

Blaxall was invited to attend a meeting in Durban on what steps to take next. He was concerned that a program to achieve the revolutionary program the Freedom Charter called for would lead to chaos and bloodshed. He wrote me (July 15, 1955), "I realize more than ever that I am treading on very thin ice by attending such meetings, but do feel that the position has become so critical that some of us must be ready to let the ice break under us, even if we are drowned in the process."

THE TRIALS

The treason arrests were the government's retaliation against the leaders of the Congress of the People and its Freedom Charter. Patrick Duncan wrote to me (December 21, 1956), "What the arrested seem to have in common is attendance at the Kliptown Congress of the People. The Public Prosecutor opened his address and all that has come through to me yet is a statement that the Congress of the People and the Freedom Charter were an attempt to set up an alternative government for the Union." Before bail was set, the accused, segregated by race, were held in a prison called the Fort in Johannesburg. Among the Africans, Lutuli led a brief ceremony. He said, "If there are any present who are sorry to be in the Fort and regret that their membership in the Congress has brought them to this pass, let them drop out of the circle."[2] No one did. After a prayer, everyone sang the African national anthem, "Nkosi Sikelél iAfrika" ("God Bless Africa").

Bail was arranged, but the accused had to stay in Johannesburg for the extensive preliminary hearings. In early January 1957, Matthews began writing me details from Johannesburg. Because no regular courtroom was large enough to hold the vast number of people involved, an old building called the Drill Hall was taken over. At first before bail was arranged, the defendants were kept in a zoolike enclosure of mesh wire. As the hearings opened, thousands of people stood outside with signs reading "We stand behind our leaders." They sang hymns and Congress songs and gave the thumbs-up salute again and again. Matthews wrote (June 1957) "The accused in this trial sit together as a mixed group without regard to race. I suppose the intention is to show that this is a group beyond redemption as far as South African mores are concerned, but we see it as a picture of the South Africa of tomorrow."

According to Matthews, the accused were a mixed group ranging from conservative tribal Africans to ultra-left whites. They included three clerics, five doctors, seven lawyers, two teachers, seven journalists, two students, and many trade unionists. Most of them were members of organizations that sponsored the Congress of the People. The prosecution was determined "to prove that these organizations are all communist or communist-influenced." Nevertheless, Matthews pointed out, some of the leading Communists in the country, such as Dr. Yusuf Dadoo, were not detained.

Those arrested were heroes to a large section of the people. Poems were written about them.

> Here are the leaders
> Here they are
> Look upon them, people

Look upon them
On their faces you will see
The look of our South Africa to be.

The whole exercise of the treason trials lasted for more than four years. It was a mammoth failure for the South African government but very costly for the defense. The legal gyrations of the prosecution made it quite apparent that the government was not well prepared. The preliminary examination lasted about 13 months and considered more than 25,000 documents.

On January 30, 1958, 65 defendants, including Chief Lutuli and Oliver Tambo, were released. The other 91 were charged with high treason for preparing to overthrow the state by violent, revolutionary methods and establish a so-called People's Democracy. A subsidiary charge was that the defendants were guilty of being Communists.

The first trial of the 91 began August 1, 1958. This phase ended in October with the government dividing the remaining defendants into two groups of 30 hard-core suspected Communists and 61 others to be tried separately, a further indication of the government's legal confusion. Matthews wrote me that the new indictment against the 91 put greater emphasis on the advocacy of Communism, although there were no specific charges under the Suppression of Communism Act, which defines a Communist as one who "aims at the encouragement of feelings of hostility between the Europeans and non-European races" or "who aims at bringing about any political, industrial, social or economic change . . . by the promotion of disturbance or disorder or by the threat of such acts." To add to the confusion about the government's position, the indictment against the 61 was quashed on April 20, 1959, that against the final 30 in March 1961. The process leading to this conclusion was long, tortuous, and expensive.

DEFENSE FUNDS

Alan Paton wrote early in 1957 from South Africa to say that a Treason Trial Defence Fund had been organized to help raise the large sums that were necessary to defend the accused. The initial goal was £100,000. Arthur Blaxall (December 13, 1956) wrote that if the government interfered, "some of us are quite determined that if we are not allowed to do this constitutionally then we will really develop underground organization."

The ACOA decided to set up its own South Africa Defense Fund in the United States to support the effort as best it could. The Very Rev. James Pike, dean of the Episcopal Cathedral of St. John the Divine in New York, and John Gunther, the author, became co-chairmen with a distinguished group of sponsors. Martin Luther King was a strong supporter of the campaign for funds and signed one of our early appeal letters.

In England a similar organization was set up. Fenner Brockway, Labour MP and leader of the Movement for Colonial Freedom, wrote (January 1,

1957), "In Association with Christian Action we were able to start a fund for legal defence and the next day cabled £100." Certainly the most successful effort for raising funds was that headed by Canon L. John Collins of St. Paul's Cathedral in London. Through his organization, Christian Action, much more was raised than in the United States. The liberal British public was much closer to the South African scene than Americans were.

The ACOA contributed about $75,000 to the legal defense over the years. At first we were fearful that it might be difficult to transmit funds to South Africa because of government interference. But at this point we found no problem and dealt directly with Anglican Bishop Ambrose Reeves in South Africa, chairman of the Treason Trial Defence Fund.

Reeves came to the United States on a speaking tour in June 1957. The ACOA held a luncheon for him in New York and gave him our initial check of $5,000. After this, for the duration of the trial, we sent him checks ranging from $1,000 to $5,000. The South African government deported Reeves back to Britain in September 1960. He continued his active support for the antiapartheid cause from there.

In September 1958 Dr. Ellen Hellmann, a leader in the South Africa Institute of Race Relations and an active supporter of the Defence Fund, wrote me that the Treason Trial Defence Fund was planning an art and antiques auction to raise money and wondered if I would approach Eleanor Roosevelt to contribute some personal item. Mrs. Roosevelt was very sympathetic. She contributed an autographed copy of her latest book, *On My Own,* which was auctioned off for a generous amount.

Not surprisingly, Mary Louise Hooper was served with an early deportation order. According to Blaxall, she was taken into custody on March 10, 1957, by order of the minister of the interior, ostensibly because she had associated herself with the ANC and this was "not for the true welfare of the native African people." She was given 30 days to clear up her affairs. Blaxall told me (March 11, 1957) he was not surprised. "In her enthusiasm to be helpful she was often alone in her car with three or four Africans; as you know, in an atmosphere like ours, anything touching on close relationships is the last thing." The ANC gave Hooper a letter of commendation signed by Lutuli and Tambo in gratitude for her identification with their cause. She slipped across the border to Southern Rhodesia before her 30 days were up. She wrote from Salisbury (May 22, 1957), "Just a hurried line to let you know that I am out of the Union, for good, I fear. I thought it best not to wait to be deported." Although the ACOA missed her reports from the spot, we gained organizationally. At home she immediately started work as West Coast representative of the ACOA's South Africa Defense Fund and made a tremendous contribution to the cause.

GRISWOLD AS AN OBSERVER

With the exception of the funds we raised for legal defense for treason trials, our most important project was arranging for Erwin Griswold, then dean of the Harvard Law School, to go to South Africa as an expert legal observer at the trial. No one was more respected than Griswold, and we agreed to raise the funds.

Griswold was eager to have material that would acquaint him with the situation in South Africa. After digesting the information I sent, he wrote (July 2, 1958), "These [books] have made it clearer to me than it was before that this is a delicate and difficult matter. I will try very hard to be discreet and to avoid any problems in South Africa. However such problems may arise and I will have to decide myself what to do about them. . . . I have no thought of being a martyr or a cause célèbre. If for any reason things should get to that pass, I will simply pick up and depart."

Because the whole matter was delicate and sensitive, the ACOA had agreed that we would not publicize the fact that we made the arrangements for him to go. Had that been known, he might never have been able to enter South Africa. We also agreed that he would allow us to arrange a press conference and other events in New York for him on his return.

We kept our bargain. Griswold wrote to me (August 19, 1958) just after he left South Africa saying, "I am sorry that I have been so distant from you this summer but I think it was better. I found that there was considerable hostility to ACOA and I think that many doors were opened to me which would not have been opened if I had come as a representative of the American Committee." Nevertheless, in his valuable and extensive private notes, he said that "financial provision for my trip has been made by and through the American Committee on Africa," and he referred to my putting him in touch with helpful people in South Africa.

Griswold's arrival in South Africa was prominently noted under the *Sunday Express* headline (July 27, 1958), "Head of Harvard Law School Comes to South Africa." He reported to us that he "received every facility and courtesy from the South African officials, including members of the government and the counsel on both sides of the case." He dispelled any doubts about the fairness of the trial. "The world need have no concern about formal adequacies of the trial . . . or about adequate procedure and fair hearing. It may well be concerned that there should be such a trial at all."[3] He reported that after two and a half weeks of argument on both sides, all indictments for Communism were dismissed, leaving only the charge of high treason. "This is a vague charge since it arises from Roman-Dutch common law without statutory definition. Counsel for the Crown has stated that any effort to coerce the government even by nonpolitical or nonviolent means would be high treason. Nonwhites in South Africa have no political power and therefore are in a dilemma."[4]

Griswold was genuinely critical of the trial. "It is hard to escape the thought," he stated, "that quite apart from the legalities involved, everything about [the trial] is a little absurd. Of course it is deadly serious and tragic for the accused."[5] Ninety-one persons were being tried on a single indictment, but there was no single group act alleged. In effect the accused were charged with opposing government policy but had not engaged in any joint act. "This is a very different kind of conspiracy than the ordinary one, to do a specific criminal act. . . . It is hard to escape the feeling that everyone (almost) on the Crown side feels that they have a bear by the tail and want to find some way to get rid of it without losing face."[6]

The ACOA organized a two-day program for Griswold in New York on September 30 and October 1. It included a press conference, radio programs, an informal meeting with the ACOA, and a joint luncheon with the Sidney Hillman Foundation, which had contributed $2,500 toward the project. I was puzzled that at this luncheon, Griswold thanked the foundation for its aid but never mentioned the ACOA. Contributors to the ACOA for the project wondered what had happened to their funds. I felt boxed in because we had agreed not to publicize our sponsorship. The only conclusion was that Griswold was trying to keep his skirts clean. But it was so unnecessary because we had never publicly claimed sponsorship.

It was another three years before the government dropped the case. As a result, the government looked "absurd," as Griswold put it, but the prestige of the ANC was enormously enhanced. Anthony Sampson wrote of the trial, "The greatest single upshot of the treason hearings was the emergence, both in black and white minds of the name Congress as a real force of black power."[7] The formation of defense funds in Britain, the United States, and elsewhere signaled the kind of international support to come as the struggle in South Africa intensified. Lutuli wrote, "I do not hesitate to say that out of the mingling of the government's opponents of all races . . . a new sense of solidarity and a new sense of direction were born."[8]

It was very pleasant to receive a letter from Ellen Hellmann (March 29, 1961):

> I always write to you when things go wrong and when in urgent trouble, and so I feel I must write to you on this very happy day. Today the treason trial ended with the acquittal of all the accused. But I do want you to know that as I sat in court in Pretoria today and heard the judgment and experienced gladness that hasn't come my way here in South Africa in many years, I thought of you and your colleagues and supporters in the Committee and felt deeply thankful for what you have done to assist us. Today I am rather giving myself over to this rare feeling of gladness.

THE DECLARATION OF CONSCIENCE CAMPAIGN

The ACOA aroused the ire of the South African government not only because of our efforts to defend the accused in the treason trials but also because in 1957 we initiated "The Declaration of Conscience Campaign." The idea was simple. We wrote a hard-hitting declaration, which stated that "Freedom and human dignity are in grave jeopardy in the Union of South Africa today. The government of that nation continues to extend relentlessly its racist policy of apartheid into the economic, educational, religious and other areas of life." The declaration called on South Africa to "honor its moral and legal obligations as a signatory to the United Nations Charter by honoring the Declaration of Human Rights."

Our declaration was designed to be international in its appeal. It called on people the world over to protest against South Africa's racism on Human Rights Day, December 10, 1957. Mrs. Roosevelt was the international chair. Dean James Pike was the U.S. national chair, and Martin Luther King, the national vice-chair. The declaration was signed by 123 world leaders, including Bertrand Russell, Pablo Casals, Arnold Toynbee, Trygvie Lie, Bruno Walter, Martin Niemoeller, Martin Buber, Erich Fromm, Julius Nyerere, Alan Paton, Ambrose Reeves, John Gunther, Walter Reuther, and Albert Lutuli.

The campaign generated a lot of public attention. There were hundreds of meetings and many statements in the United States and elsewhere on December 10. The government of South Africa became so incensed by the Declaration of Conscience that the minister of external affairs, Eric Louw, attacked the ACOA on a national radio program (December 12, 1957), branding us as "leftists." He said, "This organization has a decidedly pinkish tinge. A number of its leading members are known to be associated with left-wing organizations." He specifically stated that Mrs. Roosevelt was "not a stranger in American left-wing circles." He even called me a "known leftist" and warned, "This campaign directed against the European population of our country cannot but result in conditions of Bantu unrest and racial tension. This is what the Communists are aiming at. Do the ultra-liberals and leftists in the U.S. and elsewhere realize that they are playing into the hands of those who for their own purposes would destroy European civilization in South Africa?"

Our supporters got front-page publicity too. Bishop Reeves's reply to Louw was carried by the *Rand Daily Mail* (December 14, 1957). He commented that the ACOA's sponsorship included 4 U.S. senators, 16 members of the House, 2 university presidents, national religious leaders, and 11 authors and scholars. The paper editorialized that "Louw's speech shows that he was addressing himself not as a Minister of External Affairs to overseas opinion, but as a party politician to South African voters." Chief Lutuli said, "By branding the sponsors of the Declaration of Conscience as ultra-liberalistic and smearing them as Communist, the Minister of External Affairs did not absolve South Africa from charges made by leading individuals and statesmen throughout the world."

THE SHARPEVILLE MASSACRE

March 21, 1960, is a date to be remembered in South African history. This was the day of the Sharpeville Massacre, a turning point in the nature of the struggle for freedom. I had never heard of Sharpeville, an 11-year-old African township for the white municipality of Vereeniging, about 30 miles south of Johannesburg. Early in the morning of the fateful day, a crowd of 5,000 to 7,000 (some estimates are much greater) gathered to march in a peaceful demonstration to the municipal office and central police station of the township. They were responding to a call from Robert Sobukwe, president of the Pan Africanist Congress (PAC), to protest the hated pass system requiring Africans to carry identification papers. Each year hundreds of thousands of Africans were arrested for violating the pass laws. Sobukwe called on the people to "launch our positive, decisive action against the pass laws" but to "observe absolute nonviolence."

On the whole the response was disappointing. Perhaps there were 150 volunteers in Johannesburg. A few were arrested, including Sobukwe, when they presented themselves at the police station of the Orlando township near Johannesburg, having destroyed their passes. No demonstrations took place in such major centers as Durban, Port Elizabeth, and East London. Mass demonstrations occurred only in Cape Town, Sharpeville, and a nearby Evaton township. In Langa, a Cape Town African township, 10,000 gathered, and when the police opened fired to break up the crowd, 2 Africans were killed and 49 injured. But if it had not been for the killings at Sharpeville, the incidents of the day might have passed relatively unnoticed.

Humphrey Tyler, editor of *Drum* magazine, was an eyewitness to the Sharpeville demonstration. The ACOA carried his account in the May issue of our publication *Africa Today*. Some 300 police reinforcements were called to control the demonstrators. Five Saracen armored vehicles were on hand. The demonstrators seemed to be in a good mood. Suddenly, seemingly without a clear order, the police fired into the crowd. Tyler wrote: "We heard the chatter of a machine gun, then another, then another. There were hundreds of women [running], some of them laughing. They must have thought the police were firing blanks. . . . Hundreds of kids were running too. One little boy had an old black coat, which he held up behind his head, thinking perhaps that it might save him from the bullets." The police commented later that the crowd had "ferocious weapons." Tyler noted, "I saw no weapons, although I looked very carefully, and afterwards studied very carefully the photographs of the death scene. While I was there I saw only shoes, hats and a few bicycles left among the bodies."[9] Sixty-nine were killed, including 31 women and 19 children. This was the event that aroused such a tremendous reaction within South Africa and internationally and escalated the liberation struggle beyond all expectations.

The events of March 21 were precipitated by the Pan Africanist Congress. The PAC was a recent split-off from the ANC. The trouble had been brewing for some time. In the mid-1950s a significant caucus was organized within the ANC called the Africanists. Essentially they believed that the leadership in the liberation struggle must be securely in African hands. They opposed the ANC's alliance with the South African Indian Congress, the Coloured People's Organization, and the white Congress of Democrats. They objected to decisions based on joint meetings of the leaders of these groups. It did not make sense to them that these groups had an equal voice with the Africans of the ANC in making strategy decisions when Africans were the vast majority.

The Africanists were also opposed to the Congress of the People, which was the result of joint planning. They could not endorse the preamble to the Freedom Charter, which stated "that South Africa belongs to all who live in it, black and white." It was an African country, they argued, which had been taken away from them. They believed that only after majority rule was established could all, regardless of race, become citizens as individuals. They did not believe in special laws or rules for minority groups.

The Africanists were activists. Leaders came from the Youth League of the ANC, whose 1949 Program of Action laid the foundations for the Defiance Campaign of 1952 and became the dominant strategy for the ANC. My ANC contacts had been with Chief Lutuli, Walter Sisulu, Z.K. Matthews, and Oliver Tambo, all of whom were committed to the Freedom Charter and the joint cooperation with all sympathetic forces in the liberation struggle. Sobukwe was a new personality to me. He had not been in the limelight before he was unanimously chosen president of the newly founded PAC in April 1959. He had previously been a behind-the-scenes theoretician. Yet he had been national secretary of the Youth League in 1949 and a student leader at Fort Hare University College.

Sobukwe had been dismissed from his first teaching post because he spoke publicly in support of the Defiance Campaign. Subsequently he was a lecturer at the University of Witwatersrand. He associated himself with those in the ANC who did not identify with the Freedom Charter and the Congress of the People. In his articles and occasional public speeches, his convictions won him a significant following.

Not being allowed into South Africa, I never met Sobukwe. The anti-pass demonstrations of March 21 constituted the first major action planned by the PAC. The ANC was disturbed by the PAC action. Their own anti-pass campaign was planned to begin about 10 days later, but the aftermath of Sharpeville engulfed both groups, and new approaches had to be devised.

Repercussions set in almost immediately. A report from Patrick Duncan in Cape Town described two large demonstrations led by Philip Kgosana, regional secretary of the PAC, on March 25 and 30. "The two great demonstrations in Cape Town were not riots. They were peaceful acts of purest nonviolence, up to the highest levels obtained by Gandhi's satyagraha."[10] The vast throng of 30,000 surged into Cape Town on March 30 to request the release of certain of their arrested leaders. In Cape Town almost all the 60,000 workers went on strike. Kgosana, at the head of the marchers, had negotiated with the police. Duncan wrote, "They had agreed to take him to the Minister of Justice for an interview if he on his side would send home the huge crowd he had brought. He did this and returned for the interview later that afternoon. Instead of the interview, he was arrested."[11]

Chief Lutuli called for a national day of mourning. Hundreds of thousands of people stayed away from work in answer to this call. Lutuli burned his pass publicly in Pretoria, as did many others.

Within 48 hours the U.S. Department of State surprisingly condemned the police violence at Sharpeville. The UN Security Council called an emergency meeting on April 1 and deplored "the recent disturbances in the Union of South Africa" and "the policies and actions of the government of South Africa which have given rise to the present situation." The United States voted for the resolution. Henry Cabot Lodge, the U.S. ambassador, stated, "The source of the conflict from which the recent tragic events have flowed is the policy of apartheid followed by the government of the Union of South Africa." Only France and Britain abstained in an otherwise unanimous vote.

South Africa was shaken by the intensity of national and international reaction. On March 30 a state of emergency was declared. Meetings were banned. About 2,000 demonstrators were arrested, including 100 whites, and held without trial. The value of shares on the Johannesburg stock exchange plunged by more than £500,000 from the level of January 1. The government panicked momentarily and lifted the pass laws. For a brief moment it seemed as if the anti-pass campaign had won a momentous victory, but in a few days the pass laws were restored. On April 8 the ANC and the PAC were declared "unlawful organizations" and "a serious threat to the safety of the public." The ANC decided that Oliver Tambo should leave the country to organize international support.

In New York, the ACOA announced that our Africa Defense and Aid Fund would send funds to the families of the victims of Sharpeville. As a result of the second Africa Freedom Day observance at Town Hall, we sent a check for $10,000.

AFTERMATH

The Sharpeville Massacre was a watershed in South African affairs. As Bishop Reeves later wrote, "Until Sharpeville, violence for the most part had been used by those who were committed to the maintenance of the white minority. The fact is that [after Sharpeville] for the first time both sides . . . are now committed to violence: the white minority to preserve the status quo; the nonwhite majority to change."[12]

The banning of the ANC and the PAC led to a large-scale exodus of leaders from South Africa, perhaps 300 or 400, just as had happened in South West Africa after the police violence of December 10, 1959. Underground political work in exile began. Soon offices of banned organizations sprang up in Ghana, Algeria, Egypt, and Britain.

The overwhelming reaction to Sharpeville may seem surprising. After all, the loss of life there was slight compared with the casualties in Algeria, for instance, but international opposition to bald racism in South Africa was deep. There was very little sympathy for the violent tactics of the white minority, especially in the light of the largely nonviolent actions by the African majority. The Sharpeville Massacre stirred the conscience of most of the world in an unprecedented way.

The AAPC in 1958 had called for a boycott of South African goods but with meager results. But Sharpeville turned the effort into a mighty propaganda vehicle. Trade unions in Jamaica, Nigeria, Ghana, Tanganyika, Norway, West Germany, Cyprus, and Malaysia not only backed the boycott but called for a refusal to unload ships carrying South African goods. Even George Meany, president of the AFL-CIO, asked for a halt to the U.S. purchase of gold to demonstrate disapproval of "inhuman and callous" racial policies.

The ACOA placed an ad in the *New York Times* (May 31, 1960) signed by hundreds of people announcing, "We will not purchase South African goods until such time as the South African government abandons her racist policies." The practical problem we faced was that there were very few South African consumer goods coming into the country. It was hard to mount a serious campaign aimed only at South African rock lobster tails.

There is no doubt that the 1960 Nobel Peace Prize was awarded to Chief Lutuli as an aftermath of Sharpeville, although he was not able to go to Oslo until 1961 because of travel restrictions by the South African government.

The Sharpeville Massacre did more than any other event to spawn antiapartheid organizations in many countries around the world. Of particular importance was the British Antiapartheid Movement with which the ACOA cooperated from that point on. Other movements sprang up in Sweden, Denmark, Norway, France, Belgium, Finland, and elsewhere. Fund-raising efforts to support the victims of apartheid and to oppose South African racism increased dramatically after Sharpeville. Canon L. John Collins of St. Paul's Cathedral in London set up a Defence and Aid Fund associated with Christian Action, which over the years supplied legal defense and welfare aid to the tune of millions of pounds.

The ACOA put particular effort into organizing a coalition of groups for an ongoing campaign against apartheid. On April 21, a South Africa Emergency Committee was constituted representing about 30 groups. The lead story in the *Johannesburg Star* (April 24, 1961) was headlined "Strong Action Against Union" and subtitled, "U.S. groups will increase pressure." The story opened: "A powerful group of organizations in the U.S. is planning strong action to compel South Africa to change its apartheid policies. They are being led by the American Committee on Africa with active cooperation of the American Federation of Labor."

The focus of our action was a South Africa Emergency Conference, chaired by Jackie Robinson, held at the end of May. About 300 attended. We announced a comprehensive boycott of South Africa, recommending that unions refuse to unload ships from South Africa; that performers, athletes, and tourists not visit South Africa; that South Africa be excluded from the Rome Olympics, and that U.S. firms operating in South Africa abstain from apartheid practices. A scholarly memorandum by Professor

Thomas Hovet of New York University, "The Concept of Sanctions and Their General Application and Use," was prepared. Many of the programs enacted in later years were first outlined at this conference.

Oliver Tambo was to have been the principal speaker. Evading South African border control, he had crossed to Bechuanaland. South Africa tried to have him extradited, but he chartered a private plane and flew to Nairobi. From there he went to Ghana and finally to London. I cabled him in care of the Africa Bureau, "Congratulations on escape. Can you come here soon to help campaign against apartheid?" He quickly agreed to spend four weeks with us, beginning with our May conference.

There could have been no better person than Tambo to undertake such a speaking schedule. Fresh from South Africa, he was deputy president of the ANC and had worked closely with Chief Lutuli. From a peasant family in Pondoland, he had studied at a local mission school and then at St. Peter's school in Johannesburg. He won a scholarship to Fort Hare, where he participated in protest activities that led to his expulsion. After teaching science at St. Peter's, he studied law and then opened a law office with Nelson Mandela. All this time he was active in the ANC, played a leading role in the Defiance Campaign and Congress of the People, and was one of the accused in the treason trial of 1957.

From my associations with Tambo, I understood why Blaxall and others considered him outstanding (see chapter 3). He had a gentleness and sensitivity that was winning. His friendliness seemed in no way artificial. He was a good listener. He was the first African man I met who very naturally held my hand briefly as we were walking together. In Western society this just is not done, but it is common in Africa as an expression of friendship and compatibility. Tambo was one of the ANC leaders about whom the PAC dissidents spoke respectfully. To them he was a nationalist. They seemed to trust his word. Further, along with his commitment to the liberation cause, he maintained a Christian perspective. Father Trevor Huddleston, who had known him well at St. Peters and later on in the ANC, once said of him, "It would be hard to find a more devoted churchman than Oliver Tambo." Mainly I think of him in terms of his lifelong commitment to the liberation cause through the ANC—in exile since 1960.

The ACOA was rather surprised to learn that the U.S. government was giving Tambo problems with his visa. I called Washington and was at first told that he was "ineligible" for entry for undisclosed reasons. We feverishly organized protests to Christian Herter, then secretary of state, and finally in June the government decision was reversed. But it was too late. Tambo had missed our conference. Fortunately we were able to reschedule some speaking dates.

Another aspect of the aftermath of Sharpeville was a more rigid atmosphere in South Africa. I was made aware of it through Alan Paton and a friend in South Africa. In 1955 I learned that Paton was returning briefly to the States (I had missed his visit in 1954) and wrote to him suggesting that we meet. We did, and his subsequent letters gave information and brought issues to our attention. In 1958 he urged the ACOA to look into the question of international organizations that allowed affiliates to practice segregation. He mentioned the Lions' Club, which had a branch in Cape Town that observed the color bar. In early 1960, before Sharpeville, he wrote (March 9) "I do not think the present consumer boycott will have any material effect, but it certainly has increased the number of people who know about apartheid."

After Sharpeville, I wrote to Paton very carefully, never using letterhead and sending letters through his trusted agent and friend in New York. I had long hoped that he would be able to speak under ACOA auspices to raise funds for victims of apartheid. He agreed to do this in the fall of 1960, not unmindful of the risks involved when he returned home. He wrote (March 9) "I think that I may freely say that the days of free movement overseas are finished. However, we won't give up hope."

We lined up engagements for Paton in Chicago, Boston, and Toronto. He also spoke before the Greater Atlanta chapter of the Georgia Council on Human Relations. A story appeared in the *Atlanta Constitution* (October 14, 1960) saying that Paton had outlined a middle solution to the South Africa racial problem that might avoid a bloody conflict: countries opposed to apartheid might adopt such sanctions as refusing to buy from South Africa or fly over its territory or unload South African ships in world ports.

When Paton returned to South Africa in December, his passport was withdrawn. Louw said he was "aiding and comforting the enemies of South Africa in the U.S." I had a guilty feeling for the part I had played in setting up Paton's engagements, but I knew he was not surprised. All I could do was to send my regrets and tell him, "You did a great deal of good for the cause while you were here."

The post-Sharpeville atmosphere was especially discouraging and alarming to liberals in South Africa. A letter from a South African friend (August 17, 1960) reflected this. Violaine Junod was a scholar and a professor who was associated with Paton politically and a member of the Liberal party. I had known her well when she was teaching and doing research in the United States in the late 1950s. After she returned to South Africa, our correspondence was limited because of the feeling that letters were sometimes scrutinized by government authorities. Her August letter came from Southern Rhodesia, where she was attending an academic conference. She felt she could write freely because she sent the letter with a friend traveling to the United States. Describing the fate of all those who had been arrested after Sharpeville, she said, "In fact . . . thousands have been arrested who strictly do not fall in the category of being 'unruly elements in urban areas,' but more likely are members of [certain] organizations. As far as we can make out, they must have had lists of all ANC membership and they have tried to rope in all of them. But what is terrible is that these people just disappear and are not heard of by family." She concluded: "The sum total builds up to a pretty ugly picture, that we are fast moving to the finalization of a police state is no exaggeration." She told me that I should write her addressed to an assumed name at a box number in Durban. Such was the repressive atmosphere in South Africa after Sharpeville.

YEARS OF TURMOIL

A tumultuous period begins with the independence of the Belgian Congo (now Zaire) in 1960 and ends with the military coup in Portugal in 1974. The great hope for a new day in Africa as the Congo became independent was dashed by the reality of a politically disunited and tribally segmented country, the fruit of Belgium's unenlightened colonial policy. The struggle for control in the Congo led to the first African conflict among the world's superpowers, as the United States and the Soviet Union vied for dominance. The United Nations was powerless to control the situation. The conflict led to the death of UN Secretary General Dag Hammarskjold and the martyrdom of Patrice Lumumba, the Congo's first premier. The age of innocence in Africa's struggle against colonialism had ended.

The violence in the Congo was matched by the beginning of serious guerrilla warfare, focused particularly in the Portuguese areas of Angola, Mozambique, and Guinea-Bissau and in Rhodesia, South Africa, and South West Africa (now Namibia). The various liberation movements went through their own turmoil fueled by competition, both ideological and political, among organizations and leaders.

This was also the period when many African countries achieved independence. These new states, although lacking economic and political stability at home, began to exert themselves internationally and at the UN. The Organization of African Unity (OAU) was formed to help draw the countries together on basic programs, such as support for the efforts to win majority rule and independence in southern Africa. Africa began to occupy a more important place in U.S. policy but was still only a low-key topic.

CHAPTER TWELVE

The Congo:
An African Turning Point

In late November 1960 I was on the ferry plying its way across the wide Congo River from Brazzaville to Leopoldville (now Kinshasa). It was my fourth visit to the Congo, but this time it was bound to be different; the Congo had been independent for almost five months. Many things seemed unchanged: the ferry still made half-hourly trips; on the Leopoldville side there was very little red tape with customs or immigration (the immigration forms were the same as under Belgian rule); the paved roads were filled with bicycle and automobile traffic; relatively high buildings dotted the skyline; the factory sirens, heard throughout the city, sounded off at 6:30, 6:45, and 7:00 in the morning; and the Hausa traders were still selling ebony and ivory in the public square.

But some things had changed. It had been impossible to arrange for a visa for the Congo in New York, even though I had a pleasant chat with Cyrille Adoula, head of the delegation to the UN and later prime minister, who even wrote a letter on my behalf to the president. In the midst of the Congo controversy, no visas could be granted overseas. So, as I left the ferry, my passport was simply stamped by an official with no questions.

Police control was not very tight, as I was shortly to find out. As I walked toward waiting taxis, I was immediately besieged by several drivers. This was not unusual, but it was odd for first one and then another driver to grab my bag, struggle to keep it, and put it in his car, only to have it pulled out again by a competitor. I thought my bag would surely be torn to pieces. When it was finally secured in one of the taxis, another driver began exchanging blows with the successful driver, but then, thinking of a better strategy, he drove his car across the road, cutting off the taxi in which I was now seated. Never during all this frantic activity did the policeman standing close by intervene. I finally found my own solution. Taking my bag in hand, I walked for a block until one of the taxis caught up with me and took me to my destination.

It was different, too, seeing troops on the city streets—UN troops from Malaysia, Tunisia, and Morocco came into view immediately. Jeeploads of Congolese troops sped along the roads. It was not unusual to be stopped by Congolese troops at gunpoint. Searching the car and looking at papers did not take long, but sometimes those stopped were personally searched and held for half an hour or so. It was always a little unnerving to undergo this procedure while a gun was pointed somewhat casually at your person. The atmosphere of the capital was definitely unsettled. What had happened to change things in what the Belgians, and many others, had looked upon as a model colony?

LUMUMBA AND THE PATH TO INDEPENDENCE

I had, of course, been closely following events in the Congo well before independence on June 30. Confounded by my own experiences in the Congo, I wondered how the Belgians thought they could hold back the urgent call for independence in their colony in a continent aflame with nationalism.

WARNINGS OF UNREST

I had seen unmistakable warnings. In 1956 a group of Congolese put out *Conscience Africaine,* a manifesto that mildly demanded independence in 30 years. Shortly thereafter, a countermanifesto was issued by the Association for the Protection of Culture and Interests of the Bakongo (ABAKO), centered in Leopoldville among the Bakongo people, with which Joseph Kasavubu was associated. It said *Conscience Africaine* did not go far enough. "Our patience has passed the boundaries. Since the hour has come, we must be granted this very day the emancipation which would be delayed still another thirty years." A Belgian official told me in 1957 that these statements did not have to be taken seriously because these groups did not represent the people.

The political organizations that began to appear in the Congo were essentially regionally and tribally based, like ABAKO. In mineral-rich Katanga Province, the Confederation of Katanga Tribal Associations (CONAKAT) was formed in 1958 with Moise Tshombe as its leader. The one party with a national, not just regional, following was the National Congolese Movement (MNC). Inspired by the speech Charles de Gaulle made across the river in Brazzaville in 1958, offering French colonies independence either in association with France or separately, the MNC petitioned the Belgian government to set a date for independence. Patrice Lumumba, one of the signers of this petition, was chosen leader of the MNC soon thereafter. His political career lasted less than three years. Yet in that short time, he became not only the major political figure in the Congo but an African leader known and remembered throughout much of the world.

Lumumba's base in the Congo was Stanleyville (now Kisangani), on the Congo River, several hundred miles northeast of Leopoldville. Never formally educated beyond primary school, he worked many years as a postal clerk. In 1957 he had served six months of a two-year prison term on a questionable charge of embezzlement. Around Stanleyville, he held leading positions in as many as seven organizations. After his release from prison, he moved to Leopoldville and did public relations for a brewery. From his new base he became active in political affairs.

I first met Lumumba at the AAPC in Accra in 1958. Then 33, he attracted a great deal of attention, for he was tall, slim, and well dressed and spoke fluent French as well as Swahili. This linguistic ability was a factor in his developing a good relationship with Tom Mboya, who spoke no French, while Lumumba spoke no English.

Lumumba was friendly. Our ACOA group talked with him several times in Accra and were impressed with his commitment. The other two Congolese delegates did not draw the same kind of personal attention, although all were noteworthy because their country was large, rich, and the epitome of colonialism. Lumumba was chosen as the Congo representative on the conference Steering Committee. All these factors encouraged Kwame Nkrumah to establish a warm relationship with him.

Returning to Leopoldville, the Congo delegation reported on the conference to an excited throng of some 7,000. The AAPC resolutions at Accra were integrated into the MNC program.

RIOTS IN LEOPOLDVILLE

Only a few days later, riots broke out in Leopoldville when the Belgians banned a meeting of ABAKO. There were heavy casualties—49 Africans killed, 330 Africans and 40 Europeans injured. ABAKO was then banned and its leaders, including Kasavubu, arrested. To stave off further violent reaction the Belgian government issued a declaration committing it to leading the colony toward independence "gradually and progressively."

In early January 1959 in the Belgian Senate, Maurice van Hemelrijck, minister of the Belgian Congo, announced the process that would go into effect "to lead the Congolese people to a point where they will be capable of self-administration. . . . Universal suffrage will be established." The plan called for the election of municipal and territorial councils in 1959, but no date was set for independence. "Belgium will hand over these responsibilities as the new Congolese institutions gradually prove they are capable of maintaining order," the minister said.

I wrote to Lumumba on January 20 after the riots to express concern and to get his assessment of the situation. After nearly eight months, he wrote a long letter (August 6, 1959) detailing the turmoil following the January uprising. His response was late because he had been traveling abroad and then in the Congo. He appealed for aid, indicating great financial need—no job but a wife and four children. He hoped to come to the United States to plead his cause.

The process toward independence quickened. The Belgian settlers were incensed by what they considered pro-African statements by Van Hemelrijck. While visiting the Congo, he was pelted with tomatoes by whites. ABAKO was critical of the slow government approach and advocated a boycott of the municipal and provincial elections. In November Lumumba was arrested in Stanleyville and given a six-months sentence for inciting the people. King Baudouin visited the Congo to assess the situation and apparently was disturbed by what he saw. The Belgian government finally called for a round table in Brussels to work out a plan for the future.

CONFERENCE IN BRUSSELS

The Brussels meeting began January 20, 1960, and lasted a month. Lumumba was released from prison to attend. Fifty official delegates represented 15 political parties and 6 tribal chiefs. In an optimistic euphoria, the conference agreed on a date for independence, resolving that "As of June 30 next, the Congo . . . shall become an independent state whose inhabitants shall, under conditions to be enacted by law, have the same nationality and shall be free to move about and establish themselves within the confines of the said state." Provisions were made for elections with universal adult suffrage to choose a parliament before the date of independence.

The speeches on the final day of the conference were joyful and enthusiastic, yet some of them hinted at problems to come, such as viewing the country's provinces as separate political units. Tshombe, president of CONAKAT, indicated his satisfaction "that an end has been put to the excessive centralization under which the Congo was laboring and . . . has resulted in the acknowledgement of the former provinces as political entities, with all corresponding powers."[1] Lumumba, true to his Pan-African convictions, noted in his final statement that their African brothers in Kenya, Nyasaland, South Africa, and Angola "are still fighting for their accession to autonomy."[2] He called for the eradication of all racial discrimination.

Two beneficial results came from the Brussels conference. As reported by Thomas Kanza, a Congolese observer whom I knew and who later became a government official, "It had made possible the first meeting in the flesh of various politicians from all over the country, each of whom was looked upon as a god by his own party, region, or tribe. It also made each of them aware of the difficulty, if not the impossibility, of anyone's hoping to wield total power in so enormous and variegated a country as the Congo. Not one of them possessed a truly national popularity."[3]

When I traveled to the Congo in February 1960, it seemed amazing that independence was only four months away. A Belgian official told me that the government was doing everything possible to reassure the Congolese of Belgian intentions, but the people still doubted. Business interests were unsure of their future. Katanga, source of about 60 percent of the Congo's income, was least anxious to break ties with Belgium.

Signs of disunity were rampant. No political party had a massive national following. The May elections revealed the dominance of tribal rather than national loyalties. The MNC won 35 out of 137 seats in the lower house of Parliament, just over 25 percent, although well below the 69 votes needed for a majority. Nine parties won 7 to 14 seats each. Twenty-four seats were won by even smaller groupings. Lumumba was chosen as prime minister with 74 votes. Kasavubu was elected president three days later.

INDEPENDENCE AND ITS AFTERMATH

Independence came on June 30, as scheduled. The foundations had been abysmally laid by the Belgians, who were no longer prepared to deal with the political crises caused by upsurging nationalism, although they intended to maintain economic control. The Congo was fabulously rich but had only one trained African doctor, lawyer, army officer, and senior civil servant. Only 17 Congolese had even been to university, and most of these had not completed their studies.

The first discordant note was struck at the independence ceremony. Although an intensely committed nationalist, Lumumba was not an experienced diplomat. With the king of Belgium seated close to him, he spoke of the struggle for independence bringing "to an end the humiliating slavery imposed on us by force. Such was our lot for eighty years with the colonialist regime; our wounds are still too fresh and painful for us to be able to forget them at will."[4] This reminder of the colonial past was considered insulting to the king and the Belgian people. Belgian fears about Lumumba were reinforced.

The newly chosen, inexperienced Congolese officials were dependent on their Belgian advisers at the outset. Kanza reported on the tragicomic aspects of the first meeting of the Council of Ministers. "All of us were happy . . . at being ministers. It was playacting. . . . we, the colonized, now had titles and dignity; but we had no power at all over any of the instruments we needed to carry out the functions expected of us. . . . We discussed the allocation of ministerial cars, the choosing and allotting of ministerial residences. . . . In short, we talked endlessly, laughed ourselves silly, and concluded by generally agreeing that the Belgian colonizers were to blame for all our troubles."[5]

MILITARY REVOLT

There was no postindependence honeymoon in the Congo. The government was in no position to handle crises. It was barely equipped to handle the basic task of organization. The trouble began with the revolt of the Congolese troops just six days after independence. They locked up their Belgian officers and demanded promotions, pay increases, and the dismissal of the Belgian commander. Whites were attacked. Panic resulted. Within a few weeks only about 20,000 of the some 100,000 Belgians remained in the country. Belgium quickly sent in troops. They bombed the port of Matadi, killing many Congolese. To complicate matters further, Katanga declared independence from the Congo on July 11, unprotested by Belgium. Not only was the Congo breaking up, but it looked as if Belgium were intent upon recapturing what it had presumably just given up.

In desperation Lumumba and Kasavubu demanded that Belgian troops leave the country and appealed to the United Nations for military aid "to protect the national territory of the Congo against the present external aggression which is a threat to international peace." They also sent a message to Soviet Premier Nikita Khrushchev, urging him to follow the situation since the Congo might need Soviet help to stem the aggression.

On July 14 the UN Security Council asked Belgium to withdraw its troops and authorized Hammarskjold to provide military and technical assistance "until the national security forces may be able, in the opinion of the government, to meet fully their tasks." Within days the UN had dispatched an international force, which grew to more than 20,000 troops and 200 technical advisers. Troops from Ethiopia, Ghana, Morocco, Tunisia, Guinea, Malaysia, Sweden, and Ireland were flown in at various stages in U.S. transport planes. The Soviets ferried in food and some Ghanaian troops.

Representing Lumumba's government at the UN was Thomas Kanza, then only 26. Son of a distinguished political figure, in 1952 he had been the first Congolese to attend a university in Belgium. Then he had worked for the European Economic Community (EEC) in Brussels. He was exceedingly personable and handled himself well among seasoned diplomats at the UN during a troubled period. In the Security Council he called for evacuation of Belgian troops, UN refusal to recognize Katanga, and UN technical assistance. The council's resolution encompassed all these points.

The problems did not go away, however. Belgian troops remained in Katanga, which continued its separatist course. The United States was openly worried about Soviet involvement. Lumumba was seen by the American ambassador, Clare Timberlake, as undependable, unstable, and very possibly another Fidel Castro, in short, someone who would have to go.

Lumumba arrived in New York on July 24. He received a lot of publicity—speeches at the UN, press conferences, an enthusiastic street-corner meeting in Harlem, a meeting with Secretary of State Christian Herter in Washington. This meeting did not change the administration's opinion of him as messianic and irrational. Lumumba and Hammarskjold clearly had differing conceptions of the task of the UN. Lumumba felt that he should have UN backing, particularly on the Katanga issue, while the secretary general, as an international civil servant, faced the necessity of balancing the contending powers in the UN.

Lumumba had not forgotten me. At his huge UN press conference, he saw me and Associate ACOA Director Homer Jack standing at the edge of the crowd and came over to greet us warmly. When Peter Weiss, Jack, and I called on him later at his hotel, we assured him of the ACOA's support. With us he seemed affable, open, and sensible. Understandably, he spoke excitedly about the immensity of his task. At the same time, he was self-confident and optimistic that the UN would support him and the rebellion in Katanga would end. Whether he was whistling in the dark, I could not tell.

Back in the Congo, events were unfolding that led eventually to Lumumba's death. Since the UN was not supporting his efforts to prevent the secession not only of Katanga but also of the agriculturally important province of Kasai, he appealed directly to the Soviet Union. Khrushchev sent limited military aid—trucks, arms, planes, and advisers. In August, the Congolese troops opened an ill-fated attack on Kasai.

KASAVUBU VERSUS LUMUMBA

Division among the Congolese became insurmountable. On September 5, President Kasavubu, over the radio, dismissed Lumumba as prime minister. Incensed, Lumumba promptly proclaimed by radio Kasavubu's removal from the presidency. Parliament negated both actions by a vote of 60 to 19. In effect, there were two governments, one under the president and the other under the prime minister, neither of which was able to function. To make matters worse, Kasavubu was backed by the Western powers and Lumumba by the Soviet Union and the more radical African states. Thus the situation of near anarchy was compounded by the threat of a superpower confrontation.

The impasse was broken when the 29-year-old Col. Joseph Mobutu, a former protégé of Lumumba, who was second in command of the army, took over. On national radio he announced that the Congolese army had acted to neutralize the two rival governments and both houses of Parliament until December 31, 1960.

Lumumba now found himself under virtual house arrest. He was protected by African UN troops while a thousand Congolese troops surrounded the area to prevent his escape. Mobutu expelled the Soviet and Czech embassies, appointed a rather impotent prime minister, and put the executive functions of government into the hands of a College of Commissioners composed of young, educated, but governmentally untrained Congolese.

The UN debated the Congo issue. Third World countries were unusually well represented. Krushchev, head of the Soviet delegation, put forth his troika proposal, calling for three secretary generals of the UN, to represent the West, the Socialist bloc, and the neutral countries. This proposal reflected Soviet opposition to the perceived Western bias of Hammarskjold. A diplomatic battle over representation in the UN took place between a Lumumba delegation headed by Kanza and a Kasavubu delegation headed by Justin Bomboko. Kasavubu won by a vote of 53 to 24 with 19 abstentions.

DOWNFALL OF LUMUMBA

This was the situation when I arrived at Leopoldville. During the next week I tried to see as many of the leading figures in the struggle as possible. I talked with ambassadors; with top UN officials such as Gen.

Indar Rikye, head of the UN forces, and Sture Linner, head of UN civilian operations; with proponents and opponents of Lumumba and Kasavubu; with Congolese church leaders; and with reporters. The one thing that emerged from all these talks was that there was no easy solution to the perplexing tragic crisis. There was agreement that a power vacuum existed but none as to which aspirant should fill it.

First, the Congolese themselves were hopelessly divided—Lumumba against Kasavubu; a Lumumba faction of the MNC based in Stanleyville against a faction in Kasai led by Isaac Kalonji; Jason Sendwe's Balubakat party in northern Katanga at odds with Tshombe's CONAKAT.

Second, the African states that might have been a stabilizing influence were divided between those supporting Lumumba (Ghana, Guinea, United Arab Republic, and Morocco) and those supporting Kasavubu (mostly the newly independent former French colonies, preeminently the government of Abbe Youlou, in Congo Brazzaville).

Third, the United Nations, trying to hold the country together and keep out the cold war, was powerless to act in the face of its conflicting members.

Fourth, the United States and the Soviet Union, each with its own interests in the wealth and strategic location of the Congo, backed opposing forces. U.S. policy, strongly anti-Communist, was bent on preventing a Soviet base in the heart of Africa. I felt that to try to understand the conflict in terms of ideology was a mistake. Essentially the Congo leaders were making international alliances to advance their own cause. They thought, perhaps unrealistically, that at the right moment they could control their own destiny despite outside influences.

I had an overwhelming sense of hopelessness. Like other opponents of colonialism, I had anticipated the independence of the Congo with such enthusiasm that the reality was hard to bear. It was like being a potential Olympic medalist and breaking a leg just before the start of the race.

ATTACK ON THE GHANAIAN EMBASSY

I soon tasted the seriousness of the conflict. On the evening of November 21 I heard explosive sounds like fire crackers, unmistakably gunfire, going off a few blocks from where I was staying. It was a short-lived battle at the Ghanaian embassy between attacking Congolese and defending UN troops. Mobutu was intent on expelling the Ghanaian ambassador to punish him for supporting Lumumba. Ghanaian troops helped transport Lumumba around Leopoldville when he daringly left his house to speak to the people. The U.S. ambassador grudgingly commented, "The sad fact is that there is not anybody down there really outside Lumumba who has got the kind of energy and drive and imagination which would let him be Prime Minister, in fact, not just in name."[6] In the fracas six Tunisians and six Congolese were killed, including Joseph Nkololo, Mobutu's second in command.

The next morning I spent an hour in the Ghanaian embassy. The troops had all gone. The empty embassy and the house across the way were pockmarked, and cars on the street were riddled with bullet holes. The fox holes dug by the Congolese still looked freshly made. In the embassy a pool of blood marked where a Tunisian had fallen, and some blood-soaked bandages were lying on the floor. Not even police were in evidence. The ambassador had fled or had been expelled.

I called on the Tunisian ambassador, whom I had known well at the UN. He was understandably very upset and seemed to blame Ghana and the UN for not seeing that the ambassador left the country before fighting erupted. The atmosphere in the city was tense. The ferry to Brazzaville was closed. I found out that the U.S. embassy had tried to reach all Americans in the city to urge them to stay off the streets.

I spent a lot of time with Kanza, who had an apartment in the same building with UN headquarters. Although he felt he was a marked man because of his ties with Lumumba, he was safe there. The only way he could keep in touch with Lumumba, under house arrest, was by telephone. He feared that with the seating of the Kasavubu delegation in New York, Lumumba would try to escape to Stanleyville, where he would receive Soviet support. He strongly advised Lumumba against this. Once while I was there, he called Lumumba, with whom I also talked. He seemed to be calm and unrealistically optimistic. This conversation, as things turned out, was actually a farewell.

THE FATE OF LUMUMBA

Shortly after Kanza's call, Lumumba did escape. As predicted, he headed for Stanleyville. Only a few days later, his capture in Kasai was reported. His own courage and self-confidence had betrayed him. He could have made good his escape, but he waited at a ferry crossing for his wife and children, who had been delayed. His pursuers caught up with him and arrested him and two companions, Maurice Mpolo and Joseph Okito. The three were held at an army camp at Thysville for about six weeks, then on January 17 flown to Katanga and turned over to Tshombe's police. According to eye witnesses, they were horribly beaten on the five-hour plane trip. Most authorities believe they were killed that same night.

However, the story put out by Tshombe's spokesman on February 13 was that they escaped and were captured by villagers in Katanga and killed. Their bodies were secretly disposed of, presumably at the direction of local officials. I wrote to Kanza, who was back in New York representing the now rebel regime in Stanleyville, expressing my shock and deep sense of shame.

REACTION TO LUMUMBA'S MURDER

The emotional reaction to Lumumba's murder was swift. I was in the Security Council chamber at the UN on February 15, two days after the news. Adlai Stevenson was scheduled to speak in the Congo debate. He had hardly opened his mouth when bedlam erupted in the visitors' gallery. I had heard that a coalition of Lumumba's supporters from black nationalist organizations in Harlem were planning a protest, and I knew quite a few of those who stood up and shouted in support of Lumumba against Hammarskjold and the United States. I still remember Stevenson's startled face. It took some moments for the unarmed UN guards to eject the demonstrators. I did not see any real violence, although later reports said that a score of people were injured. Afterwards an excited organizer of the demonstration enthusiastically proclaimed to me, "We have now expanded into midtown."

I attended the third, and last, AAPC in March in Cairo. It was a month after Lumumba's murder, and the Congo issue was dominant. The neutralist theme of the previous conferences was gone. The tone was anti-West. Kanyama Chiume, only recently returned from his U.S. tour, said to me, "The Congo crisis has done terrible damage to the United States, the UN, and Hammarskjold." Slogans around the conference hall said, "Unify Congo as one country," "Death to Lumumba's murderers." Pictures of Lumumba hung on the walls. A message from G. Mennen Williams, the new assistant secretary for African Affairs, was not even circulated. The conference reflected a reality in African politics—the Congo crisis was a turning point. Something new was happening and Lumumba's death helped to trigger it.

A dynamic and forceful personality, Lumumba aroused tremendous loyalty among his friends and followers and the bitterest hatred and fear among his enemies. Indeed the U.S. government was involved, through the Central Intelligence Agency (CIA), in a plot to poison him, as revealed by a Senate investigatory committee in 1975. But his Congolese enemies murdered him first.

Although his name is associated with the chaos that enveloped the Congo after independence, he will be remembered by most Africans first and foremost as a committed nationalist and Pan-Africanist who was martyred for trying to unify his country. He tried to rise about the grievous divisions of ethnic and regional interests. With Nkrumah he shared an idealistic vision of a great union of African states. In Ghana on his way back to the Congo following his UN visit, he and Nkrumah had signed a secret agreement calling for the establishment of such an African union under a federal government with a common currency, defense, foreign policy, and economic planning and the capital in Leopoldville. At that time such a dream was unrealizable, but it was testimony to a commitment that Nkrumah and Lumumba both shared.

African city streets are named after Lumumba, and schools and organizations bear his name. Even some of those involved in his arrest and death, such as Mobutu, later president of Zaire, hypocritically invoke his name as a great national hero when seeking applause at public gatherings.

THE KATANGA PROBLEM

With Lumumba gone, Mobutu and Kasavubu ensconced in the central government, the Soviet Union expelled, and the United States the dominant international force in the Congo, a new phase in the Congo problem began. Under the new Kennedy administration, U.S. tactics changed. Stevenson at the UN, Chester Bowles as under secretary of state, and Williams as assistant secretary of state for Africa set a different tone. The emphasis was on winning African support, not simply opposing Communism. Williams, traveling in Africa, made his much publicized "Africa for the Africans" statement in Nairobi, which incensed the white settlers and later led one to assault him physically in Lusaka. When the peasant revolt broke out in Angola in March, Stevenson supported a UN resolution that criticized Portuguese policy in Angola. The administration was open to a coalition government in the Congo, even including Antoine Gizenga, based in Stanleyville, who inherited Lumumba's mantle. In March Gizenga became deputy prime minister, but in name only.

Relative stability in Leopoldville made it possible to focus attention on the secession of Katanga. The Tshombe regime was protected by about 500 Belgian troops and several hundred soldiers of fortune from South Africa, Britain, Rhodesia, and France, who were sympathetic to Belgian and white settler interests. Although Hammarskjold had preferred to settle the secession issue by negotiations, they did not lead to a solution either. Tshombe signed agreements in Leopoldville, only to renege when he returned to his stronghold in Elizabethville (now Lubumbashi).

In September 1961 UN troops and Katanga forces clashed for several days. Hammarskjold was en route to a meeting with Tshombe when his plane crashed under suspicious circumstances near Ndola in Northern Rhodesia. Everyone on board was killed. Shocked, I felt the loss in a personal way. Although I had only met Hammarskjold, I had known well one of the men with him, Heinreich Weischoff, head of the Trusteeship Division. I was happy, however, with the choice of U Thant, formerly Burma's ambassador to the UN, as the new secretary general. He was very active in the anticolonial cause, and we were on friendly terms. Shortly after he took office in November, the Security Council called for the "use of force if necessary" in Katanga, to arrest, detain, or deport the mercenaries and for all secessionist activities to cease.

UN military action to end the secession began in December. The United States supplied planes to transport reinforcements from Leopoldville. Tshombe capitulated momentarily by accepting a formula that ended secession and absorbed his military force into the national army, but, as with previous agreements, he did not honor the terms.

In the meantime, the right wing was organized in the United States to oppose the UN action. Senator Thomas Dodd said that the United States had never been committed "to a more preposterous and less defensible policy." Groups such as the American Friends of Katanga sprang up. They put out little stickers saying, "Stop UN Colonialism" and "Hands Off Katanga." The American Committee to Aid Katanga Freedom Fighters was organized "to mobilize maximum public support for the Katangan fight for self-determination against U.N. military agression . . . and U.S. support of this operation."[7]

The ACOA took the lead in countering the Katanga lobby. Our material pointed out that Tshombe's party did not have legitimate control in Katanga. It won only 25 out of 60 seats with 33.4 percent of the vote and had eliminated the opposition Balubakat party, which had won 49.4 percent, by jailing its leaders.

During the debate on Katanga, I had an unexpected visit from Dodd's executive assistant, who had seen the various ACOA statements. We exchanged ideas and information in a civilized, if not altogether friendly way. Our perceptions of the crisis were quite different. He saw it in terms of a fight against international Communism with Tshombe as the knight on a white horse. I saw the campaign of the so-called freedom fighters as "an attempt to wreck the UN and to defeat an enlightened American policy backing the UN," as an ACOA statement put it.

The facts were that the Soviets did not support UN action, and neither Prime Minister Adoula nor President Kasavubu had appealed to the Soviet Union for help against Katanga. Our statement pointed out that Tshombe's secret police were ruthlessly suppressing opposition and that the "freedom fighters" were not essentially Katanganese but white settlers and soldiers of fortune. "The real support for Tshombe comes from the European investors whose holdings produce more than $350,000,000 annually." Senator Hubert Humphrey responded, "The points you make are very good. I have noticed the spate of advertisements by the so-called Katanga Freedom Fighters. You are providing a much-needed corrective. More power to you."[8]

A few days after meeting Dodd's assistant, I sent a communication to Dodd and other senators and congressmen including a statement from U Thant that with the end of Katanga secession, there would be a general amnesty and no reprisals against any supporters of Tshombe. By return mail my covering letter to Dodd came back to me with an angry note scribbled on it by Dodd's assistant. "I am returning this letter to you because I feel there can be no discourse between people who do not share the same moral values. You are a man of blood and dishonesty—a strong statement—but after my conversation with you in New York you should at least be aware of the untruthfulness of certain of the assertions contained in your statement on Katanga."[9] Then he threatened to discuss the matter with members of the ACOA National Committee, hinting that I might be out of a job. I philosophized that people will do strange things when emotionally aroused. I was annoyed more by his failure to pass my letter on to Dodd than by what he wrote to me.

The Katanga issue was settled when the UN installed officials to take control of the provincial administration. On January 15, 1963, Tshombe finally capitulated. After two and a half years, secession was finally ended.

THE STANLEYVILLE CRISIS

Trouble in the Congo, however, was by no means over. The challenge to Congo unity now came from Stanleyville, which so far had not been securely integrated into the central government. Christophe Gbenye, formerly Lumumba's minister of the interior, who had succeeded him as head of the MNC, headed a government in Orientale Province, where Stanleyville was, which proclaimed itself a People's Republic in August 1964. To make matters worse, the UN forces, short of funds, had left the Congo in June. Prime Minister Adoula, no longer exercising real power, resigned in July, and almost unbelievably Kasavubu appointed Tshombe, symbol of secession, as prime minister. This move was certainly a formula for disaster. Plans for a military attack against Stanleyville were put in motion. Desperately trying to protect itself from invasion by Congolese forces and several hundred mercenaries from Katanga, the Stanleyville rebel regime seized some 1,600 foreign hostages, including American missionaries, the U.S. consul, and several CIA officials. The regime had some Chinese Communist support, which brought the cold war into the picture again. While negotiations on the release of the hostages were in progress in Nairobi between Kanza, representing the Stanleyville regime, and William Attwood, U.S. ambassador to Kenya, what was touted as a "rescue and humanitarian mission" took place. U.S. planes dropped 600 paratroopers into the city. After brief fighting, the rebel forces fled. They massacred 30 hostages on the spot and murdered perhaps 50 more over the next few days.

What a tragedy this whole episode was! The ACOA deplored the tactic of holding hostages as blackmail but also was critical of the U.S. involvement in the "rescue mission." Would there have been a greater loss of life if the negotiations in Nairobi had been allowed to continue? Would there have been a chance of saving lives? We wrote to Dean Rusk, secretary of state, "It's right for the U.S. to want to see a stable central government in the Congo. But is it the American responsibility to become involved further in the internal politics of a country in the heart of Africa when at least a large number of African states interpret U.S. involvement as interference for essentially cold war objectives?"

This was to be the last major diplomatic effort for Kanza. He wrote me (July 12, 1966) that he had resigned from the revolutionary movement in the Congo and hoped to be out of politics for good. His plans called for a career of writing and teaching and he asked for any help I could give him. My last contact with him was an invitation to lecture in a course he was giving at Harvard in the 1970s.

MOBUTU IN POWER

In October 1965, Kasavubu dismissed Tshombe as prime minister, and then in a bloodless coup, Mobutu deposed Kasavubu and named himself president for a five-year term, a post he has held ever since. All political parties were banned in April 1967.

Mobutu instituted an "authenticity" program. The name of the country was changed to Zaire (meaning "river"). Leopoldville was renamed Kinshasa; Stanleyville, Kinsangani; Elizabethville, Lubumbashi. In 1972 he changed his own name to Mobutu Sese Seko and made it a crime for a Zairian baby to be given a Western name. The date of Christmas was changed temporarily to June 24. Further to establish himself as an African nationalist, he nationalized small and large businesses but with little advance planning. When inexperienced Zairians replaced Europeans in foreign-backed enterprises, disaster resulted. Europeans left and bankruptcy mounted. As the cost of oil and grain imports rose and the price for exported copper fell drastically, Zaire became a major economic calamity, deep in debt. The International Monetary Fund sent in specialists to run the central bank and establish a system by which foreign banks could receive payments on their loans made to keep Zaire afloat.

Combined with this economic disorder was massive corruption as officials diverted funds from government revenues into personal accounts in foreign banks. Mobutu himself was (and is) reputed to be one of the richest men in the world. Nevertheless, he retained a strong anti-Communist image and was regarded by successive U.S. administrations as one of the West's best friends in Africa. Zaire has been one of the most-favored African recipients of U.S. aid over the years.

A TURNING POINT

The Congo's independence symbolized the beginning of a new period in Africa. Although only 1 of 17 countries to become independent in 1960, developments there had unmatched significance. Anticipation for its success had been so high that the sudden letdown was all the more traumatic. The conflict over the Congo in the UN, the murder of its first prime minister, and the death of the secretary general while trying to negotiate a peaceful settlement all combined to mark Congo independence as unique.

The Congo crisis signaled the need for a more realistic view of the revolutionary changes taking place in Africa. The romance of the anti-colonial struggle was challenged. No longer could Africa be viewed simplistically. Independence was risky to achieve and by itself would not solve the problems of ethnic conflict, economic development, and the need for an educated and experienced leadership. From this point on, the struggle against colonialism and white domination in southern Africa would be more violent. Competition between the big powers in Africa would become more frequent. Disillusionment in the West was more than matched by the deep suspicion of African nationalists that the end of political colonialism would not mean the end of economic dominance by foreign powers and that their struggle would have little help from the West.

CHAPTER THIRTEEN

Angola: The Stormy Path Toward Independence

O n my two trips to Africa in 1960 I had seen only limited evidence that an outbreak of violence in Angola would soon shatter that "kingdom of silence." Up to this time my contacts had been almost exclusively with the UPA, primarily through Barros Necaca and Holden Roberto. I knew only dimly of the MPLA, based in Luanda. It had to operate clandestinely because Portugal permitted only one political party to exist, Dictator Antonio de Oliveira Salazar's National Union.

START OF THE MPLA

The MPLA, a merger of several smaller groups, had been organized secretly in Luanda in December 1956, in contrast to the UPA, which had been organized externally. The key figures of the original nucleus were among the better-educated, middle-class, urban-based population. By 1959 it was clear that it would be difficult for the underground organization to maintain and extend itself effectively inside Angola, a police state. The secret police had stepped up their activity as a result of Portuguese apprehension about the massive riots of January 1959 in the neighboring Congo. Large-scale arrests in March and July 1959 led to a secret trial in 1960 of 57 persons accused of "attempts against the external security of the state and the unity of the nation." Among those jailed was the first president of the MPLA, Ilidio Machado.

Under these conditions, the MPLA decided in early 1960 to set up external headquarters in Conakry, in newly independent Guinea. Guinea was far from Angola, but its African nationalist atmosphere with socialist tendencies was friendly to the MPLA. Mario de Andrade, who was outside the country, was chosen president and Viriato da Cruz, secretary general.

De Andrade came from the Dembos forest area of Angola, just east of Luanda. He entered the University of Lisbon in 1948, and six years later went to the Sorbonne in Paris, where he was during the founding of the MPLA. He wrote extensively, even publishing an anthology of poetry. During these years Da Cruz was also in Paris. In Angola he had been the editor of *Mensagem* ("Message"), which published poetry and other literature to contrast Portuguese and African culture. It was banned by the government after its second issue, and Da Cruz fled the country. Lucio Lara, a third political exile, formed part of this political nucleus in Paris.

The name of Agostinho Neto was thrust into prominence by another round of arrests in Angola in June 1960. He and 51 others were taken into custody. Neto, a doctor, was no stranger to prison. He was born in the village of Bengo near Luanda in 1922. The son of a Methodist pastor, he grew up in the church. After schooling in Luanda, he worked for Ralph Dodge, an American Methodist missionary in Angola, and then spent three years in public health services in Luanda. He went to Portugal in 1947 on a Methodist scholarship and completed medical school. Because of his activity in the anti-Salazar youth movement, he was sentenced to more than two years in jail in 1955. Nevertheless, he was awarded his medical degree in 1958, married Eugenia, a Portuguese woman of unusual talent, and returned to Angola to practice.

After Neto's June 8 arrest, for the first four days and nights in prison he was tortured by not being allowed to sleep. A week later, some thousand of his neighbors of Bengo and adjacent Icolo demonstrated at the district government office in nearby Catete to protest his confinement. Soldiers attacked the protestors, killing 30 and injuring more than 200. The next day the two villages were burned. Censorship kept this incident out of the press.

With its leaders arrested or in exile, the MPLA busied itself with international activity. Representatives traveled to various parts of Africa, to London, and to China to win international support. At the AAPC in Tunis, the MPLA tried to establish an understanding with the UPA, pressuring a reluctant Roberto to sign a declaration calling for joint action in Angola. This agreement was never implemented.

Just two weeks before Congo independence, the MPLA appealed to Portugal to call a conference to discuss self-determination, release of political prisoners, and withdrawal of Portuguese forces from Angola. Portugal responded unofficially by declaring that self-determination for its overseas territories was not a matter for discussion.

ROBERTO AS LEADER OF THE UPA

After Congo independence, Roberto returned to Leopoldville and gave himself full time to leadership of the UPA, although he had no organizational title. The UPA continued to expand. Political broadcasts were beamed to Angola by permission of Patrice Lumumba. Before long, Roberto's relations with Joseph Kasavubu soured, however, because Kasavubu, as a Bakongo nationalist, acted through his tribal organization, ABAKO, which wanted to reconstitute the Pan-Bakongo traditional kingdom, and the UPA rejected the idea. This constituted an open break with Kasavubu. Hearing that Kasavubu was going to have him arrested, in September Roberto hurriedly left the Congo for Ghana.

In Accra, Roberto discovered that his relations with Kwame Nkrumah had cooled considerably. Nkrumah charged him with being too close to the

United States and with resisting a united front with the MPLA. Roberto had replied that he was a nationalist. He told me many years later that he had, in fact, feared a formal tie with the MPLA because the UPA did not then have trained leaders to hold their own, although still later he had no such fears. At any rate, he was stranded in Accra without funds until Nkrumah sent him £200, which enabled him to make his second trip to the UN.

When Roberto returned to the Congo in January 1961, he adamantly opposed the front that the UPA under Necaca had formed with the MPLA. Controversy was vigorous, but Roberto prevailed. A majority from the Steering Committee, including Necaca, resigned in protest, and Roberto became the leader, although he was not elected president for another two months. Necaca remained in the UPA but with no policy-making responsibility.

BEGINNING OF ARMED STRUGGLE

The reality of the struggle for freedom in Angola was suddenly thrust upon the international scene in 1961. The Portuguese had always been able to keep events in their African colonies out of the headlines. This changed with a series of strangely linked events.

A HIGHJACKED SHIP AND A PRISON RAID

A Portuguese luxury liner, the *Santa Maria,* was highjacked off the coast of South America on January 22 by Capt. Henrique Galvão, formerly a deputy in the Portuguese National Assembly and chief inspector of over-seas territories. A staunch opponent of Salazar, he had written a report highly critical of contract-labor abuses in Angola. As a dissident he was sentenced in 1958 to 16 years in prison. The next year he managed to escape and was given asylum in Argentina and Venezuela, where he worked to overthrow Salazar's government.

Galvão announced that he would sail the *Santa Maria* to Luanda. Although he abandoned her 11 days later in Brazil, the publicity given to this daring act drew many international news reporters to Luanda to await his arrival. I made contact with Galvão in São Paulo, Brazil, through an organization of Portuguese democrats in the United States. The ACOA invited him to speak at our Africa Freedom Day meeting in April 1961. He accepted, only to be refused a U.S. visa because Portugal claimed he was wanted for "fraudulent bankruptcy." As Galvão later said to me, how could he have been guilty of such a charge when he was in prison at the time? In fact, the United States did not want to offend Portugal because of the agreement for a U.S. air base on the Azores Islands. It was two years before Galvão could give testimony at the UN.

Another event tied in with the *Santa Maria* incident was a predawn raid on February 4 by several hundred Africans on the main prison of Luanda to free political prisoners. Militants of the MPLA planned the attack. It was their opening salvo in the struggle for independence, and February 4 is now celebrated as Angola's national day. In the attack at least 7 police and some 40 Africans were killed. The next day, European civilians, after leaving funeral services for the police, rioted and attacked African bystanders indiscriminately. The rioting spread to African sections of Luanda, and hundreds were killed. This incident, like other earlier ones, would have gone virtually unnoticed had not world reporters been on hand to cover the *Santa Maria* incident. They filed stories filled with gruesome detail.

A PEASANT REVOLT

A little more than a month later, a third event shattered any Portuguese hope for a return to colonial peace and tranquility—a peasant uprising in northern Angola. Apparently it was planned to coincide with a meeting of the UN Security Council to debate the Angolan situation after the February prison attack and the subsequent massacre. Roberto, who had arrived in New York several days before the UN debate, had warned me with words to the effect of, "Watch March 15. Something important will happen that day." Wondering if he was referring to UN action, I asked what he meant. "Just wait," he replied.

When I was in northern Angola a few months later, I heard that the peasant rebellion had begun on the Primavera plantation owned by a Portuguese named Reis. On March 15, several hundred contract laborers confronted Reis, demanding payment for several months' back wages. He had refused and in attempting to scatter them, had shot into their midst, killing one. This triggered a counterattack in which Reis was killed, then other Portuguese, including members of his family. But the uprising was not confined to Primavera. A Reuters dispatch from Lisbon on March 17 named Nova Caipemba, Nambuangogo, and Quitexe as localities of greatest violence. An estimated 200 white men, women, and children were killed on the first few days of the revolt. A British Baptist missionary in northern Angola told me later of those days: "It was a chilling demonstration of what the release of long pent-up feelings can do."

Although the UPA had been identified with the uprising, its preparation was indeed minimal. An early military chief of the UPA, who had deserted from the Portuguese Army because he had heard that the UPA was well armed and ready for battle, told me he was deeply disillusioned when he reached Leopoldville to discover the dismal preparation—only 7 guns, for example, and 11 men who were being trained at the Tunisian embassy.

In view of the limited preparation, the revolt had a surprising short-term success. For virtually the entire six months after March 15, the rebel forces moved rapidly at will, even though their tactics were not well planned. The Portuguese were forced out of 33 fortified posts and hung on to only 9 in a corner of the Uige district. A pro-Portuguese South African journalist, A. J. Venter, reported that within a month, 100 administrative posts in three districts were eliminated and more than 1500 Europeans had been killed.[1]

Coffee plantations were particularly hard hit by the war. Dozens of planters were ruined by the destruction of their crops. The mass of people in the north did not become militants, but hundreds of thousands became refugees, and many walked long distances to reach the Congo.

Portuguese reprisals began soon. A Methodist missionary friend, Malcolm McVeigh, who was working then in the Kimbundu-speaking area of Angola, talked with me of his experience. He was holding religious meetings in villages where the people were not even aware of the uprising when the local Portuguese official warned him to leave immediately because the area was going to be bombed. "The majority of those people who escaped the bombings," he told me, "were either taken prisoner or killed."

Believing unaccountably that Protestant missionaries were among the principal fomenters of the revolt, the Portuguese reacted against the churches. One American missionary reported that out of 165 Methodist pastors and teachers in the Luanda and Dembos areas, 135 were missing, dead, or in prison by early 1962. Four American Methodist missionaries were jailed for three months and then deported to the United States, charged with running a school for terrorists and storing arms.

How does one assess this peasant revolt? On the one hand, it certainly took the struggle for independence from Luanda to the rural north. It inescapably focused world attention on Portuguese colonialism and no doubt quickened the process of revolution in Guinea-Bissau and Mozambique. If it did not attract mass support outside of the north, it did attract leaders from all sections of the country. On the other hand, the uprising was poorly planned. Virtually no advance explanation was given to those who would be primarily affected. There was no clear vision about the kind of country that should result from the revolt. Had there been a clearer purpose, perhaps some of the initial indiscriminate slaughter could have been avoided. Had there been some forethought, UPA forces might have known what to do with the vast area of the north that they controlled for several months. As it was, when the Portuguese did not flee or move to negotiate, UPA was at a loss as to the next move.

GROWTH OF UPA

Nevertheless, the March 15 revolt spurred the growth of UPA. The mass base of the movement remained among the Bakongo, but anti-Portuguese dissidents were attracted from other areas of the country, as well. The top military chiefs, the vice president, the leader of a UPA-dominated trade union, and the medical officer who headed the Assistance Service for Angolan Refugees (SARA) all came from central or southern Angola.

In late 1961 Jonas Savimbi joined. He came from Chilesso in the Bie district and had a religious background, since his father had combined railroad work with work for Protestant missionaries. Savimbi not only brought in new leadership from the south but also a much-needed intellectual image to a heavily peasant-oriented UPA. He soon became secretary general. He accompanied Roberto to the Conference of Nonaligned Countries in Yugoslavia in 1961 and to the UN General Assembly that fall. When I met him at the UN he was not bearded and rather quietly followed Roberto.

In the meantime, UPA sent more than 20 men to Algerian FLN bases in Tunisia for military training. Most became officers for the newly organized UPA army and trained other men for guerrilla warfare.

WITH THE UPA REBELS

While Roberto was at the UN, I talked with him about going into northern Angola with the UPA rebels. He was supportive and I made a plan. John Marcum, an African specialist at Lincoln University, a black school near Philadelphia, who had been part of the ACOA delegation to the AAPC in Accra, wanted to go too. Knowledgeable, soft spoken, fluent in French, and easy to get along with, he seemed an ideal companion. We left at the earliest opportunity, right after Christmas.

CROSSING THE BORDER

On the heavily clouded night of January 4, 1962, we drove out of Leopoldville, intending to cross into Angola in the dark. In the car with us was José Manuel Peterson, a UPA official with responsibilities for organizing refugees, and Field Commander João Batista. Born in southern Angola, Batista had been drafted into the Portuguese army while he was still in school. Promoted to corporal and sent to northern Angola, he learned about UPA from Congolese soldiers at the border. He decided to desert and after several attempts, crossed into the Congo and got in touch with UPA. He was one of the handful of Angolans who received further military training under Tunisian direction in Leopoldville. He participated in the first action against the Portuguese in mid-March 1961 and by July was designated commander.

A few miles out of Leopoldville, the tropical rain struck. Our windshield wipers did not work and the car slowed to a crawl. Fortunately the rain had let up when we turned off onto a dirt road that led to the border. There we met, as planned, a UPA truck with eight soldiers in the back, sitting in the midst of a variety of weapons. Car and truck proceeded together in the dark on the rough road. When the car broke down at 3:00 A.M., all of us piled into the truck. Near the border, the heavily loaded truck broke through an old bridge and had to be abandoned with a small

João Batista, UPA commander, reading the Bible at a camp in Angola, 1962.

guard. We walked the last few miles through a small village of refugees, up a hill, past a line of eucalyptus trees marking the border, and into Angola. The sun was fairly high by that time, but there apparently were no officials on either side of the line, for we were not intercepted.

Despite a night of travel without sleep, I felt amazingly keyed up. The morning air was fresh and cool and the landscape was beautiful—rolling hills and valleys, forests of tall trees, grass higher than Iowa corn, and abundant water in the many streams. It was hard to realize that there was a war going on.

Only a few hundred yards across the border we came upon an impressive pile of weapons from Tunisia and Algeria, which had been brought in earlier for distribution to young nationalists who had marched many days from farther south. After a brief rest we started hiking south. The young men shouldered astoundingly heavy loads of rifles, machine guns, ammunition, and land mines.

Some five hours hike brought us wearily to our destination, an almost empty village, whose inhabitants had fled north to join the growing throng of refugees in the Congo. Here we stayed for a couple of nights in a hut while the arms were distributed and the guerrillas scattered to their various bases. Marcum and I watched, talking with the few who could speak French, and most importantly acted like medical technicians, which we were not. We did bring in 250 pounds of medicines.

A VILLAGE TOUR

During our 11-day trek through high grass and deep forest, we visited 12 villages. Sometimes we were 5, sometimes 20, but always accompanied by Peterson. The narrow paths wound up and down hill, across streams bridged usually by a single log or by several logs bound together by jungle vines, suspended high above the water. The lush grass, 15 or more feet high, had sharp edges that scratched our arms. The footing was precarious there and difficult in the forest because of roots across the path and the constant dampness beneath the impenetrable shade.

We were greeted with genuine warmth by the hundreds of people we met on the paths, many of them refugees moving north toward the Congo. Any such chance meeting meant a kind of reception line as we shook hands and spoke words of greeting. An old woman and small child stopped in front of Marcum and me, danced around us, and knelt and offered a prayer. Villagers shared their grass-and-mud huts and their food with us. Occasionally we had chicken, wild buffalo, wild pig, fish, and eel caught in one of the rivers. Usually, however, our diet consisted of luscious fruits such as bananas, mangos, pineapple, and papaya, along with generous supplies of manioc (the staple) and peanuts. We had to drink water from the streams. The simple water purifiers we carried must have done some good, for we did not suffer any serious digestive consequences.

We saw something of the effects of the war. Food and scant medical supplies were stored outside each village in case of a bombing, of which

Angolan refugees fleeing to the Congo, 1962.

there was always danger. We witnessed an attack on two villages just after we had left them. The small planes dove, dropping their incendiary bombs and rockets, then flew off. We could hear the concussion of the bombs and saw the fires that erupted. A little later someone from the villages reported that no one was injured because the people had scattered. I was given fragments of a bomb as a memento. On another occasion, while walking through a forest, we heard a plane diving near us, but no explosions. It was dropping leaflets. Soon we were given one, written in Portuguese and Kikongo, calling on the people to return to Portuguese protection. As the leaflet was read aloud, the people laughed derisively or growled in anger.

We saw burnt abandoned villages. At one, the walls of a gutted Catholic chapel bore the words, "Angola, Kimpwanza ['Independence']. Amen." I took a picture of a napalm bomb casing clearly marked, "Property of the U.S. Air Force."

A strange combination of ordinary village pursuits and military practices grew out of the exigencies of war. When we approached a village, we quite suddenly would come upon sentries, who had been standing out of sight. Our UPA travel documents, a mimeographed sheet, would be examined, perhaps signed, and then returned to us. A gate would swing open on the path and we would enter the village area. Frequently a military drill would be put on for our benefit. Almost invariably Marcum and I would be asked to give medical treatment. It was a pitiful sight as a line formed and we did what we could for raw, open sores on arms or legs. The people may have felt something important was being accomplished. We felt inadequate.

Our primary destination was the UPA field headquarters called Fuesse, near São Salvador. It was hidden from the air, deep in the forest. The young men on duty at the gate examined our papers very officially, but when they tried to examine Batista's pockets, he angrily protested. It was obvious that the authority of the field commander, coming as he did from the Cuanhama area far to the south, was very limited in this Bakongo region. After much arguing, the problem was not happily resolved, and Batista refused to make his usual speech to the militants after their dress parade. A few days later Batista continued south toward a headquarters near Bembe. We last saw him with a few UPA troops disappearing down the path into the forest. Shortly thereafter, we concluded our exciting, informative trip with the UPA forces and returned to New York.

Although I had not been able to talk directly to Batista because of the language barrier, he had impressed me—by his courage and his personal discipline in difficult circumstances. Therefore, it was sad to hear of his death less than a month afterwards. According to the official report, issued a year later, he had been killed in a battle with the Portuguese near Bembe. But quite another version came out. Marcos Kassanga, military chief of staff, had been selected to succeed Batista. Instead he held a press conference, at which he resigned and announced that Batista had been killed by the UPA Bakongos. I do not know what the truth may be. This was the first of many defections. Nevertheless, I sensed that the UPA had something going. It was not just a lot of talk. Yet its organization and leadership were obviously limited. What lay ahead was unclear.

THE FNLA AND GRAE

On the whole, 1962 was a pretty good year for UPA. Toward the end of March the National Front for the Liberation of Angola (FNLA) was formed when UPA and the Democratic Party of Angola (PDA) joined.* On April 3 they formed the Revolutionary Government of Angola in Exile (GRAE). UPA headquarters in Leopoldville became GRAE headquarters. Holden Roberto was chairman of the Executive Committee of the FNLA and president of GRAE. Emmanuel Kunzika of the PDA became first vice president. From this point on UPA was hardly ever mentioned. The terms FNLA or GRAE were used somewhat interchangeably depending on whether the movement or the government in exile was meant.

In mid-August GRAE opened up a military camp at Kinkuzu some 70 miles west of Thysville in the Congo, which had been a Congo army base. Cyrille Adoula, prime minister of the Congo, and Roberto had a good relationship, since they had known each other for years and had formerly played on the same soccer team. When I visited this base, in the company of nationalist leaders from other parts of Africa,* there were about 1,500 men there for training. Jonas Savimbi, foreign minister of GRAE, headed the delegation.

When we arrived, the men, including 200 deserters from the Portuguese Army, who were directed by officers trained in Algeria, were assembled quickly for drill. All were in uniform, most in sneakers. Only 10 percent were armed because those who had already gone into Angola had taken most of the arms with them. It was obvious that the military potential of GRAE was growing. The drill concluded with a skillful speech in Portuguese by Savimbi.

REACTION IN THE UNITED STATES

When fighting broke out in Angola in 1961, the United States was faced with a dilemma that was never satisfactorily resolved—how to remain neutral in Portugal's African wars while maintaining a military alliance with Portugal that involved an American Air Force base in the Azores. The resulting stance was in effect unfriendly to the liberation struggle. In attempting to balance policy, U.S. Ambassador to the UN Adlai Stevenson supported the UN resolution criticizing Portugal's violent response to the

---

*The PDA, formerly ALIAZO, had broadened its name to be rid of tribal connotations.

*Sam Nujoma, president of SWAPO; Ndabaningi Sithole from Southern Rhodesia, of the Zimbabwe African Peoples Union (ZAPU); and Paulo Gumane, president of a dissident Mozambique organization, the Mozambique Revolutionary Committee (COREMO).

Angola prison attack, and the United States prohibited Portugal's use of NATO military equipment outside the North Atlantic zone, but to little effect since this could not be monitored. Portugal countered by refusing to renew the agreement for the U.S. base in the Azores, although it did not interfere with continued U.S. use.

Arthur Schlesinger, formerly a member of the ACOA's National Committee, wrote:

The problem led to continued wrangling in Washington—the Bureau of European Affairs vs. the Bureau of African Affairs, the Mission to the U.N. vs. the Pentagon. . . . This left us no choice but of moderating policy on Portuguese questions in the UN—never enough for the nationalists in Africa and always too much for the Pentagon and Dr. Salazar.[2]

We in the ACOA were concerned not only with government policy but also with a Portuguese-sponsored right-wing campaign against us in the United States. In 1961 the Portuguese-American Committee on Foreign Affairs suddenly appeared. It was headquartered in Boston and chaired by a Portuguese-born Boston lawyer, Martin T. Comacho. It was financed by 40 overseas Portuguese companies. Comacho released a seven-page public statement attacking the ACOA and demanding a congressional investigation of it for "supporting communist goals" and for its financing of and connections with the "terrorist" movement in Angola. He called on prominent people on our National Committee to resign. None did. Comacho's committee also published a pamphlet, *Communists and Angola*, devoted almost exclusively to attacking the ACOA. Because we were not called communist but only described as "backing communist goals" it was difficult to take legal action.

Others picked up the attack. Fulton Lewis, Jr., a right-wing columnist, wrote that the ACOA's main target was Portugal and that our program "would probably deprive this country of a loyal and dedicated ally."[3] Senator John Tower of Texas said in the Senate that the ACOA seemed to be the agent of a foreign power, leading Comacho to ask the Department of Justice to force the ACOA to register as a foreign agent. At a conference with a government lawyer sent from Washington, we presented evidence that the ACOA received absolutely no financial backing from any government or any other foreign source. The case was dropped. I felt it was poetic justice when, a little later, Comacho was called to testify at Senate hearings on the Foreign Agent Registration Act. When it was established that his Portuguese-American Committee was financed by Portuguese companies, he had to register as a foreign agent.

THE MPLA AND ATTEMPTS TOWARD A UNITED FRONT

By early April 1961 the MPLA was confronted with a sobering set of circumstances. Fighting had broken out in Luanda and the north, and the coffee-based economy of northern Angola was in disarray. For the moment the Portuguese were in retreat and the world was aware. Yet the MPLA lacked an accessible strong base in the north, and its external headquarters was thousands of miles away in Conakry.

The MPLA made numerous attempts directly or through a third party to involve the FNLA in a united front. At the third AAPC in Cairo, I talked with Mario de Andrade, president of the MPLA, who stressed the necessity for a united front. My awareness of the issue was also sharpened by my correspondence with Bishop Ralph Dodge, who had spent many years in Angola. He wrote to me (May 23, 1961) summarizing the many MPLA attempts to bring Roberto into a united front and emphasized his fear that open conflict would begin between the two movements, thus dissipating energy that should be directed against the Salazar regime.

Agostinho Neto was under house arrest in Lisbon at this time. Many who were close to the Angola situation felt that his release was important to the future of the struggle. The ACOA joined the international campaign to press the Portuguese, unsuccessfully, for his release. With the help of the anti-Salazar underground, however, he escaped.

Neto made his way to MPLA headquarters, now in Leopoldville by government permission, and tried to bring the MPLA and the FNLA together. An official meeting of the groups was held on August 5, 1962, but no agreement was reached. The suspicions on each side were too formidable. The subsequent letters between Roberto and Neto were undiplomatic, and Roberto refused Neto's proposal for another meeting. Not only did Roberto fear the MPLA's sophisticated leadership, but his movement was in fact stronger; he felt that he had more to lose than to gain.

The MPLA certainly had a level of sophistication that UPA could not match. The neatness and orderliness of the MPLA medical office and clinic in Leopoldville were in sharp contrast to the bedlam around the comparable service of UPA. There were eight doctors, compared to one for UPA, well-kept records, and a well-stocked supply room.

In early 1962, John Marcum and I went twice to the MPLA office. In our discussions its Executive Committee indeed stressed the necessity for joint action militarily but not politically with UPA (the FNLA was set up two months later). It felt UPA had no program and no ideology and was tribalist and racist. (UPA seemed prejudiced against mulattos, who were numerous in MPLA leadership.) Furthermore, MPLA leaders were enraged by the UPA murder of 16 MPLA comrades who had been captured in Angola while trying to take ammunition to their militants in the Nambuangongo area.

In December 1962 the MPLA held its first national conference. Neto was chosen president and Mario deAndrade became head of external affairs. Viriato da Cruz, former secretary general, who had led dissidents out of the MPLA some months earlier, was officially ousted. The conference enunciated a fundamental principle of "the priority of the interior over the exterior," meaning that it must find a base for operation within Angola.

HEADY DAYS FOR THE FNLA AND GRAE

My main contact with the liberation struggle in Angola continued to be primarily with the FNLA and GRAE. I did not try to shun the MPLA; its work was just less apparent to me. The ACOA's most substantial project in Angola was medical, Emergency Relief to Angola (ERA). We launched it shortly after Marcum and I returned from northern Angola. We cooperated particularly with the FNLA medical and refugee program (SARA) and its director, Dr. José Liahuca.

IAN GILCHRIST AND SARA

When we began looking for a permanent doctor for the program, the ideal person came along. Ian Gilchrist was a young Canadian doctor who had been raised in Angola in a medical missionary family and had been trained in Canada. He had never lost his strong attachment to the Ovimbundu people with whom he had grown up.

At that time, Gilchrist had a wife and two children and was working in a hospital in Sierra Leone. We worried about Portuguese reprisals against his parents in Angola if he was working with the FNLA, but he was committed: "My family are ready. We are agreed that the time is long past for positive action and we are ready for the consequences."[4] In addition to having medical skills, Gilchrist knew Angola and could speak some Portuguese, Umbundu, and French. He also knew Liahuca, who was enthusiastic about his coming. It took months to get Roberto's approval. Gilchrist finally went to Leopoldville in January 1963 with no set salary. We took out an insurance policy and opened a small savings account for him in New York. His family joined him later.

When I met the Gilchrists in mid-1963, I was immediately attracted. Ian was slight, with reddish blonde hair and beard and a ready smile but an intense manner. Joyce was blond and quiet but gave the impression of great inner strength. They lived under almost impossible circumstances in the SARA clinic, which was in the regular FNLA compound. There were five or six buildings, once private houses, only a 15-minute walk from the center of the city. The grounds were congested with people, mostly refugees. Hundreds were settled there at any given time, as though it were a village. People cooked food over open fires and slept on the ground. Sanitation was woefully inadequate. The Gilchrists occupied one room of the clinic separated from the surgical room by a curtain. The two children could watch an operation simply by lying on their stomachs and peering under the curtain.

SARA tried to help the refugees through the Leopoldville clinic and also to send medical staff to the border villages filled with displaced Angolans. Through ERA the ACOA supplied a volkswagen van converted into an ambulance. Gilchrist's special assignment was to spend time at the border. He vividly described in a report in early 1963 what it was like to go into a village. "Here you see the lines of refugees, one line of women and

Dr. Ian Gilchrist and family
and friend in Leopoldville,
Congo, 1963.

children and one line of men. We worked away here during the whole day. The clinics start early in the morning as soon as it is light and then work through until it is dark or until supplies are exhausted."

Travel to the border had many hazards. He wrote (March 10, 1963), "We managed to get stuck three times, first in wet sand, then in mud, and finally between some deep ruts. The last time was 5:30 A.M. so we all went to sleep where we sat until the sun came up an hour or so later, then we dug out and continued on." Months later he wrote (October 13, 1963), "All the way down from Mukumbi to Kizamba we were followed by a variety of spies from the adjacent Portuguese posts [just across the border]. . . . The Portuguese spread the word that I was not really a doctor but a mulatto deserter." His experiences were made real to me when I traveled with him to the border, camping out at night, cooking food over an open fire, and holding clinics.

RECOGNITION BY THE OAU

Nineteen sixty-three was the peak year for the FNLA. Adoula, still the Congo's prime minister, sent assistance, which came also from Algeria and Tunisia. Roberto was indisputably in command. The PDA was only a junior partner both in the FNLA and GRAE. The MPLA was offering little competition. Tom Mboya wrote me from Nairobi (January 28, 1963) that the MPLA was refused affiliation with PAFMECA at their recent conference. "The conference felt that it must encourage the two groups [MPLA and GRAE] to come together rather than recognize them as separate. It is obvious from our observations that Holden Roberto commands most popular support, more than the MPLA."

At the end of May, at a conference of the heads of African independent states in Addis Ababa, which I attended as an official observer, the Organization of African Unity (OAU) was born. What a thrilling moment it was to see most of the African leaders seated at a horse shoe-shaped table with Emperor Haile Selassie in the chair. Virtually all the heroes of the freedom struggle were there—Kwame Nkrumah, Ahmed Ben Bella, Habib Bourguiba, Julius Nyerere, Sékou Touré—along with the leaders of the liberation movements. It was clear that the OAU would supplant the AAPC.

One of the principal decisions of the OAU was to establish a nine-member Coordinating Committee for the liberation movements. Each of the OAU member states was to be financially assessed in order to buiid up a special fund to aid the struggle. An important early task was to establish a Reconciliation Commission to the Congo in order to study the strengths and relations of the FNLA and the MPLA.

In October the commission recommended that support and recognition should be given to the FNLA and GRAE. Three key north African countries—Algeria, Tunisia, and Morocco—had already recognized GRAE. Roberto was particularly ecstatic about Algeria, a country he said that "has always stood by the side of the Angola people from the dawn of its revolution."

For the moment it looked as if Roberto's refusal to cooperate with the MPLA had paid off. Adoula's government officially recognized GRAE on June 29, 1963, over the opposition of Kasavubu.

At the same time the MPLA suffered harassment from the Congo government. In June its office was raided by police. Arms and explosives were seized and the MPLA was later fined. In September Neto and Lara were arrested for having false papers, although they had travel documents from African states. The MPLA clinic was closed in October and the office itself in November. The MPLA moved across the river to Brazzaville, where a friendly government had just gained control.

NEW INITIATIVES BY THE MPLA

At its new base in Brazzaville, the MPLA held a conference to try to find a new, more promising direction to establish its credibility as a formidable leader of the Angolan liberation struggle. To that end it decided to open a new fighting front in the Portuguese enclave of Cabinda, a densely forested coastal area that borders both Congo-Leopoldville and Congo-Brazzaville, Using a few hundred guerrillas, the MPLA scored some early successes. Perhaps 5,000 Portuguese troops were sent to the area to counteract the MPLA forces.

Later, the MPLA claimed to control about 50 percent of the territory. A.J. Venter said it occupied more than 90 percent.[5] After 1967, however, the Cabinda campaign lost its earlier impetus although sporadic attacks continued.

Even more important than the Cabinda campaign was the opening up of the struggle in Moxico and Cuando Cubango districts in eastern Angola, bordering on newly independent Zambia. The MPLA opened an office in Lusaka, which became its principal international headquarters. The eastern front, or Third Region (the first being the north, the second Cabinda), is a vast flat plateau, close to 4,000 feet in elevation, with many rivers, forming the drainage for the Zambezi River. In the cool season the temperature can reach freezing after sundown. There were only about 380,000 people in a few scattered villages, who cultivated rice, manioc, sorghum, and millet and fished in the rivers. The Portuguese called the area "the land at the end of the earth" and had done virtually nothing to develop it. There were a few rudimentary roads and almost no schools, hospitals, or projects for economic development. Troops held some Portuguese outposts occupied otherwise only by pioneer traders and government officials.

The eastern front was an all-important entering wedge for the MPLA. It opened the way into the heartland of Angola through the districts of Malange and Bié and thence west even to the Atlantic. The external office of the MPLA would continue to serve as liaison with Lusaka, Brazzaville, and Dar es Salaam, but the most important work would be done inside the country. By August 1968 the MPLA felt confident enough about its hold on the region to convene its first regional conference in Moxico.

The Portuguese at first saw the eastern front as only a distraction from the area of conflict in the Dembos Mountains and the north, but by mid-1970 the MPLA reportedly had from 3,000 to 5,000 fighting units on the eastern front and about another thousand units in the Dembos area.[6] They used guerrilla tactics—ambushing Portuguese patrols and posts, mining the roads, and trying to protect the villagers who fled to the forest. The overall objective was to make the region secure enough so that it could be the springboard for incursions into the heartland of Angola.

HARD TIMES FOR THE FNLA AND GRAE

The optimistic feeling of unity and success did not last long at FNLA headquarters. Any revolutionary situation is bound to have strains and stresses as factions compete for power. The FNLA was no exception.

PROBLEMS WITH ROBERTO

Some problems arose because of the way Roberto worked. I had an intimation of this at the OAU conference in Addis Ababa in May 1963.

Jonas Savimbi, who was there with Roberto, looked troubled and sent a note saying he would like to talk with me. Later at a long session, he told me things were not going well. Roberto kept everything in his own hands. He seemed to trust only a few people, usually Bakongos. For months on end he would not write to Savimbi, who was studying in Switzerland. Roberto, complained Savimbi, did not know how to delegate work to others. He had no theoretical or long-range plan and no sense of a grand strategy. Every decision was his own and no one else knew about it. All of this was causing deep dissatisfaction. Then Savimbi urged me to "speak to the president and tell him there will be problems if some changes are not made." He was wrong if he thought I could influence the way Roberto worked. Although I could talk frankly with him, my influence certainly did not extend to changing his personal behavior. Roberto did not like political criticism from the outside (or inside either).

A further indication of Roberto's inability to share responsibility appeared on his and Kunzika's trip to the UN. They were both to speak at a particular session. Roberto was to let Kunzika know the time, but he did not do so. Kunzika was elsewhere at the appointed hour, and Roberto alone appeared. Kunzika was terribly angry and frustrated by this and spoke to me bitterly about it. A trip all the way to New York, only to miss the whole purpose of it!

An inevitable result of Roberto's attempt to maintain almost absolute control was that he lost the confidence and support of potentially helpful allies, particularly those who came from other parts of Angola. I saw some of the deterioration. In July 1964 when I was briefly in Leopoldville, Dr. José Liahuca talked to me with surprising frankness. For some time his relations with Roberto had been souring. He said he felt like a prisoner, that he would like to leave but didn't know where to go. He felt that Roberto was not pressing the struggle in the south, had alienated the southerners, and was incapable of unifying the country. Indeed, the next, night, Liahuca did leave. On my return to New York a letter from Gilchrist told me (July 26, 1964), "Liahuca is gone. He escaped across the river with his family. The same night Holden arrived back unexpectedly [from Cairo], but too late to stop him."

In a resignation statement from Brazzaville (July 25, 1964), Liahuca denounced the tribalistic maneuvers of Roberto, "who was using all methods to surround himself with members of his family in the GRAE at the same time that he is alienating hundreds of Angolan military men and civilians of other ethnic origins."

At about this same time, after a year's build up, Savimbi resigned publicly from FNLA and GRAE at the OAU gathering in Cairo. I had suspected trouble when Gilchrist wrote (February 10, 1964), "Discontent is rampant in the ranks. . . . The split between Holden and Savimbi appears widening."

Relations went from bad to worse when the FNLA began discussions with Viriato da Cruz, a Marxist with good Chinese connections, about his joining the front after his faction had been ousted from the MPLA. John

Marcum wrote me from Leopoldville (April 4, 1964) that "Jonas is outraged by the entrance of Viriato da Cruz!" Savimbi cabled me from Lausanne (April 24, 1964), "Important see you before going Leopoldville. Learned Viriato joined the front. My group disagreed. If impossible [for you to] come, please call." Just a few days before he took off for Cairo he wrote (June 18, 1964), "Holden is more afraid of us than of any Communist. . . . This is unbelievable!" I was not surprised, therefore, at Savimbi's announcement in Cairo.

DIFFICULTIES FOR GILCHRIST

My main concern during this period was for the welfare of Ian Gilchrist and his family. His situation was increasingly precarious. Although initially an enthusiastic supporter of Roberto, he had slowly been drawn into sympathy with the southern Angolans and the critics of Roberto. I think he tried desperately to remain even-handed in his judgments, but being so close to the situation on a day-to-day basis, it was very difficult. His real commitment was to the overall liberation struggle, not to one particular person or movement.

Political concerns constantly interrupted medical concerns as the possibility of significant defection increased. Gilchrist wrote (August 5, 1964) that almost all the Ovimbundu officers were taken prisoner at the base [Kinkuzu], including the commander, Kalundungo. There were then only two Ovimbundu connected in any way with the GRAE.

The medical work seemed to go downhill after Liahuca's departure. There was no competent, well-trained Angolan to replace him. Furthermore the VW ambulance and a Land Rover that had been contributed for SARA use were more frequently commandeered by GRAE, making medical trips to the border impossible.

The pressure of work was as great as ever. There were an estimated 400,000 Angolan refugees in the Congo, arriving at the rate of 5,000 a month. Gilchrist's mood was not helped by a raid for recruits at the GRAE compound by Congolese soldiers and Angolan security guards. He was asked to pick out any too sick to be so conscripted. He chose about 8 out of 50—one with a critically ill wife, a man with a fractured arm, a child of about 10, an old man with gray hair. "For this the Congolese soldiers pointed their rifles at me and promised to have me locked up. . . . Several other sick persons were taken away. You can't imagine how troubled I am."[7] In addition, he wanted to finish a course in tropical medicine at Louvanium University in Leopoldville, which ran until June, so he cut his schedule at SARA to consulting only two days a week.

Barely had he finished the course when Alexander Taty, minister of defense in the GRAE cabinet, and Andre Kassinda attempted an armed coup on June 21. It failed, but during the fighting in the GRAE compound, Gilchrist was told by a nurse that the police riding in the SARA ambulance had begun to pick up persons who had been suspected of opposition to GRAE. A nurse's brother was among them. When Gilchrist protested, he was held two hours at GRAE headquarters until Roberto arrived. Roberto accused him of interfering in political affairs and demanded that he surrender the keys to the SARA vehicles. Then he was unceremoniously expelled from the compound.

It was clearly essential for Gilchrist's safety that he leave the country immediately. Without baggage he took the first available plane. En route to Canada he stopped in New York and we spent hours at my house reviewing all that had happened. His family left safely a few days later.

POLITICAL CHANGES

Roberto's problems during this period were compounded by political changes in the Congo. Moise Tshombe, who had always been sympathetic to the Portuguese, succeeded Adoula (see chapter 12) as prime minister. Furthermore, material assistance to the FNLA from African states virtually dried up. This exacerbated problems at the Kinkuzu military base, where funds were lacking for adequate food or arms for the 2,000 men in training there. Low morale and hot dissension resulted in several attempted mutinies.

Early in 1964 Roberto had announced that he planned to seek help from Communist countries, particularly China, which he proposed to visit. During this period the FNLA accepted the da Cruz faction of the MPLA for membership. But Roberto never went to China, and the small da Cruz faction was never effectively integrated into the front.

Roberto's prospects improved when Joseph Mobutu, with whom he had excellent relations, replaced Tshombe in October 1965. He once told me that he and Mobutu were more than friends, indeed, "like brothers." The opening of the eastern front by the MPLA spurred the OAU again to attempt a reconciliation between the MPLA and the FNLA. An agreement on paper was reached in Cairo in late 1966 calling for an end to hostile propaganda, a release of prisoners, and a willingness to explore ways of cooperation, but there was never a follow-up. Finally the OAU officially recognized both the MPLA and the FNLA but not GRAE. Venter commented, "The OAU has chosen wisely. Portuguese military authorities in Angola admit that the MPLA threat is the most serious they have encountered since the start of the war."[8]

THE FORMATION OF UNITA

After Savimbi resigned from the FNLA, he went to Brazzaville, where he met with but did not join the MPLA. He explained his objection in a letter to North American church contacts that the MPLA was Moscow-oriented and dominated by the Kimbundu while GRAE was Western-supported and predominantly Bakongo. What was needed, he felt, was a third movement based inside the country and representative of the majority.

Savimbi completed his studies at the University of Lausanne and then moved to Lusaka, where he made contact with exiled Ovimbundu and Chokwe compatriots from eastern and southern Angola. They decided to form a new political organization, the National Union for the Total Independence of Angola (UNITA). The organizing conference was held in Moxico in March 1966.

Savimbi traveled widely to win support for the new party. He went to Egypt, Tanzania, and Algeria. He also went to East Germany, Czechoslovakia, Hungary, and the Soviet Union, but these countries were supporting the MPLA and were not prepared to take on a new movement. In North Korea and China he met both Mao Zedong and Zhou Enlai, who offered scholarships for military training. On his return to Angola in late 1966 he was elected president of UNITA.

UNITA's first serious military action, on Christmas Day, 1966, was an attack on the eastern town of Teixeira de Sousa, including the Benguela railroad. Disrupting the railroad was a sensitive undertaking because Zambia, which was dependent on the railroad for exporting its mineral produce, as was Zaire, had warned the Angolan movements not to attack it. Savimbi immediately sent messengers telling UNITA commanders not to sabotage the railroad, but it took them a month to get through on foot, and the line was severed again before the orders arrived. Savimbi was in Baghdad in June 1967 when he heard by radio that the railroad had been blown up yet again. Hastily he returned to Zambia for discussions but was arrested and deported to Tanzania. He said in an interview, "Since I was deported from Zambia, I think this was the dark day of UNITA."

Savimbi decided to return to Angola and work from within. From mid-1968 into the 1970s, communications from him were addressed "Free Land of Angola." UNITA claimed to be working from Moxico, Cuando Cubango, and Lunda in the east to Bié, Malange, Huambo, and Cunene in the center and south. The constant theme of all their publications and speeches was that the organization was entirely inside Angola. This was mostly making a virtue of necessity; the movement was never recognized by the OAU. It did, however, have representatives in London, Geneva, and Cairo and unofficially in Lusaka.

THREE LIBERATION MOVEMENTS

All three movements separately yet somewhat effectively carried on their struggle against Portuguese colonialism.* An indication of their effectiveness was the increase in Portuguese military activity and expenditures

---

*Many journalists and political supporters of one movement or another traveled to Angola's maquis and testified to a wide range of guerrilla activities. Among them were Pierre Pascal Rossi (Switzerland), Don Barnett and Roy Harvey (USA) in 1968, Steve Valentine and Michael Marshment (Britain) in 1969, Fritz Sitte (Austria) in 1969 and 1971, Basil Davidson (Britain), Jean Jacques DuPont and Philip Latelier (France) 1970, Leon Dash (USA), Bernard Rivers (Britain), 1973.

to combat the insurgency. In the late 1960s and early 1970s Portugal was spending almost 50 percent of its national budget on the wars in Africa (including Mozambique and Guinea-Bissau), about $300,000 a day. There were about 160,000 Portuguese troops in Africa, almost half of them in Angola. Proportionally Portugal had three times as many troops in Africa as the United States had in Vietnam.[9]

Using classical counterinsurgency tactics, the Portuguese defended their militarized bases. Patrols into the countryside engaged guerrilla forces. Villages suspected of supporting guerrilla operations were burned to the ground or otherwise destroyed. Planes and helicopters shot and bombed, and crops were destroyed with herbicides.

The heart of the Portuguese protective security system in the war zones was the establishment of fortified villages, or *aldeamentos* (literally "new villages"). Under this program, dispersed groups of Africans were gathered together in larger villages along the roads patrolled by the Portuguese military. All the gardens and livestock were kept within a reasonable distance, and each family built its own hut within the village compound, where it had to sleep every night. Each village had its own militia and was required to report any strangers in the area. By November 1968, it was estimated that 70 percent of the Africans in the Lunda and Moxico districts were living in these new villages. The program did not, however, stop the incursion of Angolan nationalists. Furthermore, it did great damage to the economy since it uprooted the people from the fields they had tilled for many years and made it hard for fishermen to reach their fishing places and still return to the villages by night.

By the start of the 13th year of war in 1974, there was no end in sight. Neither the Portuguese nor the liberation movements were winning. The weapons of the three liberation movements were improving. There were more than 20,000 in their forces—estimated at 10,000 for the FNLA, 7,000 for the MPLA, and 4,000 for UNITA.[10] By 1973, all but four of the districts had seen military action.

In 1968 Roberto testified before the UN Decolonization Committee that GRAE controlled one fifth of the country. The MPLA claimed to be fighting in 10 of the 15 districts of Angola and to have some control in a third of the country. UNITA's claims were more modest. A Zambian journalist spoke of UNITA as the "Cinderella movement" of Angola in that it was so limited in supplies and equipment.

With varying degrees of success, each movement established schools and medical programs either inside Angola or in area just beyond the border.

THE FNLA PROGRAMS

I was most familiar with FNLA facilities in Zaire because I saw them at close hand. The SARA medical clinic was always congested as long as headquarters was at the FNLA compound in Kinshasa. In 1968, however, a tremendous improvement was made when GRAE purchased 20 acres of land some 25 miles outside Kinshasa. I visited there several times. About 700 people were living there in 1970, but they had increased to 2,000 three years later. A village had been built around the original dwelling, which had been converted into a hospital. In 1973 there were two doctors and 28 beds, which were usually filled with wounded from the front, expectant mothers, or postsurgical patients. The nurses had been trained in Tunisia, India, or Israel.

The nonmedical people built village-style huts and grew manioc and peanuts. A generator supplied electricity. A transmitter, which operated only at night, kept the establishment in touch with headquarters in Kinshasa and the military camps. The FNLA's preferred position in Zaire was obviously of great benefit.

Education was a major problem as floods of refugees came to Zaire. Many children were able to attend Zairian schools, but there was a language problem because the lingua franca in Zaire was French and in Angola, Portuguese. In 1964 GRAE gave up the Portuguese system and adjusted to that of Zaire, including creating a school system through the eighth grade. The education program was organized by Emmanuel Kunzika. It gave him some leeway for his own ideas, free from Roberto's constant control.

THE MPLA PROGRAMS

The MPLA carried on its external medical program from Congo-Brazzaville and Zambia. In Dolisie, near the Cabinda border, there was a hospital with only 12 beds. Another was being built at Sikongo in western Zambia. There was also a network of local clinics and dispensaries.

The MPLA had 40 primary schools in its semiliberated areas with more than 3,000 pupils in 1971. There were secondary schools at Dolisie and in the Sikongo-Kassamba area. The MPLA was much more ideological in its education program than the other movements. It emphasized a several-months course of study in Centers for Revolutionary Instruction (CIR) established in eastern Angola soon after the front was opened in 1966.

The MPLA called itself socialist, but it had no party documents outlining a socialist or Marxist program. In a speech over Tanzanian radio Neto defined it as essentially ending exploitation: "We don't intend to allow either Angolans or foreigners to exploit others in our country."[11]

UNITA'S PROGRAMS

UNITA's medical program was quite limited. It had no doctors, one medical assistant at the base hospital, and only about 20 nurses, who had been trained either by the Portuguese or missionaries. There were five rudimentary hospitals in three districts. They had very little medicine and

performed amputations without anesthetic. According to UNITA statistics, 25,000 persons were treated in the six years from 1966 to 1972.

In UNITA areas there were 10 boarding schools with up to 150 students
in each. As with the other movements, the schools inside Angola (UNITA
had none outside) were protected from air attack by forests. They had
virtually no books. Adult literacy classes made use of old hymnals and
Bibles. Boards painted black were used as blackboards. A 1972 UNITA
publication reported that there were 12,000 children and adults in various
primary schools.

A CIA CONNECTION?

A persistant and vexatious rumor during my years of African work was
that the ACOA and I had been a conduit for U.S. government funds
through the CIA to Holden Roberto. I probably should have shrugged off
the rumor as an occupational hazard. It disturbed me, however, because
some of our supposed friends and organizational allies picked it up. The
rumor began in Leopoldville, where in the troubled environment in the
early 1960s rumors were rife. I was frequently in and out of the city, and
since I always spent some time with Roberto or at FNLA headquarters, it
was easy for false impressions to arise. In 1962 a Congo paper, *Courrier
d'Afrique* (February 5, 1962), reported that the ACOA was giving the UPA
substantial material and financial support from the U.S. government, on
condition that the UPA not ally itself with the MPLA, "which American
circles accuse of being pro-communist." This information was prefaced by
the phrase "if one believes numerous bits of gossip in circulation." To my
great chagrin, the rumor tended to become fact in the minds of some. It
was repeated in enough places so that over a period of time it could be
footnoted from diverse sources. The Portuguese government, in an official
1973 publication entitled *Portuguese Africa*, even gave us credit for creating
GRAE. "The first of these three [GRAE] was created by the American
Committee on Africa to forestall the second [MPLA] which is inspired and
aided by communist powers."

Particularly disturbing was a 1969 pamphlet published by the Angola
Committee of Holland entitled *Portugal and NATO*, which reported: "A
stop was put to the use of public funds by the American Committee on
Africa for work in Angola. An agent of the Portuguese secret police had
discovered that Roberto Holden's Angola independence movement,
GRAE, was supported with money from the American taxpayers via this
committee." I corresponded with Dr. E.J. Bosgra, one of the authors of
their pamphlet, and subsequently met him at a conference on the Struggle
Against Portuguese Colonialism in Rome in June 1970. He thought the
information was reliable because it came from a Social Democratic source
in West Germany. Nevertheless, the sentences were deleted from later
reprints of the pamphlet.

I was not surprised that the MPLA picked up the rumor. After all, it helped its cause politically to have "proof" that the FNLA was a tool of the CIA. My long association with Roberto plus the spread of this rumor made the MPLA regard me and the ACOA with suspicion. To counter it, in May 1969 when I was in Dar es Salaam I went to the MPLA office to talk with Neto and a key lieutenant, Daniel Chipenda. I told them that originally I had supported Roberto's movement as the only viable approach to the Angolan struggle. I said the ACOA supported the struggle, was not committed to any organization, and certainly was no conduit for the CIA. Whatever the long-range effect of this statement, at least it broke the ice. In a memorandum for limited distribution I wrote: "How could I fool my close associates" if I had been an instrument of the CIA? "I would have to be either a very successful Jekyll-Hyde character or an amazingly adroit Scarlet Pimpernel. . . . I wouldn't have lasted a moment [as director of the ACOA] if I was suspected of this kind of double dealing."

The question of which Angolan movement the ACOA should assist had been no problem in the early days. The UPA-FNLA-GRAE were uncontested in their superiority. By and large we followed the OAU policy—supporting those movements it recognized and aided. UNITA was never recognized. But the MPLA gradually gained in strength after 1966, complications plagued GRAE, and many of my colleagues became dissatisfied with the FNLA. I myself had come to the conclusion that Roberto could not lead the country to independence. I admired his courage; up to 1974 he drove round Kinshasa in his own car without a bodyguard despite his many enemies. As late as 1973 he had driven me to his home, several miles from headquarters, with no security, although his office and house were guarded. Yet he was not a charismatic leader or a man of the people. He did not visit his troops or the villages inside Angola. He worked through his aides, whom he could dominate, but suspected potential leaders who could challenge him. He could not unify varied ethnic and racial groups.

In spring 1969, at a special policy meeting, the ACOA agreed to recognize the "primacy of the MPLA." We would not cease all contact with the FNLA or UNITA, but we recognized the MPLA as having the initiative and the greatest potential for leadership of an independent Angola.

THE CONTINUING PROBLEM OF UNITY

The liberation struggle was plagued by disunity among movements and within them.

The OAU constantly emphasized the theme of unity among liberation movements in Angola. In 1971 another attempt at unity was made. The OAU set up a Commission of Conciliation, which was to report at its annual conference in Rabat, Morocco, June 1972. Attending this conference, I learned that Neto and Roberto were then meeting in Brazzaville. As I continued my journey south, I hoped to see them in Brazzaville, but they had already left for Rabat to give concrete evidence of the steps toward unity. I was later told that (with some embarrassment) they even embraced in front of the conference.

DISUNITY AMONG MOVEMENTS

The formal agreement of unity, the "Angolan Liberation Movements Re-Conciliation Agreement," was signed six months later in Kinshasa. It established a Supreme Council for the Liberation of Angola and two subordinate councils, one military and one political, with equal representation on each. Each side agreed to the "establishment of a climate of peace and fraternity. . . , the immediate cessation of all acts of hostility and of all attacks by radio, press and television."

Each side made some attempt to be faithful to the agreement. An MPLA representative was suspended for distributing a leaflet attacking the FNLA at a conference in Oslo in April 1973. At the July Pan-African Youth Festival in Tunis, the two movements marched together in the parade. In Kinshasa at about that time I noted that the terminology of a government in exile, including the name GRAE, was not in evidence and the FNLA called its functional units departments instead of ministries.

Yet by 1974, there was still no real substance to the agreement. None of the three councils had met. After I talked with Roberto in mid-1973 in Kinshasa, my impression was that the agreement could not work. The suspicions were too great. Neither side wanted to divulge its military strength or areas of control. Neto told me in Lusaka in October 1974 that the agreement with Roberto was dead.

DISUNITY WITHIN MOVEMENTS.

In the meantime, each movement had its own problem of internal unity. An attempted insurrection at the FNLA military base at Kinkuzu threatened Roberto's leadership. Twenty-two of the 33 military leaders signed a letter to Roberto complaining that the base was too small and food and clothing inadequate and threatening to take further steps if something was not done.

Roberto met with the leaders at the base. The problems were not resolved, but provision for future meetings was agreed upon. An eyewitness told me what happened as Roberto was leaving. The officer who had instigated the complaint refused to open the gate and then ordered some soldiers to shoot Roberto. Showing great courage, Roberto got out of his car and confronted the soldiers, who ran away, one of them even giving Roberto his gun. The gate was opened and Roberto left.

Subsequently fighting broke out between officers and troops loyal to Roberto and those who chose to rebel. Mobutu sent an armored battalion and a parachute battalion from Zaire to take over the base. They prevailed, with considerable loss of life among the Angolans, and the camp was turned back to the FNLA in a public ceremony.

This episode had extensive repercussions. Thirteen officers were tried, found guilty, and shot. At the political level, the GRAE minister of defense was demoted. Kunzika and other PDA leaders were expelled for suspected complicity. Organization was tightened. The PDA was in effect liquidated.

The MPLA was also threatened by splits in its ranks, especially in 1974 after the coup in Portugal, just when the three rival movements needed their full strength. Neto's leadership was challenged by two factions. One, the Revolt of the East, was led by his long-time lieutenant, Chipenda, who had played an important role when the MPLA's eastern front was opened. It had a following of about 3,000 guerrillas, largely from the Chokwe of the east. The other, the Active Revolt, was based in Brazzaville, led by Mario de Andrade and later his brother, Father Jaoquim Pinto de Andrade, who had been released after 14 years in a Portuguese prison.

Strenuous efforts were made by the OAU Conciliation Commission to heal this three-way breach, but a congress in Lusaka in early August fell apart when the Neto and deAndrade delegations separately walked out. An attempted reconciliation failed and Chipenda opened up an office in Kinshasa in a cooperation with the FNLA.

When I was in Africa in late October 1974, I saw both Neto and Chipenda. In Dar es Salaam Neto was more open and friendly than I had ever seen him. Behind locked doors we discussed Chipenda, who had been with us at our previous conference. According to Neto the split had occurred because of a power struggle—Chipenda wanted to be president. Neto affirmed that all agreements with the FNLA or Chipenda's faction of the MPLA were dead. Yet he hoped for some kind of joint discussions with the new Portuguese government in Lisbon.

In Kinshasa in his new office Chipenda talked in much more detail about his differences with Neto, about the cleavages between the people of the east and those from the Kimbundu region, about Neto's delay in calling an MPLA congress, about his unavailability (on account of travel) for discussion of crucial strategy, and about his making critical decisions unilaterally. Chipenda had good relations with Mobutu, who was giving him material support. He was optimistic that he, Roberto, and Savimbi would be able to agree on a basis for negotiating with the Portuguese that would leave Neto out in the cold. This seemed to me an unjustified conclusion, given Neto's strength in Luanda and his support from both Communists and Socialists in Lisbon and from the Soviet Union.

THE MILITARY COUP IN PORTUGAL AND THE AFRICAN RESPONSE

On April 24, 1974, I lunched in New York with an old friend, Ruth First. She was a white South African who had been writing on South African issues from exile in London. She was known as a brilliant and active opponent of apartheid. I knew she had been a leader in the banned South African Communist party. I shared the high respect in which she was generally held. We discussed at length Portugal and its African wars. In spite of liberation advances in Angola, Guinea-Bissau, and Mozambique, no military victory was in sight. We agreed that the struggle was to be protracted.*

What poor prophets we were. The very next day came the astounding news of the military revolt in Portugal overthrowing the regime of Marcello Caetano. The signs of decay in the regime, however, had been obvious. There was serious opposition in Portugal to the African wars, not unlike the widespread opposition among Americans to the Vietnam War. Military casualties had already reached 40,000 dead and wounded. Some 100,000 draft resisters had fled the country. Sabotage by antiwar groups was on the increase. In addition, faced with a deteriorating economy and the highest inflation in Europe, more than 1.5 million Portuguese had left the country to find jobs elsewhere.

In February 1974, General Antonio de Spinola, a military hero and governor of Guinea-Bissau, published a book, *Portugal and the Future,* which took the forthright position that Portugal could not win a military victory in Africa. The book reinforced opposition to the African wars. Thus the coup, when it came, was virtually bloodless. The overthrown leaders were exiled to Madeira and then to Brazil. The new military government set about negotiating an end to Portuguese expeditions in Africa.

For the Africans, the coup meant the beginning of the end of fighting against a European force. It also meant a critical point had been reached for the movements struggling for power in revolutionary African countries. In Angola with three contending movements, the situation was particularly serious.

In November, I spent some time at the FNLA office in Kinshasa. The atmosphere was now very tight. A high wall guarded by soldiers surrounded the premises. This time I had difficulty gaining admittance. A soldier through a peephole in the solid gate asked me for identification. With the language barrier and a closed gate, this was not easy. Finally an old friend came along and vouched for me. Roberto was very much preoccupied. He greeted me briefly and asked me to return two hours later. I never saw him again. He went to the airport to see off the representatives to his newly opened headquarters in Luanda, where the FNLA had moved more than a hundred of its people.

The MPLA and UNITA opened offices in Luanda too, but the FNLA appeared to be in a strong position with a large military establishment, Chinese military instructors, financial and logistical backing from Mobutu, half a million Angolan refugees in Zaire to call upon, and access to the long border with Zaire. The final stage in the power struggle was about to begin.

*Eight years later, in 1982, Ruth First was tragically killed by a parcel bomb sent from South Africa that exploded in her faculty office at Eduardo Mondlane University in Mozambique.

CHAPTER FOURTEEN

Mozambique:
A Dream the Size of Freedom

> How can we tell you the size
> of our dream?
>
> During centuries
> we waited
> that a Messiah might free
> us . . .
> Until we understood.
> Today
> our Revolution
> is a great flower
> to which each day
> new petals are added.
>
> The petals are the land
> reconquered,
> the people freed,
> the fields cultivated,
> schools and hospitals.
>
> Our Dream has the size
> of Freedom.
> —FRELIMO

EDUARDO MONDLANE

No struggle for freedom from colonial domination had more idealism, optimism, and hope for a radical change in the way of life than that in Mozambique. The 1969 greeting card from the Front for the Liberation of Mozambique (FRELIMO), which opens this chapter, caught this spirit. I was one of many in Africa and around the world who looked to Mozambique with particular hope and faith. Although many Mozambicans contributed to the special glow of their country's struggle, none did so more than the first president of FRELIMO, Eduardo Chivambo Mondlane.

Mondlane was 32 when I met him in September 1951. We were at a conference site along Lake Erie near Oberlin College, where Mondlane had just come to finish his studies. He was very dark, quite tall, with thinning hair. Outgoing, exuberant, with a booming voice, he had a presence no one could miss. Over the next few years I heard about him from time to time as a most unusual and talented African who was bound to have a leadership position some day. I developed a friendship with him in the late 1950s, while he was a researcher at the UN, where I also spent much time. Yet I never fully appreciated his remarkable life until I visited his home in Mozambique years later in 1975. By then his country was newly independent, and he had been dead, by assassination, six years. So my visit was filled with bitter-sweet memories of this man who played such an essential role in the Mozambican struggle.

Mondlane was born in Gaza Province in southern Mozambique about 10 miles from Manjacaze, the provincial capital. I was driven by FRELIMO friends to his home area, Nwajdahane, starting out in a Mercedes and then changing to a Land Rover, for reasons that soon became clear. When we turned off the main highway for the Mondlane place, the road became what looked like a cowpath in the bush. It was slow going, but I had a chance to see the countryside from which Mondlane had emerged. We drove past homesteads consisting of collections of round huts, each with a cultivated area for small-scale farming. Usually a few farm animals and chickens were in evidence. Occasionally there would be a well from which women or children were drawing water in buckets let down by a long rope. The area was flat, dusty, and sandy. When we finally arrived, it was just another homestead with three huts, two for sleeping and one for cooking.

The only unusual structure in the compound was the half-constructed shell of a fairly large rectangular building for his family, for which Mondlane had provided funds on a visit in 1961. Since the secret police had stopped the construction, it was still standing unfinished and unusable. In the pitiful garden area, some maize was struggling to grow through the dusty soil. I saw a few chickens and ducks but no cattle. There were perhaps a dozen to 15 people around, mostly children and older women. The senior person was Paulina Mondlane, Eduardo's niece. Her youngest child, who looked about 9 or 10, was also named Eduardo Chivambo Mondlane. He was neatly dressed, having just returned from his twice-daily 10-mile walk to school in Manjacaze.

Fifty yards from the living area was a small, fenced-in graveyard. Posts marked the graves—one for Eduardo's father and close by one for his mother, his father's third wife. Other relatives were all buried in this plot, each post indicating the relationship to Eduardo Mondlane, "the first president of FRELIMO."

Now that I could see the humble circumstances of his origin, I was all the more amazed at the rise of such an unusual person. Until he was 10, he herded cattle, sheep, and goats. Then he went to government and mission schools, receiving his primary school certificate, the highest degree then available to an African in Mozambique, in Lourenço Marques (now Maputo). With missionary aid he took a course in farming, which he subsequently taught in Gaza. At 24, again through church sponsorship, he won a scholarship to a secondary school in South Africa. Then he studied at the Jan Hofmeyer School for Social Work in Johannesburg. He entered Witwatersrand University in 1948, when the National Party came to power and instituted apartheid. One of the few nonwhite students, he became an obvious target because of his popularity and outspoken leadership. He was expelled from the country in 1949.

Back in Mozambique, Mondlane's troubles continued as he helped organize the National Union of Mozambican Students. Since the government was suspicious of this organization, he was picked up by the authorities for questioning that lasted three days and nights and thereafter was put under surveillance. To avoid this and to advance his education, he decided to study at the University of Lisbon. The Portuguese government was agreeable because they wanted him out of Mozambique. During his year in Portugal he met future leaders from other Portuguese colonies, such as Agostinho Neto, Amilcar Cabral, and Mario de Andrade. But harassment by the secret police—regular monthly ransacking of his room and constant surveillance—made him decide to transfer to the United States. He received a scholarship from the Phelps Stokes Fund to attend Oberlin College. After graduating in 1953, he studied at Northwestern University and Harvard, and in 1960 took a Ph.D. at Northwestern, where he worked under the noted anthropologist and Africanist Melville J. Herskovits. By this time he was doing research for the Trusteeship Division of the UN.

From our first lengthy talks at the UN, it was clear to me that Mondlane never lost his obsession with returning home to take part in the liberation struggle. In a sense, he was marking time in the United States waiting for the right moment to return to Africa. Yet he conscientiously undertook the tasks before him and followed the rules for an international civil servant. He did a lot of speaking, some of which the ACOA arranged. Unfailingly he would tell me first to clear his engagements with his department head.

Mondlane was fortunate in his marriage. He met Janet Rae Johnson when he was a workshop leader at a 1951 summer Christian youth conference. She was an idealistic high school participant with an ambition to be a missionary in Africa. Thus a relationship began that lasted until his death. Her white, middle-class family in Indianapolis was strongly opposed to an interracial marriage. It took many years of determined effort by both Eduardo and Janet to reach a reconciliation with them. Their success is itself a comment on their character. They were married in 1956. Over the years I came to know Janet and to admire her great commitment and strength. She became not only a partner to Eduardo but a comrade in the liberation struggle.

The year 1961 was critical for Mondlane. His chance to return to Africa came when he was sent with a UN team to supervise a plebiscite in the Cameroons. Afterward he extended his time in Africa to visit Mozambique with Janet, who had preceded him. A Lourenço Marques newspaper reported his return, and he also wrote a report, not for publication, of this trip. Hundreds of people came to see him singly or in small groups, to discuss many issues. Every time he appeared in the streets or after church, he attracted large crowds. Africans accosted him to ask advice on how to leave the country to join nationalists organizing against the Portuguese. He answered carefully, knowing that some such requests were government inspired. Some of his former schoolmates were in prison. The secret police spied on him to find out who was visiting him, especially at night.

Mondlane returned to New York from this momentous experience exuberant about the possibilities of launching a successful campaign in Africa and playing a special role in it. The Portuguese, aware of his potential as a nationalist leader, kept an eye on him at the UN. I recall stopping at his office one day just as two men were leaving. With a quiet laugh Mondlane explained that they had just offered him a teaching post in Portugal. "I told them I was not ready to change positions yet. They keep an eye on me all the time. I have been offered many jobs. I just keep them guessing, but maintain cordiality. They don't want me back in Mozambique."

In the summer of 1961 Mondlane became a lecturer in anthropology at Syracuse University to free himself from the strictures of being an international civil servant. He could now more easily keep in touch with newly forming groups in East Africa.

ORGANIZATION OF POLITICAL GROUPS

Through Eduardo Mondlane and other friends and contacts and visits to Dar es Salaam, I began to learn about the new anticolonial groups being organized in Mozambique.

MANU

One group was formed by some northern Mozambicans who had taken jobs in Tanganyika. They were Makondes, who lived on both sides of the Mozambican-Tanganyikan border and were skilled wood carvers. In Tanganyika they organized the Mozambique African National Union (MANU) in 1960. Their president, Matthew Mmole, and their secretary general, L. Mallinga Millinga, wrote me occasionally until I finally met them in Dar es Salaam in 1962. They hoped the ACOA could finance and sponsor the visit of a delegation to the UN, where they could present their grievances. They claimed that MANU had some 2,000 members drawn from the 60,000 Mozambicans working on the plantations and in the port cities of British East Africa. Although they were interesting to meet, I felt their base was much too narrow to lead the struggle for independence.

UDENAMO

I had told a black American friend, Joe Ridgeway, a merchant seaman with an intense interest in Africa, of my contacts with MANU. In the fall of 1961, when his ship stopped in Dar es Salaam, he dropped by its office.

He did not think much of Mmole, Millinga, or MANU, but he was impressed by Jaime Rivaz Sigauke, who ran an office for the Democratic National Union of Mozambique (UDENAMO), a newly formed nationalist movement of Mozambicans from farther south.

UDENAMO had been organized in Salisbury, Southern Rhodesia. Its president, Adelino Gwambe, had originally been sent by the Portuguese secret police to Salisbury to spy on his fellow Mozambicans. But once there, he shifted his loyalty and joined them. The secretary was Uria Simango, a Protestant missionary from Beira who worked among Mozambicans in Southern Rhodesia. He helped to organize the Mozambican Burial Society, an outwardly cultural and self-help organization that served as a convenient front for political activity. Simango, whom I came to know in Dar es Salaam, told me they had 5,000 to 6,000 members who paid for burial insurance. About 250 formed the political underground, which met weekly. He had met Mondlane in 1961 in Mozambique and had fled to Dar es Salaam in 1962 to escape arrest when his underground activities were discovered by the Portuguese.

UNAMI

J.B.C. Chagonga, a former member of the Mozambique medical department, wrote me from Dar es Salaam about a third group. During his 30 years' service his duties had taken him to the major towns around the country, where he had been disturbed by bad conditions. As he developed anticolonialist ideas, he felt unsafe in Mozambique and left the country. In Nyasaland he met Dr. Kamuzu Banda, who had introduced him to me in a letter, and established the African National Union of Independent Mozambique (UNAMI). Its constituency was essentially Mozambicans from Tete Province, his own home area, which bordered Nyasaland. Still feeling unsafe, he fled to Tanganyika. He wrote me hoping we could supply a ticket for him to come to the UN.

I discussed my correspondence and contacts with the three organizations with Mondlane. He felt they were complementary—one representing peasants of northern Mozambique working mainly in Tanganyika, one representing urban elements from central and southern Mozambique, and the third representing Tete people, many of them in Nyasaland. This approach was typical of Mondlane. Neither overly critical nor a joiner, he tried to work with all elements and merge them into a working whole.

FRELIMO

FRELIMO, one of the few successful efforts to form a front of competing nationalist groups, was organized at a conference in Dar es Salaam June 25, 1962. Mondlane, in New York, was kept informed of the preliminary meeting. He passed on his inner excitement to me. He was invited to the June conference, where he was elected president with 95 percent of the

vote. Back in New York he informed me with his characteristic enthusiasm that the first Congress of FRELIMO would be held without delay.

The Congress was held in late September in Dar es Salaam. Eighty delegates were chosen from organized elements sympathetic to FRELIMO's cause, and there were more than 500 observers. FRELIMO's purpose was "to promote the efficient organization of the struggle of the Mozambican people for national liberation." Plans were made to set up an underground organization inside Mozambique and seek the cooperation of trade unions, students, youth, and women's organizations in the struggle. A Central Committee was chosen. The way was paved for the next phase of the struggle.

EARLY PROTEST AND DISSENSION

FRELIMO's aim was to overthrow the four-century-old exploitive system of Portuguese control. In our many talks, Mondlane had given me some insight into the injustices that motivated the Mozambican struggle.[1] Early Portuguese enterprises had inaugurated a commerical system of barter, mostly in gold and ivory from a few centers along the 1,700-mile coast, which developed into a grab for land. A major center was the island of Mozambique, from which the country took its name. Settlers seized great tracts particularly along the Zambesi River. From this practice sprang the *prazo*, or plantation system, in which the lord of the estate controlled the labor of all those on his land. Slave labor, contract labor, and a compulsory crop-raising system derived from the *prazo*. Some 10,000 to 25,000 slaves were exported annually, the trade continuing even after slavery was outlawed in 1836. Mondlane emphasized that the principal legacy of Portuguese colonialism in Mozambique was labor exploitation, just as it was in Angola.

Mondlane was particularly aroused against Portugal's pretense that it was constructing a nonracial society. Theoretically any nonwhite could become an *assimilado* ("assimilated person") by patterning his life after the Portuguese, but only about 1 percent of Mozambican Africans achieved this status. The most the *assimilado* system did was to create a few "honorary whites."

Mondlane also talked with me about the long tradition of anticolonial protest in Mozambique; the sporadic revolts in the 19th and early 20th centuries; and the variety of organizations that were formed, especially among the educated elite, to give voice to dissatisfactions. We talked about the important role of the urban labor force, such as striking the docks in Lourenço Marques in 1947, again in 1956 when 49 strikers were killed, and in 1963 in Beira and Nacala. Protests took place in small towns too, strengthening the spirit of revolt, notably in Mueda on June 16, 1960, when 600 people were mowed down by gun fire for daring to protest to the Portuguese administrator against conditions.

External factors also contributed to the successful organization of FRELIMO: the large number of Mozambicans living in bordering countries, the phenomenal growth of Pan-Africanism in the 1950s, and Tanganyika's imminent independence with Nyerere strongly supporting a unified Mozambican movement.

FRELIMO early decided to set up an education program. Janet Mondlane told me that on Eduardo's 1961 visit to Mozambique so many people had asked them for scholarships or other aid that they knew some kind of program would have to be established. Mondlane approached the Ford Foundation in New York and received $100,000. With this money the Mozambique Institute was set up in 1963 as an extension of FRELIMO but with its own separate budget and board of trustees. It built a secondary school in Dar es Salaam attended by Mozambican refugees. Gradually its work was coordinated with the various departments of FRELIMO—education, health, information, and foreign affairs. Other organizations and individuals could contribute directly to these programs without endorsing all FRELIMO's political and military projects.

The Ford grant became a bone of contention within the Ford Foundation. The Portuguese foreign minister attacked the foundation for allegedly financing FRELIMO. This was enough to cancel any plans for further foundation contributions. According to the *New York Times* (December 21, 1964), "The Ford Foundation is reported to have assured the government of Premier Salazar that it would be consulted before any future grants were given to African areas of particular interest in Portugal."

FRELIMO's direct military preparations began in January 1963, when 50 Mozambicans went to Algeria for training.* Two more groups of 70 each followed. Samora Machel, the first president of Mozambique, was

---

*The first Mozambicans to receive military training went before FRELIMO was formed. Under the aegis of UDENAMO, Gwambe had arranged with Kwame Nkrumah for a few Mozambicans to train in Ghana in early 1962.

part of the third group. When the men returned from Algeria in 1963–1964, they received further training at the first FRELIMO military camp in Tanganyika, at Bagamoyo, an historically important village set with palms on the Indian Ocean about 40 miles north of Dar es Salaam. They also helped train others. In little more than a year, some of these soldiers began infiltrating into Mozambique to establish bases and stock pile arms and ammunition. Bagamoyo, which I visited many times, later became the site of the Mozambique Institute's secondary school.

In its early years, FRELIMO found it hard going. There were strains and stresses as previously separated organizations were drawn together in a united front. When Mondlane, immediately after FRELIMO's formation, returned to Syracuse University to finish his teaching assignment, problems arose. To enhance his own position, Leo Milas, FRELIMO's publicity secretary, who had been left in charge of certain aspects of the work, contrived not only to expel David Mabunda, secretary general, and Paulo Gumane, his deputy, but to have them deported from Tanganyika. His weapon was a letter naming them as Portuguese agents, a letter, which, it was later discovered, he had not "found" but had himself forged.

Later Mondlane personally investigated Milas's background and discovered that he was an Afro-American from California masquerading as a Mozambican. But the damage had been done. Gumane and Mabunda proceeded to Cairo, where they reconstituted UDENAMO. Mondlane returned to Africa from Syracuse in 1963, went to Cairo to appeal to the dissidents to return, but failed. FRELIMO did not suffer unduly, however, since Cairo was far removed from Mozambique and potential UDENAMO supporters in East Africa. Later Gumane became president of a potential rival organization, the Mozambique Revolutionary Committee (COREMO), with headquarters in Lusaka.

BEGINNING OF THE WAR FOR LIBERATION

In mid-October 1964, on a plane from Cairo to Nairobi, to my great pleasure, I met Eduardo Mondlane. We sat together and talked all the way. I remember three things about our conversation. One, an incidental item, was that on his visit to East Germany, he had been given several hundred cameras for FRELIMO's use. When he asked me whether the ACOA would be able to contribute a Land Rover to the Mozambique Institute, I said yes and added jokingly, "In exchange, can you save one of the cameras for us?" It was agreed, with a laugh.

A second point referred to his own personal security. Three young men guarded the house where he and his family lived. Matter-of-factly he said, "There is always the possibility of assassination." He felt safest traveling in Eastern Europe because it would be more difficult for the Portuguese to hire someone to kill him there.

The third point was the most pressing—FRELIMO had begun the

armed struggle. I had seen only brief news items about it. He filled me in. It was only the beginning, he explained. It would be a protracted struggle, but with his usual optimism, he added, "We will be victorious." He and others were convinced of the inevitability of armed struggle. Janet had written me (February 26, 1964): "Somewhere at the back of my head I had hoped that [war] wouldn't be necessary, but Portugal doesn't learn a stitch of a lesson from her other colonies [the Angolan and Guinea-Bissau armed struggles were already in progress], so wars in other territories don't help to get independence peacefully for Mozambique."

The outbreak of hostilities had been set for September 25, Mondlane told me. There were only about 250 trained men, although the military force grew rapidly—2,000 by 1965, 8,000 by 1967, and 12,000 by 1974, with twice that many in village militias. At first, action was concentrated in the northern provinces of Cabo Delgado and Niassa.

The Portuguese, unlike in Angola, were not entirely unprepared. They evacuated the people from the Ruvuma River area on the Tanzanian border, constructed air strips in the far north, and set up *aldeamentos*. Thousands of Mozambicans streamed into southern Tanzania as the Portuguese burned villages in the war zone in reprisal.

A series of articles in the conservative *Evening Standard* of London in 1965 by Lord Kilbracken attested to the seriousness and effectiveness of FRELIMO's campaign. Following a Portuguese-sponsored trip into the war zone of Niassa, he wrote, "The scale of fighting in this bitter, unsung war has steadily increased since the first minor incidents just a year ago. . . . In 3,000 terrorized square miles the Portuguese, both civil and military, are now confined to five small isolated garrisons." He had visited all five garrisons. He wrote of FRELIMO that they "are a tough and elusive enemy. They generally operate in very small units, often of only half a dozen men. . . . They are at home in the jungle and bush, where they live off the country, striking silently by night, withdrawing swiftly into the dense cover if the Portuguese reply in strength."

The war was expensive for the Portuguese. They had between 60,000 and 70,000 troops in Mozambique. Military expenditures were $195 million in 1963 and shot up to $217 million in 1968. Casualty figures were not reliable. Official Portuguese figures estimated losses in killed and wounded at approximately 4,000 in the first three years of the war. FRELIMO set the figure at more like 9,000.

By the end of 1965 FRELIMO controlled virtually all of Cabo Delgado and significant portions of Niassa, although its strategy was a holding action to allow time for additional troops to be trained. It confined itself to laying mines and setting ambushes. No great supply lines were necessary because the troops grew their own food and were supported by the local people.

The principal Portuguese response was aerial warfare. Civilians were the main victims, but crops, villages, schools, and clinics were bombed. This increased the flow of refugees north across the Ruvuma River, where the Tanzanian government and FRELIMO refugee services helped them.

In March 1968 FRELIMO decided to extend the war to Tete Province, farther south, bordering Malawi and Zambia. Tete, one of the richest provinces of Mozambique, had untapped mineral resources, abundant cattle, and important agricultural potential. It was looked upon as strategically important because it was the site of the large hydroelectric project at Cabora Bassa on the Zambezi River. Work began on the dam in 1969. It was to be a concrete wall 510 feet high and 1,000 feet across, which would form a 1,600-square-mile reservoir stretching all the way to the Zambian border in order to irrigate 3 million acres and provide electric power for South Africa. The project was funded by a consortium headed by South African entrepreneur Harry Oppenheimer. I visited it in 1975 when it was nearing completion. FRELIMO, however during the liberation war, had looked upon the dam as a threat. The overall Portuguese plan was to use the dam to encourage large-scale European immigration into the Zambezi Valley. FRELIMO did not plan a frontal attack on the dam, which would have been suicidal, but its ambushes and landmining were effective enough to delay construction. Samora Machel told me, "We'll eat away at the project, making it more expensive and taking longer to construct."

FRELIMO's problem was to establish a base from which to enter Tete. Mozambique is such a long, narrow country that it was not easy, with Tanzania as a base, to contemplate opening up a front in the central and southern provinces. To have men portaging military supplies on their heads for a thousand miles or so was almost impossible. South Africa and Rhodesia on the south and west were hardly sympathetic to FRELIMO. Theoretically, Malawi should have offered aid and sanctuary, but Banda did not. On a visit to the United States he told me he did not trust Mondlane, then still employed at the UN, because he understood Mondlane was talking with Portuguese officials, meaning that he was a possible sellout. Then Banda asked me to keep an eye on Mondlane and let him know if I noted anything suspicious.

I discussed Banda's surprising half-accusation with Mondlane, who in turn brought up Banda's ambition to reestablish a Greater Malawi. To that end he would have had to make a deal with the Portuguese who would cede to landlocked Malawi a portion of Mozambique in order to give Malawi a corridor to the Indian Ocean. When I reported to Banda, quite truthfully, that Mondlane's only talks with the Portuguese related to their efforts to induce him to pursue his vocation in Portugal, Banda let the matter drop, as far as I knew.

I had another indication of Banda's policy toward FRELIMO beginning with my arrival by air as a guest at Malawi's independence celebration in July 1964. Almost simultaneously another aircraft brought an official delegation of Portuguese guests, who were greeted on behalf of the soon-to-be-independent Malawi government by my old friend Kanyama Chiume, the foreign minister designate. Embarrassed, he explained, in answer to my whispered question, that the Portuguese were guests of the government.

Not long after, Banda sent Chiume on a trip to some African capitals to feel out such leaders as Julius Nyerere in Tanzania and Ahmed Ben Bella in Algeria on the idea of a Greater Malawi and the corridor to the sea. Later, after Chiume and other Malawi leaders had broken with Banda and fled the country, Chiume with his irrepressible humor described this strange trip. "Could you imagine me talking seriously with these African nationalist leaders, who had struggled against European domination so vigorously, about making a deal with Portugal?" He never brought up the subject in his discussions with them. Then he reported to Banda that the idea was not acceptable to African leaders.*

MONDLANE'S LEADERSHIP

During the early days of FRELIMO's conflict with Portugal, Eduardo Mondlane's leadership was critical. Not only was he personally committed, but he was a highly disciplined individual. In one of his many letters to Janet, which she occasionally shared with me, Eduardo described his early morning regimen. He rose at 6:45, ran to the beach for a swim, and then did some pushups and other exercises before taking another swim and shower. After a walk and breakfast, he was ready for the day's work. He maintained this kind of discipline even when traveling abroad.

Mondlane generally reflected an enthusiastic and positive attitude that affected those around him. He was ecstatic about the formative OAU conference in Addis Ababa in 1963, which he described in another letter to Janet. The Ethiopian emperor's opening address was "superb"; Balewa's [of Nigeria] the "most conservative"; Nkrumah's "the most forward-looking . . . most unlikely to be accepted by most statesmen present"; Nyerere's "the most pragmatic." He was enthusiastic about the many countries pledging 1 percent of their budgets to support the freedom fighters.

In yet another letter he described a trip to southern Tanzania, where he asked a responsive stadium crowd of a thousand Mozambicans to demonstrate their support by giving a shilling each. They collected 590 shillings on the spot, a tidy amount from displaced peasants and workers. "The people are really eager," he wrote.

At this time, Mondlane's personal ideology was nationalist and pragmatic with a socialist bias. He wrote to me about a trip to New York he planned for October 1963, asking the ACOA to help arrange some dates. In this letter (September 10, 1963) he gave vent to some of his negative feelings toward Holden Roberto, whom he nevertheless wanted to meet in New York, a "confrontation" he called it.

I heard that [Roberto] has asked UDENAMO people to accompany him in order to help him prove that FRELIMO was a Communist set-up. For your information, I'd like to state that FRELIMO is a purely Africanist party. It carries

---

*Chiume discusses Banda's policy toward Portugal in his *Kwacha: An Autobiography* (1975).

Eduardo Mondlane, president of FRELIMO, speaking to the people inside
Mozambique, 1968.
ACOA files.

no brief for either Western capitalists or Eastern communists. We, of course,
believe in socialism, but one type only typical to Africa, as exemplified by a
number of African states, e.g., Guinea, Tanganyika, Ghana, etc. I believe that all
African states will end up following some form of socialism or other.

I did arrange for the two to meet, but Roberto, after reluctantly agreeing,
failed to show up.

The relations of various African liberation movements toward one
another were affected by international alignments. This was no doubt a
factor in the Mondlane-Roberto problem. FRELIMO and the FNLA
were never organizationally aligned; the MPLA was FRELIMO's counterpart in Angola. When, in 1963, Cyril Adoula, as Congo prime minister,
hoped to establish a Liberation Center in Leopoldville, UDENAMO and
later COREMO were included rather than FRELIMO. These alignments
were a constant subject for discussion. In one conversation (May 1967),
Mondlane explained alignments in terms of the Soviet-Chinese cold war.
One group of movements leaned toward the Soviet Union, which sent
them significant military support. Another group tended towards China.
The Western governments were not much of a factor because no official
help came from them, although many Western organizations sent private
aid. The tendency toward alignments was codified at a conference in

Khartoum in 1968 sponsored by Soviet-aligned international organizations. The liberation movements invited were the so-called authentic six—the ANC in South Africa, Zimbabwe African People's Union (ZAPU), South West Africa People's Organization (SWAPO), African Party for the Independence of Guinea and Cape Verde (PAIGC), MPLA, and FRELIMO. Excluded as not "authentic" were the PAC of South Africa, Zimbabwe African National Union (ZANU), FNLA, COREMO, and other smaller movements from Namibia and Guinea-Bissau.

Mondlane attended the Khartoum conference of necessity. Most of the military hardware for FRELIMO came from Soviet-aligned countries. Nevertheless, he, more than any other liberation leader, did not cut himself off from any governments and organizations, East or West, that were willing to help. I heard a conversation between Roberto and Gumane in Kinshasa in which they credited Simango with having the Chinese connections and Marcelino dos Santos as having the Soviet connections. They claimed that Mondlane was a figurehead. He laughed at this when we talked about it. He had enemies, of course, but he had friends in the right places all over the world. The OAU recognized only FRELIMO, never COREMO. Both Nyerere and Kaunda told me that they supported FRELIMO. COREMO had an office in Lusaka but was never allowed to open one in Dar es Salaam.

Although the United States was looked upon as an ally of Portugal, Mondlane maintained friendly relations with Americans, such as Attorney General Robert Kennedy. As an academician, Mondlane was sought after in university circles. His 10 years in the United States had made him seem almost American. He was an avid sports fan, for example, and was always eager to know professional football scores.

I knew something of Mondlane's approach to the American scene. In 1967 the ACOA had agreed to try to raise funds to support the opening of a FRELIMO office in New York. Just about this time the exposé about the CIA using private American organizations as conduits hit the U.S. press. It did not affect the ACOA because we were never named, but I wrote to Mondlane asking if he felt the exposure should affect the timing of opening the FRELIMO office. He replied (April 10, 1967):

> If each time there is a scandal in any of the countries which support us, we stampeded out, the Portuguese government would conveniently arrange to create such commotion. . . . I believe the CIA scandal was an American tragedy, not ours. . . . It will not help anyone for Americans to warn everybody away from accepting any and all help from the U.S. for fear that they may be labeled as agents.

Both the FRELIMO military effort and the Mozambique Institute cost millions of dollars a year. Aid came from many sources. In the fund-raising effort one could see the practical value of Mondlane's cultivation of all sides on the international scene. Virtually all military aid, including not only weapons and armaments but also clothing, medicine, and food, came from socialist countries. Western European countries and North American humanitarian and religious organizations contributed educational and medical supplies. Both the People's Republic of China and the USSR gave material support. About 20 percent of FRELIMO's needs were met through the OAU and Tanzania, Egypt, Algeria, and Zambia. FRELIMO had offices in Dar es Salaam, Lusaka, Algiers, and Cairo and overseas in Moscow, Stockholm, and New York.

The ACOA was instrumental in opening the New York office and maintained a close connection with its head, Sharfudine Khan. We coordinated fund raising for this office among church agencies, trade unions, and individuals and, as promised, raised funds for a Land Rover. We shipped it to my friend Rashidi Kawawa, the second vice president of Tanzania, and thus avoided paying duty. Mondlane reported (January 26, 1966), "[The Land Rover] is already in service and tomorrow morning is going to start on its first long safari between Dar es Salaam and the southeastern part of Tanzania to pick up a number of refugees who are sick." On my next trip to Dar es Salaam in 1967, as I prepared to board the plane, Simango, who was seeing me off, thrust a camera into my hands. It was one of the East German cameras that Mondlane had told me about on that plane ride three years earlier. I had forgotten about our joking agreement, but he had remembered.

MONDLANE'S ASSASSINATION

FRELIMO had to face internal conflicts and tensions that might have doomed a less solidly based organization.One such test came in March 1968, when some students at the Mozambique Institute's secondary school at Kurasini in Dar es Salaam rebelled against FRELIMO's expectation that they would serve FRELIMO and Mozambique when called to do so. The dissension was fanned by Father Mateus Gwenjere, a Mozambican priest, who convinced some of the students that their education had prepared them for higher duties. Violence erupted and the school was closed for two and a half years before reopening in Bagamoyo.

Another test came when Lazaro Kavandame, an important leader in the cooperative FRELIMO People's Stores in Cabo Delgado, was discovered to be transferring some of the clothing earmarked for these stores, in which manufactured goods were bartered for farmers' produce, to his own stores, where sales benefitted only him. Following a decision of FRELIMO's Executive Committee, Mondlane wrote a letter expelling him from the movement. Subsequently Kavandame called upon the Makonde people to end their struggle against Portugal, and he himself defected to the Portuguese. The Portuguese played this up as evidence of a major split in FRELIMO, which was far from true.

Such signs of internal dissension were nothing compared to the crisis of Mondlane's assassination in Dar es Salaam on February 3, 1969. I received the shattering news by telephone. Mondlane had been alone about 11:20 A.M. opening his mail, as he sometimes did, at the home of a friend. A bomb placed in a package containing a book exploded, killing him immediately. Police investigation revealed that Portuguese secret police who had infiltrated FRELIMO had carried the package from Lourenço Marques to Tanzania and delivered it to the post office. There it was put in FRELIMO's private bag and taken to its office, where Mondlane picked it up on that fateful Monday morning.

Janet Mondlane, who was on a fund-raising mission in Europe, hurried back to Tanzania. Eduardo was buried with all the honor ordinarily paid a head of state. Later, on the anniversary of his death, FRELIMO made a simple statement: "The enemy hoped they could disorganize the liberation movement [by the assassination] and halt the struggle . . . but they failed."

A few weeks later Janet wrote me a moving letter (March 11, 1969).

In a most fundamental way life has changed for me since I saw you in New York. There are so many things I could say about myself since that catastrophic day when Eduardo was killed. But I can't say them now because I don't know how to say them. Somewhere inside, what must be said is waiting. I haven't quite found that part of me that has been lost in order to put it together. So many things have been

Eduardo and Janet Mondlane and daughter in Dar es Salaam, Tanzania, mid-1960s.

said over and over again in all parts of the world. He seemed to belong to so many others that have had the strength to describe what he was. I have benefitted from their ability to speak out what I could not. Perhaps some day in the future I shall speak too, but then it will perhaps be only for myself.

A leadership crisis ensued. A collective Council of the Presidency, formed of three leaders—Machel, Simango, and Dos Santos—was short-lived. Simango, the vice president, had assumed that he would automatically become president, but he lacked the leadership potential to pull together the elements that Mondlane had molded into a working whole. In November 1969 he issued a 13-page document, "Gloomy Situation in FRELIMO," outlining serious grievances against other leaders in the movement and airing internal disputes. For some reason he was particularly virulent in attacks on Janet Mondlane. In response to my questions, she wrote (December 10, 1969):

There is certainly nothing secret about events surrounding [Simango's] case. He himself made very sure of that, for instead of breathing a word to the Council of the Presidency of his complaints, or the Executive Committee, or to any other organ of FRELIMO for that matter, he literally distributed a libelous 13 page pamphlet throughout the world. I myself was included in his accusations saying, among other things, that I and nine other people planned the murder of Nungu [a FRELIMO leader] and made plans for the assassination of others. . . . Simango's big problem was that he did not succeed Mondlane in the Presidency and he just couldn't get over that hurdle.

At a meeting of the OAU Liberation Committee, Simango accused FRELIMO leaders of being imperialist agents. Consequently he was expelled from the party. Later he was ordered out of Tanzania and became secretary for international affairs for COREMO.

In May 1970 FRELIMO's Central Committee elected Machel president and Dos Santos, vice president. A month later I met Machel and from that and two lengthy subsequent meetings derived my impressions of him. Dark and heavily bearded, he seemed much taller than his five feet nine inches because he held himself so erect. He was impressive. Everything about him seemed dynamic—his ideas, his easy laughter and many gestures, his erect and rapid walking pace. He did not like to talk about himself. When I asked about his personal background, he responded, "That is not important. What is important is the movement!" "We have no Che's in FRELIMO," he said, referring to the Cuban Leader Che Guevara. "We don't believe in personality cult."

Like Mondlane, Samora Machel came from Gaza Province in southern Mozambique. He was born in 1933 in a peasant family. He had four years in a Catholic mission school and further training as a medical assistant. He was working in a hospital in Lourenço Marques in 1961, when he met Mondlane and became an early recruit to FRELIMO.

Machel had the reputation of being pragmatic. He was always on the move, especially in the liberated areas inside Mozambique. "My headquarters is in my pocket," he said. He greatly admired Mondlane, Nyerere,

Samora Machel (left), president of FRELIMO, and Joaquim Chissano (right), FRELIMO leader, in Dar es Salaam, Tanzania, 1972.

and Kaunda and appreciated a direct style. He said, "When I want to see someone, I don't want a bureaucracy to stand in my way to protect me."

EXPANDING EFFORTS

Under Machel's leadership the work of FRELIMO continued to expand. On my various visits I marveled at the growth of the Mozambique Institute, still headed by Janet Mondlane. It had headquarters in Dar es Salaam, a secondary school in Bagamoyo, a women's and children's center in Tunduru in southern Tanzania, and a hospital at Mtwara, also in the south.

The main objective was never lost sight of—preparing to go back to an independent Mozambique. At Bagamoyo, as I saw on my 1970 visit, they tried to approximate conditions in the bush inside Mozambique—a well with a pump instead of running water, no electricity, petrol lamps, outside privies, prefabricated dormitories, cooking done over an open fire—to make it easier to transport the school to Mozambique at the appropriate time. The students raised some of their own food. A year later they had more than 200 students with another hundred waiting to come. About 20 buildings were either constructed or in the process.

In Mtwara I had a good view of FRELIMO's new Americo Boavida hospital, named after the MPLA doctor killed in Angola in 1968, to which the ACOA Africa Fund had contributed an initial $25,000. A Bulgarian surgeon and his wife, a general practitioner, were in charge. There was a staff of 37 and 70 beds. Thirty-five nurses in training were preparing to go back to serve FRELIMO clinics in Niassa, Cabo Delgado, and Tete. Most of the serious cases, both civilian and military, came from inside Mozambique.

The primary school in Tunduru began in 1966 with 25 children from Niassa, who were either orphaned or lost after Portuguese bombings. As Janet Mondlane explained it, one of the liberation fighters, disturbed by the plight of the children, began with others to "collect" them, walking across the Tanzanian border to Tunduru, carrying some children while others followed on foot. By 1973 there were about 1,200 children in primary and preschool programs. Eight hundred women were in the center also, mothers of the children or wives of men at the fighting front. The women were learning to read. The center grew rapidly, especially with generous aid from Sweden. Eight buildings were constructed in 1973 alone.

Meanwhile FRELIMO faced its greatest military challenge between May and September 1970. The Portuguese launched a major offensive against FRELIMO strongholds. A new commander, Gen. Kaulza Oliveira de Arriaga, led some 50,000 Portuguese troops. Large-scale aerial bombardments and helicopter attacks followed by infantry occupation were the tactics. FRELIMO, receiving advance intelligence reports, relocated its bases and supplies. Although the offensive was not a military success for Portugal, crops were destroyed and food shortages resulted. A year later Portugal still had 20,000 troops in Tete, but FRELIMO was also still there.

One result of this campaign was to drive FRELIMO's military efforts farther south into Manica and Sofala provinces. According to the *Johannesburg Star*, "Even their most ardent detractors now grudgingly admit that FRELIMO's military attacks on Mozambique are making formidable strides."[2] In two years the struggle had advanced from the extreme north into the center of the country. In 1973 FRELIMO acquired the new SAM 7 missiles, increasing its attacks on aircraft. The rail line from Salisbury, Rhodesia, to Beira, a major seaport, was vulnerable to sabotage, affecting exports and imports for the white minority government. Furthermore, increased cooperation between ZANU forces and FRELIMO created an obvious challenge to the white minority in both Mozambique and Rhodesia.

The Portuguese responded by expanding their system of *aldeamentos*.

By 1973 an estimated million people were living in almost 900 such villages in the northern provinces with another 200 or more being constructed in Manica and Sofala.

I was in Dar es Salaam in July 1973, when news flashed around the world of a massacre of hundreds of peasants in the village of Wiriyamu in Tete Province on December 16, 1972. Spanish missionaries near the spot were finally able to publicize the tragedy. Although FRELIMO leaders were disturbed, they were not surprised. As Jorge Rebelo, secretary for information, told me, "We have been releasing information about such mass attacks on defenseless civilians for a long time. No one listened. We are grateful that the world is listening to the missionaries."

In October 1975, after Mozambican independence, I arranged to visit Wiriyamu. It was both a moving and an eerie experience. As we drove along a dirt road, we passed a few isolated huts but no villages. Wiriyamu was a wide open, uninhabited clearing. Practically no structures remained standing. It had been a new village where people had been compelled to move by the Portuguese, but it was not a regular *aldeamento*. No troops had been stationed there.

I was given a graphic description of what had happened. Suspecting that the villagers were helping FRELIMO guerrillas, agents of the secret police came to the village to announce a meeting. A company of Portuguese troops surrounded the village. All the people were lined up—children, old people, men, and women in four separate lines. Then the troops suddenly began firing. The idea was to kill everyone. Some 400 died. The only villagers to escape were the badly wounded who feigned death and a few who were doing laundry at the river nearby. Then all the huts were burned and with them a few old and sick people who could not have attended the "meeting." All that remained were scorched hut posts, scattered pots and pans, and a small thatched-roofed structure with open sides in which a chest filled with skulls and bones sat on a pile of rocks. Right next to this structure was a large mound of earth, perhaps 20 feet by 10 and 4 feet high, with a cross on top, containing the remains of the people of Wiriyamu.

PUTTING PRINCIPLES INTO PRACTICE

I was attracted to FRELIMO because it was an effective movement with unusual leaders interested not only in independence but also in creating a positive experience for the people in place of an exploitative one. Eduardo Mondlane made the point that "Liberation is to us not simply a matter of expelling the Portuguese; it means reorganizing the life of the country and setting it on the road to sound national development." FRELIMO made valiant efforts to put its principles into practice. By 1973 there were more than a million Mozambicans living in liberated areas, almost 20 percent of the population. In both the liberated areas and in Tanzania, one could get a pretty good idea of FRELIMO's dedication. I was impressed by its services in exile at Bagamoyo and Mtwara and inside Mozambique, where thousands were being taught to read and write and thousands were being vaccinated against disease.

I was also impressed by FRELIMO's egalitarianism. Titles for officials were eschewed. Everyone was "comrade," or known simply as a *responsavel*, that is, one who had responsibility for a particular task. I was impressed too by FRELIMO's commitment to the nontribal, nonracial principle. Mozambique has 42 tribes. Yet I never came across tribal tensions between leaders, although they may have existed. FRELIMO tried to combat any such tendencies. Several leaders in addition to Mondlane married across racial lines. Mozambicans of Asian background were integrated into the organization.

A prime objective of FRELIMO was to change the role of women. It had made a brave beginning by forming a Women's Detachment in 1967 with responsibility for the movement of food to the fighting front, for social services such as caring for orphans, for medical assistance, and for literacy campaigns. The Organization of Mozambican Women was set up in 1972, and the first women's conference was held in 1973.

FRELIMO made no attempt to idealize the war. The leaders made no assumption that liberation could be achieved everywhere only by armed struggle. Methods used must be adapted to the concrete situation. The distinction between military and civilian was looked upon as functional. Most of the FRELIMO guerrillas were themselves peasants.

Since Mozambique is basically an agricultural country, a foremost problem was to organize the use of the land in liberated areas. By 1973 FRELIMO was carrying on a limited international trade in Mozambican farm products—cashews, castor seeds, peanuts, tobacco, sesame. I discussed this extensively with Joaquim Chissano, who was responsible for FRELIMO's commerce and other activities in Tanzania. People's Stores were organized deep inside Mozambique and on the Tanzanian border. There farmers brought their crops to trade for hoes, hatchets, salt, matches, clothes, and blankets made available through FRELIMO's international outreach.

I was impressed by the breadth of FRELIMO's international contacts, a legacy of Mondlane's work. According to Chissano, it had excellent relations with both China and the Soviet Union and with Scandinavia. "Mondlane's policy is really paying off at this time." he said. Yet relations with the U.S. government, beyond polite personal embassy contact, were almost nonexistent. Chissano told me that when a U.S. embassy spokesman in Dar es Salaam asked how Chissano would respond to a dinner invitation, Chissano said he would turn it down, explaining, "Because you are my enemy. Not you personally but your government."

U.S. support of Portugal in NATO made a good relationship with liberation movements in Portuguese colonies impossible. Against the background of wars in Africa, U.S. aid to Portugal could be seen by the movements only as an act of enmity. Portugal had 150,000 soldiers in Africa and spent close to 50 percent of its budget on the war. In 1971 the United States sold to Portugal 707 and 747 aircraft to be used for troop transport in Africa and five Bell helicopters for use in Mozambique and gave $2.5 million in direct military assistance. To cap it, in December the United States and Portugal signed a five-year agreement that the United States would continue to use the air and naval base in the Azores and would give Portugal more than $400 million in loans and grants in economic aid.

I was one of those who testified before the Senate Foreign Relations Committee opposing this decision. I was also one of a handful of people who, at his request, advised Charles Diggs, chair of the House Subcommittee on Africa, to resign from the U.S. delegation to the UN in protest, which he did.

A NEW MOOD IN SOUTHERN AFRICA

The army coup in Portugal in April 1974 radically changed the situation. When I was in Africa a few months later, a transitional government had been set up in Lourenço Marques. I had hoped to visit Mozambique. However, both Rebelo, the transitional minister of information, and Mariano Matsinhe, minister of labor, whom I saw in Zambia, suggested that I wait until after independence in June. "It is still a transitional government," they explained. "We are telling our friends we can organize a better program to see the country after independence." So I somewhat reluctantly postponed my trip.

In Dar es Salaam there was much excitement at FRELIMO headquarters. Chissano had just been installed as interim prime minister in Lourenço Marques. Big decisions were being made. When should Machel return to Lourenço Marques? What should be done about the Bagamoyo and Tunduru schools, the hospital in Mtwara?

At the Mozambique Institute and later at the Mondlane home, I had a long talk with Machel, with Janet Mondlane and a FRELIMO aide interpreting. Although Machel spoke and understood some English, he was more comfortable in Portuguese. We munched Mozambique cashews as we talked. He was happy about reports from Mozambique, particularly about the deportment of the FRELIMO troops in Lourenço Marques. "We trained them well," he said. "We had hundreds of Portuguese soldiers imprisoned. Not one was executed." They respected the rank of Portuguese officers. "Even if our own troops were in rags, we always saw that captured officers were neat and clean." There was not a reported case of mistreated civilians or women raped.

According to Machel, there were four categories of Portuguese in Mozambique. One consisted of the reactionaries and fascists who feared what would happen when FRELIMO took over. A second were those who had committed crimes and feared punishment. A third were either fearful or hopeful, depending on what they heard from others. A fourth, notably the Portuguese officers, were FRELIMO sympathizers.

I gained further perspective from Tony Avirgan, a journalist friend in Tanzania, who had just returned from Lourenço Marques. He reported that Europeans were obviously apprehensive about what would happen when FRELIMO troops came in. After all, they had been fed a steady stream of propaganda about terrorists and they expected thousands of whites to be killed. This fear was in part dispelled by Chissano's quiet, forceful, intelligent handling of his first press conference.

Avirgan and the people with whom he talked were impressed by the way the FRELIMO soldiers handled themselves. They lined the streets in strategic areas. Although not fraternizing with the people, they would put their guns aside and talk openly with anyone who asked them questions. Avirgan emphasized particularly the soldiers' restraint in areas of Lourenço Marques notorious for wild night life. Because Samora had initially spoken vigorously against prostitution, it was expected that soldiers would close bars and brothels on "Sin Street." Instead they quietly and persistently presented the FRELIMO position but took no other action. Fears eased and hope was implanted of a peaceful transition into independence.

The coup in Portugal and the forthcoming independence of Mozambique ushered in a triumphal mood of expectancy in Africa. Even South Africa was hopeful as Prime Minister John Vorster and President Kenneth Kaunda talked of a detente. There was no one with whom I talked who did not reflect a great optimism. A leader in the ANC said to me, "This is the most hopeful time we have ever had in South Africa."

CHAPTER FIFTEEN

Guinea-Bissau:
"Our People Are Our Mountains"

The guerrilla manuals once told us that without mountains you cannot make guerrilla war. But in my country there are no mountains, only the people.
—Amilcar Cabral

In July 1983 I spent an hour in Dar es Salaam reminiscing with Tanzanian President Julius Nyerere, my friend of more than 25 years. I had just retired from the ACOA, and he had announced his plan not to seek reelection in two years time. After he had commented on some of the African leaders we both had known, who had all died, he said pensively of Amilcar Cabral, "He may have been the greatest leader of all in Africa." Nyerere had been more impressed by him than by any other individual. He told me he had given Cabral a copy of a book Nyerere had written and had inscribed in it, "Win the war. Stay alive. Africa needs you."

Tragically and ironically Cabral was assassinated the year before the cause for which he gave his life was realized. I received the devastating news by telephone on a Sunday afternoon from Janet Hooper, a colleague at the ACOA, who had heard a radio report that Cabral had been shot late the night before (January 20, 1973) at his headquarters in Conakry. After an awful moment, questions immediately crowded my mind: Why? Who did it? What did it mean for the future of the struggle in Portuguese Guinea?*

AMILCAR CABRAL

Amilcar Cabral had been the inspired genius of the liberation movement in Portuguese Guinea, the African Party for the Independence of Guinea and Cape Verde (PAIGC). I had first met him in January 1960 at the second AAPC in Tunis. He kept a very low profile, even using a pseudonym, Abel Djassi, so that the Portuguese would not know he was there. I met him again in Cairo at the third AAPC. This time he wrote his real name in my notebook and the box number of the new external PAIGC headquarters in Conakry. Cabral was only a passing figure to me then. He was of moderate height with a round face, rather light skin, and a hairline beard running from his sideburns to his chin. His glasses gave him the look of the

*Portuguese Guinea officially took the name Guinea-Bissau in 1974.

intellectual that he was. He certainly did not fit my mental image of a revolutionary leader. Over the years, particularly from 1969, as I had increased contact with Cabral, my admiration for him grew. His great organizing ability, clarity of purpose, clear analysis, superb tactical sense, and innovative ideas made him a leader almost without peer in the African liberation struggle.

The PAIGC was probably the most successful and advanced of all the freedom organizations in Africa in the 1960s and early 1970s. Cabral's death was bound to have an enormous effect. Yet the foundation of the movement was so secure that rather than faltering, the struggle actually quickened in 1973.

A few weeks after the assassination I had a letter (February 1973) from Gil Fernandes, PAIGC representative in the United States and later the first ambassador from Guinea-Bissau to the United States and the UN.

Now that I can muster enough courage after that terrible tragedy, I have decided to drop you a line and let you know where things are. First of all I should let you know that the struggle continues. A bunch of Portuguese agents will never be able to stop the great work initiated by Amilcar. They will not prevent us from becoming free. It was a terrible setback, but . . . in fact the struggle has picked up since.

In Conakry, just five months after Cabral's murder, I asked many people what they thought the effect of his death would be. While expressing grief and a profound sense of loss, they echoed Fernandes: "His death has heightened our resolve. We miss his counsel, but our decisions were collective ones. We will carry on as before."

CONDITIONS IN PORTUGUESE GUINEA

Portuguese Guinea, the third of Portugal's major African colonies, seems an unlikely place to have given rise to such an outstanding leader. It is a small country in the bulge of West Africa with a population estimated at less than a million in the 1960s. Sandwiched between Senegal and the Republic of Guinea (both former French colonies), it was off the beaten track and difficult to reach. Yet it was a focal point for the liberation struggle. Under the leadership of Cabral, the PAIGC was the most effective anticolonial movement.

The word Guinea is from the Arabic and means "the land of black men." The bulge of West Africa was once known simply as the Guinea coast. During the colonial period the countries named Guinea were distinguished by the adjectives French and Portuguese. Later the names of the capital cities, Bissau and Conakry, were added to "Guinea" to distinguish them.

My knowledge of Angola and Mozambique helped me greatly to understand Portuguese Guinea. But the country is different. It is much smaller in both area and population. It is hot and humid with no mountains, and the economy is based on subsistence agriculture. Most of the people live in small villages. There is little in the way of exploitable natural resources, although bauxite and phosphate are present. Consequently, unlike the other Portuguese territories, it did not attract European settlers; there were never more than 3,000 Portuguese in residence.

Although the land was too inhospitable for large-scale Portuguese settlement, Portugal fought for a foothold there against British and French encroachment. Finally, in 1886 Portugal's control over the area was recognized in Europe. But the indigenous people resisted, and it took six military campaigns, the latest ending in 1915, to pacify the area.

Forced labor was not a principal grievance of the people in Portuguese Guinea, as it was in Angola and Mozambique, because it affected only a small part of the population. In a country where the infrastructure was so underdeveloped, labor was not recruited for private use, as it was in the larger colonies, but mainly for construction work on roads and bridges. Impetus for revolution grew out of the combination of political and economic domination on the one hand and Portugal's callous policy of ignoring development needs on the other. Cabral put it this way:

We are not only underdeveloped, but not developed at all. The situation in my country, before the struggle, was that agriculture was the main basis of our economy. About 60 percent of the exportation in the country were peanuts. We didn't have any kind of industry. Only fourteen persons had passed the university until 1960 . . . 99.7 percent . . . were illiterate. We had only two hospitals . . . only 300 beds for the sick people. The mortality for children in some regions was about 80 percent. You can realize what kind of situation we had after . . . more than 500 years of Portuguese presence in our country.[1]

The 10 Cape Verde Islands, some 300 miles off the coast of Senegal, are historically tied to the mainland. When I visited them in 1975, I was struck by the dreadful irony of drought conditions on land surrounded by the sparkling blue waters of the Atlantic. Cape Verde is the same latitude as the Sahel and in some areas is covered by deep sand, which has been blown across the ocean from the Sahara, far to the east. Like the mainland deserts, it is chronically affected by drought.

When Portuguese navigators discovered the islands, they were uninhabited. The first settlers were Portuguese, and the islands served as a point of departure for slaves sent to the new world. Portugal administered the islands and the mainland together until 1874. Today some 200,000 people live on the islands with more than that number of Cape Verdeans scattered elsewhere in the world. Largely of mixed blood, they are descendants of Portuguese settlers and Africans brought in as workers or slaves. A Portuguese culture developed on the islands, and during the colonial period all the people were considered Portuguese citizens. On the mainland, by contrast, only 2 percent of the people were "civilized" by Por-

---

*French Guinea became the Republic of Guinea in 1958. Portuguese Guinea became the independent state of Guinea-Bissau in 1974.

tuguese definition in 1950. The lingua franca of both Guinea-Bissau and Cape Verde is Creole, a cross between the Portuguese and African languages. Many Cape Verdeans live in Guinea-Bissau. Having had greater access to education, large numbers of them were in the Portuguese civil service. Many of them have played a significant role in the PAIGC.

CABRAL AND THE PAIGC

Although no successful organization can be attributed to the work of only one person, the PAIGC had the indelible stamp of Amilcar Cabral's ideas and ways of working. Without him, it undoubtedly would have been organized, but it would have been different. Cabral was born in September 1924 in Bafata, Portuguese Guinea. When he was nine, his parents separated and he was sent to Cape Verde to live for a time with his father's family. He went to primary school in Praia, the capital, on São Tiago and to secondary school on São Vicente. An outstanding student, he went to Lisbon on scholarship to study agronomy. After five years he received an engineering degree. Although he associated with students from other Portuguese colonies who later became leaders, such as Agostinho Neto of Angola, he was not then active in politics.

After returning to Portuguese Guinea, Cabral, one of four university graduates in the country, took a job as a government agricultural engineer. His principal duty, to prepare the way for an agricultural census, gave him the opportunity to travel from one end of the country to the other from 1952 to 1954. Not only did he do his job well, but he made good use of his travels to acquaint himself with the country, to meet the people, and to develop his ideas for a political party. In Bissau, where he was headquartered, he began to meet quietly with others, initially Cape Verdeans who shared his conviction that political organization was necessary to challenge Portuguese domination. At that time, Cabral explained later, "We didn't think about independence. We hoped in that moment to change, to have civil rights, to be men, not treated like animals in general. . . . We wanted at that moment . . . to pass from the situation of being second-class Portuguese to being Portuguese like Portuguese. We received as answer only repression, imprisonment, torture."[2]

Among those with whom Cabral formed a close association was Aristedes Pereira, a civil servant in the post office, who, after Cabral's death, succeeded him as secretary general of the PAIGC and subsequently became the first president of an independent Cape Verde. Another close associate was Amilcar's half brother, Luis Cabral, a bookkeeper in a private firm. A third associate was Fernando Fortes, also a civil servant in the post office with Pereira. According to Pereira, the group met for the first time during the Portuguese election campaign of 1954, drawn together by their support for the opposition candidate to Antonio de Oliveira Salazar.

Since Cabral was traveling around the country a great deal at this time, his meetings with others were fleeting. As Fortes explained to me, they had to be exceedingly careful, for the secret police were very watchful. They met clandestinely with Cabral in different places, sometimes even in Luis Cabral's car, usually only two or three at a time. They organized a sports club to be used partly as a front for political discussion, but the government banned it. The authorities became suspicious of Cabral. He was warned by the governor, who respected his work, that he was in danger of being arrested and should leave the country.

Cabral went to Lisbon in 1955, where he took a job with an Angolan company based in Portugal. This work necessitated frequent and extensive trips to Angola. He spent enough time there to be on hand when the MPLA was organized in late 1956.

Over the next three years, Cabral made only an occasional trip to Portuguese Guinea. On one visit, in September 1956, he and five trusted friends organized the PAIGC. They agreed on their objectives—independence for Guinea and Cape Verde, democratization and emancipation of the African people, and rapid economic progress. The work of organizing was done carefully and quietly, principally in urban areas among dockworkers, truckers, and other workers.

Each of the six original PAIGC members had responsibilities and his own circle of contacts. In this way the party expanded slowly through small secret meetings. Those who organized the dockworkers were most active. There was some precedence for small strikes, chiefly over low pay. Cooks in Portuguese homes had struck once. Sailors had gone on strike. The Pidjiguiti dock strike of early August 1959, which, according to Pereira, was planned by the infant PAIGC, proved to be a turning point in the liberation struggle. Fifty dock workers were killed and more than a hundred wounded in the so-called Pidjiguiti Massacre.

I stood on the Pidjiguiti dock 16 years after the police onslaught against the striking dockworkers and visualized what had happened. A striking worker, José Gomes, who was still employed there in 1975, recounted how the strike began in the last days of July as a demand for higher pay. Wages amounted to a few dollars a month. Pay day was August 3. About 200 dockworkers struck, and 60 armed police were called in to quell the disturbance. About 3:00 P.M. the police opened fire. Since the exit from the dock was blocked, many escaping workers jumped into the water and were drowned. Those who were not killed were arrested, Gomes among them. He told me that the next day he and others were forced to return to the dock from jail to wash off the blood. He spent five months in prison.

Nothing appeared in the Bissau press about Pidjiguiti. The Lisbon press referred to the incident as a minor police action—nothing about killed and wounded. But for the PAIGC it was a major event. Cabral heard about the massacre in Angola and returned to Bissau in September. Twelve PAIGC members met September 19 and decided on an entirely new approach to the struggle in line with Cabral's analysis. From then on it was agreed that the peasants, rather than the city workers, should be the principal force in the struggle for national liberation. Party organizational work in the urban areas would continue, but very secretly, avoiding public demonstrations. A training program would begin to prepare the greatest possible number of people for political leadership.

A decision was made to transfer the secretariat of the PAIGC to Conakry, capital of the Republic of Guinea. From there it could carry out a training program and keep in touch with the independent African states and African nationalist organizations. In effect, the decisions made in September 1959 laid the groundwork for an eventual armed conflict with Portugal—an ambitious undertaking for an organization that may have had no more than 50 members.

LAYING THE FOUNDATION FOR THE STRUGGLE

By January 1960, Cabral had decided to give all of his time and energy to the struggle. He left Lisbon to take up his headquarters in Conakry. The president of the Republic of Guinea, Sékou Touré, gave him a job as an agronomist, and a house, which became the headquarters of the PAIGC and his home up to the time of his assassination. A cluster of other buildings, mostly prefabricated, were built around Cabral's small house to make up the external headquarters of the PAIGC until independence.

Other PAIGC leaders gravitated toward Conakry to join Cabral during this period. Without giving notice, Pereira quietly left his job in Bissau in May 1960 and via Cape Verde and Lisbon joined Cabral in Conakry in January 1961.

For two years Cabral carried on an intensive education campaign aimed at winning the support of the peasants. This was not easy. Although peasants were virtually the whole population of the country, they had very little contact with the Portuguese.

The people were touched by colonialism principally through a 10 percent head tax and in some areas an enforced growing of certain crops such as peanuts. There was no direct competition between Africans and Portuguese for land since the Portuguese were less than 1 percent of the population, located mostly in urban administrative positions. Thus the people did not necessarily associate their economic plight with Portuguese exploitation.

Another difficulty, Cabral explained, was that the Portuguese used traditional chiefs as agents of authority where they could. Two principal tribes, the Balante and the Fula, had quite different traditions. The Balante, with no chiefs, were not drawn into administrative posts by the Portuguese. But the Fula chiefs became part of the administrative system. Consequently, at the outset of the struggle, the PAIGC had greater success among the Balante and met more resistance from the Fula.

The PAIGC also had to win support from people in urban areas. Among what Cabral called the petite bourgeoisie were officials in the Portuguese administration, others with nationalist sympathies in varied occupations, and wage earners. On the whole, those working within the administration were not open to the aims of the PAIGC. Principal support came from the other two groups.

The task of the party was to bring together the various elements in the society to win independence. Cabral was convinced that the first step should be a careful political campaign of education and persuasion among the mass of the people. He opened a political school in Conakry in 1960 with about 50 trainees. They lived together for two or three months before returning to Portuguese Guinea to organize. Then another group came. Cabral handled most of the study and lecture program himself. Over a two-year period, 800 to 1,000 cadres were trained in the school.

I did not see Cabral at work, but from my discussions with others and my reading I know that he handled this instruction with care and sensitivity. He was dealing with many recruits who could not read or write, which made teaching basic literacy a priority. His wife, Maria Helena Rodrigues, whom he met in Portugal, observed: "He was very gifted. He started teaching these young people and he absolutely transformed them. He knew how to listen to them and explain things to them in a kind, thoughtful and unaggressive way."[3]

Leaders of the PAIGC were not anxious for armed conflict. In 1960 and 1961 they made several appeals to the Portuguese for discussions, release of political prisoners, and some steps toward decolonization. Portugal never responded.

On the second anniversary of the Pidjiguiti Massacre (August 3, 1961), PAIGC leaders decided the time had come for direct action. It would take the form of sabotage. In June 1973, seated on a crude bench in a thick growth of tall trees at the southern headquarters of the PAIGC forces, I discussed this period with João Bernardo Vieira (nicknamed Nino), the commander of the PAIGC forces and later the second president of independent Guinea-Bissau. He came from Bissau and had been an electrician. Shortly after the Pidjiguiti strike he went to Conakry, where he met Cabral and participated in the PAIGC training program. When the sabotage campaign began, he was a leader in the south. They cut telephone wires, destroyed small bridges, and cut down trees to block roads. For a brief period they virtually halted communication from Bissau to the outside world.

The Portuguese reacted to this PAIGC initiative by widespread repression. The secret police rounded up suspects, attacked the underground headquarters of the party, and seized party material. Among those arrested was Raphael Barbosa, a government worker who was chairman of the party's Central Committee. He spent several years in prison and later publicly renounced his party association as a result of Portuguese pressure.

During this period, Cabral gave some attention to international contacts. He wrote me in early 1962 asking about sending a delegation to the UN and seeking the aid of the ACOA. When he finally arrived in New York in December 1962, he made a long, impressive statement to the UN, clearly presenting the exploitive nature of Portuguese rule in Guinea.

João Bernardo Vieira (Nino, center), commander of the PAIGC forces inside
Guinea-Bissau, and Vasco Cabral (right), PAIGC leader, 1973.

PERIOD OF ARMED STRUGGLE

PAIGC volunteers had received military training in China, Algeria,
Tunisia, and Morocco. The fighting began early in 1963 in the southern
part of the country and spread to the north by midyear. In that same
conversation of June 1973, Vieira told me that he was in charge of a
guerrilla group at Quattiore in the south. Although they had only seven
pistols and some old hunting rifles and explosives, they laid ambushes
against the Portuguese. The action was effective, he pointed out, simply
because the Portuguese were not expecting it.

The pattern for the conflict was quickly established as the guerrillas
took control of large rural areas. The Portuguese administrative posts were
in the towns or in fortified settlements. Ambushes made the few roads
almost unusable.

PAIGC VICTORIES

The first crucial battle in January 1964 was for control of the island of
Como, an important PAIGC base just off the southwestern coast. Vieira
led the defensive forces of some 300 men, pitted against about 3,000
Portuguese troops, including reinforcements from Angola. The battle

raged for 75 days with the Portuguese suffering tremendous losses. The PAIGC were not dislodged. The battle was not only a military but a psychological defeat for the Portuguese.

The overall struggle had made such rapid progress and had attracted so much countrywide support that reorganization was a necessity. The first congress of the PAIGC was called. For a full week about 100 delegates met to decide about program and policies, even while the battle for Como was in progress.

A major decision was to establish a regular army called the People's Revolutionary Armed Forces (FARP) in addition to the local semi-autonomous guerrilla units. The national army counteracted tendencies toward regionalism and tribalism, which the movement decried. Thereafter, the military force of the PAIGC consisted of both the uniformed regular army and the guerrilla units, who formed a militia with the task simply of defending their own villages.

PAIGC military effectiveness grew considerably over the years. An initial few hundred guerrillas increased to 8,000 soldiers by 1972 with another 10,000 in the village militia. At first they received military training mostly in the Republic of Guinea with Soviet, later Algerian, instructors. But soon all training was inside Portuguese Guinea. In 1963 the Portuguese had 80 garrisons in the country. By 1971 they were reduced to 35, and the PAIGC controlled three fourths of the country.

The Portuguese military strategy was built around complete air supremacy. Suspected PAIGC strongholds were bombed regularly. This was the greatest threat to the Guinean villages, as I saw when I accompanied a small PAIGC contingent into southern Portuguese Guinea in June 1973. We stopped at a PAIGC school, which had just moved near the border of the Republic of Guinea to escape the bombings. It was now carefully located under tall trees so that it could not be seen from the air. Trenches were dug on the grounds in case of air attack. Only two days before I arrived, bombs had been dropped close by: two teachers showed me their fragments. The children sang a song, "We have the land. The Portuguese have only the sky."

Portuguese ground forces went on missions from their garrisons by day and returned before dark. As the war went on, they became increasingly isolated. Portuguese patrols could hardly venture forth without facing devastating attack. They had to be supplied by air because the roads were controlled by the PAIGC.

TRIP TO GUILEGE

One of the objectives of my trip in June 1973 was to go to Guilege, the site of an important garrison of 160 about 20 miles from the Republic of Guinea border, where the PAIGC had won a five-day battle only a few days earlier. It had a rudimentary air strip for small planes, its only means of receiving supplies. We set out in late afternoon to minimize the risk of an air attack. Once across the border we could still drive because the PAIGC controlled the road. Our small caravan—a jeep, a Land Rover, and two armored trucks—found the "road" almost impassable. It reminded me of a mountain streambed filled with water, rocks, and boulders because of the heavy rains (June was the rainy season). The going was rough and slow, at times like riding a bucking bronco. At one point the jeep and a truck were stuck in the mud. It took careful work for the other truck to tow them out. The 15 or 20 miles we covered took more than two hours, and my muscles ached for days afterwards.

It was after seven in the evening when we left our vehicles and walked the last mile to Guilege, almost too late for taking pictures. When the rain and hurricanelike winds struck for 15 minutes, we had no protection. We just stood there and took it. Although I had light rain gear in my shoulder bag, no one else had anything. Laughingly I solved this personal dilemma by getting soaked rather than produce a raincoat that would somehow have made me seem a privilged character. As a result, I caught a raging cold.

Guilege covered about 20 acres cut right out of a thickly forested area. Now it was almost completely leveled with only two or three small huts still standing. Cement bunkers were exposed like open basements. As I scrambled about in the ruins, taking pictures, I was warned to watch out for land mines. Naively I had not expected anything like this. The barbed wire fencing still surrounded the plot where the base once stood. Although many of the floodlights pointing outward to brighten the surrounding forest (in order to lessen the likelihood of surprise night attacks) were still in place, the generator had been taken intact by the PAIGC. They had also seized a six-months supply of food and a large quantity of military equipment. One wrecked five-seater plane was still on the runway. The only sign of life was a frightened puppy, which was immediately adopted and named "Guilege." Portuguese books lay in the mud, their pages soaked and flapping in the wind, and letters and other personal items lay scattered about. Barely 10 miles away we could hear the guns of another battle in progress for the garrison at Gadamael. It had been going for three weeks but was expected to end soon in victory for the PAIGC. The destruction and muffled sound of battle were grim reminders that a war was going on.

PAIGC PROGRAMS

Much too late the Portuguese tried to win the support of the people by proposing some reforms and offering rewards. The "Better Guinea" program was instituted in 1968, when Gen. Antonio Spinola became governor. Ethnically based congresses of the Balante and Fula were supported by the Portuguese. Some schools were built, trips to Portugal were offered, and scholarships were granted. Spinola even hinted at some kind of self-government, eventually with a "Portuguese Africa basically governed by Portuguese Africans."

Perhaps the Portuguese hoped that these reforms would compete with PAIGC programs aimed at meeting the needs of the people. The effective control of the countryside by the PAIGC had brought the agricultural economy of the Portuguese almost to a standstill. The export of peanuts, the principal product, was radically curtailed. Villagers were cut off from the money economy of the Portuguese. It was under these circumstances that the PAIGC established People's Shops. It encouraged farmers to grow crops beyond the needs of their own family and especially to increase rice production. Then through the shops, the PAIGC began buying agricultural products from the peasants and in turn sold consumer goods such as clothing, shoes, and salt. This trading was all done by barter.

In 1973 I visited one of the 32 such shops scattered around the country. About 50 villagers came to trade every day. The shop consisted of half a dozen African village-style structures made of slender tree trunks with thatched roofs situated in a heavily forested area for protection from bombing. The buildings were warehouses for storing rice, kola nuts, bees wax, honey, animal skins, and palm products. They also held trade items such as blankets, soap, sugar, salt, and cigarettes.

The *responsavel* for the shop told me that a peasant who brought in three kilos of rice, for example, could receive in exchange one pair of trousers. One kilo of rice was worth a pair of women's shoes or a kilo of sugar; two kilos of cola nuts equaled one blanket, and so on. The peasant would receive more in goods for his produce than he would have received in the Portuguese money economy. The manufactured goods were gifts from friendly countries, notably in Scandinavia and Eastern Europe, and private organizations in the West.

The PAIGC also emphasized a broad educational program. The Portuguese provided only 11 government schools with 2,000 children. In addition there were 45 mission schools. Education expanded dramatically in PAIGC areas. On visits in 1970 and 1973 I spent much time with Domingos Brito, director of the Friendship Institute, which sponsored the education program. A short, energetic man with graying hair, he had been a bookkeeper with a Portuguese firm in Bissau. He joined the party in 1963. For a time he worked with children in the liberated areas until the Friendship Institute was started in 1965. By 1973, according to Brito's careful records, there were 164 schools, 258 teachers, and 14,531 students. In addition, 420 students had studied in Europe, and 35 had university degrees.

I was greatly impressed by the way the schools functioned under the adverse conditions of jungle warfare. On my way to Guilege, I spent time at one of the five boarding schools, or *internatos*. This, serving the southern part of the country, was named after Areolina Lopes da Cruz, a young hero of the movement who had been killed several years earlier. The term boarding school should not conjure up an image of a school for the privileged. This school looked like a small African village—a large circle of thatched huts, which served as classrooms or dormitories. There were 82 students and 7 teachers. The school course covered four years. The best students went on to the Pilot School in Conakry for a fifth year. I was deeply impressed by the neatness and organization of the school. Each bed

Students in a PAIGC school in Guinea-Bissau standing near a bomb casing used as a gong, during the liberation struggle, 1973.

in the crowded huts was carefully made up. Old ammunition boxes were used as small closets. The outside metal casing of a bomb hanging in the "courtyard" served as a gong for calling meetings or warning of approaching aircraft. At a moving farewell ceremony, the students presented me with a bracelet and a facsimile of a traditional wooden stirring spoon bearing the message in English "PAIGC needs peace."

In Conakry I visited the Pilot School with its 120 students—80 boys and 40 girls. Fifty of the students were chosen every year for further study in Europe. One of the eight teachers was the son of a Portuguese army officer in Angola. He was one of the thousands of Portuguese who rebelled against the colonial wars and in his case found a way of serving and being accepted.

The organization of student life was handled by the students themselves with a teacher as an adviser. I asked a teacher if there were any discipline problems. "No," she replied. "The students know how fortunate they are to be here. Also there is a bond between them and the teachers because of the liberation struggle." The dormitory rooms had from 4 to 12 double-decker bunks. In each room one person was responsible for seeing that everyone did his or her work. Every Friday evening the student body met to discuss any problems that had developed during the week. The place was so neat and so smoothly run that I asked if it had been specially prepared for a visitor. I was told they had not been forewarned of my coming. This was just the way it was.

PAIGC workers on an inoculation campaign in Guinea-Bissau, 1975.

The other principal program of the PAIGC concerned health. There were seven regional hospitals in the liberated areas of Portuguese Guinea, each with a doctor, and 12 other medical centers. The main hospital, Solidarity Hospital, was at Boké over the border in the Republic of Guinea, where it was relatively safe from bombing. I spent several hours there. The director, Dr. Manuel Boal, was an Angolan who had studied in Lisbon and worked with the Angolan MPLA medical program in Leopoldville. There was an international flavor to the medical staff. The head surgeon was Yugoslavian, as were four medical technicians. Two Cuban doctors, a French woman doctor, and a trained nurse from Algeria made up the team.

Solidarity Hospital had been constructed in 1969 out of prefabricated material donated by the Republic of Guinea. Its wards could accommodate 120 beds. Just a few weeks before my arrival, strong winds had torn the roof off a section, leaving 10 beds open to the elements. As if to make this real to me, a 20-minute rain and wind storm struck while I was there. I could feel the walls quiver. The staff watched with apprehension, but the building held together.

ORGANIZING A STATE

Portuguese Guinea was comparable at this time to "an independent state part of whose national territory is occupied by foreign military forces," Cabral wrote in early 1973. Why therefore should the PAIGC not adopt a constitution and elect a national assembly and proclaim its state? Perhaps the most inventive and unique strategy Cabral devised was the initiative of holding an election for a representative People's National Assembly even while Portuguese troops occupied limited areas of the country. He was not interested in a government in exile or in declaring independence. He wanted to proclaim a reality that already existed. These elections were a witness to Cabral's tactical genius.

For eight months, from January to August 1972, extensive educational work about the forthcoming election was done, as debates and discussions were held at party and public rallies in the liberated areas. The plan called for the People's National Assembly to have 120 members—80 (not necessarily party members) to be elected by the people and 40 to be chosen by the party. Anyone could vote who was 15 or older and who had registered during the eight-month prepatatory period.

In reality the most important part of the process was the preparation period, when the village people nominated their 80 representatives. Competition for these seats was hot and heavy. More than 80,000 people voted for the slate of candidates, who were approved by about 97 percent. The groundwork for the state was laid.

CABRAL, THE ACOA, AND THE UN

Following Cabral's mission to the United Nations in 1962, I had not been in direct contact with him for several years. The limited time and funds of the ACOA were directed elsewhere. I was encouraged to reestablish a direct relationship with the PAIGC, partly as a result of the quickening liberation struggle, but also by a conversation in London with the historian Basil Davidson, who had written of his own expedition with Cabral into the liberated areas of the country. Davidson told me that Cabral wanted to develop a closer relationship with groups in Western countries. I wrote to Cabral (May 13, 1969) telling him we would like to give what help we could to the PAIGC educational and health programs. He replied with information about the Friendship Institute and the Solidarity Hospital. Since then the ACOA developed a continuing program of financial and material assistance to the PAIGC.

By 1972 the PAIGC felt secure enough in its control of the southern part of the country to invite a UN delegation to visit. Representatives from Uruguay, Tunisia, and Sweden spent a week with the PAIGC forces in April. The Portuguese, of course, knew of the visit and tried to harass it by the most intensive bombing ever experienced in the area. Portuguese troops were dispatched to the south to try to stop the mission. Cabral reported, "The Portuguese dropped napalm and fragmentation bombs, landed special troops along rivers which they assumed the U.N. visitors would use, and attacked large villages, killing 25 civilians."[4] They were not successful.

Cabral made two more visits to the United States—in February 1970 and October 1972, just after the election for the National Assembly. The

PAIGC representative, Gil Fernandes, and I arranged for Cabral to give testimony to the House Subcommittee on Africa and to be heard at the UN. A personal high point for him was receiving an honorary degree from Lincoln University in 1972.

I became better acquainted with Cabral during these visits, gaining some insight into his character and personality. It was agreed that for security reasons there would be no advance notice of his coming. Fernandes would meet him at the airport and escort him to the Commodore Hotel, where I had reserved a room. But a mixup occurred. Cabral's plane arrived early and Fernandes was not there. So Cabral went to the hotel alone and called my office. I dashed to the hotel and spent the next hour and a half talking to my guest. Since there was no word from Fernandes, I became concerned and told Cabral that I was going to call the police. He calmly responded, "Don't be concerned. He will be here. I know my people." We waited some more. Then on a sudden inspiration, I walked down the hall to a room reserved for Fernandes. I knocked, and to my relief and surprise, he opened the door. He was agitated when I told him Cabral had already arrived. Since he had missed Cabral's plane and could not reach me at the office, he had waited in his room. Hurriedly we went to Cabral's room, where he embraced Fernandes as if nothing had happened.

THE ASSASSINATION

After the election for the People's National Assembly, it remained for the PAIGC's Supreme Council to make arrangements for the Assembly to meet and proclaim the existence of the state. Then came a shattering blow—Amilcar Cabral was assassinated. Several months later in June, at PAIGC headquarters in Conakry I was given the essential facts by Aristedes Pereira.

Pereira was working late in his office on Saturday evening January 20, 1973, when Cabral, accompanied by his wife, returned from a Polish diplomatic reception. As he drove into the PAIGC compound, a car blocked the way. He was accosted by Inocencio Kani, who had been relieved of his responsibilities for the PAIGC motor launches in 1971 for selling a motor for personal gain. Kani accompanied by two others, ordered Cabral to follow him.

Guns were drawn. Cabral tried to talk things over, but when Kani tried to tie his arms, Cabral told Kani it could not be done, especially by him. Shots rang and Cabral fell to the ground dead. Apparently the objective had not been to kill him but to turn him over to the Portuguese, but this plan went awry as Cabral resisted capture.

Pereira himself was shot at, but the bullet only grazed his head and he fainted. The attackers then tied him securely and took him to a small PAIGC launch anchored close by. Now the top PAIGC official, he was to be turned over to the Portuguese. The boat headed toward Bissau. Pereira felt he owed his life and certainly his freedom to the fact that launches of the Republic of Guinea intercepted the PAIGC boat shortly before it entered Guinea-Bissau waters. He was freed, and his captors were returned to Conakry, where they were put in the hands of the PAIGC. Pereira had suffered serious injuries during his several hours of captivity. Not only had he been beaten, but the rope tying his arms made severe wounds. For months thereafter he needed hospitalization and medical care. When I saw him he was still weak and the rope scars were quite visible. Luis Cabral came from Dakar to Conakry to handle urgent party affairs.

Other PAIGC leaders were also taken captive on the night of January 20. Jose Araujo, in charge of information, had been at a meeting with visiting leaders of Frelimo. He told me he had taken Joaquim Chissano of FRELIMO back to his hotel after the meeting and then decided to go by the office before returning home. When he approached the PAIGC office at about 11:30, he saw a large crowd gathered. He got out of his car to ask what was going on and was told there was serious trouble and he should not go in. Araujo then drove home, intending to get his gun and return. He and five other party leaders lived communally with their families at a place near headquarters where too late he discovered that the plotters had stationed armed men. He was taken prisoner and at gun point with fellow leaders who had already been captured, he was taken to what had been the PAIGC prison and locked up. They were told they would be shot in the morning but were released a few hours later when troops of the Republic of Guinea intervened.

The circumstances leading to the assassination reveal a lot about Cabral's unusual character and the nature of his leadership. According to Pereira, the two key men in the plot, early party members who had spent years in prison, came from Bissau in November 1971. They said they had escaped from Bissau and were welcomed as old comrades.

It was not discovered until March 1972 that a plot to overthrow PAIGC leadership was in preparation. The two recent arrivals from Bissau were placed under house arrest. The party set up a commission of inquiry to discover the extent of Portuguese infiltration within its ranks. Cabral had wanted to play down the revelation of subversion; he thought it would be possible to win back the dissidents. They had once been loyal comrades, he reasoned, and could be again. As Fernandes later wrote to me, "Cabral was killed because one of his biggest weaknesses was that he trusted people very much. One of the brains of the operation was an agent sent by the Portuguese. Our security services discovered the plot and recommended that he should be shot. Cabral personally intervened on his behalf. . . . The whole tragedy . . . was perpetrated by people Amilcar himself decided to rehabilitate."

There were several motivations for the attempted coup: (1) the plotters were promised well-paying positions by the Portuguese in Bissau; (2) Guinea-Bissau could have a kind of independence, under new leadership, separate from Cape Verde, within a Portuguese commonwealth; (3) Cape Verde leadership would be eliminated from the party.

The house arrest of the two recent arrivals from Bissau did not stop the plot, which had 9 or 10 ring leaders. Forty-five were arrested for complicity, of whom 9 were executed.

From the Portuguese perspective, the attempted coup was a desperate effort to stem the PAIGC when it was in the position of growing strength and to save Portugal's colonial structure when it was in a precarious position, not only in Portuguese Guinea but in Angola and Mozambique as well. The plot utterly failed to weaken the PAIGC, as my trip to Guilege, five months after Cabral's death, testified.

PROCLAMATION OF AN INDEPENDENT STATE

The death of Cabral briefly delayed the proclamation of the State of Guinea-Bissau. When I returned to New York in July 1973, a long cable from the PAIGC Executive Committee, announcing the results of the second party congress, was awaiting me. It had selected Aristedes Pereira as secretary general to succeed Cabral and chosen a permanent secretariat, consisting of Pereira, Luis Cabral, João Bernardo Vieira (Nino), and Francisco Mendes (Chico). The National Assembly was to meet on September 21–23.

The People's National Assembly proclaimed "the self-determination of our people and the de facto existence of an efficiently functioning State structure." The proclamation made clear that the State of Guinea-Bissau was confined to the mainland and the immediate offshore islands, such as the Bissagos. A claim of statehood was not made for Cape Verde but only for "the complete liberation of the people of Guinea-Bissasu and Cape Verde and the forging of a union between the two territories." The proclamation ended with an appeal to all independent states to give de jure recognition and announced the determination of the new state to seek participation in the United Nations. Luis Cabral was chosen as president of the Council of State, to exercise authority between meetings of the Assembly. A Council of Commissioners was set up like a cabinet with functional responsibilities. Vieira was commissioner of the armed forces. Guinea-Bissau was a one-party state with the general secretary of the party having no position in the government.

Within a few weeks after the proclamation, some 70 countries recognized the new state, including 38 African countries, all those in the Chinese and Soviet camps, many Asian and Middle Eastern countries, and very few Latin American countries. No Western country took this diplomatic step.

In New York we organized a committee to campaign for the recognition of Guinea-Bissau, since every U.S. administration had been careful not to embarrass the Lisbon government. For example, the U.S. ambassador to the Republic of Guinea in 1970 told me that in the months since his arrival he had had no contact with the PAIGC, indeed considered it unwise "for obvious reasons," and had not met Cabral.

Five months after the proclamation, the coup took place in Portugal. Unlike Angola and Mozambique, everything was in place for the independence of Guinea-Bissau. It had the People's National Assembly and the Council of State and Council of Commissioners, and the PAIGC was in control of most of the country. The morale of the Portuguese forces was so low that they welcomed the end of the war without the urging of Lisbon. Fraternizing among the troops of both sides began spontaneously. The PAIGC commander for the Bafata region, who had had the first contact with the Portuguese military after the coup, told me how a cease fire was quickly agreed upon and on condition that none of the Portuguese troops would leave their camps or transport munitions. By September, Portugal had agreed to recognize Guinea-Bissau's independence, which was declared September 24.

AN ASSESSMENT OF AMILCAR CABRAL

A little more than two years after Cabral's assassination and about six months after independence, I arrived in Bissau for the first time, accompanied by my friend and colleague Ray Gould. Flying in from Dakar, an open map on my lap, I had a good view of the city as we approached the small airport. I saw no other planes but noted a few concrete pill boxes, which had been part of the Portuguese defense system. Signs along the edge of the landing area warned of possible unexploded land mines. We were met by the chief of protocol and taken to a small hotel.

Reporters assigned to Bissau had usually given the impression that it was a dreary, lazy, hot, and humid town, which a visitor would want to leave as soon as possible. Perhaps I was so excited about actually being in a place I had read so much about that I created my own reality, but I had a different reaction. I was impressed by the cleanliness of the city, the people on the street who looked at me with curiosity but without a hint of hostility, and by the lack of tension in the air. Only about 200 Portuguese still remained of the some 3,000 who had been there before independence, but they were beginning to return and were quite visible. The city seemed sleepy only during the siesta from 12:30 to 3:00. In the evening a gentle, refreshing breeze blew from the water, at least at that time of year.

There were few political graffiti on the walls. Some shop windows displayed PAIGC leaflets. Most prominent were pictures of Cabral with the caption (in Portuguese): "Eternal glory to the martyr of national liberation."

One evening Gould and I were taken to dinner by a group of men who had been in the struggle from the early days. As we sat around the table in the Pidjiguiti Hotel, formerly a naval barracks, we talked about Cabral. All these men had known him well. I was especially struck by the affection, almost veneration, in which they held him. I had felt this myself when I talked with him personally, especially in 1972, and when I heard him talking with small groups. He spoke firmly, definitely, and quietly. He

Amilcar Cabral, president of
the PAIGC, at the UN, 1972.
United Nations. Photo by Y.
Nagata/ARA.

took his listeners along with him. I could understand how both Pereira and
Fortes, of the original six who launched the PAIGC in 1956, could say that
Cabral was the key to their organization. Julio Semedo, whom I met in
New York when Guinea-Bissau was setting up its first official office there,
said to me, "I will never meet another person as great as Cabral."

Our hosts agreed that Cabral was even more brilliant as a tactician than
as a political and social theorist. We discussed both aspects of the man, for
it was the combination that made him unique. They reiterated that it was
his analysis that led the PAIGC to see the peasant as the basis of their
revolution. He saw the importance of the training period in Conakry
before beginning the armed struggle. He was not only a man of ideas, they
felt, but he had the genious to put these ideas into practice. He was not a
dogmatic ideologist but a pragmatist. I recalled that at the U.S. House
Subcommittee on Africa in 1970, when Congressman Brad Morse asked
him about the ideology of the movement, Cabral replied, "Our ideology is
nationalism, to get our independence absolutely . . . but to cooperate with
all other peoples in order to realize the development of our country."[5]

Our PAIGC hosts felt that Cabral had been concerned not just with
distant objectives. The schools, hospitals, and People's Shops were monu-
ments to his pragmatism. The objective of the revolution was not only to
win freedom but also to achieve a better way of life for the people. He was
innovative, and his timing was good. He knew when to change tactics after
the Pidjiguiti massacre. He knew when it was time to develop the army

from local guerrilla movements into a united, mobile, national force. He knew when it was possible, even in the midst of struggle, for the PAIGC to organize elections. Cabral, like Eduardo Mondlane, was also pragmatic in his efforts to obtain aid from abroad. Although most military aid came from Eastern Europe, humanitarian projects received wide support from agencies in Western Europe, especially Scandinavia, Britain, and the United States.

Cabral combined his pragmatism with a most unusual human-itarianism. He listened to people. Those who went through the course of training with him in Conakry believed that he was genuinely interested in them. He opposed the use of terrorist methods that would endanger the lives of innocent people. He believed optimistically in the possibility of rehabilitating the defectors from the party who later killed him. He frowned on the use of the death penalty. He always made clear that the struggle was not against the Portuguese people but the policy of the Portuguese government. Twice in 1968 the PAIGC turned Portuguese prisoners over to the Senegalese Red Cross to be returned to Portugal.

Over our meal that evening, I asked our hosts whether at times they wondered what Cabral would have said about a particular problem they faced. They replied that they knew his ideas, which were in his writings and speeches. They had no Cabral now, but collectively they were trying to plan their way along the lines he would have wanted. Then one said. "He so affected every facet of the life of the organization that we still feel his presence. It is as if he is sitting in our meetings, strangely enough." Then he quickly added, "But it is not a religion."

CHAPTER SIXTEEN

Zimbabwe:
The Making of a Nation

During the celebration of Zambia's* independence in October 1964, I had an experience that reinforced my prejudices against the government of Southern Rhodesia. An extracurricular highlight for the guests was a trip to Victoria Falls. I looked forward with pleasure to the one-day expedition to the site on the Zambezi River, which formed a natural boundary between Zambia and Southern Rhodesia.

We arrived at the Livingstone airport in midmorning and proceeded by bus to the falls. Although it was the low-water season, the spray from the falls rose high above the river, and the water plunged over the huge drop with a deafening roar. On the boat ride above the cataracts leading to the falls, we saw hippos, crocodiles, monkeys, and other animals. The afternoon plan was for the guests to cross the bridge spanning the great chasm formed by the river to see the falls from the Rhodesian side.

On the boat ride I had already had the first intimation of difficulty. A voice on the public address system asked the persons whose names were called to see the officer in charge when the boat docked. Three names were called, mine among them. When I introduced myself to the proper British official, he seemed embarrassed but explained that I would not be included with the guests going to the Rhodesian side. The Rhodesian government had given the Zambian officials the prohibited names for Southern Rhodesia, and of course, I was on the list.

With apologies the official informed me that I would be taken instead to a small game park near Livingstone, along with a Soviet and an East German guest. They both spoke good English and joined in uproarious but sympathetic laughter that an American and two Communists should be brought together by a prohibited status in Rhodesia. Although the game park was not very interesting, our conversation and good humor were stimulating. Later I discovered that one of the buses with guests had turned back at the Rhodesian border in protest when the officials tried to set apart African and European guests. Thus I gained yet another indication of white racist practices imposed on southern Africa.

BACKGROUND TO CONFLICT

Although I had never been permitted in Southern Rhodesia, I felt I understood the basis of the problems. I concluded that Southern Rhodesia

---

*Zambia was formerly Northern Rhodesia.

was a schizophrenic society—a single country with two separate peoples, each with its own history, each looking upon the country as theirs. The former name of the country, Rhodesia, reflected the European incursion into a territory in search of agreeable climate, good land, and a chance of achieving great wealth through the discovery of minerals. The country was named for Cecil Rhodes, a Briton who went to South Africa at the age of 17 in 1870 and made a fortune in diamonds. Then with dreams of building a railroad from the Cape to Cairo and extending the British Empire, in 1888 he expanded his interests into the country of the Mashona and the Ndebele, which the British called Zambesia.

The present-day name of the country, Zimbabwe, reflects the African history of the area. The name is Shona; it comes from stone ruins near the town of Masvingo (formerly Fort Victoria) and means "house of stones." Although there has been much speculation about who built these massive stone structures and when, it is now generally assumed that they were built by Africans to their own design at least as early as the 11th century. When I first visited what is now called Great Zimbabwe in 1980, I was awestruck by this evidence of engineering achievement.

The basis of conflict between the Europeans and the Africans was laid when the whites took land by guile and conquest from the blacks who were there, constructed an affluent society, and designed their laws and constitution to maintain what they taken. The Shona and the Ndebele struggled to stave off the European invasion, and having lost, fought to win back the land and resources taken from them in order to construct a way of life of their own choosing.

The British foothold began with a concession for exclusive mining rights, granted in 1888 by Lobengula, king of the Ndebele. A year later the British Crown authorized Rhodes to set up the British South Africa Company, which was for the next 25 years the effective government for Europeans in Rhodesia. The first Rhodesians were a couple of hundred young recruits (called the Pioneer Column) selected by Rhodes, who marched to Fort Salisbury, later the capital, and raised the Union Jack on September 12, 1890. The Europeans celebrated this date as Occupation Day.

The agreement for mineral exploration became an excuse for an invasion of the country by white settlers. The Shona and the Ndebele resisted the foreign incursion in two wars, 1893 and 1896–1897, but were defeated, and Lobengula himself lost his life in flight. Spears and arrows were no match for firearms. The country was taken over by European settlers, resistance was virtually wiped out, and violent protest did not reappear for more than 70 years.

Although never more than 5 percent of the total population, the European settlers grew from 1,500 in 1892 to about 280,000 in the 1970s. The laws and constitution were designed to protect their interests and keep the African majority subservient. Gradually power shifted from the British South Africa Company directly to the settlers. By referendum in 1922 approximately 60 percent of the settlers voted to establish a government separate from the company, while 40 percent voted to join the newly formed Union of South Africa. Thus Rhodesia became a "self governing colony" with loose ties to Britain.

The fundamental issues between the Europeans and the Africans involved land, labor, and political rights. One third of the land was in the hands of 1/20 of the population. The cities were controlled by whites. Africans were restricted as to the number of cattle they could have on their limited acreage, while no such restrictions applied to Europeans. African laborers generally received only 1/10 of the pay of their European counterparts, and their rights of collective bargaining and striking were severely restricted. The right to vote was not absolutely denied to Africans, but the educational, property, and financial qualifications were set so high that only an insignificant minority could ever hope to cast a ballot. For example, the 1969 constitution was adopted with fewer than 7,000 Africans qualified to vote out of more than 5 million. Furthermore, effective African political action was hampered by restrictive laws, and police could ban protest organizations, prohibit meetings, and arrest leaders at any critical time.

Very early I was convinced that fundamental change would come primarily through African action. Weak as the African nationalists in Rhodesia were during much of this period, they alone could force a confrontation with the white minority. They adopted the slogan, "We are our own liberators."

THE LIBERAL PHASE

African organizations had appealed to the white government for small reforms after World War II, but the struggle really took shape in 1955, when the Southern Rhodesian African National Youth League was organized. It was founded and led by young men who were impatient for change and openly skeptical about the pseudo-liberalism in vogue and the slogan of racial partnership proclaimed by the leaders of the Central African Federation.

I learned a great deal about the Youth League through contacts with two of its principal leaders, James Chikerema and George Nyandoro. After schooling in Rhodesia and Basutoland (now Lesotho), Chikerema entered Cape Town University, where he was head of the local Youth League of the ANC. He was forced to return suddenly to Rhodesia to escape arrest for his political activities. He brought with him the South African Youth League constitution, which became a guideline for the Youth League that he helped set up in Salisbury.

Nyandoro, vice president of the Youth League, had been educated at an Anglican school and had been active in politics from the age of 17. An exuberant man, he almost always gave the impression of bubbling over with excitement.

The Youth League in its 18 months of existence, ushered in a new style of African political activity. Its program was reminiscent of the nonviolent civil rights movement in the United States. I was fascinated by the incidents of civil disobedience Chikerema and Nyandoro described to me, such as using the toilets in the native commissioner's office, encouraging the preparation of the African home brew called "chukuba," and encouraging Africans to cultivate a potato crop on private land, all in defiance of regulations. The league's greatest triumph was a bus boycott to protest a fare increase for Africans traveling to work in Salisbury from Harare African township. For three days the buses were virtually empty.

The league's most significant contribution, however, was that it inspired the formation of the first truly countrywide nationalist organization, the Southern Rhodesia African National Congress (SRANC). The new body, which was intended to attract a more mature following than the Youth League, was launched on a significant date, September 12, 1957, the 67th anniversary of Occupation Day. The SRANC was a protest organization, not a revolutionary one, which aimed to work within the existing society. At that time, the ideas of multiracialism and partnership were still acceptable to many Africans. Ultimate African independence and majority rule were more implied than demanded.

It was not easy to find the right president for the new organization. Chikerema and his other Youth League colleagues agreed that a student, such as Chikerema himself, could not bring the proper prestige to the SRANC. An older and better-established person was needed. Various people turned down the offer of the post, some fearing that their jobs might be jeopardized. Joshua Nkomo was ready to take the risk. He represented a moderate African leadership that could not be dismissed out of hand by the more established blacks. He had already gained some prominence, not only through his work with the railway union, but as an African representative in the London discussions about the establishment of the Central African Federation, which he opposed.

The SRANC's main following came from the workers and the peasantry—on the bottom rung of the social and economic ladder. The educated elite—teachers, business men, professionals—were not attracted. They still believed in the idea of the federation and in multiracialism, not the sort of struggle the SRANC proposed.

Nonracial in its approach, the SRANC included about a hundred European members. It particularly contested racial laws and practices that closed certain facilities to Africans. Their members demanded service in hotels and restaurants and on trains. Although they were almost always refused, their action showed up the false pretensions of partnership of white Rhodesians.

The SRANC was Pan-African in outlook. It had a close working relationship with the corresponding ANCs in Northern Rhodesia and Nyasaland, especially in condemning the Central African Federation.

During the period of the Youth League and the founding of the SRANC, Garfield Todd was prime minister (1953–1958). He was about as liberal as a white in government could afford to be and still hold an elective post. A New Zealander, he had come to Southern Rhodesia in 1934 as a missionary. It was years later, after he had been badly defeated because the whites considered him too friendly to blacks, that I came to know him.

Todd's fall from power marked a turning point in the struggle between whites and blacks in Rhodesia. Sir Edgar Whitehead, to the right of Todd politically, became prime minister. In a little more than six months the SRANC was banned (February 26, 1959) under the Unlawful Organizations Act, because the government feared its mass demonstrations and growing support would threaten law and order. Nkomo was out of the country at this time. Other major leaders were arrested and imprisoned, including Chikerema and Nyandoro, who spent nearly four years behind bars.

THE CONSTITUTIONAL PHASE

In January 1960 a new nationalist organization was set up, the National Democratic Party (NDP), which lasted for almost two years, until December 9, 1961. This was an important period of change elsewhere in Africa—the Sharpeville Massacre, Macmillan's "wind of change" speech, the UN resolution calling for decolonization, the beginning of armed revolt in Angola, the independence of so many countries. The Central African Federation was breaking up. Kenneth Kaunda and Kamuzu Banda, arrested in 1959, were released. Independence for Northern Rhodesia and Nyasaland was not far away.

No such changes, however, were envisioned by the white minority in Southern Rhodesia. The NDP was less interested in Africans winning equality of treatment in public places than in majority rule. Nkomo put it dramatically: "We don't want to swim in your swimming pools. We want to swim with you in Parliament."[1]

The focus and style of the NDP were instrumental in attracting as leaders many well-educated Africans—Robert Mugabe, Ndabaningi Sithole, Herbert Chitepo. Those in prison had a hand in its formation. Nyandoro told me that he, Chikerema, and several others had drafted a constitution, which was smuggled page by page out of prison through visitors, bribed prison guards, and even in the rectums of released prisoners. Nkomo assumed the presidency when he returned from voluntary exile.

The government had to take the NDP seriously because of its mass support. It raided party headquarters in the African township of Highfield, near Salisbury, ransacked the homes of three NDP leaders, and arrested them. This action triggered a spontaneous strike and a mass march of an estimated 40,000 to the prime minister's office. Four thousand spent the night in protest outside the police station where the leaders were being held, and 12 Africans were killed.

In this time of tension, the British initiated talks on a new constitution for Southern Rhodesia. The NDP demanded universal adult franchise and a bill of rights that would protect Africans from discriminatory legislation. What finally emerged was a compromise, in which the bill of rights was accepted by the British and 15 seats in a parliament of 50 would be reserved for Africans. This was far from the NDP's demand for majority rule.

When Nkomo and I met at the AAPC in Cairo, he said he had reluctantly accepted the compromise as the best terms that could be obtained at that time. The temptation to be recognized as leader of 15 African members in Parliament (for the NDP could undoubtedly have won all the seats) must have been great. Later he reported to an NDP meeting that "we were able to move the mountain . . . an inch by getting the declaration of human rights . . . enshrined in the Constitution." But bitter controversy emerged in the party as the issue was debated. The NDP put the contitutional proposals to an unofficial public referendum in which only 471 out of some 370,000 voted favorably. Leopold Takawira, NDP director for external and international affairs, sent me the results of the referendum, proclaiming, "Our people rejected it."

In contrast, in an official referendum sponsored by the white minority government and boycotted by the NDP, the proposals were accepted by almost 42,000 out of more than 63,000 voting. Nkomo later opposed the compromise. He sent me a copy of the NDP resolution categorically rejecting the new constitution, which he called a "white man to white man agreement [which] shall be resisted by the majority of the people." His vacillation cost him the confidence of some influential NDP leaders.

By rejecting the constitution, the NDP put itself outside the legal political framework. Confrontation was sure to follow. Nkomo wrote to me in November 1961 that the government was stepping up arrests. More than 500 were in prisons and hundreds awaited trial. He asked if we could send funds for legal defense.

NDP rallies in the African townships increased, with hugh crowds attending, even in the presence of troops. The Salisbury and Bulawayo city councils banned all open-air NDP meetings. And then the organization as a whole was banned on December 9.

THE NATIONALIST SPLIT

The NDP leadership had prepared for its banning. ZAPU picked up where the NDP ended, December 9, 1961, with almost all the same leadership and continued mass support. Nkomo assumed the presidency as soon as he returned from attending Tanzania's independence celebration in Dar es Salaam. He came to New York with a ZAPU delegation to the UN in 1962. Returning to Salisbury, he was greeted by about 20,000 followers, according to the *New York Times*.

ZAPU, like the NDP, was committed to universal suffrage, Pan-Africanism, liquidation of colonialism, respect for human rights, and cooperation with all like-minded international bodies. But it was on a collision course with the white government, which reacted to ZAPU's mass rallies as it had to the NDP. Security laws were tightened. Frequently meetings were broken up by police and the speakers arrested. Gradually disillusioned Africans accepted the necessity of violent response to such interference. ZAPU sent some men abroad for military training—to Algeria, Ghana, Czechoslovakia, and China. I saw a widely circulated announcement by a "General Chedu" that a Zimbabwe Liberation Army had been formed. There was no General Chedu. The name, which means "ours" in Shona, was chosen by a group of militant nationalists convinced that violence was necessary.

ZAPU leaders knew it was only a matter of time until ZAPU would be banned. They planned not to organize a new group but to go underground. When the ban fell in September 1962, some 1,600 leaders were rounded up and detained three months. Nkomo, again out of the country, delayed his return in order to talk with Julius Nyerere in Dar es Salaam about next steps. As Nyerere recounted the meeting to me, Nkomo wanted to set up a government-in-exile in Dar, but Nyerere did not believe in the efficacy of governments-in-exile. Although he agreed to have a ZAPU office in Dar, he strongly urged Nkomo to return to Rhodesia. Nkomo did so and was arrested and given the same three months detention as the other leaders, but his delayed return caused some bitter criticism by some of his colleagues.

A wave of violence spread throughout the country after the banning of ZAPU. Schools and other government buildings were burned, and forests of the British South Africa Company were set afire. In reaction, the white minority became more conservative. In the December 1962 elections they turned to the right-wing Dominion Party, which took 70 percent of the seats in Parliament. Winston Field, a prominent farmer, became prime minister.

The next few months were confusing and frustrating for African nationalists. The white minority were talking about an independence that would put them indefinitely in power at the expense of the African majority. One thing was clear; the banning of ZAPU meant that there was no legal way to continue the struggle for majority rule. The options were few—either quicken underground activity inside Rhodesia or work from a freer base outside. Either way, violence was bound to increase. ZAPU leaders could not agree on a common strategy, and tension mounted.

Much to my disappointment, a major issue that divided the leadership revolved around Nkomo. He had been the uncontested leader for many years, unrivaled at home and widely known abroad because of his extensive travels. Apparently he wanted to launch a Zimbabwe government in exile, if, as was expected, the white minority made a unilateral declaration of independence (UDI) without British approval. The way was paved for such a move with the dissolution of the Central African Federation in June 1963.

The government-in-exile idea was not to be implemented. Within ZAPU, Sithole and Mugabe, among others, opposed it, but it couldn't work for another overwhelming reason. The logical location for it was Dar es Salaam, but Nyerere was unalterably opposed. He told me that in his follow-up discussions with Nkomo he sternly reemphasized that Nkomo's place was inside Rhodesia, and he would be declared a prohibited immigrant in Tanzania if he did not leave. Nyerere also voiced his regret that he might have unwittingly played a part in the split within ZAPU by this strong admonition. Nkomo returned to Rhodesia and convinced ZAPU leaders to meet in Dar es Salaam even though some, including Mugabe, would have to jump bail to attend.

At this meeting it was agreed that an office (not a government) should be set up. Apparently Nkomo's critics in ZAPU had not at this time decided to form a new organization, although they felt Nkomo had been too vacillating and was trying to solve their struggle through international diplomacy rather than direct confrontation. I had no hint of an imminent split when I had long talks with Sithole, a dissident leader.

The ways parted in July 1963. After the Dar meeting, Nkomo went back to Rhodesia, where some correspondence fell into his hands that clearly identified opposition to his leadership. He called a press conference suspending Sithole (national chairman), Takawira (secretary for external affairs), Mugabe (publicity secretary), and Moton Malianga (secretary general). These four in turn, in Dar, deposed Nkomo as president and elected Sithole in his place. Three other ZAPU leaders, including Jason Moyo, walked out, dissociating themselves from the dissidents.

I had a letter from Eddison Zvobgo (July 20, 1963), who had studied in the United States and enthusiastically supported the revolt against Nkomo. "Nkomo is doomed. That is what things are boiling down to. The revolt against Joshua has now spread beyond bounds. . . . I predict that in another month the game will be all over. . . . Sithole is likely to lead as things stand. His popularity is spreading like wild fire by the hour." In his enthusiasm Zvobgo was underestimating Nkomo.

ZANU was organized in early August 1963 after Sithole returned from Dar. Its policy statement had little to distinguish it from ZAPU. Pan-Africanist, nonracial, committed to universal suffrage, vaguely socialistic, it called for nationalization of major industries but allowed for private enterprise. Thus the split did not seem to be primarily ideological.

Nkomo called a large, representative gathering at Cold Comfort Farm near Salisbury to settle the leadership question. Although a thousand were expected, at least 5,000 came. They hailed Nkomo as "the only national leader and life president" of the movement and called on Britain to transfer power to the majority. They urged the people to engage in active resistance to colonialism. Since ZAPU was banned, a new body, the People's Caretaker Council (PCC), was set up to rival ZANU, as yet too new to be illegal. The PCC was organized in cells in every 40th house in the African townships, the cell leaders to be in close touch with Nkomo.

ZANU held its inaugural congress May 21 to 23, 1964, attended by more than 1200 delegates. They endorsed the constitution and policy statement and elected officers. Sithole just managed to win the presidency from Mugabe, who was elected secretary general; Takawira was vice president; Zvobgo, vice secretary general; Chitepo, national chairman.

Sithole, born in Rhodesia in 1920, was educated in Methodist schools and ordained. He did graduate work at Andover-Newton Theological Seminary in Massachusetts and on his return was made principal of a government primary school. Active in the NDP, he had to give up his teaching post when he was elected secretary general in 1960. He was chosen national chairman of ZAPU. I saw him frequently in the United States and Africa.

Sithole was regarded as a hard-hitting nationalist. He was arrested when he returned to Salisbury from Dar es Salaam in late 1962 for a letter he had written urging a boycott of the December elections. When he finished a year at hard labor in May 1965, he was given a five-year restriction order. According to his book, *African Nationalism*, there were 51 charges against him between July 30, 1963, and June 22, 1964.

The bitter split in the nationalist ranks broke into occasional violence. Nevertheless, the struggle against the white government intensified. Railways and electrical installations were sabotaged. A bomb was exploded at a sports gathering attended by the prime minister. A train was derailed near Bulawayo.

The leaders of both ZAPU and ZANU were arrested. Nkomo was put under long-term restriction in a remote area without a specific charge on April 16, 1964, shortly after Ian Smith replaced Winston Field as prime minister. By the end of 1964, almost 2,000 Africans were in detention, and ZANU and the PCC, as well as ZAPU were declared illegal.

I was dismayed by the split in ZAPU. We supporters of the liberation struggle had to decide how we should relate to the new creation, ZANU. Although I knew Nkomo best, I also knew and respected many ZANU leaders. Without a clear ideological or tactical distinction, there was no objective basis for supporting one group rather than the other. The OAU recognized both. President Kaunda tended to favor ZAPU, but both groups had offices in Lusaka and in Dar es Salaam and used Zambian facilities for beaming radio broadcasts to Rhodesia.

We decided to maintain contact with both ZAPU and ZANU. I met Mugabe several times when he came to the UN in October 1963 on behalf of ZANU, and wrote to Zvobgo that he had made a good presentation. I did not, however, accept ZANU's charges that Nkomo was out of the country each time a group was banned because he feared arrest. He had stood up against the white minority government too often to make me believe that, and his travels were necessary to his work. Stylistically he was a politician more than an activist seeking confrontation.

I had many discussions with leaders in both groups about whether tribal differences affected the split. Although it is terribly difficult for an outsider to assess, I tended to discount such influence. Certainly among the mass of people, Nkomo remained the most popular. At rallies, he far outdrew Shona leaders even in the most heavily Shona areas. About 80 percent of the country is Shona-speaking. The rest speak Ndebele. But the Shona have distinct subgroups such as the Karanga, Manica, Korekore, and Zezuru. To complicate the matter still further, Nkomo was identified as Kalanga, a group that derives ethnically from the Shona but speaks Ndebele. The only safe generalization was that ZANU had its main following among the Shona but had some Ndebele leaders. ZAPU had a Ndebele base but a significant Shona following and some Shona leaders. I concluded that to translate tribe into political bias was an oversimplification but could not be completely ignored. We foreign supporters of the struggle had to adjust to the fact that there were two viable movements after the split in 1963.

UDI AND SANCTIONS

The three letters UDI (Unilateral Declaration of Independence) became a code phrase eliciting differing reactions. To the British it stood for an embarrassing rebellion by a white minority in a colony. To most white Rhodesians it conjured up visions of determinedly going it alone to preserve "Christian" white civilization against threats within and without their country. To most Africans whom I met it was a matter of indifference. Whether white-dominated Rhodesia was a self-governing colony or an "independent" country made little difference to their way of life. They wanted majority rule.

UDI finally became a reality in November 1965 with Prime Minister Ian Smith as its architect. Unlike most white Rhodesians, who were post-World War II immigrants and in 1969 had been in the country less than 20 years, Smith was born in Rhodesia, in 1919. He went to university in South Africa and then became a successful farmer. A hard-liner of the Rhodesian Front, he epitomized the white minority and prophesied that white rule in Rhodesia would last a thousand years. His political rise was probably inevitable as the situation became critical and the British insisted on maintaining some limited role in order to protect the black majority. As deputy prime minister, he had been told in London by Commonwealth Secretary Duncan Sandys that Rhodesia could not be granted independence like Zambia and Malawi because the Rhodesian "franchise is incomparably more restrictive than that of any other British territory to which independence has hitherto been granted."[2]

Neither the British Prime Minister, Harold Wilson, nor Ian Smith seriously believed that the UDI issue would be protracted or that many years of civil war would follow. The African nationalists were not then a power to contend with. Guerrilla warfare was yet to come. Wilson unrealistically proclaimed that the rebellion would be ended "in months if not weeks" as a result of the limited economic sanctions that the British asked the UN to adopt.

Most Africans I talked with were bitter because Wilson would not use force to quell the white revolt. If it had been non-Europeans revolting against whites, there would have been little hesitation about sending troops. British troops had gone to Cyprus, Singapore, and Kenya when trouble arose. James Chikerema expressed African opinion when he told me, "If Britain really wanted to take over their colony, which they always say is still their colony, they could have done so." Africans felt that the racist argument that white Rhodesians were "kith and kin" dictated the British response.

Limited sanctions against the wayward colony were imposed, as the British boycotted tobacco and sugar, which accounted for about three fourths of Rhodesia's exports. Agreeing to a British request, the UN called for voluntary compliance with sanctions prohibiting the import of Rhodesian asbestos, iron ore, chrome, copper, meat, tobacco, and sugar and forbidding the export to Rhodesia of arms, military equipment, and oil. In 1968 these sanctions, implemented in the United States by executive order, were made mandatory and were extended to include investment, trade, and recognition of passports.

Although the sanctions had some effect, they certainly did not come close to bringing down the government. Trade to Rhodesia went through its neighbors, South Africa, which owned many Rhodesian firms, and Mozambique. Oil sanctions, which might have led to an economic collapse in Rhodesia, were ineffective because of refineries and depots in those countries.

Since the Rhodesian rebellion was obviously not going to end quickly, the British had a continuing responsibility. They felt they could not extricate themselves until there was an agreement moving in the direction of majority rule. Highly publicized discussions took place between Wilson and Smith on board the British destroyer *Tiger* in the Mediterranean in 1966 and on the *Fearless* in 1968. Neither meeting was successful. The British announced "five principles," insisting on progress toward majority rule and an end to racial discrimination if they were to withdraw. Smith rejected these conditions as infringing on "Rhodesian sovereignty." Instead, the Rhodesian government adopted a new constitution in 1969 setting forth the principle that at some future date, when Africans qualified to vote in sufficient numbers (by virtue of higher monetary, property, and educational status), they would compose half the members of Parliament. After new negotiations in 1971 under a Conservative government, a slight amendment allowed for an ultimate 10-seat African majority in Parliament. How long would this take? Smith reported to his fellow whites that it would take so long that "no European need harbor any anxiety about the security of his future in Rhodesia."[3]

YEARS OF DETENTION AND EXILE

While the British were trying to forestall UDI, Africans in Rhodesia were victims of government crackdowns, especially in the decade 1964 to 1974.

Frequent declarations of a state of emergency gave police and army the power to arrest people without warrant for such infractions as taking unauthorized photographs or making controversial statements. Not only were political organizations banned, but at least 10 publications were closed down, and political meetings were disallowed. Virtually all black leaders were placed in prison or detention camps. Some were able to escape and pursue their political work outside the country.

One of the best known of the nine detention camps was Gonakudzingwa, where Nkomo was sent in 1964. Jane Ngwenya, a top ZAPU leader, who was there for about six and a half years, gave me a graphic description. I had met her in 1961 at the AAPC in Cairo, and we renewed our friendship after her release in 1970. In 1964 Gonakudzingwa had more than 900 inmates. In the southeast, about 400 miles by road from Salisbury, it was flat, semidesert country that was very hot in daytime. Populated by many wild animals, the area was a game preserve.Near the convergence of Rhodesia, South Africa, and Mozambique, at one time it had served as an escape route for South African criminals. The camp inmates lived in barracks made of corrugated metal sheets and cooked their meals from raw food provided weekly.

At first, there was relatively little discipline or supervision. On weekends hundreds of ZAPU supporters made a pilgrimage by car to visit their leaders. The inmates had about four miles in which to move around. No one ever escaped, Ngwenya told me. Nkomo would address the visitors. For a time the detainees even published *The Africa Home News*, a bulletin reporting on the camp. Nkomo was given the title "Chibwechitedze," meaning "the Unconquerable" in Ndebele. Literally it meant a large round boulder so smooth that no one could climb on it. On May 28, 1965, however, when a state of emergency was declared, troops stopped visitors from coming to hear Nkomo.

I was surprised by an early postcard from Nkomo (May 1964): "Just to say hello to you all. I am restricted at the above address. . . . We are adjusting ourselves well and becoming friendly to lions and elephants." Once he wrote saying he had heard me on the Voice of America radio braodcast after I had testified to a congressional committee. His notes were usually innocuous because of censorship, for example thanking me for attending his daughter's wedding in New York and congratulating me on my daughter's wedding, ending with, "We are keeping very much fit and always looking on the bright side of things" (February 5, 1972).

One letter smuggled out had more feeling (December 19, 1969): "The people in control of our country are bigoted racialists. There can be no compromise with them."

Among ZANU leaders, I probably had most contact with Eddison Zvobgo, whom I had known when he was the NDP-ZAPU representative in the United States while attending Tufts University. He was imprisoned in Salisbury for about a year. He wrote to me (July 1965):

At long last I have been released from Salisbury Prison. I gained my "freedom" on Saturday, 10th of July, but I was picked up at the prison front gate and served with a new five year restriction order. I was immediately hustled to the car and driven to this camp [Sikombela Restriction Area near Que Que]. You must have heard that our whole group . . . were moved last month to this area. The restriction area is about 15 miles long by 10 miles wide. There is a huge forest all over here and no people live anywhere near here. It is a new experience. I hope we will be able to survive the isolation. . . . [He reported that the top ZANU leaders were there—Sithole, Mugabe, Takawira.] It's a nice team in temporary exile.

Zvobgo, like many other detainees, made good use of his time in confinement. He earned degrees by correspondence from the University of South Africa and the University of London. The ACOA sent him and others books and tuition, usually through the Rev. Jack Grant, a missionary and head of Christian Care, an organization that helped detainees and their families. Grant wrote in his newsletter (November 20, 1971),

Eddison was excited, if not confused by his sudden release after seven and a half years of detention. He was deposited on a friend's doorstep in Highfield without a penny in his pocket. Within 24 hours he was informed by the superintendent of the township that he could not stay at that place. . . . He could not join his wife and children in England as he is restricted to Highfield and environs. He broke down when I emptied my purse and gave him the few pounds I had in it.

There were sad episodes. Leopold Takawira, vice president of ZANU, died in Salisbury prison in June 1970. Because of his diabetic condition he asked the authorities for hospital care as early as 1967, but this was denied. Although he was in a coma for three days, the prison authorities would not respond to the urgent appeals of his comrades, and the prison doctor reported that he died of "natural causes."

The Rhodesian government also took action against its white critics and opponents. In December 1970 Guy Clutton-Brock, a white member of the banned SRANC, was deprived of his citizenship and deported. Shortly thereafter Cold Comfort Farm, the interracial cooperative he helped found, was closed down and his African associate, Didymus Mutasa, was arrested and imprisoned.

Another white casualty was Jack Halpern, former editor of the liberal *Central African Examiner,* whom I had known several years. His letter to me of October 4, 1963 (in answer to my query about my daughter Martha's plan to study in Nigeria) began, "About your daughter . . ." and went no further. Weeks later when I received it, it went on, "sorry but on the day I started this letter . . . two polite gentlemen arrived to hand me a notice declaring me a prohibited immigrant. No reasons, no legal challenge possible but just get out."

One of the most prominent whites to be imprisoned and then banned was Garfield Todd, whom I met at various times over many years. A former missionary and prime minister and a convincing and polished speaker, who was too liberal to have a significant European following during the Ian Smith years, he seemed a most unlikely candidate for arrest. Yet he and his daughter Judith, who was very outspoken against the government, were picked up in 1972 as security risks under the Law and

Order Maintenance Act. They were held in prison for 10 weeks, Judy in Marandellas and Garfield in Gatooma.

Todd gave me a fascinating account of his ordeal. As the only white prisoner, he was kept in isolation from the Africans. He was allowed half an hour a day alone in the yard as his only exercise. Then quite suddenly he and Judy were released. For four years, he was confined to within 80 paces of his house, while Judy was able to leave the country. He was released only when he was invited by Nkomo to be an adviser to the ZAPU delegation at negotiations in Geneva in 1976.

During this whole restrictive period, the ACOA responded to requests of both ZAPU and ZANU—expenses for the ZAPU representative in New York; funds for books and magazines; stationery and a photostat machine and typewriter for their offices; helping with arrangements and expenses for a North American tour for the ZANU secretary for external affairs; funds for correspondence courses for political detainees, as noted earlier. I was in fairly regular contact with ZAPU and ZANU offices in Lusaka and Dar es Salaam both by letter and visits.

ZAPU and ZANU, working underground, became consciously committed to armed struggle. At first, not all leaders thought sending nationalists abroad for military training was wise. Later, hesitancy disappeared, and ZANU recruits were sent to China, Cuba, and Ghana; ZAPU recruits to the Soviet Union, Bulgaria, North Korea, and Cuba. These trained men then infiltrated back into Rhodesia and became the nucleus for later guerrilla activity.

The first relatively large-scale military action was a series of encounters from August 1967 to July 1968. Later in 1967 Oliver Tambo of the ANC and James Chikerema of ZAPU held a joint press conference to announce the formation of an ANC-ZAPU military alliance. Hundreds of nationalists clashed with Rhodesian forces. The ANC, of course, wanted access to South Africa through Rhodesia. The military action was serious enough that, for the first time, South African troops joined Rhodesians, with Prime Minister Vorster proclaiming, "We are good friends [with Rhodesia] and good friends know what their duty is when the neighbor's house is on fire."

This combined military action was not a success. Nyandoro, with whom I talked in Lusaka, called it a "disaster" but said they had learned a great deal from it and would not make the same mistakes again. They should not have sent military units into the country in uniforms and carrying arms because that helped to identify them. They should not have hidden in caves and forests because when discovered, they were already isolated and easily attacked. They had violated the cardinal rule of guerrilla warfare. They had not quietly infiltrated and mingled with the people as ordinary villagers "like fish in the water." Nor had they prepared the way for their military effort by an educational effort among the people.

For ZANU the war had officially begun earlier, April 28, 1966, when 21 ZANU guerrillas clashed with Rhodesian troops supported by helicopters in the battle of Sinoia. Seven died. The date is remembered as Chimurenga

Day. "Chimurenga" is a Shona word, which stands for the wars of resistance of the 1890s.

A NEW CHANCE

The British hoped that their 1971 agreement with Ian Smith, allowing for an eventual 10-seat African majority in Parliament, would end the strife in Rhodesia. But this agreement had to meet the "test of acceptability" one of the "five principles" put forth by Harold Wilson years before. Lord Pearce, a distinguished British peer, was chosen to lead a commission to Rhodesia to assess opinion, black and white, toward the proposed settlement. From January 11, 1972, to March 11, the Pearce Commission received more than 45,000 letters and memoranda and about 2,000 petitions. It traveled throughout the country in cities and rural areas, where it held 50 meetings attended by 20,000 people, explaining the proposed settlement.[4]

I learned a great deal about what happened from Michael Mawema, a nationalist leader and a major objector to the proposals, when he came to the United States. "Overnight," he explained, "the Zimbabwe political scene was transformed." The African National Council had been organized to mobilize opposition to the proposals and purposely given the same initials as the old Southern Rhodesian African National Congress. New leaders had to be found for it because virtually all the old leaders were detained or exiled. But the detained leaders were consulted. They approved as candidate for president Abel Muzorewa, the Methodist bishop for Rhodesia, who had close ties to American Methodists. Not previously politically active, he was a distinguished public figure and acceptable to almost everyone.

In spite of the protection offered by the Pearce Commission, the new ANC found the going difficult. Mawema explained to the UN, "The Council operated under very trying and difficult circumstances. The state of emergency was still in force; public meetings remained banned despite undertakings that normal political activities would be permitted during the test of acceptability." The ANC was a single-issue organization intended to last only so long as the test of acceptability was in progress.

"We went flat out for victory," Mawema told the UN. The ANC distributed millions of leaflets, stickers, and pieces of literature. But the government tried to frustrate its organizing efforts, rejecting all 200 ANC applications for meetings in tribal trust lands. Some meetings were stopped by police violence, as in Umtali, where a meeting scheduled with the Pearce Commission was canceled at the last moment by the authorities. The crowd refused to disperse. Dogs and tear gas were used to control them, and finally machine guns were fired. Fifteen Africans were killed. After the commission had done its work, the Rhodesian government itself reported that in those two months, 1,736 people had been arrested, of whom 923 had been released and 689 convicted, with the cases of the remainder pending.

The Pearce Commission finally reported succinctly: "We are satisfied . . . that the proposals are acceptable to the great majority of Europeans. We are equally satisfied . . . that the majority of Africans rejected the proposals." Consequently, the Anglo-Rhodesian settlement was turned down.

I met Bishop Muzorewa for the first time in March 1972 in New York. We had a reception for him. When I asked him about ZAPU and ZANU, he replied that they hardly existed anymore, that everything was now being done through the ANC. I wondered if that was an accurate statement.

THE BYRD AMENDMENT—U.S. VIOLATION OF SANCTIONS

Although the rebellion led by Ian Smith received considerable attention in the United States, the government gave African issues low priority and tried not to become involved. Further, the Richard Nixon administration, guided by Secretary of State Henry Kissinger, assumed that any change in southern Africa would not be through African action. According to National Security Study Memorandum No. 39, the white governments in South Africa, Rhodesia, and the Portuguese territories were the effective agents to deal with because they were there to stay. Ultimately the United States supported sanctions against Rhodesia because the British requested it. In early 1970 the United States closed its consulate in Salisbury.

Ian Smith had his staunch U.S. supporters. Shortly after UDI, I began to receive communications from right-wing groups. The National Coordinating Committee of the Friends of Rhodesian Independence wrote (February 22, 1966), "Rhodesia is the key to the West's precarious position in the Afro-Asian world. If Rhodesia falls, South Africa and Portuguese Africa will inevitably follow like dominoes leaving the entire continent in anti-Western hands."

The Friends of Rhodesia, another organization, sponsored all-expense-paid tours to Rhodesia for influential Americans, who found, not surprisingly, that "Rhodesia is a model nation for peace and stability and for harmony and understanding between the races." The bulletin of the American-Southern Africa Council reported that "Sanctions are designed to lead to the destruction of the only firm bastions of anti-communism and Western civilization on the African continent."[5] They were undertaking to have a million letters sent to the White House by the end of the year to show that Rhodesia had massive U.S. support.

Smith's sympathizers adopted a clever legislative strategy. In cooperation with conservative Democratic Senator Harry F. Byrd, an amendment to the Military Procurement Bill was adopted in October 1971, which stipulated that the President could not prohibit the importation into the United States of any strategic material so long as it was not prohibited from a Communist country. Chrome, for example, could be imported from Rhodesia because it was also coming from the Soviet Union. The State Deparment had actually lobbied against this Byrd Amendment, recognizing the damage it would do to U.S. prestige at the UN and in Africa. Union Carbide and the Foote Mineral Company, the largest chrome producers in Rhodesia, lobbied hard for the measure. Nixon finally signed the bill with the amendment on January 24, 1972. Seventy-two strategic items were thus eliminated from the materials prohibited by sanctions, in spite of the fact that the United States had a stockpile of 2.2 million tons of chrome in excess of foreseeable needs. Other strategic materials that could be imported included nickel, copper, asbestos, manganese, and ferrochrome. The *New York Times* (January 26, 1972) editorialized: "The Nixon administration has now taken an action which puts the U.S. in violation of the U.N. Charter and gives moral support to the Rhodesian minority government." The timing of Nixon's signing of the bill was blatantly provocative for it was simultaneous with the work of the Pearce Commission.

The Byrd Amendment became a major political issue before it was finally repealed in December 1973. During these two years of sanctions breaking, U.S. imports came to $413.3 million. The ACOA, among other groups, worked hard for its repeal. Our Washington office, established in 1967, was expanded and became jointly sponsored by the Methodists, Episcopalians, Presbyterians, and the United Church of Christ and later by other denominations and labor unions. It was formally renamed the Washington Office on Africa. Edgar (Ted) Lockwood, an Episcopal clergyman, a lawyer, and member of ACOA's Executive Board, was executive director. He and Christine Root, delaying her studies at Oberlin, served as an effective team.

In New York the ACOA concentrated on community action. Henry Lieberg would sometimes spend all night in the office sending cables to ships suspected of carrying Rhodesian cargo in order to ascertain their port destination. We then called organizations that were prepared to protest. The ACOA tracked eight such ships and reported the arrival of another four to the International Longshoremen's Association (ILA), the UN Sanctions Committee, the chairman of the House Subcommittee on Africa, and others. Three ships were diverted as a result of threatened demonstrations. The ILA refused to unload Rhodesian cargo. Major demonstrations occurred in New York, Philadelphia, and ports in Louisiana and Maryland. Although these efforts did not stop the cargo from being off-loaded ultimately, they did call public attention to U.S. disregard of UN sanctions and added impetus to efforts to repeal the Byrd Amendment.

NEW NATIONALIST DIVISIONS IN EXILE

While the African National Council was winning a tremendous victory inside Rhodesia by forestalling the imposition of the Anglo-Rhodesian

George Nyandoro and Jason Moyo, leaders of ZAPU, at the ZAPU office in Lusaka, Zambia, 1978.

proposals, a new set of problems plagued the nationalist movement in exile. This was a painful period for exiled ZAPU and ZANU and their supporters abroad. Their main task was to publicize the cause and build up military strength. The bickering, intrigue, and infighting among the leaders, particularly in ZAPU, almost negated their efforts for a time. Although one could argue that this was just part of the frustration of political exile, it did not make the situation any less damaging.

A new split among ZAPU leaders came to a head in early 1970. Nkomo, confined to Gonakudzingwa, could not be consulted. External leadership was in the hands of the five stalwarts in Lusaka. Chikerema was acting chairman, working closely with Nyandoro, national secretary. Jason Moyo, treasurer; George Silundika, publicity officer; and Edward Ndlovu, deputy national secretary, were not in Chikerema's confidence and increasingly drew together in opposition to him. I did not realize the extent of the tension until I received a copy of a memorandum (February 25, 1970) from Moyo, "Observations on Our Struggle" pointing to the lack of discipline in the military as well as in the political organization. It protested vigorously against Chikerema's unilateral decision, which Moyo learned about only through the daily press, to allow a British television team to produce a program at ZAPU's military camp in Zambia. This act had also angered the Zambian government because it had always claimed that no liberation movement had a training camp on its soil.

Weeks later in a stinging reply, Chikerema exerted his authority as the inheritor of Nkomo's mantle. He wrote in a memorandum:

Our Zimbabwe society here abroad has become a hotbed of tribal intrigue, nepotism and corruption. I have left this drift for too long in the interest of revolutionary democracy. . . . I am the leader of this organization—a leader among equals—but my authority and mandate is above that of all my colleagues. [Then Chikerema announced drastic steps:] I have therefore dissolved the whole military command. . . . I am taking direct control of foreign affairs . . . and of all external accounts of party funds.

By this action he was attempting to wrest their powers from Silundika and Moyo. They replied immediately in a memo declaring Chikerema's action "null and void."

This split led to violence at Zimbabwe House, a ZAPU hostel in Lusaka. The Zambian police intervened and the government threatened, "If we close all ZAPU's offices in Zambia, it will be ZAPU's fault, not ours." Kaunda told me soon after that he had called the five ZAPU leaders to the state house and sternly told them that they must come to some agreement or close down their operations.

The leaders made an effort and came to an awkward working accommodation. On several visits to the ZAPU office in 1970, I never saw Chikerema there. He worked privately elsewhere. But I met the other four leaders. Their relationship was polite but strained. They never contradicted one another publicly, but privately Moyo, Silundika, and Ndlovu criticized Chikerema. Apparently the split had tribal overtones—Zezuru (Chikerema and Nyandoro) versus Kalanga. Nevertheless, they said,"We must make a go of it." Since they hadn't even been speaking to one another previously, perhaps this was progress.

This uneasy relationship did not last long. In late 1970 Chikerema began unity discussions with Nathan Shamuyarira, a ZANU leader, and a little later with Herbert Chitepo, who headed the external office of ZANU. The fact that Chikerema proceeded with the discussions without consulting his ZAPU comrades exacerbated their bad relationship. The OAU cut off all but military assistance to ZAPU, and that was to go indirectly through the Zambian government. ZANU on its side called a conference, which voted not to continue unity talks and put Shamuyarira off the Supreme Council.

A new organization did emerge from these talks, in October 1971, the Front for the Liberation of Zimbabwe (FROLIZI). It claimed to represent a united ZAPU-ZANU, which it considered "dead and buried." The reality was far different. The OAU never recognized FROLIZI, and President Nyerere refused to allow it to open an office in Tanzania. Its existence, however, helped clarify the leadership question in ZAPU. Chikerema and Nyandoro were expelled "with dishonor." After a few months, Chikerema took over as president of FROLIZI with Nyandoro in charge of foreign affairs. Subsequently, Shamuyarira left the organization. He told me that it soon became clear to him that it had no potential as a real united front. Nevertheless, as a result of all this maneuvering, there were now four nationalist organizations either in Rhodesia or in exile—ZAPU, ZANU, the ANC, and FROLIZI.

THE NEW OFFENSIVE

Word of a greatly intensified armed struggle filtered out of Rhodesia in December 1972. The new offensive, the beginning of the final phase of the struggle between African nationalists and Rhodesians, was the work of the Zimbabwe African National Liberation Army (ZANLA), the military wing of ZANU. In preparation, ZANLA militants had crossed into Rhodesia without arms or uniforms and lived as ordinary villagers for at least six months. The ZANU publication *Zimbabwe News* (November 1972) commented even before the offensive began, "ZANLA fighters are now moving among the masses like fish in the water." The *Johannesburg Star* (February 10, 1975) pointed out that "The newcomers infiltrated across an unmarked border with Mozambique in an extremely rugged area of bush and escarpment. They traveled via Mozambique with the help of the FRELIMO guerrillas attacking there."

A new factor in the offensive was the cooperation between ZANU and FRELIMO, indicating the pragmatic approach of the Mozambique movement. Their longtime ally, ZAPU, was based in Zambia and was entering Rhodesia from the west and northwest. ZANU, however, made inroads into Rhodesia on the east and northeast, bordering Mozambique. Since Rhodesia and Mozambique share a very long border, the cooperation between the two movements was especially important. They began coordinated attacks on the railway and road links from Umtali, in eastern Rhodesia to Beira, the second major Mozambique port.

The ZANLA attacks started on December 21, near the town of Centenary. Objectives were the Altena Farm and the Whistlefield Farm, which was a command post for the Rhodesian army. A truckload of 35 Rhodesian soldiers was blown up by antitank mines, two other troop trucks were destroyed, and a locomotive engine was exploded. The statistical information emanating from each side at the end of a year differed greatly, but the guerrillas were operating with increased effectiveness. The *London Daily Telegraph* (April 13, 1973) observed, "Mr. [Ian] Smith has now accepted that the present guerrilla offensive is the most serious security threat the country has faced."

The military campaign changed the way of life of the whites, especially in the northeast. Women were mustered for field reservist duties and trained in the use of firearms, first aid, and radio operation. Men had both farm and patrol duty. Either social life was limited to daylight hours, or dinner guests spent the night. Road signs warned of the danger of travel after 3:00 P.M. Most farmers laid warning trip mines and alarms. House windows were covered with mesh to stop grenades, and walls and windows were sandbagged.

The Rhodesian government created a "no-go" area of 200 miles along the Mozambique border and herded Africans into "protected villages," like the Portuguese *aldeamentos*. For the first time, reserve units of men of 38 or more were called up. An exodus of whites began. Tourism in 1973 was the lowest on record. The government announced the "Settler '74" campaign to increase white immigration. In January full-page advertisement in the *Rhodesian Herald* asked readers to give names and addresses of people who might want to move to Rhodesia.

In the meantime, in 1973 Ian Smith and Muzorewa of the African National Council met several times to consider the possibility of a negotiated solution. Muzorewa asked for parity in Parliament (not one man, one vote), a British veto on any discriminatory amendments to the constitution, an integrated school system, and amnesty for guerrillas outside the country. Smith rejected these proposals as "totally and absolutely unacceptable." The other nationalist movements felt that the time for negotiation was past. They were committed only to the principle of majority rule.

DETENTE

In October 1974 at the celebration of the 10th anniversary of Zambia's independence in Lusaka, I sat beside Henry Hamadziripi, treasurer of ZANU, whom I had known for several years. As a veteran of the nationalist struggle, he knew the inside of many a Rhodesian prison. He remarked that change would come soon, not without further bitter struggle, but "now we are assured of victory." ZANU's offensive in the north and east was expanding, ZAPU forces were infiltrating into the west, and even FROLIZI was involved in limited action.

I also talked with Jane Ngwenya of ZAPU. While returning from Botswana a short time before, she noted that the trains from Rhodesia heading south through Botswana to South Africa were loaded with white Rhodesians; on northbound trains virtually no Europeans were evident. The white exodus was on. The Rhodesian government was taking desperate measures. I learned that Nkomo had just been moved from the Gonakudzingwa detention camp near the Mozambique border to Salisbury prison, lest FRELIMO forces attack across the border to free the veteran leader. The camp was in fact soon closed down. Ngwenya told me how, in her presence, Ethan Dube, a ZAPU leader with her in Botswana, had been clubbed unconscious while in a private home and then driven by two Europeans into Rhodesia, where he disappeared. Edson Sithole, a ZANU leader, was kidnapped outside a hotel in downtown Salisbury and never seen again. The ZANU office at the Liberation Center in Lusaka was bombed in the middle of the night shortly before the 10th anniversary celebration.

When I went to the Liberation Center, although I had often been there and knew the Zambian in charge, I could not go beyond the reception room. Only a few designated members of each movement were allowed inside the compound. Armed police were on hand to enforce the regulation.

Inside Rhodesia there was a feeling that transition to majority rule was not far away, and even those Africans in government pay were ready to defy the government. Ian Smith called an *indaba* (a conference of chiefs and leaders) to discuss problems between the government and the Africans. Only about 20 of the 150 invited (more or less beholden to him) showed up.

Early in the morning of my departure from Lusaka I had an unexpected invitation to meet with President Kaunda privately. He had been so busy meeting guests for the celebration that this was quite special. As I entered the hall of the president's house, previously the British governor's mansion, I sidestepped the leopard rug, feeling as though I would be treading on something alive. I was seated in a waiting room and offered fruit juice. Soon the president arrived, dressed in a neat safari-type suit with a kerchief around his neck. We went into a private lounge where he seemed to give me his undivided attention. Although his hair was graying and he was heavier than on his first U.S. visit 14 years earlier, he looked good. The strain of his responsibilities did not seem to be taking a toll. It was then 8:00 A.M. and at 8:50 I was due at the airport, a 30-minute drive away.

This was an important time to see Kaunda. Three days earlier he had given a speech at the University of Zambia in response to one by Prime Minister Vorster. Actually the two speeches, in both content and timing, had been carefully orchestrated to inaugurate a brief period of detente. Vorster had said that South Africa would not interfere with Mozambique (on the verge of independence), wanted to normalize relations with black African states, and would offer economic aid if requested. Kaunda called Vorster's speech "the voice of reason for which Africa and the world have waited for years." Speaking of Rhodesia, he said,

a military victory for the Smith regime is impossible, but a black victory inevitable. . . . Mr. Smith must now opt for a political solution. . . . we therefore reaffirm our pledge to call upon the liberation movements to desist from armed struggles if Mr. Smith accepts negotiations with the . . . legitimate and authentic leaders of the African people. . . . [Speaking directly to South Africa, he said] The time has come for the South African government to make a choice . . . either the road to peace, progress and development or the escalation of conflict in southern Africa.

He called on South Africa to disengage from Rhodesia and ended with the hope that South Africa would support "peaceful change."

Kaunda told me that he expected a further response from Vorster soon. He expected South Africa to put pressure on Smith because with Mozambique and Angola independent, Smith would have to come to terms with a new reality in southern Africa. Kaunda hoped to be able to invite Nkomo and Sithole, both incarcerated in Rhodesia, to come to Zambia soon to discuss unity in their country.

When I remembered to check my watch, it was 8:45. Kaunda had someone call the airport and hold the plane. As I left, he gave me his picture inscribed, "George. Always remember, keep smiling as you serve your fellow man. God's blessings, Kenneth." Then I was driven to the airport, where I was the last passenger to board the plane.

Soon after my return to New York, the startling news came out that the Rhodesian government had released Nkomo and Sithole for meetings in Lusaka, which turned out to be a real summit meeting on Rhodesia. It was attended by the presidents of Tanzania, Botswana, and Zambia, who were joined by Nkomo, Sithole, Muzorewa, and Chikerema. The resulting Lusaka Agreement stated that the movements "hereby agree to unite in the African National Council." The separate organizations were to dissolve, join the ANC for an interim four months, and then participate in a congress to draft a new constitution and elect new leadership. The purpose of this unity was to prepare for "any conference for the transfer of power to the majority [in Rhodesia] that might be called." At the same time it was recognized that the armed struggle would continue until total liberation was won.

Hope for a detente seemed justified when Ian Smith announced the release of African leaders to engage in normal legal activity. "This will I believe create the right atmosphere for the holding of the constitutional conference," he said. It was soon obvious, however, that things would not run smoothly. The Smith government made clear that it was not ready to hand over power to the majority. Also, there were leadership problems among the nationalists. In New York a little later, Nkomo made disparaging remarks to me about Muzorewa. The bishop now had political ambitions and wanted more permanant power in the ANC, which was not about to go out of business. This did not sit well with Nkomo, who felt responsible for Muzorewa's original designation as ANC chairman.

Even more serious was the leadership problem in ZANU. Although Sithole still held the title of president, he had lost his power while in prison. Zvobgo explained to me that Sithole and the other imprisoned leaders communicated with one another daily when they were together from early morning till 4:00 P.M. in an enclosed bull pen. In such circumstances, he said, "You naturally get to know the strengths and weaknesses of your comrades quite well." Sithole's gradual loss of his cellmates' confidence and respect culminated in his attempt to make a deal with the government in order to avoid six more years in prison for promoting a plot (smuggled out in letters) to assassinate Ian Smith. He told the authorities he would convince his fellow ZANU leaders to renounce violence if his sentence were commuted. He stated in court, "I wish publicly to dissociate myself in word, thought, and deed from any subversive activities . . . and from any form of violence." Yet he privately told his comrades that once released they could carry on as before. The ZANU leaders felt this two-faced position could not be explained to their members and they flatly refused to accept it.

When Sithole, the ZANU president, was called to the Lusaka meeting in December 1974, the ZANU executive in Salisbury prison sent Mugabe to represent them instead. Mugabe, whom I had known at the UN during the NDP years, was a quietly impressive man, not given to dramatics. Over the years I was impressed by his disciplined strength and dedication to principle. Born in 1924 in a small village northwest of Salisbury, he had

had a religious upbringing in a Jesuit mission. He told me the most important influences on his life were the year he spent at Fort Hare University College in South Africa in 1950 and his contact with the Youth League of the ANC of South Africa just before the Defiance Campaign. He was strongly influenced by Gandhian nonviolence and by Kwame Nkrumah while he (Mugabe) taught in Ghana just after its independence. When he returned to Rhodesia, he began his career as a nationalist leader in the just organized NDP. A measure of his discipline is that during the nearly 11 years he spent in prison and detention, he earned three university degrees by correspondence, which the ACOA helped finance.

When Mugabe appeared at Lusaka instead of Sithole, the four presidents were nonplussed. They had known nothing of the rupture in ZANU. When talking to me in 1983, Nyerere recalled with a smile that he had been very rough on Mugabe. "Who is Mugabe? We don't know Mugabe. We know Sithole. He is the person who was elected president of ZANU." So Mugabe was sent back to the Rhodesian prison, and Sithole came, accompanied, at the insistence of the imprisoned ZANU leaders, by one of their members, Maurice Nyagumbo, to keep an eye on him.

CHAPTER SEVENTEEN

The Struggle for Namibia

The sun had not yet risen when a group of five of us headed for the airport in Lusaka, Zambia, on December 6, 1967. I was nervous, as I am sure my companions were. It wasn't just that we were embarking on a risky project but on one that, after nine months of work, was finally coming to pass. For this was the day we were flying into South West Africa (now Namibia) in two small chartered planes without South African visas and therefore in defiance of South Africa's de facto control of the area. We had put so much time, effort, and money into the project that we couldn't take the expedition lightly.

CONFRONTATION—A MILE HIGH

The project had started casually, almost as an intriguing intellectual exercise, back in February. I was lunching with my old friend Lyle Tatum. We had both been pacifists in World War II. He had then worked for the American Friends Service Committee in Africa and was now executive secretary of Farmers and World Affairs. We talked of South West Africa. The area had been through a frustrating six years, 1960–1966, during which the UN had waited for the International Court of Justice (ICJ) to decide on South Africa's legal right to continue its League of Nations mandate to administer the former German territory. By an eight to seven vote, the court ruled that it could give no verdict because the plaintiffs, Ethiopia and Liberia, had no legal standing to bring the case. In effect there was no decision at all. So in October 1966, the UN General Assembly took action and passed Resolution 2145, declaring that because South Africa had failed to ensure the moral and material well being of the indigenous inhabitants of South West Africa, "the Mandate . . . is therefore terminated . . . and henceforth South West Africa comes under the direct responsibility of the U.N."

Spurred by this development, Tatum and I began to speculate on what could be done to implement the UN resolution. During brainstorming sessions over the ensuing months, we developed a plan of action. In the meantime the UN passed Resolution 2248 to establish the UN Council for South West Africa to administer the area. The problem, of course, was that South Africa refused to recognize the UN resolutions.

As our weekly planning sessions went on, we were joined by two men with broad African experience—Walter Martin from London, director of the Quaker Mission to the UN, and Jim Bristol, from Philadelphia, working with the American Friends Service Committee.

243

Increasingly I saw a parallel between our present desire to implement the UN resolution and my feeling 20 years earlier that the U.S. Supreme Court decision in the Irene Morgan case to outlaw segregation in interstate travel needed to be tested. A group of us, black and white, had done so in 1947 by taking freedom rides in the south. That project helped to highlight the continuing disregard in southern states for Supreme Court decisions about segregation in travel.

Although there was certainly a practical difference between U.S. Supreme Court decisions and UN resolutions, still we felt the need to develop a viable plan to challenge South Africa's continued defiance of the UN. We organized the Ad Hoc Committee for the Development of an Independent South West Africa and recruited some volunteer specialists to attempt to fly into the country to develop projects in farming, nutrition, health, and cooperatives. We raised funds to cover expenses estimated at $20,000. We discussed the project with the UN Council, received the support of SWAPO, sought and received essential cooperation from President Kenneth Kaunda of Zambia, who assigned Vernon Mwaanga, later Zambian ambassador to the UN and foreign minister, to give us every assistance on the African end.

In addition to Lyle Tatum and me, our team that December morning consisted of John L.S. Holloman, M.D., former president of the National Medical Association and the Medical Committee for Human Rights and later New York City commissioner of health and hospitals; Professor Flemmie P. Kittrell, a nutrition specialist at Howard University; and Samuel F. Ashelman, economic consultant with the International Cooperative Development Association. Jim Bristol, who had been involved in the detailed planning, suffered a heart attack, which made his participation impossible. Walter Martin, who had done a lot of advance work, did not join us because it was less complicated to make the group all American in case of later legal action. Joining the five of us were three journalists for the London *Times* and two Zambian papers. Thus, including the pilots, there were 10 on two planes. No advance public notice had been given of our planned flight. We told Robert Good, U.S. ambassador to Zambia, the day before we left Lusaka and told the newspapers that evening.

The two planes, Piper-Aztecs, took off shortly after a cloudy dawn. I sat next to the pilot in the lead plane. I had never flown on such a small plane before. The cabin was quite intimate, almost like riding in the front seat of a car. It was difficult at first to talk to the American pilot, David Bobman, because he did not know anything about our project. If he had known, undoubtedly the planes would not have been available. The other pilot was a white Rhodesian.

The pilots first realized that they were involved in an unusual project after we had refueled at Livingstone, about an hour and a half flight from Lusaka, and had taken a turn around the spectacular Victoria Falls lying just below us. Then as we started the three-hour flight across the desolate expanse of Botswana, our plane was radioed by South African police. A voice with a heavy Afrikaans accent said: "We know what your mission is. You will not be allowed to land in Windhoek. What is your intention?" The puzzled pilot turned to me and asked what this was all about.

We had prepared a brief written statement explaining that we had no visas, did not recognize South African administration in South West Africa, and planned to land there to identify projects to help in the transition to independence. Grim-faced, the pilot said, "This is a gritty position." He told the South African police that we would fly on. Thus we passed the first crisis. No further word came over the radio for some time. The pilot turned to me and commented, "You can probably get the visa problem straightened out at the Windhoek airport." I said nothing, realizing that the real confrontation was yet to come.

The flight itself was pleasant—scattered clouds, no rain, not very bumpy. We flew at an altitude of 4,000 to 5,000 feet. Below was the great desertlike emptiness of Botswana. When the pilot announced that we had crossed into South West Africa, the radio came to life again. An Afrikaans voice asked for the names of all passengers. The pilot complied. Then the voice said: "Listen carefully and note this important message. You will not be allowed to land at Strijdom Airport [at Windhoek] or any other airport in South West Africa unless all documents of crew and passengers meet all local legal requirements. We know the reason for your mission and should you land against this instruction, you shall have to bear the consequences."

Without a word the pilot turned the craft around and radioed the other plane, which was always out of sight, to do likewise. We argued with the pilot that our contract was to land us at Windhoek. He asked, "Have you got £20,000 to pay for the plane?" Then he added, "I am not going to jail for this."

I had a sinking feeling. Then we all realized that we had a different crisis. The fuel needle was almost on empty. The pilot's request to land for fuel was denied. "Find Ghanzi or Maun," we were told. They were just spots in the desert. We could not see Ghanzi. The pilot said we could not make Livingstone. I perspired profusely as we looked for Maun.

The plane jerked and the left motor went dead. This was frightening. Not knowing the plane had an emergency tank, I peered frantically for a place to land. As the pilot turned on the emergency tank, the right motor stopped, and the propeller went limp. The second emergency tank came on. We could go a little farther. Finally a faint signal appeared in the navigation equipment. The other plane (now in front of us) radioed, "We see it. Look for body of water on the right." We landed and refueled at the Maun airstrip. Our group went through an agonizing discussion. Should we, according to our backup plan, be dropped at a town near the Caprivi Strip and try to enter South West Africa by Land Rover? We decided against it. The planes took off again, and in three hours we arrived back in Lusaka after dark, hungry and dead tired, to face reporters.

I had never felt more let down. We had worked so hard, and then it was all over in one day without a satisfactory ending. We had wanted a confrontation on the ground. Instead, as Tatum pointed out, "We had our confrontation a mile high."

The incident received a lot of publicity. Headlines in the South African and South West African press read: "Intruders Test South Africa Control of South West Africa," "Yankees Turn Back Without Landing," "Americans Sent Back." The London *Times, New York Times,* and *Washington Post* all had stories. Prime Minister John Vorster was quoted in *Die Transvaler,* a leading Afrikaans paper (December 7, 1967), "Mr. George Houser . . . was well known for his interference in South African affairs, and his action was arrogant and provocative. . . . The whole move was merely an attempt to revive the South West Africa debate in the U.N. . . . Nobody will be allowed in South Africa or South West Africa without proper documents and Houser will definitely, with or without documents, not be permitted."

There was a sad sequel to this experience. A year later on the main street in Lusaka I ran into David Bobman, the pilot. He greeted me as an old friend and we stopped for coffee. He told me that of all his experiences in flying charters "ours took the cake." Then he said he would like to try again. I was elated to feel that we had a new ally, and we agreed to keep in touch. A week later in New York I saw in the *Times of Zambia* (December 16, 1967) a front-page story of the crash of a chartered flight caught in a storm near Lusaka. The plane had "suddenly plunged into the bush and exploded eight miles from the International airport. The five occupants, including the pilot, David Bobman, were all killed." I felt as if I had lost a friend. I didn't have the heart to plan another expedition at that time.

EXILE POLITICS

Our attempted "fly-in" was one of many events that signaled that a new active period had begun after the UN termination of South Africa's mandate. The preceding six years had been a period of waiting on the part of African nationalists while South Africa went ahead with plans to extend apartheid to South West Africa. In 1964 the South African government produced the Odendaal Plan, which formally recommended imposing the "homelands" policy of South Africa on South West Africa. The theory was that the area, like South Africa, was made up of many "nations" (ethnic units), all of which should have the right of self-government—a perfect divide-and-rule device, dishonestly and cynically using the language of self-government. About 40 percent of the territory would be partitioned into self-governing homelands and more than 50 percent, including the industrialized and mineral-rich areas, would remain permanently under white control.

During these six confusing years, many black nationalists had fled the country after the violence of December 10, 1959, in the Old Location at Windhoek. Some gravitated to New York, where, after making presentations to the UN, they were not sure of their next moves. Quasi-refugees, they were cut off from events back home and had to scrounge for financial backing both politically and personally. One could not make a profession out of telling one's story again and again to the UN.

In this realm of exile politics it took some time to organize internationally, particularly for South West Africans, who had had little experience outside their country. I saw something of their travail. Sam Nujoma arrived in New York following his escape from banishment to Ovamboland. Here I met him. Then he went to Cairo to the third AAPC and thence to Dar es Salaam, Tanzania, to establish the first SWAPO office in exile. Jacob Kuhangua arrived in New York next with his harrowing tale of arrest and deportation to Ovamboland, and then his escape across Africa. He was national secretary of SWAPO and began his own travels through Africa and Europe on its behalf.

New York was not the only gathering point. Dar es Salaam drew political refugees like a magnet. In January 1962 I spent hours talking with some 20 SWAPO refugees there. Only one had a job. Julius Nyerere told me that TANU was spending about £400 a month to help them and couldn't keep it up.

Kuhangua told me there were about 130 SWAPO refugees, some at a camp and others in a SWAPO-run house. They needed food and clothing. When the Tanzanian government had to drop its 21 shilling-per-person-per-day subsidy for refugees, the Christian Council of Tanzania refugee program and other private bodies picked it up.

In Accra, Ghana, I met Peter Mueshihange, later SWAPO secretary for foreign affairs. He had worked in Cape Town in the 1950s and helped found the OPO. Arrested in the demonstrations in Cape Town at the time of the Sharpeville Massacre in 1960, he had served three months in jail and was then deported to South West Africa. From there he escaped and eventually obtained a UN scholarship to a government school in Ghana.

My path frequently crossed that of Sam Nujoma. He took me to a refugee center near Lusaka. All 57 new arrivals were crowded into a dwelling for 20. Some bunks, hardly wide enough for one person, held two. After several days they were to move on to Dar es Salaam, where a few might receive scholarships and others would just have to survive.

In Kinshasa, Zaire, I met Andreas Shipanga, later SWAPO information and publicity secretary. After eight months exile he felt destitute and discouraged but also responsible for a half dozen or so South West Africans who depended on him. He had made an odyssey from Ovamboland by bicycle across to Angola in the early 1950s, then on through Rhodesia to the Johannesburg mines and finally to Cape Town during the founding days of OPO. He had tried to escape from South West Africa through Botswana in 1963, was kidnapped by South African police, but was eventually released to the Botswana authorities. He ended up in Kinshasa with a number of SWAPO members to pave the way for training at the UPA military camp at Kinkuzu in the Congo. I talked with one of his discouraged comrades who had been at Kinkuzu for nine months. All the trainees wanted to move on to Dar es Salaam. They had no money, could not speak French, and felt isolated.

During these six years, exiled leaders worked constantly either to establish a united front of various nationalist organizations or to ensure the preeminence of one group over another. But no political party was prepared to dissolve. As in other countries, the existence of separate and competing movements was a continuing problem for the ACOA and other supporters. Whom should they primarily relate to? Which movement was most effective? It wasn't always easy to tell. We maintained neutrality by responding to legitimate requests from any group as best we could, and we also helped individuals.

Frequently it was difficult to differentiate between personal and organizational appeals. The Rev. Markus Kooper was a case in point. He had suffered physical abuse from the South African government when he opposed South Africa's control. He was removed from his congregation and with all his family was cast into an isolated desert place miles from his home area. We sent funds through Chief Kutako to help sustain him until he escaped. He came to New York and spent 16 years at odd jobs and as a perpetual petitioner at the UN. Not until the mid-1970s was he able to return home.

Jacob Kuhangua suffered a severe personal tragedy. He was a vibrant person, committed to SWAPO and ambitious to lead. I was shocked to learn that in Dar es Salaam he had been stabbed in a fit of anger by his SWAPO roommate the last day of 1965. His spine was severed, so that he was paralyzed from the waist down. His leadership in SWAPO was over. Although painfully confined to a wheelchair in New York, he earned a degree from Long Island University. He finally returned home in the late 1970s but needed constant hospital care.

A CHANGE OF STRATEGY

Changed circumstances in Africa influenced new strategies in the South West African independence struggle in the mid-1960s. Most important was the realization that neither the ICJ nor the United Nations could effect fundamental change. Events inside the country would determine the future.

Of special importance to SWAPO was the opening up of a military base in the Congo by the UPA. In 1962 Kuhangua had, on behalf of SWAPO, signed an agreement with Holden Roberto calling for military collaboration. This action signaled their rather idealistic desire "to form a federation of the independent states of Angola, Bechuanaland [Botswana] and South West Africa, governed by a central government which would eventually become part of the federal states of Africa." That same year at an unpublicized conference in Mbeya, Tanzania, SWAPO had decided to form a liberation army and to prepare its people for armed struggle. When

I visited the Kinkuzu base in June 1963, Sam Nujoma was one of the liberation leaders there.

The development in 1963 of the Caprivi African National Union (CANU) was important to SWAPO. The Caprivi Strip* is a panhandle about 80 miles wide by 300 miles long running east of Namibia to Zambia between Botswana on the south and Angola in the north. Heavy forests and many rivers, particularly in the eastern part, make it good guerrilla country. CANU merged with SWAPO in 1964, making Caprivi an entering wedge into South West Africa.

SWAPO had been quietly moving young men out of the country for some time. Small groups of two to five made their way to SWAPO headquarters in Francistown, Botswana, and then to Tanzania for orientation before being sent elsewhere for study or training. The South African government was aware of SWAPO's preparations. The venerable SWAPO leader Herman Toivo Ja-Toivo (he later dropped "Herman" for "Andimba"), imprisoned for 18 years, whom I met at the UN, told me that supposedly trusted SWAPO comrades gave away the position of a SWAPO training camp in the bush and the method of supplying it. Thus South African authorities knew when the first SWAPO militants infiltrated back into their country in September 1965.

The armed struggle actually began August 26, 1966, hardly a month after the ICJ's nondecision, when the South African police attacked the SWAPO camp. Taken by surprise, at least two SWAPO soldiers were killed and eight captured, along with a quantity of arms.

The conflict continued on a low level, which, nevertheless, South Africa had to take seriously. It more than doubled the police force in South West Africa. The press reported increasingly frequent incidents: an attack on a Bantu administration office and residence in Oshikango in September 1966, an attack on two tribal headmen in the pay of South Africa in November, a skirmish with 10 guerrillas who escaped to the Caprivi Strip in March 1967, the death of the SWAPO leader Tobias Heinjeko at a crossing of the Zambezi River in May.

The Caprivi Strip became the focus for armed clashes. The South African journalist A.J. Venter reported, "African terrorists based in Zambia have invaded the South African-controlled Caprivi Strip. . . . They attacked a post near South Africa's big airforce base at Katima Mulilo. Another attack was made near the South Africa administrative center of Runtu some miles to the west."[1] The London *Times* (May 25, 1971)

---

*The Germans had gained control of the Caprivi Strip, named after the German imperial chancellor, Count Leo de Caprivi, in 1893 to have access to the Zambezi River, then considered potentially navigable. They also hoped to link South West Africa to their colony of Tanganyika and thus have a corridor across Africa, an ambition frustrated by Cecil Rhodes's northward thrust. Rhodesians occupied the strip until 1914, when the British took over administration of South West Africa until South Africa obtained the League of Nations mandate.

reported two South African policemen killed and seven injured when a Land Rover struck a powerful land mine in the Caprivi.

In response to this violence, South Africa's forces in Namibia were expanded to 40,000 by 1970. SWAPO alleged that the South African police and army waged a campaign of retaliation against villagers. Water resources were poisoned in villages suspected of aiding guerrillas, and forests were burned in order to facilitate spotting SWAPO militants. The refugee problem in adjacent countries, especially Zambia, grew rapidly. It was reported that 2,000 had crossed into Zambia and Botswana during one three-day period in 1968. Two camps were organized in Zambia to help deal with the influx.

South Africa regarded the Namibian resistance as just part of a wider Communist conspiracy and took stringent legal measures to try to stamp it out. A rash of arrests were made. They were brought closer to me when Hidipo Hamutenya, now a major SWAPO leader, who was then a student at Lincoln University, wrote me that his father along with many others, was being held in prison in Pretoria under terrible conditions.

The most renowned person arrested was Toivo Ja-Toivo. He had not, at first, favored the use of violence. Nevertheless, as SWAPO representative in Ovamboland, he had felt it his duty to assist the SWAPO militants in the bush. His own livelihood came from a small store he operated out of his house. His part in the struggle was betrayed by his supposed comrades.

Only after these multiple arrests did the South African Parliament enact laws to legitimize what had been done. In June 1967 it passed the Terrorism Act as an amendment to the Suppression of Communism Act and made it retroactive to 1962. It was made applicable to South West Africa. "Terrorism" was defined as an act committed anywhere with the intent to endanger law and order in South Africa or South West Africa. The accused could be arrested without warrant and held in solitary confinement indefinitely for interrogation without access to lawyers or family. A trial under this act was by judge alone, without a jury, and the accused had the onus of proving innocence beyond a reasonable doubt. Penalties ranged from five years imprisonment to execution. Thirty-seven black South West Africans were arrested and held in solitary confinement for at least 200 days waiting for the Terrorism Act to be passed so that they could be formally charged.

I shuddered to hear how the prisoners were tortured while supposedly being interrogated. The gruesome details—electric shock treatment, hanging by the arms with only the toes touching the floor, beatings—are described by one of the accused, John Ya-Otto, a school teacher and secretary of SWAPO in his *Battlefront Namibia* (1982). One prisoner died.

The episode became real to us at the ACOA when Joel Carlson, lawyer for the accused, arrived in New York. One of the few South African lawyers who was prepared to defend opponents of the government, he suffered the consequences, as he described in his book *No Neutral Ground* (1973). The threats against his family, the anonymous calls, the bullets fired into his office, and the bomb threats finally made him decide to leave South Africa. In 1967, however, his task was to save the lives of the 37 accused. He decided, after talking with them, that it was essential to sensitize the international community to what South Africa was doing in South West Africa.

In New York Carlson worked like a man tormented. He was greatly helped by Jennifer Davis, who was doing research at the ACOA; Mike Davis, formerly a lawyer in South Africa; and the attorney Peter Weiss, then president of the ACOA. In two frantic weeks of meetings in New York and Washington with organizations and influential Americans, both in and out of government, Carlson was responsible for activating many people to help save the accused from the death penalty. He also went to London and Geneva. The UN adopted a resolution (with only South Africa and Portugal opposed) demanding that South Africa call off the trial.

After this international exposure, some of the worst abuses surrounding the trial ended. Police dogs at the entrance to the court house in Pretoria disappeared. Distinguished international observers were on hand, such as Richard Falk, a Princeton professor representing the International Commission of Jurists, and Arthur Larsen from the World Lutheran Federation.

On January 26, 1968, 19 of the accused were given life imprisonment, 9 (including Toivo) received 20-year sentences, and 2 had 5-year terms. Others received suspended 5-year sentences. Only 2 were acquitted.

A LONG-TERM CONFRONTATION

The struggle for Namibia's independence has proceeded on two levels—outside the country and inside. External action has quickened in response to urgent internal developments. The beginning of the armed struggle and the terrorism trial sparked the UN Security Council in March 1969 to endorse the Assembly's resolution ending South Africa's mandate and calling for its immediate withdrawal. In June 1971 in reconsidering its case, the ICJ finally declared South Africa's occupation of Namibia illegal. The international community was unwilling, however, to back up these decisions with power.

The two significant nationalist movements operating outside the country were SWAPO and SWANU. Along with practically every other African nationalist movement, SWAPO is nontribalist in principle. Still, it has been strengthened by a firm traditional base among the Ovambos, who are almost half the population. SWAPO has had surprisingly stable leadership, given the strains of exile politics. Sam Nujoma has been president from the beginning. Few major leaders have left. Those who have (such as Mburumba Kerina and Shipanga) have not been able to organize successful competing movements or cause a schism.

SWAPO's political program is straightforward: "to establish a free democratic government in Namibia founded upon the will and participation of all the people of our country." It accepts both public and privately

owned industry. Forced contract labor will be abolished, and the land of absentee owners will be confiscated. Until the mid-1970s SWAPO followed a neutralist policy internationally. It was one of the few liberation groups that occasionally consulted with U.S. embassies in Dar es Salaam or Lusaka. Although aligned with other groups then acceptable to the Soviet Union, it also worked with Holden Roberto's FNLA and Jonas Savimbi's UNITA, a position that later changed.

In the fall of 1971, SWAPO had five key leaders at the UN for almost three months. Nujoma set a precedent by being the first representative of an African liberation movement to be heard by the Security Council. In 1972 SWAPO sponsored a full-time representative at the UN, Theo Ben-Gurirab. By then SWAPO was in a strong enough position to organize an international conference on Namibia in Brussels. I was among the more than 400 attendees and reported to the ACOA: "It is very doubtful that any other Namibian organization could have successfully put together such a conference. Therefore it helped to establish SWAPO as the one Namibian nationalist organization with significant international following." It was the only such movement recognized by the OAU.

SWANU never achieved the standing of SWAPO. Its dominant figure at the outset was Jariretundu Kozonguizi, whom I met in New York in 1959. He always spoke his mind in our long conversations, yet he had a puzzling naiveté. For example, on a trip to China in 1960, he gave an address over Peking radio (August 19, 1960, monitored in Washington) that was not designed to win official American favor. "The sooner I am back [in Africa] the better for all of us who are urging the struggle against the common enemy—World Imperialism—headed by the United States of America." He was interviewed by Hsinhua, the Chinese news agency, and quoted as saying that "U.S. and British imperialism and the colonialism of the Union of South Africa which they supported were the main enemies of the current national independence movement in South West Africa." He ruffled feathers at the UN by saying that "the UN seems to be a tool of the U.S. and the other Western big powers."

I wasn't personally upset by Kozonguizi's speech. I figured he was responding to the atmosphere in China, but for one who was planning to be back in New York at the UN, his language was unrestrained and undiplomatic. When some reactions to his remarks reached him, he wrote me (October 6, 1960), "I see that there seems to be some panic over there over statements I am alleged to have made in Peking. . . . could you please write to me about the general atmosphere there and if possible send me the circulated statements?" He asked me to give him "a hand in arranging some forum or avenue through which I can put forward my case. . . . I don't intend to be apologetic at all but I shall have to put facts straight."

Whatever else he accomplished, Kozonguizi was not providing SWANU with stable leadership. In 1966 he resigned as president and in 1969 as a member when a SWANU publication (*Windhoek Review*) asked in a headline, "Kozonguizi a South Africa Spy?" I discounted this charge, for my own experiences with him belied his playing a double role. Yet this sort of thing sapped the strength of SWANU. He dropped out of politics while finishing his law studies in London. In 1971 when he announced he would again become politically active, he had no base. He developed a good relationship with SWAPO, however, and told me in London that SWAPO was the only external movement with any credibility. Yet he never joined.

Many of us who supported Namibian independence began to concentrate our efforts in another area—the exploitation of Namibia's natural resources by foreign corporations. The country is potentially one of the richest in Africa with great mineral reserves, lucrative fishing resources, and a promising agricultural potential.

Foreign corporations controlled most of these resources—diamonds through the South African-dominated Consolidated Diamond Mines; uranium through the British Rio Tinto Zinc; copper, lead, and zinc at Tsumeb Mines, through the American corporations of Newmont Mining and American Metal Climax. Both in the United States and Britain, the ACOA and other private organizations called for corporations to sever their relations with Namibia if it meant working through South Africa.

The UN Council for Namibia took its own action. Realizing that Namibia's supply of minerals was not inexhaustible, the council adopted Decree No. 1 as a protective measure. The initiative came from Sean MacBride, appointed UN commissioner for Namibia in 1974, who instituted a whole set of measures to curb South Africa and activate the UN. The decree disallowed the exploration for, or exportation of, any resource from Namibia without the permission of the council. Any ship or other conveyance carrying such resource was subject to seizure, and any entity or corporation contravening the decree could be liable for damages by a future independent Namibia. The problem, of course, was implementation. No country was immediately prepared to seize such a ship.

In keeping with the concern about investments, the Richard Nixon administration took limited action. Charles W. Yost, ambassador to the UN, announced (May 20, 1970) that henceforth the United States would actively discourage American investment in Namibia as long as South Africa continued its rule in defiance of the UN. The Export-Import Bank would no longer provide credit guarantees for trade with South Africa. At this time U.S. economic relations with Namibia amounted to about $11 million in investments and about $45 million chiefly in mineral exploration ventures.

South Africa tried to ignore all outside efforts to curb its control of Namibia. Defying the decision of the ICJ, Prime Minister Vorster announced that South Africa would not only continue its administration but implement its policy of "self-determination for all population groups," its apartheid Bantustan program.

At a special session in Addis Ababa, Ethiopia, in early 1972, the UN Security Council instructed Secretary General Kurt Waldheim to work with all parties involved to enable the people of Namibia to move on to independence. His subsequent three-day visit to South Africa and Namibia did not lead to anything substantial.

In the meantime, quite unexpectedly, contract workers in Namibia went on strike. There had been strikes before, but they had been short and local. Namibian sympathizers assumed this new strike would fit the same pattern, but it was different. The strike spread rapidly. Almost 6,000 struck in Windhoek, including garbage collectors, porters, and hotel and airport workers. Nearly 2,000 contract laborers in Walvis Bay joined in. About 4,000 employees in the Tsumeb Mine stopped working. Other mine workers in Namibia joined the action; the number rose to 25,000 in some 20 centers.

To some extent the strike was spontaneous, but a great deal of planning and hard work went into it as well. John Otto said in *Battlefront Namibia* that SWAPO had spent nine months organizing the effort. The strike was essentially a protest by Ovambo workers against the contract labor system. It may have been triggered by the remark of Jannie de Wet, native commissioner for Ovomboland, that "the Ovambos are quite happy with the contract labor system."[2] This angered the workers, who participated in contract labor not from choice but for lack of an alternative.

South Africa tried to break the strike. Suspected leaders were arrested. Strike breakers were brought in, and strikers were threatened with being returned to Ovamboland. This policy had the unintentional result of causing thousands of contract workers to return north voluntarily, and Ovamboland became a tense area. Protest meetings were forbidden by the Bantustan legislative council. Colin Winter, the Anglican bishop of Namibia, after a visit to Ovamboland, said the area "looked like occupied territory, . . . it was obvious that the strike was to be broken at all costs by smashing down resistance of the people."[3] Atrocities were committed by the young South African recruits suddenly placed in the charged atmosphere of Ovamboland. On "Bloody Sunday," January 30, as people were leaving an Anglican church in Epinga, they were attacked by an armed patrol of South African-recruits. Six parishioners were killed and others wounded. For his report on this tragedy, Winter was forbidden to enter Ovamboland again and a year later was deported from Namibia.

The ACOA held an open-air press conference outside the headquarters of the Newmont Mining Corporation in New York, calling for an end to cooperation with South Africa's illegal administration of Namibia. I recall the dramatic gesture of Joel Carlson, who said, "I take off my hat to the striking workers of Namibia," as he stood bareheaded in a chilling February wind.

In spite of international protests and resistance inside the country, South Africa continued to apply its Bantustan policy of separate development to Namibia. A "two-track" policy was put into effect, one international and the other internal. On the one hand, South Africa did not reject meetings with the UN secretary general or his special representative. Pro forma discussions took place from time to time. On the other hand, no change in domestic in policy resulted. In 1972 South Africa declared Ovamboland a self-governing region. Elections were announced for August 1973. SWAPO called for a boycott, which was overwhelmingly successful. Only 2.5 percent of eligible voters cast ballots, thus clearly labeling the elections a farce.

After the coup in Portugal in 1974, the protection that South Africa had always had from the Salazar-Caetano government was in jeopardy at the Angola-Namibia border. This danger increased South Africa's determination to apply apartheid in Namibia. Plans were laid for establishing a coalition government under white domination with Africans participating only as representatives of ethnically separated "nations." For African nationalists, however, the Portuguese coup was a sign of hope. Angolan independence would signal new opportunities to change Namibia's dependence on South Africa.

CHAPTER EIGHTEEN

South Africa:
"No Easy Walk to Freedom"

The **14 years** from the Sharpeville Massacre to the 1974 coup in
Portugal were difficult ones for Africans and their sympathizers in
South Africa. Nelson Mandela, volunteer-in-chief of the Defiance Campaign, prophetically forecast the tribulations to come in a speech for the
ANC right after the campaign. "You can see that there is no easy walk to
freedom anywhere, and many of us will have to pass through the valley of
the shadow of death again and again before we reach the mountain tops of
our desires." The language sounds surprisingly like that of Martin Luther
King.

I probably felt closer to South Africa than to any other area of Africa
partly because my long concern with U.S. racism was quite transferable to
South Africa and partly because my own country has been more economically and strategically involved there than in any other part of the continent. Moreover, the struggle in South Africa is certainly the most endur-
ing problem on the continent and the most threatening to world peace.

After the Sharpeville Massacre, those who wanted basic change had to
adopt a new realism. The idealistic hope that the white minority government would disintegrate had to be discarded. The apartheid state did not
wither away but gained in strength. It overwhelmed its opposition and
banned the organizations and individuals dedicated to its overthrow. The
opposition adjusted itself to a protracted struggle, and with leaders outlawed, the liberation movements had no concrete successes.

LIBERATION MOVEMENTS IN EXILE

A long period of underground and exile politics began for both the ANC
and the PAC. Oliver Tambo was sent abroad to head the external organization of the ANC. Peter Molotsi and Nana Mahomo did the same for the
PAC. Robert Sobukwe, head of the PAC, was in prison after Sharpeville,
as was Potlako Leballo, who was later the controversial external chief of
the PAC. But the person who attracted the most attention and indeed
became almost a legendary figure was Nelson Mandela.

MANDELA AND OTHER ANC LEADERS

Mandela was under ban or in prison during virtually all the years I
traversed Africa, so I never met him. He came from the Transkei and was

the eldest son of a Tembu chief. At Fort Hare University College he met Oliver Tambo in the midst of a student strike. Later, in Johannesburg, he met Walter Sisulu, who urged him to study law. Mandela got his B.A. degree by correspondence and his law degree from the University of Witwatersrand. He, Sisulu, and Tambo were founders of the Youth League of the ANC in 1944.

After Sharpeville and the Treason Trial, where he was one of the accused, Mandela played a leading part in the banned ANC. He went underground after organizing a less-than-successful three-day "stay-at-home" strike. He moved around skillfully under cover, often in disguise, issued press statements from telephone booths, and even appeared on a BBC television interview from a secret rendezvous. He helped organize the military wing of the ANC, Umkonto we Sizwe ("Spear of the Nation"), geared to sabotage as a resistance tactic. "Sabotage did not involve loss of life and it offered the best hope for future race relations," he later explained. For several months Mandela traveled outside South Africa visiting African heads of state. His exploits during this period added to his mystique and won him the nickname "the Black Pimpernel."

Shortly after his return he was betrayed and arrested, August 5, 1962, while masquerading as a chauffeur. He was sentenced to five years in prison. Tambo cabled me (August 10, 1962), "Arrest of Nelson Mandela powerful underground leader in South Africa has increased our traveling and related expenses beyond our means." He asked for the ACOA's assistance.

Sisulu as arrested early the next year and convicted on the charge of furthering the aims of the banned ANC. He received a six-year sentence. While this decision was being appealed and he was out on bail, he went underground.

Although more than 3,300 people were detained in 1963, major international attention was riveted on the Rivonia case. In July the police raided the underground headquarters of Umkonto we Sizwe at a farm in Rivonia outside Johannesburg and arrested Sisulu and other leaders. They discovered 250 documents, many on how to manufacture explosives. Six of the accused were African, including Mandela, who was recalled from prison to stand trial again, two were white, and one was Indian. They were accused of planning 192 specific acts of sabotage, such as derailing trains, bombing government offices, and setting fire to schools. Eight of the accused were given life imprisonment instead of a death sentence.

THE PAC IN EXILE

The PAC had a difficult time pulling itself together right after Sharpeville. It suffered from the fact that two of its top leaders were imprisoned, while others were sent abroad. Leballo was released after serving a two-year sentence and set up headquarters in Maseru, capital of Basutoland (now Lesotho). Sobukwe completed his three-year term but was kept in prison indefinitely under a specially enacted "Sobukwe clause" of the General

Laws Amendment Act. He was held at Robben Island until 1969, when he released and then put under ban. He was never again in a position to exert political leadership. He died in 1978.

Outside South Africa in 1960 the PAC and the ANC established a short-lived united front. The leaders worked in teams of two, one from each group. But before they could arrange for travel to the United States or for a conference on South Africa, the front collapsed. A letter from Vusumzi Make of the PAC informed me of its demise. "I feel there is no cause for alarm or disappointment. I have no doubt that it served its purpose and whatever the future holds, we will be able to learn a lot from the mistakes which led to its dissolution. The struggle in South Africa is such that the need for another grouping will make itself felt sooner rather than later."[1]

But no ANC-PAC front was to be tried again. Mutual bad feeling persisted. At the first OAU conference in Addis Ababa, I talked with exiled leaders of both groups. Mahomo, Molotsi, and Make belittled the ANC by saying that it had a small following inside South Africa and was mostly making a lot of noise outside. Joe Matthews, however, who was also there, said, "Time will tell which movement is the stronger. Where is the PAC? They make claims, but they don't produce anything."

The underground PAC, like the ANC, gave up an allegiance to non-violence. Going even further, it rejected sabotage as ineffective and perpetrated sporadic and not too well planned acts of violence in the western Cape. In November 1962 PAC elements attacked a police station in Paarl, in which two whites and five Africans were killed. Leballo, in Maseru, announced plans for widespread action. A new underground guerrilla group called Poqo became tenuously identified with the PAC. Basuto police, under pressure from South Africa, raided PAC headquarters in Maseru and confiscated thousands of documents and a mailing addressed to PAC and Poqo sympathizers. This action led to a mass arrest of the addressees. Parliament passed the General Laws Amendment Act of 1963, permitting the state to hold any person in solitary confinement for 90 days without charge.

After the raids at Rivonia and Maseru, effective underground activity by the movements inside South Africa was greatly curtailed. Stability was difficult to maintain. It was impossible to hold annual conferences. The external leadership, frustrated by lack of contact with its internal constituency, turned to infighting. The ANC generally kept its internal differences quiet, but PAC problems received considerable public attention. Sometimes rifts went so far that some leaders refused to work with one another and even expelled one another at separate meetings.

I witnessed some of these difficulties in 1964. Leballo expelled both Mahomo in London and Molotsi in Dar es Salaam from the organization. This affected loyalties of others. In Leopoldville five PAC men lived in one house, three in the Mahomo faction and two in the Leballo faction, all scrounging for sustenance. Both factions appealed to me for aid. One man told me privately that any aid to him should not go through the leader of the Leballo faction, for if it did, he would never receive it. In London

Mahomo told me that he would never work with Leballo again because Leballo was only after power.

My old friend Patrick Duncan, the first white member of the PAC, who was working under Leballo attached to the Algiers office of the PAC, wrote me that Mahomo and Molotsi were in the United States to raise funds ostensibly for the PAC, but in fact they had been removed from their PAC offices. Leballo added a handwritten postscript: "They do not represent the Pan Africanist Congress of South Africa, having been divested of all authority in the movement. They represent nobody but themselves."[2]

I found Duncan's new position puzzling. In the PAC he certainly would have to sacrifice some of his characteristic independence. I knew he gradually developed his PAC orientation out of sympathy for the PAC-sponsored anti-pass demonstrations that precipitated the Sharpeville massacre. Further, as a principled anti-Communist, he was critical of the ANC because its leaders included former members of the banned Communist Party of South Africa. But the PAC itself developed strong ties with China. A picture of Mao Zedong was prominent in its Dar es Salaam office. Its *Azania News* was clearly China oriented. It claimed that the Chinese did not interfere with inner PAC workings but that the Soviets did in the ANC.

I was personally fond of Pat Duncan. We had gone together to the memorable march on Washington in the summer of 1963. He was not well, and he died in London in 1967. I have always been grateful that I was able to attend his memorial service July 9. A large number of exiled South Africans in London—including whites and blacks, liberals, Marxists, and ANC and PAC members—were present in an act of solidarity. Duncan was honored for his convictions and courage, even by those who disagreed with him.

The PAC leadership felt that the ACOA and I were oriented more toward the ANC than to the PAC. We did tilt that way, although we tried to be neutral. The open multiracialism of the ANC; our long relationship; our affirmative response to the Freedom Charter; my personal relationship with Oliver Tambo, Z.K. Matthews, and others were all contributing factors. Besides, the internal difficulties in the PAC and the erratic leadership of Leballo made it almost impossible to back it wholeheartedly.

THE ANC IN EXILE

The ANC, like the PAC, had difficulties in exile, but it was a much more disciplined organization. Internal differences were dealt with primarily within its own councils. Unlike the PAC, there was very little open controversy. Of course, rumors circulated. One was that Oliver Tambo, although respected as a nationalist without foreign allegiance, was not really in charge in spite of his title of acting president. I never questioned his leadership in the ANC. I saw him enough times under various circumstances to feel that he was no one's captive. I viewed him as a consensus leader respected by all and better able than others to keep antagonists from splitting apart.

In 1967 I visited Tambo at ANC headquarters in Morogoro, Tanzania, a town about 120 miles by road west of Dar es Salaam in picturesque low mountains, where the cooler, drier climate was a relief to his asthma. While he and I talked, other top leaders, such as Moses Kotane and J.B. Marks, both former members of the South African Communist party, were in and out, deferentially following his firm yet gentle orders. Tambo and I discussed ANC strategy, which was geared to the overthrow of the South African government. Although he gave no hint of it, this was only a few months before the joint ANC-ZAPU Wankie expedition into Rhodesia, which must have been on his mind. Only in retrospect could I see what he meant when he said he was spending most of his time supervising the training program.

In 1973 I spent considerable time with Tambo in Lusaka, where the main ANC office was then. Again I saw him in the company of other senior leaders, such as Duma Nokwe and Tom Nkobi. It was clear to me that Tambo was in command. He did not act as if someone was looking over his shoulder.

During these years, it was impossible to know what was happening underground inside South Africa. Developments outside were easier to follow. In Dar es Salaam, a center for the southern African liberation movements prior to Zambia independence, the ANC had a very active office. They were obviously getting more assistance than most of the movements because they had a few cars at their disposal. Also political refugees were coming through Dar enroute for study or military training, frequently in eastern Europe. On a visit to Dar in 1964 I went with an ANC representative to a house where 20 or so of these young men were temporarily staying. In a spirited discussion with them they took the offensive, reflecting a strong anti-American bias, not knowing much about me. Could I prove that I wasn't a U.S. government agent? Did I realize that the United States, by backing the Henrik Verwoerd government, was in a war against all of Africa? The most I could convey was that not all Americans agreed with their government's policy.

During this period, Chief Lutuli was killed in July 1967 when a train struck him near his house in Groutville, Natal. Shortly thereafter, Dr. W.Z. Conco, a stalwart of the ANC, wrote me (July 1967), "The violent death of Chief Lutuli was the most shocking news of the year. The majority of Africans, . . . regarded Lutuli as the unbending, unyielding, staunch personification of a true leader of their struggle." Lutuli's funeral was an occasion for long-suppressed emotions against the government to come into the open. Thousands displayed ANC flags and sang freedom songs; some took the microphone to deliver political attacks.

Operating externally, the ANC took on some projects for public relations. One was the establishment of the Lutuli Memorial Foundation, which had plans for a tombstone, education and scholarship programs, a counseling service, a research program, and self-help projects. I thought it was too ambitious and that the technical business of operating a foundation successfully was not the role of a liberation movement. Happily the foundation did erect a tombstone, placed in July 1972 at a celebration attended by 3,000 people.

Z.K. AND JOE MATTHEWS

My old friend Z.K. Matthews died in Washington in 1968. He had resigned his teaching post at Fort Hare when the government took control of the University College. He had written me (November 30, 1959), "I feel that I cannot subscribe to the principles and the basis on which the college will be run in the future." It was a courageous act, for he was jobless, and he lost his pension. He opened a law office in Alice, then worked for the World Council of Churches in Geneva, and finally became the first ambassador to the United States and the UN for Botswana, his ancestral home. Joe Matthews came to the United States for the funeral. Afterward he wrote to me from London (July 12, 1968). "My mother has been particularly comforted by the absolutely overwhelmingly kind things that have been said and done since the old man passed away. . . . I will never forget the gesture of the President of the U.S. [Johnson] in making a plane available to take the body and the family home."

Joe Matthews was a fascinating conversationalist with a stimulating breadth of ideas. I felt a special association with him, growing out of our experience of being interrogated by the police in Port Elizabeth in 1954. When I passed through London in 1967, we must have talked for five hours about South Africa. He discussed the necessity of a two-track policy (my term, not his) for the ANC. In addition to a campaign of sabotage and preparation for an armed struggle, he said the ANC needed to nurture projects for community self-development inside South Africa. He was concerned that the ANC in exile was losing contact with the people. Most of them were not prepared to take up arms and be slaughtered, but they could participate in projects for self-betterment. He asked me to send him material on some of the projects sponsored by the Urban League in U.S. black communities. He told me that the ANC was not ready to adopt this policy yet, but he wanted to work on it. He feared that the ANC would lose its leadership position and that a political vacuum would form.

BLACK CONSCIOUSNESS

The absence of above-ground liberation organizations in South Africa did create a vacuum. Under these circumstances in the late 1960s the black consciousness movement arose, which at the beginning was a tendency, a mind-set among young Africans. To white liberals, who felt rejected by it, it smacked of black racism, as Africans emphasized that they must go it alone.

The movement arose in the liberal, multiracial student organization, the National Union of South African Students (NUSAS). After the banning of the ANC and the PAC, African students, who had no political party available, turned toward NUSAS in larger numbers.* Student organizations were not parties and membership was open to Africans. This had the effect of making NUSAS a more militant organization, but its leadership was essentially white. Functioning in a deeply segregated society, the organization had to make compromises. For example, at a 1967 conference at Rhodes University, NUSAS had to accept segregated housing. This compromise helped to trigger a separatist move among African students.

The person who gave voice and inspiration to this new mood was Steve Biko, a most extraordinary young man. He came on the scene quite suddenly when elected president of the all-black South African Students' Organization (SASO), which split off from NUSAS in 1968. Its philosophy was black consciousness, and Biko was its most eloquent spokesman. Although I never met him, I was impressed by the clarity of his writing and what I learned about his spirit and leadership.

Biko, born in 1946, came from King William's Town in the Cape. He attended a Catholic secondary school in Natal and then the University of Natal Medical School, where he was elected to the Students' Representative Council. This opened the way for wider involvement in NUSAS. In this environment his ideas of black consciousness took shape. "The philosophy of Black Consciousness . . . expresses group pride and the determination by the Blacks to rise and attain the envisaged self."[3]

That Biko was no black racist is evident from the glowing accounts given by South African whites who became his friends. Donald Woods, a newspaper editor in East London, called Biko, 13 years his junior, "the greatest man I ever met. . . . He was simply not a hater of people, . . . [In spite of harassment and frustration by his bannings and detention,] he remained the most modest and most moderate and tolerant of men."[4]

SASO became a new rallying point for African students. In 1972 they founded another organization, the Black People's Convention (BPC), for the students needed a body through which to act after their student days were over. Through SASO and the BPC a whole new generation of black leadership was thrust up. At first the government was tolerant of the black consciousness movement, mistakenly seeing it as not contradictory to apartheid. It did not immediately recognize the movement as a new expression of nationalism. Its perception changed as SASO and the BPC condemned the bantustans, engaged in actions opposing white domination, and supported the liberation struggle in other parts of Africa. In early 1973 the major leaders of the BPC, including Biko, were banned.

The black consciousness movement had an impact on the South African liberation organizations in exile. PAC leaders saw in it an extension of their own nationalist philosophy. ANC leaders looked on it with great interest

*Even the Liberal Party dissolved in 1968 rather than attempting to carry on after the government forbade multiracial political parties.

and tried to follow it as closely as possible. Neither organization could claim credit for the rise of the movement. I know that after the formation of the BPC in 1972, black consciousness was a lively topic whenever I met South African political leaders in exile.

I found my discussions with Alfred Kgokong interesting and provocative. For years, in Dar es Salaam he edited the ANC newsletter *Spotlight on South Africa*. Until 1972 he always seemed like a loyal ANC leader, but obviously the frustrations were getting to him. He was living on $6 or $7 a month and hoping he could place articles in magazines for an honorarium. I tried unsuccessfully to place some in American publications, but they were not geared to American readers.

One of Kgokong's articles argued that the movements in exile were of limited effect, cut off as they were from events inside the country. He implied criticism of the ANC by saying that external movements gave the impression that political activity inside South Africa could be guided from abroad. He was thoroughly in sympathy with the objective of the BPC "to liberate the black people from psychological and physical oppression" and to unite and solidify the blacks.

It was unusual for an ANC leader to talk frankly about problems within the organization, and Kgokong did so very carefully. Yet it was clear that he was unhappy with decisions made at an ANC conference at Morogoro in 1969, notably that membership in the ANC should be opened to all three groups in the Congress Alliance—Indians, Coloureds, and whites—each of which had previously had a life of its own. Further, the National Executive Committee was reduced from 23 to 10, necessary, according to the conference report, "to create the . . . framework for a more vigorous prosecution of the armed struggle." Kgokong, however, was disturbed by the fact that this reorganization involved dropping such nationalists as himself, Tennyson Makiwane, and Robert Resha. He stated the same concerns voiced earlier by Joe Matthews—the ANC needed to be related to the day-to-day problems inside the country and should not be building a strategy wholly around the armed struggle. Part of the appeal of the black consciousness movement was that it had developed community health and education projects in which the average black person could participate.

RISKY CONTACTS

The repressive atmosphere in South Africa was such that activists outside had to be very careful in communication with opponents of apartheid inside. The two following experiences vividly illustrate this.

One experience grew out of my long association with Arthur Blaxall. Religiously opposed to apartheid, he was inevitably in touch with anti-apartheid movements, although he was not a member of any. As the secretary of the South African Christian Council, he had frequently been asked to aid those accused of violating apartheid laws or their families. He was among those arrested in 1963 for aiding unlawful organizations under the Suppression of Communism Act. He was also charged with possession of unlawful literature, including a pamphlet I co-authored, *The South African Crisis and U.S. Policy*. He wrote me a note the day after his arrest (April 18, 1963) saying, "I am profoundly sorry to tell you that your pamphlet has been taken away by the Special Branch of the police during a search of my house and office yesterday. . . . I do hope this stupidity on my part will not embarrass you." I could not figure out why he blamed himself for the police action. If anything, it was my stupidity in sending it to him that helped put him in the spot he was in. In his seventies, Blaxall was found guilty and sentenced to six months in prison. He served only one horrible day, however, and then was released with six months on parole and 22 months suspended sentence. He described the whole shocking experience in his book *Suspended Sentence* (1965).

Arthur and Florence Blaxall soon thereafter moved to London. When I saw him there in 1964 he told me that the whole experience with the police had shaken up Florence even more than him. He didn't want to talk in her presence about details on South Africa because it was too hard on her. His only "crime" had been to transmit funds to opponents of apartheid for legal defense and welfare as a measure of reconciliation. The last time I saw him he was 80. How ironic, I felt, that a man of such good will should have been caught up by the police.

My second experience of risky contacts grew out of my correspondence with John Clarke in 1965. An Australian who had emigrated to South Africa, he was a copywriter for an advertising firm in Johannesburg. He got in touch with me through a mutual friend because he wanted to correspond with an American involved with Africa. Clarke apparently had a lot to get off his mind. He wrote eight- or nine-page letters, single-spaced, dealing usually with South African propaganda. He said that South Africa's military buildup was enhanced by the use of U.S. Piper Cub planes (not covered by the military embargo) and that South Africa's claim that the white man arrived before the Bantu was false. I found the letters interesting and often helpful.

He exercised some caution. He asked that my letters to him not go on ACOA letterhead. He gave me an alternative address and usually wrote under the name of Slocombe. He had no personal contact with any of the "movement" people; he was just an individual who hated apartheid, was frustrated in his job, and probably found an outlet through these letters. Our correspondence lasted less than a year. I wrote short notes of acknowledgment and carefully said a little bit about the ACOA's work. When he finally asked why I didn't write longer replies, I said that I feared he might get in some difficulty. His response was: "Don't worry about me. The most the authorities can do to me is deport me to Australia." So I wrote a more substantive letter to him, asking if there was any way of getting information about the use of convict or forced labor on farms in South Africa. We wanted this information as a handle to prohibit U.S. import of some goods, which are excluded if produced by forced labor.

After a long silence, a letter came from Australia (May 12, 1966). He had indeed been deported. "Actually I am pretty sure that the Afrikaner nationalist director of the ad agency I was working for started going through my desk and then reported me to the security police. The police then began intercepting my mail." He was arrested on March 21, 1966, and served with a deportation order "for which no reason was given. [They] parked me for two weeks in the central police station cells in Johannesburg, and then put me on a plane for Australia." The press vilified him as "being one of South Africa's 'leading communists' and similar slanderous lies . . . anyway I think I'm well out of it. It really is a pleasure to breathe the air of a free and decent country again and to be away from the petty hatreds and gross self interests of the South African scene."

I felt terribly guilty about Clarke's deportation. It was good of him to write to me (April 6, 1966) that "no blame attaches to you for my deportation, so please don't worry about that side of it. . . . I am neither bitter nor angry about this, as that's the way the cookie crumbles, and one must accept these things." John and his wife, Lucille, later moved to the London area. We maintain our friendship by letters and visits.* Lucille died in 1987.

BLACK POWER AND THE ACOA

During the U.S. civil rights struggle in the 1960s, I had to face an inner conflict about my work. Again and again I was told that my task lay at home rather than in a struggle thousands of miles away, yet I felt that in a universal sense they were the same struggle. Although my schedule precluded my participating in the many critical campaigns on the home front, somehow I never felt fully detached from the domestic struggle because I was involved in the international one. Further, through the work of the ACOA I was in close touch with many figures in the civil rights movement. One such person was A. Philip Randolph, a union leader and the originator of the first march on Washington in the Roosevelt era, whom I had worked with since the mid-1940s. Because of both his reputation and his deep convictions, he was always a tower of strength. He became co-chairman of the ACOA with Donald Harrington in 1961.

The ACOA was interracial. Our board happened to be almost equally divided between black and white. Hope Stevens, a lawyer and president of the Uptown Chamber of Commerce in Harlem, was vice president.†

---

*He has written a couple of books on South African propaganda under the pen name of John Laurence: *The Seeds of Disaster* (1968) and *Race, Propaganda and South Africa* (1979).

†Other members included Jim Farmer of CORE; Farrell Jones of the State Commission Against Discrimination; David Jones, deputy commissioner in the New York Department of Correction; Percy Sutton, president of the New York NAACP; Robert Browne, economist at Fairleigh Dickinson University; Bayard Rustin, organizer of the 1963 march on Washington; civil rights lawyer Conrad Lynn, Robert Van Lierop, lawyer and film maker.

Martin Luther King, Jr., was on our National Committee and co-chaired with Chief Lutuli the 1962 campaign "An Appeal for Action Against Apartheid." He was the principal speaker at a Human Rights Day Rally that we sponsored December 10, 1965. In his address, one of the few he devoted to the South African situation, he blasted the U.S. policy of

muted and peripheral denunciation of South African racial practices. We pat them on the wrist in permitting racially mixed receptions in our embassy but we give them massive support through American investments in motor and rubber industries and by extending millions in loans through our most distinguished banks and financial institutions.

He called for a massive international nonviolent boycott movement. "The time has come for an international alliance of peoples of all nations against racism."

Believing that pressure from the black community could have great influence on U.S. policy toward Africa, the ACOA proposed to leaders of civil rights groups that an organization be set up in which they could join forces to press the government on African issues. We called a meeting, at which I presented a plan for this coalition. The result was the formation of the American Negro Leadership Conference on Africa (ANLCA) in mid-1962. Theodore (Ted) Brown, long on the staff of the Brotherhood of Sleeping Car Porters, was hired as executive director.

A prestigious body, the ANLCA had a "call committee" of the big six of the civil rights movement.* It held a number of influential conferences in the 1960s. Eventually 28 national organizations were sponsors, and many members of Congress were involved. It never lived up to its potential, however, because as an elite group, it was never able to establish an independent base in the black community. Thus it could not raise a budget for its own program but had to depend on its constituent groups, who were overwhelmed by their own programs. Gradually the effort died out.

The U.S. counterpart to the black consciousness movement in South Africa was the black power movement. Several experiences dramatically brought it to my attention. One was at a symposium on southern Africa at Cornell in 1969. When the university president was explaining to an audience of 800 why Cornell had voted not to sell its stocks in banks loaning money to South Africa, two black students jumped onto the stage, collared him, and yanked him from the podium. The audience was stunned. The audacious students, who belonged to the Cornell Afro-American Society, were later disciplined by the university.

On another occasion I saw black power manifested at the stormy 1969 meeting of the African Studies Association (ASA) in Montreal. Thirty of the 55 seminars were canceled, as blacks, revolting against a seeming domination by white scholars, disrupted and stayed away from sessions.

---

*Roy Wilkins of the NAACP; Whitney Young of the National Urban League; Martin Luther King, Jr; A. Philip Randolph; James Farmer of CORE; and Dorothy Height of the National Council of Negro Women.

Distinguished African visitors, such as Robert Gardiner, director of the UN Economic Commission for Africa, and Gabriel d'Arboussier, Senegalese ambassador to the UN, supported the revolt. The result was reforms in the ASA and the formation of a new group of black scholars, the African Heritage Studies Association.

Within the ACOA, black power made itself felt. A strong nucleus of black staff and board members felt deep ties with the black consciousness movement. They must have discussed among themselves the desirability of black leadership in the ACOA. I myself thought it would have been a real advantage for the ACOA to have a black executive, and I seriously considered resigning. But I didn't, and the ACOA, unlike many groups affected by the black revolt, maintained itself as an interracial organization.

Quite unconnected with the pressures of black power was the choice of William Booth, a lawyer and leader in the black community, a former New York City commissioner for human rights, and a district court judge, to succeed Peter Weiss as president of the ACOA in 1972. He was deeply affected by his attendance, on behalf of the Episcopal Church, at a trial of antiracist Anglican leaders in South Africa. His leadership of the ACOA was a source of great strength.

REACTING TO U.S. POLICY ON SOUTH AFRICA

In the period from Sharpeville to the coup in Portugal, a series of concrete issues in U.S. relations with South Africa arose. Among them were political asylum for dissident South Africans in the United States; permission for South African Airways to begin regular flights to the United States; and setting up U.S. satellite-tracking stations in segregated South African facilities. Other issues were discrimination against black American naval personnel on shore leave in South African ports and, of central importance, growing U.S. economic ties to South Africa.

It was not easy for the ACOA to work on these issues effectively. American interest in Africa was not great. Activists were concentrating on the civil rights struggle and the war in Vietnam. Furthermore, an unwarranted feeling of optimism about progress in South Africa pervaded the consciousness of many people, despite Sharpeville. The perception was that things were rapidly changing in Africa; with the birth of so many independent states, the white-dominated governments of Rhodesia, the Portuguese colonies, and South Africa would have to recognize the signs of the times. Only later in the 1960s, as oppression increased in South Africa and guerrilla fighting expanded elsewhere, was the new reality of a long drawn-out struggle recognized.

Congressional involvement was not great. The Senate Subcommittee on Africa was almost moribund. The House Subcommittee was more active, but friendly members of Congress told me that they could not win many votes for speeches on South Africa or Rhodesia.

The various administrations also reflected a low level of activity on Africa. Common threads ran through their policies: (1) African issues had a low priority; (2) peaceful change, rather than confrontation, was emphasized; (3) South Africa must be kept open for investment and trade; (4) policy was geared toward the reality of white domination with little contact with liberation movements; (5) the strategic importance of South Africa was emphasized as the United States reacted to Soviet moves.

There were, nevertheless, some differences resulting in part from changes in circumstances and in part from differing perceptions of America's role. During the Eisenhower years, initiative was almost nonexistent. The United States even opposed the formation of the UN Commission on the Racial Situation in South Africa, on the grounds that the UN was not competent to deal with the internal affairs of a member, and refused to accept the word condemn in a UN resolution on apartheid.

Nevertheless, changes in Africa began to influence U.S. policies. A Bureau of African Affairs was formed in 1958; the State Department sponsored U.S. tours for Sékou Touré of French Guinea and Julius Nyerere of Tanganyika. Yet the government continued to look to its European allies for leadership in Africa. It supported the French in opposing the abandonment of nuclear tests in the Sahara, supported the British in opposing setting a target date for Tanganyikan independence, and abstained in a UN vote to urge negotiations to end the war in Algeria.

The Kennedy administration brought liberals to Washington—Chester Bowles as under secretary of state, the historian Arthur Schlesinger, Jr., and Michigan Governor G. Mennen Williams. Williams was assistant secretary for Africa with the liberal Wayne Fredericks as second in command.

The United States inaugurated a scholarship program for students from southern Africa partly to try to match a Soviet one that outdrew the United States nine students to one. At the UN the United States spoke more forcefully. Francis Plimpton said, "The United States abhors apartheid." The United States voted for the release of political prisoners in South Africa and an end to political trials. Adlai Stevenson, ambassador to the UN, made a hard-hitting speech on August 2, 1963, saying that all efforts to urge South Africa to change had "yielded no tangible results." Instead there had been "calculated retrogression." Then he announced that the United States expected "to bring to an end the sale of all military equipment to the government of South Africa by the end of this calendar year." Only existing contracts would be honored. At the same time he decried overall sanctions as "bad law and bad policy."

One of the innovations of Williams and Fredericks in the Africa Bureau was to establish an Advisory Council made up of about 20 academics and 20 specialists from labor, business, the church, the black community, and other civic groups. My invitation to join this council said they wanted to draw on "expert knowledge of persons outside the U.S. government who, like yourself, are active in the field of African affairs." The only condition of acceptance was that "the information and opinions brought out in these meetings would not be disclosed to persons outside the government." The ACOA board agreed that I should accept.

The council met spasmodically. Its main value to me was the contacts I made at the six meetings I attended in four years. I don't believe I ever received any inside information that would have been worth divulging to those outside the government, and it is doubtful that our discussions were very helpful to policymakers.

The ACOA kept in touch with Senator Hubert Humphrey, an early member of our National Committee, who was always ready to meet African leaders whom we sponsored. We invited him to speak at our Africa Freedom Day observance in New York April 17, 1961.* He seemed excited about the program and said he would introduce a resolution in the Senate designating April 15 as Africa Freedom Day. He asked us to draft a statement he might use, which we did.

The date of our meeting by chance coincided with the Bay of Pigs attack on Cuba. When Humphrey spoke of the United States standing for freedom, many people interrupted with loud boos. He didn't seem to understand why. He appropriately resigned from our National Committee when he became vice president under Lyndon Johnson.

Under Richard Nixon, even as demands by the independent African states became more urgent, the United States no longer abstained from voting on colonial issues at the UN but voted negatively. In 1972, for example, it voted against seven out of eight key resolutions on colonial issues and abstained on the other.

Secretary of State Henry Kissinger's National Security Study Memorandum 39 was the guide to U.S. policy. It voiced the "tar baby option" based on the premise that "the whites are here [in southern Africa] to stay and the only way that constructive change can come about is through them." Kissinger was a globalist. In his perception, southern Africa did not play an important part in the global competition between the United States and the Soviet Union.

In Kissinger's first UN speech he didn't even mention Africa. At a luncheon at the U.S. Mission to the UN in September 1974, I heard him half apologize to African ambassadors for his lack of involvement in Africa and jokingly say he would take a trip there sometime. The "joke" did not sit well with the ambassadors. The next two years forced him to become serious about Africa.

ECONOMIC DISENGAGEMENT

The ACOA's task in the 1960s was to raise the consciousness of Americans about Africa, specifically South Africa. One major thrust was to advocate

*Outstanding speakers and performers for this program included the Africans Oliver Tambo, Kenneth Kaunda, Joshua Nkomo, Tom Mboya, and Holden Roberto, all visiting the UN, and the Americans James Baldwin and Humphrey. James Farmer was master of ceremonies. Performers included Miriam Makeba, Dizzie Gillespie's Quintet, Herbie Mann's Afro Jazz Sextet, the Dinizulu Dancers, and the Billy Taylor Trio. That program was a sellout.

economic disengagement with South Africa. That put us in opposition to U.S. policy, which was neither to encourage nor discourage investment and trade with South Africa. This neutral-sounding attitude actually resulted in encouraging business contact, for potential profits were high. In the early 1960s the Department of Commerce put the average rate of profit for the approximately 240 American firms then investing about $600 million in South Africa at 17.1 percent. U.S. trade and investment would continue to increase.

The ACOA played an active part in the growing public controversy over U.S. economic relations with South Africa. I appeared before House and Senate committees many times. We published many studies developing our position. The January 1966 issue of *Africa Today* was devoted to a "Special Report on Involvement in the South Africa Economy," which expressed the hope that "by economic disengagement the U.S., in cooperation with other nations, can play a role in bringing down the apartheid republic so that a hoped-for non-racial society may be created in its stead." The *New York Times* (April 18, 1971) carried a written debate between Ulric Haynes, who had been on the National Security Council staff, and me. In my contribution, "Investment Dollars Bolster Apartheid," I developed the thesis that as American investment has grown, apartheid has worsened; that apartheid laws make fundamental change in the position of Africans impossible; and that through investment the United States is helping South Africa build a self-sufficient economy.

In the 1960s, long before pressures for divestiture were felt, business interests either kept silent on their activities in South Africa or defended the system. When Congressman Barrett O'Hara of Illinois, as chairman of the House Subcommittee on Africa, made every effort short of issuing subpoenas to persuade business representatives to appear in hearings, none agreed to do so.

THE BANK CAMPAIGN

Perhaps the ACOA's most important campaign was against U.S. bank loans to South Africa. In coalition with the University Christian Movement we organized the Committee of Conscience Against Apartheid headed by A. Philip Randolph, with more than 120 prominent sponsors. One aspect of the campaign was to urge individuals and organizations to withdraw funds from Chase Manhattan and First National City Bank (now Citibank) by Human Rights Day, December 10, 1966. By that date we knew of $22 million that had been withdrawn.

Another aspect of the campaign was to direct pressure on a consortium of ten banks involved in a $40 million loan to South Africa.* Pressure on

---

*In addition to Chase and First National City, the other banks were Bank of America, Manufacturers Hanover Trust, Morgan Guaranty Trust Co., Irving Trust Co., Continental Illinois National Bank and Trust Co., and First National Bank (Chicago).

these banks had grown year by year as their loans became the symbol of direct U.S. support for a brutal, racist police state. Many churches debated the issue and some withdrew accounts. Students pressured their colleges to end their relationships with offending banks.

We were taken by surprise when on November 21, 1969, the Associated Press reported an announcement by the South African foreign minister that the consortium loan would end "because of the Republic's strong gold and foreign exchange position." The banks had to face public relations problems as a result of the activities we helped generate. They must have reasoned that the highly visible loan was more bother than it was worth, especially since South Africa had not drawn on the loan fund recently.

The bank campaign was an opening wedge for a much broader economic challenge, particularly by some churches. The major denominations had significant investments in corporations doing business in South Africa. The question was how to use their investments as leverage to influence corporate policy. From this concern grew the Interfaith Center on Corporate Responsibility (ICCR).

THE POLAROID EXPERIMENT

Differences in strategy toward change in South Africa were highlighted by the Polaroid Corporation. In late 1970 a group of black workers at the company's headquarters in Cambridge, Massachusetts, protested the company's involvement in South Africa, especially because Polaroid furnished materials for preparing the identification passes Africans must carry, which are basic to the apartheid system. They called for a boycott of Polaroid products.

Polaroid directors responded by taking out expensive full-page ads in seven influential daily newspapers and 20 black weeklies.* They announced a "Polaroid experiment," which was to stay in business in South Africa in order to be a catalyst for change. They promised that their equipment would not be used for the hated pass system. They would, however, train black employees for important positions, commit a portion of their profits for black education, generally raise black wages, and make a grant to bring some blacks to the United States in an exchange program.

We and other critics of the Polaroid experiment pointed out its ineffectiveness and maintained that it would provide a rationale to businesses to stay in South Africa under the comfortable but false assumption that they could help end racism while making a tidy profit. We campaigned against Polaroid at stockholder meetings and directly to their president, Edwin H. Land.

The Polaroid effort ended rather suddenly in 1977 when it was discovered that their equipment was still being used in the pass system.

New York Times, Boston Globe, Christian Science Monitor, Wall Street Journal, Washington Post, Chicago Tribune, Los Angeles Times.

Indres Naidoo, a South African released in 1973 after 10 years imprisonment for sabotage, worked for three years with Polaroid's Johannesburg
distributor, Frank and Hirsch. He had incontrovertible evidence (a sales
receipt) that Polaroid film was delivered to the Bantu Reference Bureau,
responsible for Africans' passes, despite the distributor's agreement not to
sell to the government. He sent the evidence to my ACOA colleague Paul
Irish, whom he had met at Mozambique's independence celebration in
1975. Irish informed Polaroid officials, who immediately checked facts
and then terminated the relationship, adding, "We do not plan to establish
another one." The *Boston Globe* headlines of November 22, 1977, announced "Polaroid Halts Its South Africa Shipments."

OPPOSITION TO CHARLES W. ENGELHARD

The single most powerful American businessman involved in South Africa
was Charles W. Engelhard. He was chairman of the Rand Mines group,
which employed about 100,000 people and produced chrome, coal, cement, uranium, and about 17 percent of South Africa's gold. He was a
director of the Chamber of Mines and also of two organizations recruiting
black miners. He had helped engineer the $30 million credit that helped
buoy up the faltering South African economy after Sharpeville. He was
also American chairman of the South Africa Foundation, set up by a few
industrialists in 1960 to counteract South Africa's bad international image.
He had the reputation, however, of being a liberal and was a heavy
contributor to the Democratic Party. President Lyndon Johnson called
him "a humanitarian of the first order" and appointed him head of the
U.S. delegation to Zambia's independence celebration in Lusaka in 1964.

The ACOA had already drawn attention to Engelhard's South African
role in a special issue of *Africa Today* (March 1964) titled "Partners in
Apartheid." We were astounded that such a man should head a delegation
to an African country that was backing UN moves for sanctions against
South Africa. From an African perspective, it was insulting. Engelhard
was greeted by a picket line at the airport. His picture appeared in the
Zambian press with comment on his role in South Africa. I was introduced
to him at a garden party outside the State House. He knew my name, for
he had seen the ACOA study. Surprisingly friendly, he said our information was accurate and added, "You even listed some directorships I had
forgotten about." Then he said that we must get together back home and
asked me to write him.

We never managed to meet back home, although we exchanged notes.
Early in 1966 I was notified that the New Jersey region of the National
Conference of Christians and Jews (NCCJ) was giving Engelhard, who was
a generous contributor, their annual Brotherhood Award. The ACOA
protested vigorously and mounted a campaign to persuade the NCCJ to
reconsider, although we realized there was little likelihood of a change of
mind. Hundreds of protests bombarded the NCCJ office in Newark. On
the day of the dinner, 500 chanting demonstrators from the NAACP,

CORE, United Auto Workers, Drug and Hospital Workers, church people, and students formed a solid barrier at the entrance of the Robert Treat Hotel in Newark. Red-faced and flustered, surrounded by police, Engelhard pressed through the picketers. The dinner went on and the award was given.

BOYCOTTING THE SPRINGBOKS*

Another area for the ACOA to stress in focusing American attention on South Africa was racism in sports. South Africa is a country bristling with competitive sports fever. Therefore, it was a blow to white South Africa when its team was excluded from the 1964 Olympic Games in Tokyo. It was impossible to view this action from other than a political perspective, for the exclusion was directly related to the government's apartheid policy.

South Africa's sports policy had become internationalized in the late 1950s, when the nonracial South Africa Sports Association (SASA) organized a campaign to remove the color bar in sports. The internationally recognized sports body, the South African Olympic Games Association (SAOGA), was all white. At the Rome meeting of the International Olympic Committee (IOC) in 1960, SASA submitted a detailed report on racial discrimination practiced by SAOGA. A SASA representative could not attend because he was denied a passport. Nevertheless, the IOC took note of the complaint and warned that if the policy of racial discrimination did not change, SAOGA would be suspended. In the meantime, the South Africa Non-Racial Olympic Committee (SANROC) devoted exclusively to the question of South Africa's participation in the Olympics, was established under Dennis Brutus's leadership.

Dennis Brutus was born in Rhodesia in 1924 of Afrikaner and black African parents and therefore was designated "Coloured" in South African parlance. He was educated in South Africa and taught there for 14 years, winning an international reputation as a writer and poet. For his anti-apartheid activity, particularly in SANROC, he was banned from the classroom in 1961; his writings were banned the next year. In 1963 he was arrested for contravening his ban by trying to meet a visiting IOC official. While on bail he tried to escape to attend an IOC meeting in Baden-Baden, Germany, to represent the SANROC cause against South Africa's participation in the 1964 Olympics. While traveling through Mozambique on his Rhodesian passport, he was arrested and handed over to the South African police.

Then he disappeared. He later explained, "No one knew I was back in South Africa. The police could have done anything to me—no one would have known." So he desperately tried to jump from the police car in which

---

*The springbok is a gazelle, native to South Africa. It was the name of a South African rugby team and has become the symbol and the nickname of white South African teams in international sports.

he was being driven. He was shot in the back. Fortunately he recovered. He served 18 months in prison. The charge was "furthering the aims of Communism," although the judge said he saw no connection between Communism and trying to attend a sports meeting. He was released in 1965, with 12 new bans placed against him, including house detention.

Unable to support his wife and seven children, Brutus left for London on an exit permit (which makes it illegal for him to return to South Africa) to work with the International Defence and Aid Fund. That was where we first met. I had already heard about him from an antiapartheid South African rabbi, Dr. Andre Ungar, who described Brutus glowingly as "a most brilliant young writer who hopes to get the support of the international sports authorities to break racial discrimination in that field in his country." In one of our many talks Brutus spoke of the anguish of his eight months in solitary confinement, which had made him deeply religious and guilt-ridden. He told me that he even tried to commit suicide by cutting his wrists with rocks.*

With SANROC playing an important role, the IOC did suspend South Africa from the 1964 games. The South African government began a campaign to have its suspension lifted so that a team could participate in the 1968 games in Mexico City. Prime Minister John Vorster outlined a new sports policy, which would allow a multiracial team to represent South Africa in international events, but its members would be chosen in racially segregated trials. Inside South Africa there would be no mixed sporting events, a decision on which there could be "no compromise, negotiations, or abandonment of principles." At first the IOC accepted this new policy and decided South Africa could compete in Mexico City.

This reversal of the IOC position, which did not alter apartheid sports practices inside South Africa, met spirited opposition. The Supreme Council for Sport in Africa (representing the independent African countries in international sports) threatened a boycott of the Mexico City games. Dennis Brutus, in London, worked through SANROC to encourage such a boycott.

The ACOA organized a boycott campaign in cooperation with SANROC. Jackie Robinson, the first black major league professional baseball player, took the lead. At an ACOA press conference, February 8, 1968, he called for the continued suspension of South Africa because "racial discrimination is a violation of the Olympic rules."

Two months later, the ACOA circulated a statement among athletes and induced an impressive number to agree to support a boycott of the 1968 games if South Africa was participating. These men, a who's who in sports, included Jackie Robinson, Jim Bouton, Reuben Amaro, Arthur Ashe, Wilt Chamberlain, Lee Evans, John Carlos, Calvin Hill, Jim

---

*Many years later Dennis Brutus taught English at Northwestern University and subsequently at the University of Pittsburgh. In 1983 he won a celebrated case for political asylum in the United States against deportation to Zimbabwe.

McMillan, Oscar Robertson, Maury Wills, and Lenny Wilkens. Similar efforts took place in other countries.

Faced with the very real threat of a massive boycott, the IOC reconsidered and suspended South Africa again. Brutus urged me to accompany him and Chris de Broglio, a white SANROC leader and former South African national weight-lifting champion also exiled, to Mexico City to counteract lobbying efforts for reinstatement by South African sports representatives. I could not leave home base at the time but arranged for Jim Bouton, pitcher for the New York Yankees, and Steve Makone, an outstanding black South African soccer player studying in the United States, to go as our representatives. We wanted not only to keep South Africa out of the Olympics but to extend the boycott to international sports federations, such as wrestling and table tennis.

Bouton reported on their efforts. "Probably our most significant impact was simply our presence which had the effect of making every delegate aware that their days of operating in secrecy are over." The most astonishing obstacle they faced was "the direct opposition of the U.S. Olympic Committee officials to our presence in Mexico City." When he cornered Douglas Roby, chairman of the U.S. Olympic Committee, in a hotel lobby, Roby made the hostile remark, "The Russians pay your transportation down here? You working with the commies?" The press chief of the committee, Bob Paul, blurted out to Bouton, "You're the most un-American man in this room." Bouton was accused of trying to disrupt the Olympics and corrupt the athletes. Nevertheless, the exclusion of South African teams from the Olympics continues to this day.

We pressed our sports boycott in other ways. In a public relations effort, the South African golf champion Gary Player invited Lee Elder, a black American professional golfer, to join him in an exhibition match in South Africa. We urged Elder not to go on the grounds that by doing so he would be "supporting the South African government's plans to relieve international pressure against apartheid by allowing nonwhite athletes to participate with whites in special events that they choose to define as 'international.'" Despite pressure from the black community, Elder went to South Africa. Years later he said he would not go again.

We joined with Black Concern, a group led by the writer Louise Meriwether and the historian John Henrik Clarke, in opposing a Muhammad Ali fight to be staged in South Africa in 1972. The fight was canceled after considerable outcry in the black community.

Better known was the case involving the black tennis player Arthur Ashe, whom I had met in the late 1960s. He had supported the proposed boycott of the Mexico City Olympics. When his application for a visa to South Africa in 1969 to take part in the South Africa Tennis Open was turned down, we arranged for him to appear in hearings before both the UN Special Committee Against Apartheid and the House Subcommittee on Africa.

Enough pressure was applied to South Africa through government and other channels that a couple of years later, a successful application for a visa for Ashe seemed probable. He asked several people, including me, whether he should go. I strongly advised him not to because it would add falsely to the "liberal" image of South Africa. Nevertheless, he went. His conditions, such as not playing before segregated audiences, were met, but he reported in his book *Off the Court* (1981) that the "whites" and "nonwhites" signs did not come down. They just weren't enforced for his matches. Today Ashe backs the sports boycott.

Closely associated with the sports boycott was the campaign, organized by my colleague Mary Louise Hooper, to oppose apartheid in cultural contacts with South Africa. In 1965 the ACOA initiated the Declaration of American Artists Against Apartheid entitled "We Say 'No' to Apartheid." The signers of the declaration pledged themselves to refuse any encouragement of, or indeed any "personal or professional association with, the present Republic of South Africa: this until the day when all its people—black and white—shall equally enjoy the educational and cultural advantages of this rich and lovely land."

Frederick O'Neal, president of Actors Equity, hosted a party to launch the declaration. The actor Henry Fonda read the pledge and announced the names of all 65 signers, who made up a star-studded list—Tallulah Bankhead, Harry Belafonte, Leonard Bernstein, Victor Borge, Carol Burnett, Diahann Carroll, Sammy Davis, Jr., Ossie Davis, Ruby Dee, Julie Harris, Van Heflin, Lena Horne, Langston Hughes, Johnny Mathis, Burgess Meredith, Arthur Miller, Sidney Poitier, Paul Robeson, Nina Simone, Ed Sullivan, and Eli Wallach. Although some later fell by the wayside, on the whole, the artists' boycott stood up.

OTHER ACTIONS AGAINST APARTHEID

The ACOA campaigned in 1964 to have deportation proceedings dropped against five black South Africans who had come to New York to play in the Broadway musical *Sponono*. After a short run, the musical closed and the five asked for political asylum on the ground that they would face physical persecution if they returned to South Africa. It was a mixed victory. The Immigration and Naturalization Service (INS) dropped the deportation order but refused to recognize the principle that a political refugee from South Africa faced "physical persecution" if forced to return home.

We also worked hard to keep South African Airways from initiating flights into New York's Kennedy International Airport. In 1947, before the Afrikaner Nationalists came to power, the United States and South Africa had signed a Bilateral Air Transport Agreement permitting flights between the two countries. Pan American soon initiated flights but South Africa did not until 1968, when President Johnson authorized South African Airways to begin flights. The company quickly began a campaign with a full-page ad in the *New York Times* headlined "South African Airways invites 139 distinguished Americans to be among the first to fly the last ocean."

The ACOA organized an ad in reply signed by 139 black Americans, who responded, "We know the welcome of South African Airways is not meant for us. The tourism which you promote is racist. Racism is not welcome here." The signers were among the most distinguished of American blacks.*

A bill was introduced in Congress, and hearings were held by the Subcommittee on Africa. Nevertheless, the first SAA flight arrived at Kennedy on the cold, snowy night of February 23, 1969. About 200 shivering protestors were at the airport with picket signs, although because of the size of the airport, we never knew where or when the plane actually came in.

Interracial issues arose regarding personnel at the three U.S. satellite-tracking stations in South Africa. An agreement between the two governments was signed in September 1960. South Africa claimed that the United States had accepted racial restrictions at the stations in that agreement, which the Americans denied. The United States did refuse to abide by apartheid restrictions in principle but avoided the issue in practice by not having black personnel on hand. The stations were finally moved.

The issue of U.S. black personnel in South Africa arose again in May 1965, when the aircraft carrier *Independence* was due to land at Cape Town. The issue was resolved by having it bypass that port. In 1967, however, the scheduled landing of the aircraft carrier *Franklin D. Roosevelt*, carrying 400 black servicemen, became a political issue. Donald Fraser of Minnesota took leadership in the House. He wrote me as follows (February 6, 1967):

Last week I was in Germany when your letter arrived on the visit of the U.S. aircraft carrier *Franklin D. Roosevelt* to South Africa. However my staff reached me by phone and then were able to organize a protest in the House. The letter to the President signed by 38 Congressmen is enclosed. . . . In addition there were some other more senior members who indicate that they will privately protest. . . . Thanks for bringing the whole matter to my attention.

This and other incidents led to a government decision to cancel operational port calls in South Africa rather than accept the racial conditions imposed by South Africa.

At the end of 1965, the United Nations established a Trust Fund for South Africa to raise funds from member states to aid the victims of apartheid and their families. It was to be an international, governmental fund. Three months later, on the sixth anniversary of the Sharpeville Massacre, the ACOA held a commemorative public meeting at a church in Harlem, at which both E.S. Reddy, the secretary of the Special Committee Against Apartheid, and I stressed the importance of this fund. A collection was taken as a token of our support.

---

*Among the signers were Muhammed Ali, Ralph Abernathy, Roy Campanella, Harry Belafonte, Count Basie, Arthur Ashe, Julian Bond, A. Philip Randolph, Nina Simone, and many members of Congress.

A day or so later, a young man who had attended this meeting called and asked to meet with me. Deeply impressed by our Harlem gathering, and as a protest against GM involvement in South Africa, he wanted to turn over to our Africa Fund hundreds of shares of General Motors stock he had inherited. The Africa Fund would then make a significant contribution to the UN Trust Fund. A few months later, the Rev. Edler Hawkins, a trustee of our Africa Fund, and I presented a check for $50,000 to the UN Trust Fund.

Although the United States had voted for the UN Trust Fund (only South Africa had voted against it), it was not until two and half years later that it made a contribution, only $25,000.

THE FINAL CONFLICT

The overthrow of the government in Lisbon by the Armed Forces Movement (MFA) on April 25, 1974, had far-reaching effects on the African liberation struggles. The new government was committed to independence for its African colonies. The way was paved for almost immediate independence for Guinea-Bissau. In Mozambique the testing time had come for FRELIMO to set up a government that would realize its egalitarian principles for the whole country. In Angola the skirmishes for ascendance among the three nationalist movements would now become a determined struggle for dominance. Their ideological and ethnic differences would take on international proportions as the big powers aligned themselves with the movements they felt would strengthen their own global positions.

The coup also affected Rhodesia. The long eastern frontier bordered on a now-independent Mozambique, a situation that strengthened the black nationalists and was regarded as a threat by the white minority. Furthermore, the military victory in Portugal and the consequent independence of all Portugal's colonies made Spain the last Western European country with a dependent area in Africa, Spanish Sahara, and therefore subject to challenge.

Most important, the change in Portugal quickened immeasurably the struggles of the black majority against the entrenched white minority for control in Namibia and South Africa, struggles that were certain to be the final liberation contests on the continent.

CHAPTER NINETEEN

Angola: After the Coup

With mixed feelings I boarded a plane in Lisbon, bound for Luanda, shortly after midnight on March 15, 1975. My excitement was slightly dampened by a sense of foreboding. This was my first trip to Angola's capital in 21 years. My hiking expedition 13 years earlier was still a fresh memory, but that had been quite different. The liberation war had just started then and it was a clandestine trip to rural Angola. Now I was journeying to the capital after the war against Portugal and at a time when a transitional government was supposedly leading the way to peace, stability, and independence. As the plane flew south, I wondered if the Alvor Agreement, recognizing an uneasy alliance among the three liberation movements forming the transitional government, could hold until independence, November 11. I knew how tenuous their cooperation was. Thus my sense of foreboding.

The plane landed in Luanda about 9:00 A.M., by coincidence on the National Day of the FNLA. I was quickly settled at the Hotel Continental near the center of a large city of about 600,000. No one knew I was coming, for my visa had been granted only a few days earlier in Guinea-Bissau. Although very tired after the all-night flight, I excitedly spent my first few hours in Luanda trying to find my bearings.

I walked to the nearby promontory on which perched the 17th-century fort of São Miguel. There the Portuguese had defeated the Dutch in 1648. A plaque still commemorated the arrival of the Portuguese explorer Diogo Cão in 1483. The fort commands a view of the city's high buildings, which border the beautiful crescent bay, and the sea beyond. On this hot, sunny March Saturday, streams of cars drove bumper to bumper toward the nearby miles of idyllic beaches.

My first impression was that Luanda was still dominated by Europeans. The streets were full of pedestrians, black and white. Most shops were still owned by Portuguese. The heavy traffic, almost exclusively with Portuguese drivers, was regulated by few lights. Of the some 300,000 Portuguese who had lived in Angola, about 50,000 had left since the coup in Portugal. The rest were staying to see what would happen. I felt little tension as I walked about the downtown area.

Things were different, though, as evidenced by political graffiti on the walls, fences, and benches and the posters plastered on other open spaces, especially those advertising the FNLA and UNITA. Everywhere I turned I was greeted by a picture of Holden Roberto in his dark glasses or bearded Jonas Savimbi with the UNITA symbol of the rooster and the rising sun behind him over the words "Kwacha UNITA." Less often did I see

Agostinho Neto's picture and posters of the MPLA. People were obviously exercising their long-denied freedom of expression.

Another difference was the presence of troops on the streets and in the backs of military trucks. Some wore armbands to distinguish them from regular Portuguese forces. They were part of the new integrated army drawn from the liberation movements and the Portuguese. Perhaps the troops were more in evidence than usual because this was FNLA Day, and incidents could happen. (Each of the movements, now transformed into a political party, had designated its national day.) FNLA activities were confined to the *musseques*, where most of the people lived, and no incidents disturbed the peace. The U.S. consul general, Tom Killoran, with whom I talked, took this as a hopeful sign that the three-party coalition might actually work.

THE ALVOR AGREEMENT

In the 10 days at the end of my African journey, my primary task was to make contact with each of the movements so that I could assess the prospects for an orderly transition to independence. Virtually everyone was caught unprepared by the coup in Portugal. Neto, for example, was on a trip to Canada. The transfers of power in Guinea-Bissau and Mozambique were fairly simple, since no movements could compete with the PAIGC and FRELIMO. In Angola it was more complicated because each of the three movements dominated specific areas.

Within two months after the April coup, UNITA had signed a cease-fire with the Portuguese. The MPLA and the FNLA did not do so until October. Then each movement quickly set up offices in Luanda and other centers, where for the first time they could operate openly.

The beginning was hopeful. Chaired by President Jomo Kenyatta of Kenya, and supported by the OAU, Neto, Roberto, and Savimbi met in January 1975 in Mombasa, Kenya, and agreed to cooperate in Angola's reconstruction. A few days later at Alvor in southern Portugal, they agreed to set up a transitional government to exercise authority for about 10 months. Elections were set for late October, independence for November 11.

The transitional government, very logically, was headed by a Portuguese-appointed high commissioner and a cabinet of 12 ministers, 3 each for the Portuguese and the three movements. In addition, there was a Presidential Council, with one representative of each movement and monthly rotating chairmanship. An integrated defense force was to be formed from the four existing armies. When I arrived in Luanda in March, it had about 3,000 men, 500 from each movement and a matching 1,500 from the Portuguese. The goal was 8,000 from each movement with a matching 24,000 from the Portuguese. Then, after independence, the Portuguese would gradually withdraw.

The problem was that the transitional government never really had power. Power still lay with the three separate movements, which continued their long-standing animosities and suspicions. Their tenuous coalition began to break down while I was there. My observations and discussions gave me ample evidence of the difficulties lying ahead.

I met several times with Tim Killoran. When I first saw him, he had just returned from a trip to the main coffee-growing area around Carmona to the north. Because of unsettled conditions, many workers who were from the south, were returning to their home area, leaving few laborers to clear the weeds and underbrush. Consequently, Killoran thought the coffee crop, the country's main export, would be about 40 percent of normal, a bad omen for the economy.

Killoran, who expressed no bias, thought there would be violence at least in Luanda and that the FNLA and UNITA would likely join forces against the MPLA, based in Luanda. He saw no evidence of CIA involvement: perhaps he really did not know about the $300,000 it gave to the FNLA in covert assistance in January, although later it was common knowledge. He specifically told me that Roberto was not receiving U.S. aid but, ironically, was being pilloried for it. I think Killoran may not have been informed about U.S. covert aid authorized by the National Security Council's "40 Committee," but if he did know, he had no reason to tell me.

On my first day in Luanda, I heard that the FNLA was giving a party to celebrate its National Day in a public garden across from the palace, still the seat of government. I walked to the garden, and since I had no invitation I had to drop names of FNLA leaders I had known in order to persuade the soldiers at the entrance to let me in. Immediately I was faced by a huge picture of Holden Roberto, who was still in Zaire. Other leaders were present, including Johnny Eduardo, the FNLA representative on the Presidential Council; Paul Tuba, his assistant; and Hendrick Vaal Neto, minister of information. The diplomatic community was well represented, and a large UNITA delegation was on hand; there were even some MPLA leaders such as Saydi Mingas, minister of finance and planning. The advantage of my being there was that I was able to make appointments for the days ahead.

FNLA STRENGTH

I met several times with Paul Tuba, who had represented the FNLA in New York. He was now in a key position, and the information he gave me presented a decidedly pessimistic view of the future, including the possibility of civil war. He described clashes in the *musseques* between FNLA and MPLA troops. The FNLA was opening a large military training camp near Ambriz on the seacoast north of Luanda. It had 5,000 troops in the Luanda vicinity, many more than the integrated army. There was no limit on the size of the military forces of the three movements,★ and each had its own uniform. Tuba impressed upon me that violence was an ever present reality. As we disembarked from his car at a restaurant one evening, he took a revolver out of his glove compartment and carefully put it in a holster at his side.

Both the Soviet Union and China were involved in Angola, Tuba said, supporting the MPLA and the FNLA respectively. He observed with a laugh that the FNLA might be responsible for bringing China and the United States together, since both were assisting the FNLA. Chinese instructors were training FNLA troops at the Kinkuzu base in Zaire. Tuba felt optimistic about the FNLA's strength. It had just purchased the TV equipment the Portuguese had left and, unlike the other movements, planned to begin its own TV program soon.

Tuba said Roberto would not come to Angola until his public relations advisers had had time to build up "the myth of Holden." Then when he arrived shortly before the October election, he would have an aura of mystery that would attract the masses. The theory was that Neto and Savimbi, as known factors, would be less appealing. It was clear, however, that the FNLA's struggle lay not with UNITA but with the MPLA.

IMPRESSIONS OF UNITA

In the dining room of my hotel, I noticed a group of Angolans wearing UNITA buttons. I approached one of them, who spoke some English, and he introduced me to others. About 20 UNITA members who worked in the three UNITA-led ministries were staying in the hotel. Through them I made contact with Jeremias Kalandulah Chitunda, minister of natural resources. I had met him in the United States, for he had studied at Lincoln University in 1964 and in Arizona. He invited me to his home. We had friends in common because he had gone to school at the Dondi Mission, where Ian Gilchrist had grown up and Larry Henderson had worked. Our discussion reinforced certain impressions I already had. The conflict shaping up did not emanate from the ministerial representatives, who met regularly and fairly harmoniously, but the real power wasn't with them. Chitunda felt UNITA was gaining in popularity even in Luanda, the MPLA's chief base. Savimbi had attracted hundreds of thousands to his campaign rallies in Lobito and Nova Lisboa (now Huambo).† No ideological problems divided UNITA and the FNLA, although they had basically different ethnic followings. Chitunda thought both UNITA and the MPLA were expanding beyond their tribal base but not the FNLA. He hinted at ideological differences with the MPLA. If the movements did

---

★At this time the military forces were approximately 21,000 for the FNLA; 8,000 for the MPLA; 2,000 for Daniel Chipenda's organization, which affiliated with the FNLA after breaking with the MPLA; and 3,000 for UNITA.
†I was told 400,000 in Lobito and 800,000 in Nova Lisboa.

not work together, civil war would result. "I pray it doesn't come to that," he said.

It seemed to me that UNITA was putting its emphasis on political recruiting. I visited its chaotic headquarters in Luanda. Interspersed among the mainly African crowd were white Portuguese. The people were trying to register with UNITA and pay their membership dues. Similar activities were taking place at the headquarters of the other movements.

A few days later I flew to Lobito, south of Luanda, an area with a strong UNITA following. I had known Jorge Valentim, who was in charge of UNITA work there, as an exuberant student in the United States. He had then been an avid enthusiast for Holden Roberto. In 1963 he continued his studies in Europe and joined UNITA when it was formed. As soon as I was settled, I went to UNITA headquarters. As in Luanda, hundreds of people, mostly African, crowded the building. Some wanted to join; others had unemployment or housing difficulties. It took a while for me to get a message to Valentim. Finally a lad motioned for me to follow him onto the street, where another person beckoned me. An armed UNITA soldier led us several blocks to a hotel and upstairs past three more armed soldiers. I found Valentim at a desk surrounded by piles of membership forms, which he was going over one by one. On the walls were pictures of Savimbi and huge crowds. As Valentim stood up and greeted me with a smile, I couldn't help but notice a revolver at his side. We talked for two hours.

Valentim was bitterly anti-MPLA and anti-Communist. He didn't say the MPLA was Communist but that it was allied with Communists and that it was also backed by the MFA in Portugal. Although UNITA and the FNLA were competing, they were not divided ideologically, he said. He was concerned about Portugal's nationalization of the banks and its effect on the private sugar companies, in which the banks owned a large share. He was also concerned about the slowdown, sponsored by the MPLA-affiliated trade union, in unloading ships in Lobito and Luanda, and about the MPLA introducing "politics" into the school curriculum. He worried about land redistribution too, since as late as 1962 Portuguese had simply taken what land they wanted and ordered the occupants off. But there was as yet no plan for an orderly redressing of these wrongs.

Valentim assigned a tall, slim UNITA sergeant, probably still in his teens to show me around Lobito. He wore a revolver on his hip, but he brought his fiancée with him, he said, so no one would think I was under arrest. We attracted a lot of attention as we walked around, he openly holding hands with his shy girl. We communicated in simple phrases. His name was Miguel Gilchristo Higino, in honor of Ian Gilchrist's father, Dr. Sid Gilchrist, who had been the much-loved doctor at the Dondi Mission and had delivered Miguel.

My guide had been in UNITA for four years, two of them in Moxico district, where he had been wounded in the knee in battle with the MPLA forces. He was deeply suspicious of the MPLA, which, he said simplistically, would turn Angola over to "foreigners." He was generally favorable toward the FNLA and rather well disposed toward Portuguese and other whites. On the strength of his uniform, we were picked up several times by whites driving cars as we trudged around Lobito, a frequent occurrence, he said. In two more days he was leaving for a period of officer's training.

I didn't want to leave this part of Angola without visiting Nova Lisboa and the Dondi Mission, about which I had heard so much. I also wanted to ride on the famed Benguela railroad, which was such an important link between Angola on the Atlantic and Mozambique on the Indian Ocean. So I boarded the train in the evening and 12 hours later was in the cool Angola highlands about a mile above sea level. (The trip by car takes only about three hours.) Much of the ride was in the morning so that I saw each of the many villages at which we stopped along the way. Even in this heavily UNITA region, each movement had an office, marked by flying banners.

I went by taxi to the Dondi Mission, where I met Joyce Myers of the staff. She had been in Angola 11 years. On our tour of the school, hospital, and villages, we talked about the difference between the parties' present struggle for power and the much less complex struggle against Portugal. After the April coup, people gradually realized their new freedom. At a large celebration, according to Myers, nearly everyone came in traditional African dress, which the Portuguese had always discouraged. In school, classes were often conducted in Umbundu rather than Portuguese. Myers thought that the people in the area were 90 to 95 percent for UNITA, probably because of ethnic affinity.

The American vice consul had held a meeting with all the local missionaries the week before. He told them they ought to start storing their possessions and plan a way of leaving in case of trouble. None of the missionaries, however, were then prepared to think realistically about such an eventuality.

IMPRESSIONS OF THE MPLA

When I first arrived in Luanda, I had sought out the Methodist bishop, Emilio de Carvalho. I had never met him, although he had gone to Garrett Biblical Institute, in Evanston, Illinois. He knew my name because of my African work and my Methodist connection and was very helpful. As we toured the city in his car, I was especially interested in his account of the MPLA-sponsored attacks on the prisons in February 1961 and the brutal Portuguese response to the uprising in the north a month later. He himself had been arrested in August 1961 and held for 25 months. He described how he and other pastors were beaten and tortured with electric shocks as the Portuguese tried to extract information about the suspected subversive activities of American missionaries and church leaders. About 30 pastors just disappeared. His own release came unexpectedly without explanation.

Luanda was tense the day we toured. Fighting had broken out in the *musseques* between FNLA and MPLA troops. We did not enter the *musseques* because, Carvalho said, it was not safe. Portuguese no longer lived there. A big supermarket was closed because of the fighting the day before. We saw gutted and burned out Portuguese-owned stores that had been attacked shortly after the Lisbon coup, in retaliation against white violence. We also saw the wrecked headquarters of the Daniel Chipenda organization, which the MPLA had driven from its independent position into the FNLA. The building was now guarded by FNLA troops, and Chipenda was made secretary general of the FNLA.

The bishop drove me to the Ministry of Finance and Planning, where I had an appointment with the MPLA minister, Saydi Mingas. We intercepted him as he was dashing away, obviously highly agitated. He stopped just long enough to apologize and tell me he had just been shot at by an FNLA militant.

I had a long talk with Lucio Lara, head of the MPLA office. People filled the street and courtyard outside headquarters. Inside, I had a hard time working my way through the crowded reception room to someone who could help me find him. Finally I was ushered into a quiet inner office on the second floor. Lara was an impressive man, light-skinned with a prominent moustache and a low voice. He was not propagandistic but pragmatic. A key leader almost from the beginning, he combined theoretical knowledge and practical organizational skills. He had been in Portugal studying when the MPLA was organized in 1956, had returned to Angola in November 1974, and had established the Luanda office of the MPLA after the coup.

The MPLA was very strong in Luanda, he said, but the FNLA was strong in the north and UNITA in the central plateau. They didn't trust one another, and if they didn't learn to work together, he said, there would be serious difficulties. Lara thought they could work out their ideological differences on a pragmatic basis. He discussed some of the problems. The people were poor and there had to be changes in control of land and foreign corporations. But Gulf Oil, for example, could not be told just to get out of the country. They were needed and practical adjustments had to be made.

I was especially glad to have a private talk with Dr. Agostinho Neto. Lara drove me to his fairly large house with a fine view of the sea. MPLA soldiers were on guard. Neto and I sat in the living room for our hour-and-a-half discussion. We had talked five months previously in Dar es Salaam before the Alvor Agreement. He had returned to Luanda on February 4, the MPLA's National Day, and had been greeted by an estimated 300,000 people.

In spite of the Alvor Agreement, Neto said, not much had changed in the relations between the three movements. He thought the FNLA and UNITA might very well join forces against the MPLA, which although it might not sweep the country in the elections, would not be last. The settlers, as he called the resident Portuguese, tended to support UNITA and the FNLA. The MFA supported the MPLA, but the police did not.

He was unhappy about the Portuguese high commissioner, Gen. Silva Cardoso, who had previously headed the Air Force in Angola.★

I was interested in Neto's characterization of Roberto and Savimbi in their negotiating sessions. Roberto took a very firm position, which had been worked out in advance, and resisted any deviation. Savimbi, by contrast, was ready to negotiate. In regard to a peaceful solution in the relationship of the three movements, he said, "We always hope." I had the feeling, however, that they were irreconcilable.

My last day in Luanda, March 25, I heard gunfire from time to time. The transitional government had already begun to unravel. My appointment with General Cardoso was canceled at the last minute because fighting had broken out. Nothing that I had seen or heard gave me the feeling that political campaigning could proceed peacefully toward elections in October. It was not long before the civil war erupted in full force.

CIVIL WAR

I was barely back in New York when news came about an FNLA attack on an MPLA training camp north of Luanda, in which 50 young recruits had been killed. At this time, the FNLA still had the largest and best-equipped military organization. From that point on, the fighting spread with increasing intensity. The Soviet Union, the United States, China, South Africa, Zaire, and Cuba were all involved.

I concluded that the FNLA leadership felt that the Alvor Agreement could not last and that its best chance for control of all Angola was to try to eliminate MPLA power in Luanda without delay. This feeling was bolstered by the support it had from the Zairian military.

The intensity of the confrontation mounted during April and May, as the FNLA attacked MPLA suboffices in the *musseques* of Luanda, and the MPLA called upon the Soviet Union for more sophisticated armaments. Further, the MPLA army was reinforced by several thousand Katanganese gendarmes, who had been in Angola ever since Katanga's attempted secession from the Congo. UNITA, the weakest of the movements militarily, drew closer to the FNLA as its offices in Luanda were attacked by MPLA forces. UNITA's support from the Angolan Portuguese strengthened the MPLA perception that it was facing a military threat from both the other movements.

One last attempt was made to prevent the incipient civil war. Again chaired by Jomo Kenyatta and backed by the OAU, a conference in Nakuru, Kenya, in June, brought together Roberto, Neto, and Savimbi.

★The first high commissioner had been Admiral Rosa Coutinho, who had been replaced by Cardoso after the Alvor Agreement. Both the FNLA and UNITA felt that Coutinho was too sympathetic to the MPLA. However, the UNITA and FNLA representatives I talked with liked Cardoso.

They agreed to renounce force and to prepare for a peaceful transfer of power. But it was already too late. Heavy fighting occurred in July. The strengthened MPLA drove the FNLA out of Luanda and extended its control along the corridor to Malange and all the way to Henrique de Carvalho in the east. The FNLA in turn forced the MPLA out of the northern districts of Uige and Zaire.

South Africa's active entrance into the conflict marked a turning point. Savimbi had met Prime Minister John Vorster in May, even calling him a "responsible leader," to begin a long-continuing relationship. South Africa supplied personnel to train UNITA troops. It seemed contradictory that South Africa should be militarily in Angola precisely when a detente in the Rhodesian conflict was supposedly in effect.

Nevertheless, as early as August, South African forces occupied the area of the Cunene hydroelectric dam in southern Angola near the Namibian border. The principal South African invasion did not begin until late October when two columns of troops, backed by UNITA and Chipenda's FNLA-related soldiers, crossed into Angola.

The so-called Zulu Column rapidly advanced north. On November 4, they took Benguela and Lobito. They were not halted until late November, some 120 miles south of Luanda at the Queve River, by hastily summoned Cuban reinforcements.

Cuban support for the MPLA was not new. Cuban military advisers had been on hand when the MPLA was headquartered in Brazzaville in the 1960s. Cuban doctors had worked with the MPLA medical program long before the coup in Portugal. Angolan youth sympathetic to the MPLA had for years been given scholarships to study in Cuba. Furthermore, Cuban military advisers came to Angola in spring 1975, as the fighting heated up, to help train MPLA forces. At the time of the October South African invasion, several hundred Cubans were advising and supporting the MPLA, but the airlifting of thousands of Cuban soldiers in Operation Carlota did not take place until November 7, in response to an urgent appeal from Neto, when Luanda was threatened not only with the South African-led force from the south but by the FNLA-Zairian forces of Roberto from the north. Caught in a military pincer, the MPLA was faced with a crisis of survival.

Roberto's objective was to take the capital by November 11. The Portuguese military had already withdrawn, and the transition government had been declared dead in August. A critical battle took place at Kifongondo, 14 miles north of Luanda, which I visited almost six years later in 1981. It is a small village on a hill overlooking the Bengo River where the road from Caxito to Luanda crosses it. The MPLA and newly arrived Cuban troops had a commanding hilltop position. At this point the road is bordered by marshes, making an escape on the flanks almost impossible. As it was explained to me, the MPLA strategy was to allow part of the advancing FNLA-Zaire force to cross the bridge and then destroy it, thus dividing the attackers. Then the MPLA could let loose with the frightening mobile 122mm rocket launchers newly acquired from the Soviet Union. In his book *In Search of Enemies*, John Stockwell, the former head of the CIA's task force in Angola, credits the MPLA victory to this weapon as much as any other factor. The strategy worked as planned and the Roberto forces were decimated. To mark this major MPLA victory, Angolan and Cuban flags were flying side by side on the hilltop.

In the midst of this hectic military action, the MPLA declared itself the government of independent Angola with Agostinho Neto as president. The FNLA and UNITA countered by attempting to set up the Democratic People's Republic of Angola in Huambo, but it never got off the ground. The two movements never resolved their mutual suspicions. Roberto, for example, never allowed UNITA forces to enter his stronghold in the north.

The retreating Zulu Column had completely withdrawn from Angola by March 1976. The MPLA army drove the FNLA out of the north, captured the FNLA headquarters at Ambriz in January, and took Noqui on the Zairian border by early March. Roberto, back in Zaire, had only the remnants of a political organization. He even lost the 14-year-long support of his great benefactor, as President Mobutu Sese Seko signed a declaration normalizing relations with Angola on March 23, and the FLNA center in Kinshasa that I had so often visited was vacated.*

The People's Republic of Angola was barely two weeks old when it was recognized by Nigeria, Tanzania, Ghana, and the Sudan, in part at least because of South African intervention.

AMERICAN INVOLVEMENT

On the home front the ACOA's objective was to stop U.S. intervention in Angola. My colleagues and I had long been critics of the U.S. pro-Portuguese policy. Secretary of State Henry Kissinger did not really become concerned about the anticolonial struggle in Africa until the reality of the competition for power in Angola was thrust upon him. And then he saw it not in terms of an Angolan struggle but as a global conflict between a Soviet-backed movement and one having U.S. support. He hoped that CIA funds for military equipment would tip the contest toward an FNLA-UNITA victory. Thus several hundred thousand dollars went covertly to Roberto in January 1975 and $14 million in July; he requested another $27 million late in the year, which Congress turned down.

The issue for U.S. policymakers was not what might be the best movement for Angola but simply U.S.-Soviet competition. In a letter to all the African heads of state in fall 1975, President Gerald Ford called Soviet

---

*Roberto was finally expelled from Zaire in 1979 after he accused Mobutu of embezzling millions of dollars in aid intended for the FNLA during the civil war, a charge that Stockwell verifies.

support of the MPLA "intervention 8,000 miles from its borders." The American press inevitably described the MPLA as "Soviet-backed" or "Marxist" and the other two movements as "pro-West." No attempt was made to explain what "Marxist" or "pro-West" meant in terms of a program in Angola.

This White House policy had some tough sledding in other government circles. Kissinger ran into problems with his own assistant secretary for Africa, Donald Easum. I knew from Samora Machel (soon-to-be president of Mozambique) that he had received a sympathetic hearing in Dar es Salaam in 1974 from Easum, who hoped the United States would be able to open up a new, positive era with Mozambique and try to make amends for years of support for Portugal. Easum was cool toward U.S. intervention in Angola. He was relieved of his post shortly after he returned to Washington.

Nathaniel Davis, U.S. ambassador to Chile during the coup against Salvatore Allende, was nominated to succeed Easum. The ACOA had joined with other groups to oppose his nomination. We felt this was no time to send such a man to a country fraught with cold war implications. How wrong we were. Davis proved to be independent and hardheaded in analyzing the Angolan situation. He rightly saw U.S. support for FNLA-UNITA as a no-win affair. He resigned in August.

It was in Congress, however, the interventionist policy in Angola ran into the most severe opposition. Sen. Dick Clark of Iowa, chairman of the Senate Subcommittee on African Affairs, twice held hearings on U.S. policy toward Angola. After a trip to Angola, he wrote in an Op Ed piece in the *New York Times* (January 29, 1976), "I returned convinced that our involvement was a mistake." In spite of his objections, covert U.S. aid increased four times in four months. He finally offered the Clark Amendment to the Security Assistance Act to prevent funds from being spent in Angola without specific congressional approval. It lasted 10 years until it was repealed in July 1985. Further, an amendment to the Defense Appropriation Act barring further funds for Angola, sponsored by Sen. John Tunney of California, was overwhelmingly passed by both houses. After Vietnam, Americans were not anxious to be involved in another conflict thousands of miles away.

The ACOA tried to pull together what nongovernmental forces we could to form a coalition to stop U.S. intervention in Angola. More than 40 organizations responded. A rally was held in Washington in support of the Tunney Amendment, and the coalition sponsored newspaper ads likening U.S. involvement in Angola to U.S. involvement in Vietnam.

I wrote an Op Ed piece in the *New York Times* (December 14, 1975), "Communism and the War in Angola," and appeared in hearings before the Clark subcommittee in February 1976, along with my friends John Marcum and Larry Henderson.

By this time the immediate internal struggle in Angola was virtually over. The MPLA was established in Luanda and had military control in other major centers. U.S. assistance to other groups was cut off through the Clark and Tunney amendments, and the MPLA government was recognized by 41 nations.

I learned from this experience that it was much more difficult to win public support for a campaign involving the cold war than for an anti-apartheid effort. The American people did not know much about Angola. One had to appeal to their fear of another Vietnam and their distaste that U.S. support for an anti-MPLA movement put the country in a de facto alliance with South Africa. Black leadership in Congress was united in opposition. Virtually the only noticeable black support for U.S. intervention was in a campaign by Roy Innis, head of CORE, to recruit black Vietnam veterans to fight with the FNLA to defeat "communism" in Africa. I don't think any volunteers reached Angola, fortunately for them. At best they would have landed in a quagmire of disorganization and at worst they would have been captured or killed.

THE CIA AGAIN

From time to time, the old rumor surfaced about CIA funds going through the ACOA to Roberto. A friend called my attention to a book by the Soviet journalist Oleg Ignatiev, *Secret Weapon in Africa*. Chapter 2 asserted that Roberto was receiving CIA assistance and that during much of the 1960s it came through the ACOA. Ignatiev's contention that Roberto had received CIA aid was not in dispute, but his information, quite apart from his main error in positing a CIA connection between the ACOA and the FNLA, was factually incorrect on so many details that I probably should have dismissed it. I decided, however, to write him a letter pointing out specific errors and sent it in care of his publisher in Moscow. We exchanged two letters, and I received a near retraction. In the first (December 17, 1978), translated at the Soviet Embassy, he wrote, "I want to say that there is nothing in the book . . . that would give grounds for any conclusion that you have contacts with the U.S. Central Intelligence Agency . . . none of the material I had gathered for the book links your name directly with the CIA." This sentence contradicted his linking me and the ACOA to the CIA by implication. In the second, he thanked me for my letters and said, "I shall not omit to take them into account in preparing the second revised edition of my book." I did not see the revision, so I don't know what he did with my information.

This kind of attack helped to balance attacks from the extreme right. For example, the *National Review Bulletin* (April 21, 1978) wrote that I, a white Methodist minister, was executive director of the ACOA described by *Information Digest* as "the leading U.S. support group for the Soviet-aligned Marxist terrorist movement in Africa." Congressman Larry McDonald had described the ACOA and me almost identically in a speech in the House (September 9, 1977) as serving "for more than two decades as the principal support group for Marxist terrorist movements on the African continent."

Philosophically I reasoned that if I was publicly involved in controversial issues, I had to expect a certain amount of unjustified smearing.

THE EFFORT TO REBUILD

My next visit to Angola, more than five years after the civil war, was not an easy experience. The scene in Luanda was rather appalling. Most of the busy stores I had seen in 1975 were closed in 1981. Long queues formed in front of stores rumored to have food. The streets, with their few cars, were nothing like the bustling thoroughfares of a few years earlier. City dwellers went into the country to buy food. The government had instituted an austerity program to limit borrowing from sources abroad and was running up huge foreign debts.

All but 10 percent of the Portuguese had fled the country during the fighting in 1975. This meant that most professionals were gone, and much of the equipment they had not taken with them such as trucks and tractors, was sabotaged. The coffee plantations, which had once produced about 200,000 tons of coffee a year, the country's principal export, had been so grievously neglected that production was more than cut in half. Sugar production was at a standstill. Diamond production was reduced by 80 percent. Fishing from Portuguese trawlers, now gone or unusable, ceased, and traditional fishing from small boats or canoes was woefully inadequate. Roads were in disrepair. Nearly 150 bridges had been destroyed in the war, and rebuilding could be done only with foreign aid, chiefly from socialist countries.

Food shortages were constant; almost 50 percent of flour, sugar, cooking oil, and powdered milk had to be imported. A sharp drop in the world prices of coffee and oil meant that the country faced a critical economic situation. At the same time, most of the 300,000 refugees who had been in Zaire and some 30,000 in Zambia returned.

In addition to its economic problems, the MPLA government faced political crises. Barely a year and a half after independence, Nito Alves, minister of internal administration, attempted a coup on May 27, 1977, against Neto. Alves's forces had briefly taken control of the radio station and a prison and had taken a few MPLA leaders (including my friend Saydi Mingas) as hostages before the government reasserted its authority. Alves opposed Neto's nonalignment policy, advocated scrapping the private sector in the economy such as the contractual relationship with Cabinda Gulf Oil, and favored putting whites and mesticos in subordinate positions. The Neto policy, however, prevailed.

Later the same year the MPLA held its first full congress and formed the MPLA Worker's Party, transforming itself from a broad liberation movement into a political party following Marxist-Leninist principles. Banks had already been nationalized, but the process was rapidly applied to breweries, sugar plants, and cement and textile factories. The last companies to be nationalized were Diamang, the diamond company, and

Cabinda Gulf. Three fourths of American investment in Angola was through Gulf. The nationalization of oil through Sonangol, the state oil company with 51 percent control of Cabinda Gulf, which was finalized in September 1978, did not change the company's good working relationship with the government. Angola received about $500 million annually from Gulf in taxes and royalties. The president of Gulf Oil (the parent company), appearing in congressional hearings and speaking in favor of U.S. recognition of Angola, said, "Gulf has encountered no ideological or discriminatory problems of any significance. . . . [Angola follows] a highly nationalistic and yet pragmatic policy toward foreign investments."[1] Angola pursued an expedient policy of getting help where it was available. Most military matériel came through the Soviet Union, costing Angola an estimated $2 billion from 1983 to 1985.[2] Cubans served in both military and technical roles with Angola covering the cost of room and board. More than 400 Cubans filled important health posts, leading Andrew Young, U.S. ambassador to the UN, to make the controversial statement after he visited Angola in 1977 that "Cubans bring a certain stability and order" to Angola. Yugoslavs and East Germans were especially helpful in rebuilding bridges and roads. Help came from the West too. Swedish bankers offered technical advice in restructuring the National Bank of Angola; the French helped to restore coffee production; Austrians assisted in the production of iron ore.

To compound the problems of Angola, Neto died in September 1979. He was succeeded by José Eduardo dos Santos, who was trained as a petroleum engineer. Most devastating for Angola was the destabilizing effect of South Africa's continued intervention through UNITA. The rationale was that Angola offered support and sanctuary to the South West Africa People's Organization (SWAPO) in the struggle for independence in Namibia. The rationale for U.S. refusal to recognize the Angola government and for overt-covert aid to UNITA was the presence of Cuban troops. Yet as long as South Africa intervened, Cuban help was needed. A report to an MPLA congress in December 1985 summarized South African actions in Angola in the 1980s: 4,000 violations of air space, 168 aerial bombardments, 230 airborne troop landings, 90 strafing attacks, 74 land attacks, and 4 naval landings.

UNITA's guerrilla activities in the Angolan highlands, making it unsafe for the farmers to till the land, tragically disrupted the production of food. This area, once the breadbasket of Angola, reportedly had 200,000 people suffering from malnutrition. Only 3 percent of the arable land was under cultivation. A Red Cross report in late 1985 indicated that 400 tons of food were flown weekly into the area. This dreadful situation did not result from drought, as in the other hungry areas of Africa, but from UNITA's destabilizing campaign, which had turned Angola from a net exporter of food stuffs into a country dependent on imported food.

CHAPTER TWENTY

Mozambique:
The FRELIMO Victory

Mozambique had been independent for just four months when, in
October 1975, I visited it for the first time. To me, Mozambique
was the most exciting independent country in Africa just then, not simply
because the liberation struggle had been won but also because of the
integrity of the FRELIMO leadership. Yet it was clear that the testing time
was just beginning.

As the plane landed at Lourenço Marques (Maputo after February
1976), I was fascinated by the city's imposing skyline. My friends were
away and so could not meet me at the airport, but by lucky chance,
Alberto Sithole, whom I had known as the FRELIMO representative in
Lusaka and who was then with the Ministry of Foreign Affairs, was there.
He drove me to the plush Polana Hotel, which had a spectacular view of
the Indian Ocean, a large outdoor swimming pool, and an extensive
subtropical garden. The hotel was a vestige of the colonial past. One of the
staff told me that 90 percent of the guests used to be South Africans on
holiday, but now there were only 6 South Africans of 60 guests. The hotel
could accommodate 200. Thus one of the realities of independent Mozambique was impressed on me.

PROBLEMS AND ASSETS

In spite of the hope and the enthusiasm FRELIMO brought to the task of
rebuilding the country, the movement had inherited serious problems.
Most of the Portuguese residents in the south never came to terms with the
reality of a FRELIMO victory. The heavy fighting had taken place hundreds of miles to the north, and to them the possibility of the "terrorists"
winning a victory was like a bad dream. Nevertheless, the accord between
FRELIMO and Portugal was signed in Lusaka in early September 1974.

Some adamant resident Portuguese made an attempt at revolt against
the transitional government and even called for a white-controlled unilateral declaration of independence, as in Rhodesia. A contingent of armed
dissidents had briefly taken over the radio station in Lourenço Marques in
September, only to be driven out by the remaining Portuguese troops. A
month later, dissident Portuguese attacked FRELIMO soldiers on police
duty. This time the people retailiated by attacking Portuguese establishments. Several hundred people were killed or injured.

A Portuguese exodus began—doctors, lawyers, teachers, business people, technicians, farmers. A year after independence the Portuguese population had declined 90 percent, to about 20,000. Just as in Angola, they often took with them what machinery or farm equipment they could and destroyed the rest. Factories and stores were abandoned, as there were no managers or technicians to run them. Most Africans had not been trained to do so. Farms and plantations were likewise abandoned, some 4,000 in the fertile Limpopo River valley alone, north of Lourenço Marques, where much of the food for the capital area was grown. The ports and the railroad lost 7,000 skilled and semiskilled workers. Eighty percent of the doctors departed. Tourism came to a halt, and servants of the Portuguese joined the unemployed.

Furthermore, FRELIMO inherited a lopsided economy from the Portuguese. Exports were half as great as imports. The country could not feed itself. Trade, at the time of independence, was a classic example of a colonial economy—78 percent of the exports were raw materials and agricultural produce, and 85 percent of imports were manufactured goods. The economy was geared to and dominated by the relationship to South Africa. The ports and the railroads were dependent on South African traffic. About 125,000 Mozambicans were employed in the South African mines. When, in 1976, South Africa cut this number to 40,000, it simply added to Mozambique's economic woes.

Mozambique suffered from its relationship with Rhodesia as well. Within six months, President Samora Machel closed the border. This cut off Rhodesia's use of the railroad and the port facilities at Beira, but the loss of revenue from these services and from migrant labor payments cost Mozambique more than $150 million a year.

In spite of these problems, FRELIMO tackled the task at hand with vigor and determination. I sensed the air of optimism and excitement everywhere. FRELIMO had a lot of things going for it. Mozambique was not without natural resources—a lot of land, water, potential energy, vast reserves of coal, some minerals and iron ore. Furthermore, there was no large group of wealthy land owners to stand in the way of socialization, to which FRELIMO was committed, nor was there a large group of landless peasants. In 1975 there was even a small balance of payments surplus because imports were curtailed while exports continued at the regular pace for a short time.

A DEDICATED PEOPLE

The country's main asset, however, was the dedication of leaders and people to tackling their new responsibilities. It was thrilling for me to see the reunion of former comrades who had once shared prison cells. I spent several days with a young FELIMO party worker, Inacio Cossa, who came from southern Gaza Province. He went with me on my visit to the home of Eduardo Mondlane described in chapter 14. He was one of 75 nationalists caught by South African police as they were trying to escape from Mozambique through the Transvaal to join FRELIMO in Dar es Salaam. They were turned over the Portuguese authorities. After five years in prison near Lourenço Marques, he was released in 1969 and then forced to join the Portuguese army and not allowed out of the Lourenço Marques area. If he had been, he would have deserted, he said. On our trip we met two of his fellow prisoners, the head of FRELIMO for Gaza and the governmental administrator for the district of Manjacaze. The men's greeting and embrace, accompanied by laughing and back slapping, signified a special bond forged through a common experience in the liberation struggle.

Basic FRELIMO organizational practices were just being worked out. At that time, only those who had been in the armed forces or who had lived in the liberated areas during the struggle were party members. But the constitutional means of establishing membership was being discussed.

The new flag carried symbols of FRELIMO principles—the hoe for agriculture, the star for solidarity with people everywhere committed to liberation, the gun for struggle, and the book for education.

I was impressed by the enthusiasm of new FRELIMO recruits of Portuguese extraction. I spent long hours with a young teacher of English at the local high school, walking around the capital, visiting the docks, noting the half empty apartment buildings vacated by fleeing Portuguese and now beginning to fill up with Africans, noting the former houses of prostitution closed or converted to other uses. My companion was waiting for a call to do national reconstruction work in a northern village for which he and four friends had volunteered.

GDS AND PEOPLE'S SHOPS

My companion first explained to me the importance of the so-called Dynamizing Groups (Grupes Dinamezadores, GDs), which were set up in neighborhoods, schools, and business establishments to raise the political consciousness of the people and initiate them in programs supportive of FRELIMO. They were not an intergral part of the movement, although they were nurtured by it. Participation was entirely voluntary, but everyone was encouraged to be active in a GD. They had weekly meetings, chose their own leaders, and enjoyed a lot of give and take among the members.

Each GD had operational sections devoted to women's organization, political work, information and propaganda, cultural emphases, and social affairs. One volunteer was responsible for each section. I saw evidence of the work of the GDs in neighborhood clean-up squads and local vigilance committees, which patrolled day and night to discourage petty thieving and make people aware of security problems. I was once challenged by a young girl when I was taking movies of FRELIMO slogans written on the side of a school building. Our "conversation" consisted of gestures and my showing her a letter from a FRELIMO leader granting me the right to take pictures. She smiled, we shook hands, and I continued my photography. For the first two years of independence, the GDs served an important role in introducing many people in areas far removed from the liberation struggle to community action and responsible work.

My companion appraised the GDs realistically. There was a lot of apathy to contend with. When they organized GDs at his school, about 2,000 students turned out, but after a series of discussions on FRELIMO ideology and the GDs, only about 300 elected the secretariat and the key *responsavals* to head the operational sections.

When I visited FRELIMO headquarters, it seemed to me that the section encouraging the GDs, where Cossa worked, was the most active. Various GD delegations came in for help in solving problems ranging from unemployment to violation of women's rights, to isolated acts of racial discrimination. When he and I visited a clothing factory and a cashew plant, he called for the GD representatives to join us. These units were like trade unions, and through them grievances could be presented to management.

I visited some People's Shops, a carryover from the independence struggle. On a Saturday afternoon, about a hundred people were queued up at the door. They were let in a few at a time to prevent overcrowding. The shop was one of seven in the city, all owned by the state and operated for the benefit of the people. Prices were about 10 percent lower than those in an ordinary shop. There was not much stock, however, and the future of the shops was in doubt. They seemed better adapted to their original role as barter trading posts than to competition with other stores in the city.

CULTURE AND HEALTH

On Saturday afternoon in the crowded outlying areas of the city, the narrow, unpaved roads were thronged with pedestrians. In open spaces between the small houses constructed of sheets of metal and odd pieces of boarding, drumming and dancing were in progress. For blocks away the rhythmic sounds were compelling. In the Malhangalene area a FRELIMO flag was flying inside a low fenced enclosure, and a couple of hundred people were participating in festivities, sponsored by the cultural section of the neighborhood GD. I talked with the *responsaval* for culture, a woman, who explained that they were teaching the children the traditional dances. The drumming was done by women. Boys and girls were decked out in straw skirts and straw anklets. A man was leading the dancing. The rediscovery of the people's culture was under way.

I spent a lot of time with Dr. Helder Martins, the minister of health, with whom I had worked when the ACOA had contributed to the health program of FRELIMO for the long years of the struggle. He explained that despite the serious problem caused by the exodus of doctors, they were making some changes. Medical services had been nationalized. A long-term plan was in effect emphasizing preventive medicine and health education. The 1976 budget called for constructing one hospital in each province. Martins was hopeful about training new doctors. Of the current crop of graduates from the university medical school, only 12 out of 25 were staying in the country with government contracts, but in the next year's graduating class only 3 were leaving. Plans were moving ahead for an accelerated training program for medical assistants and nurses, the construction of local clinics and sanitary posts (under the Portuguese 89 percent of private doctors had worked in the capital) and mass immunization campaigns.

FRELIMO's priorities were reflected in the budget. President Machel had announced that education and culture were first, followed by agriculture, health, and, last, the armed services. The emphasis paid off in education, for in the first five years primary school attendance increased by about 100 percent to almost 1,400,000 in school, and secondary school students rose from 20,000 to 35,000. Literacy rose from about 5 percent to 25 percent.

RURAL COMMUNITIES

I went on a trip to Tete Province hundreds of miles north of Lourenço Marques. This had been the area of heavy armed struggle between FRELIMO and the Portuguese. Here the Portuguese had forced people into *aldeamentos*. In one small district there were 14. Several hundred people lived in the village of Nchamba. It had been set up in 1972 and included a military post composed of African soldiers in the Portuguese army. This prompted a villager to comment to me, "FRELIMO sees no differences in race. We have some friends who are white, and some enemies who are black." Since independence, some of the people had moved back to their old homesteads, but most had stayed on. The village now had a school, a rudimentary health post, and an active GD.

The most important feature of FRELIMO's plan for rural community life, however, was the establishment of communal villages. This was given highest priority. It was hoped that the *aldeamentos* could fit within their structure. The process of building the villages was just beginning. In the southern part of Maputo Province, I saw a village where fertile land was already being worked in common by peasants even before new houses were constructed. Joaquim Chissano, the foreign minister, explained to me that they would range from 500 to 1,000 families in size. A tremendous educational campaign was being planned to explain to the people, who had traditionally lived in separate homesteads and worked small plots, the advantages of communal life. Schools, clinics, stores, transportation, and communication facilities would be more available in a village. The land would be worked in common and the income from the produce would be shared, but families would have private plots as well. The blueprint sounded good, I thought, but would it work?

NATIONALIZATION

The process of nationalization had just begun when I was there. I discussed it with Marcelino dos Santos, minister of development and economic planning. The legal profession, the education and health systems, and funerals had been nationalized almost immediately. The idea was to stop exploitation of the common people. Nationalizing of funerals was particularly popular because of the exploitive practices of funeral directors. Unused land and rental apartment buildings were also controlled by the government, but not private homes, private industries, or stores.

RELATIONS WITH SOUTH AFRICA

I was particularly eager to know how FRELIMO would relate to South Africa, which is only 40 miles from the capital. Mozambique had inherited an economy geared to South Africa; thousands of men were employed in South African mines; its railroad and port facilities were made for South African use, and its Cabora Bassa Dam produced power for South Africa. Furthermore, FRELIMO was closely associated with the South African ANC dedicated to the overthrow of the apartheid government. How would South Africa respond to an independent Mozambique?

Security in Mozambique did not seem unusually tight. I had no qualms about walking around Lourenço Marques any time of the day or night. On the highways outside the city there were occasionally police roadblocks and checkpoints, but it was pretty routine as long as a driver had a permit for the trip.

Chissano and I discussed the relationship of the two countries. He took a pragmatic view about the Cabora Bassa Dam. I had spent some hours at this most impressive site in a deep gorge where the Zambezi must have flowed swiftly before the construction of the dam and the lake, which stretched back about 125 miles to the Rhodesian border. Only two of the five turbines were completed and in operation then, with all the electricity going to South Africa. About 1,000 workers out of an original 7,000 were still on the job.

The Mozambique goverment was not planning to interrupt the construction or cut off the flow of power to South Africa, Chissano explained to me. "The current which is flowing in the wires from Cabora Bassa to South Africa is like a river. It would be difficult to stop and stopping it would not change the situation in South Africa." Maybe the situation would change later, but in any event, FRELIMO would take its lead from the liberation movement in South Africa. The more serious problem with South Africa, he thought, involved the migrant miners and the use of the port facilities, where some 10,000 were employed. Obviously this was an inherited economic fact of life for Mozambique, which could not be precipitously changed.

NOT A SIMPLE SUCCESS STORY

I have been back to Mozambique several times since 1975 and have had a wide variety of experiences—sobering, exciting, disappointing, and satisfying. Mozambique cannot be regarded as a simple success story. The problems of daily existence make that impossible. Drought followed by floods in southern Mozambique in 1982–1983, for example, had terrible effects. Rainfall had been half the normal amount, and tens of thousands of people were starving. Efforts to send in food were sabotaged by the South African-backed Mozambique National Resistance (MNR), an anti-FRELIMO guerrilla group. It was dangerous to travel by car outside urban areas in many provinces. The UN World Food Program was unable to operate in Gaza and Inhambane because of MNR harrassment.

I was told that the long lines of people waiting to enter restaurants in Maputo were the result not of a lack of money but of a shortage of food. Maputo had a rationing system. Toward the end of the month, many people had used up their allotments and had to go to restaurants to eat.

Facilities at even some formerly first-class hotels were dismal. Frequently the main elevator was not running, as no spare parts were available for repairs. There was no soap or hot water; running water was sometimes turned off for many hours of the day, and flush toilets frequently did not work properly. Breakfast consisted of dry toast and tea or coffee. People who knew the ropes brought their own butter, jelly, or milk. The government gave low priority to tourism. Casual visitors were not likely to be drawn to Mozambique.

In spite of FRELIMO's vigorous attack on its problems, tremendous difficulties persisted. To be sure, in the first five years of independence the number of primary and secondary school students rose dramatically. But there was a great shortage of trained teachers. There were few text books, and frequently the only way to obtain reference material was laboriously to make copies from single available books.

The number of communal villages grew slowly. In 1978 the head of the program in Gaza told me there were about 860 in the entire country. Four years later there were 500 more. The government hoped to increase the population in such villages from 1.5 million to 5 million by 1990, a seemingly impossible goal.

I found my visits to communal villages fascinating—the welcome by the leaders, the singing and the discussions (frequently involving translation from the local language into Portuguese and then to English) interspersed with an easy comradery. I witnessed open-air literacy classes for adults and elementary classes for children (frequently within reed fences), poorly stocked cooperative stores, and lines at the well and the clinic. The people worked in the communal fields from 7:00 A.M. to 2:30 P.M. and then in their family plots. It was a hard life. They suffered from the same problems affecting the country as a whole—drought or floods, MNR attacks, and lack of machinery and consumer goods.

By the early 1980s the number of doctors had risen to about 350, many of them from overseas. About half were serving in Maputo. The shortage was a contant problem. Nevertheless, in the country at large, mass vaccination campaigns have been important in knocking out smallpox and attacking serious diseases such as measles.

I knew something of the destruction caused by the MNR from my visits, news accounts, and talks with officials. The amount of physical damage credited to the MNR was sobering. Machel recounted the cost in a speech made in 1984: 840 schools, 186 health posts and centers, 24 maternity clinics, 900 shops destroyed. The oil pipe line and the railroad from Beira to Zimbabwe were blown up. Foreign technicians were kidnapped and four had been killed. Sawmills, tea factories, and cotton gins had been destroyed. On top of FRELIMO's other problems, these losses were overwhelming. The MNR was a natural successor to the force of right-wing Portuguese and Rhodesian white supremacists and anti-FRELIMO Mozambicans that had operated against black nationalist forces during the struggle for the independence of Zimbabwe. After independence, they had fled to South Africa, on which they depended for support.

FRELIMO and the South African ANC had a close relationship of longstanding. Time and again leaders of both movements told me they vowed support for each other to the end. Mozambican independence was looked upon as a victory for the ANC too because it meant that the ANC had a friendly neighbor. Oliver Tambo was treated almost like a head of state when he came to Mozambique.

That is why the highly publicized Nkomati Accord signed by President P.W. Botha of South Africa and President Machel of Mozambique in March 1984 in an atmosphere of friendliness and a mutual sense of victory came as an unexpected shock to many sympathizers with FRELIMO. It was a nonaggression pact in which each country agreed to respect the sovereignty of the other, to settle disputes peacefully, to prohibit propaganda against the other, and to forbid the use of its territories by an enemy of the other planning violence. How could such a friendly document come about after years of mutual recrimination and the sudden night attacks by

South African commandos and planes on nonmilitary buildings in Matola, a suburb of Maputo?

I had visited the sites of two such attacks. In 1981 three houses of South African ANC members had been damaged and 12 people killed. When I saw the houses, they were in the same condition as the day of the attack except for the removal of the bodies—huge holes in the walls; bullet marks on the floors, ceilings, and walls; blood stains on the walls and steps, marking the exit route of those trying to escape. Scattered on the floor were ANC and SWAPO pamphlets, a copy of *Newsweek,* the book *Five Seconds to Live,* a toy pistol, broken glass, and personal effects.

In 1983 a jam factory had been bombed on the pretext that it was an ANC stronghold. Three workers had been killed and one injured. A nursery close by had been hit, but fortunately no children were there so early in the morning.

After all this destruction, many ANC leaders were understandably bitter about the accord and especially about Mozambique's air of victory. In November 1984 in Algiers at the 30th anniversary of the struggle against the French, an ANC leader told me he was convinced that South Africa was still supporting the MNR eight months after the accord. And yet, Mozambique had expelled all but 10 members of the ANC diplomatic mission in holding up its part of the accord. He said he had not lost faith in FRELIMO, but he believed the agreement could not last.*

Also in Algiers a FRELIMO leader told me that he recognized the ANC's disappointment but that the accord was a necessity. He realistically commented that the "bandits" of the MNR were gaining strength and it was hoped the accord would at least slow them down. In private I found no Mozambicans who looked upon the accord as a victory. Obviously it represented FRELIMO's inability to stamp out the MNR or respond forcefully to South African aggression.

HOPE IN SPITE OF ADVERSITY

The many economic and other problems burdening Mozambique notwith-standing, I cling to a great hope for the country. For one thing, I respond positively to the pragmatism of FRELIMO leaders, to their openness, self-criticism, and willingness to change their approach if it is not working effectively. I have sensed the efforts to change direction several times even in the decade or so since independence. For example, at the beginning, in an atmosphere of optimism the GDs were enthusiastically promoted. Yet

---

*A year later South Africa admitted violating the accord. A headline in the *New York Times* (September 20, 1985) announced: "South Africa Admits Breaking Mozambique Pact." The deputy foreign minister, Louis Nel, admitted he had made three secret trips to rebel headquarters in Mozambique and rebel officers had been ferried in and out of the country by submarine.

when I returned to Mozambique three years later, I was surprised to find they had been superseded. It was explained to me that the GDs were important for the transition period, but something more was needed for the long haul. They hadn't ceased to exist but were no longer central to the organization of the country.

THE THIRD CONGRESS

FRELIMO's third congress,* in 1977, adopted a grand development plan. Members and candidates soon rose from about 15,000 to 100,000. It was not easy to become a member, for only the most committed could win the commendation of their fellow workers, a prerequisite for membership.

Economically the plan called for the establishment of large state enterprises. The farms and plantations abandoned by the departed Portuguese would be transformed into state farms as the most effective way of meeting food requirements. Simultaneously, state-owned heavy industry was supposed to produce necessary consumer goods. I spent a day at a state farm at Umbeluzi, about 30 miles from Maputo. It covered about 6,000 acres and had some 1,500 workers, who were paid $50 a month and given housing. Previously the land had been divided into several privately owned farms operated by Italian and Portuguese farmers. Large blocks of the state farm specialized in citrus fruit, growing some 50,000 trees. Farmers were trying to develop a sunflower hybrid whose seeds would produce a superior oil and were experimenting with 12 varieties of maize, onions, and other vegetables. The farm looked impressive, but I could not judge the overall effectiveness of the system. There were about 50 state farms in Maputo Province.

My firsthand view of Mozambican industry was limited. The country had been one of the top 10 industrialized countries in Africa. Cashews, primarily, followed by tea, cotton, sisal, and sugar were processed for export. Rice, meat, and dairy products were processed for local consumption. In addition, plants manufactured textiles, clothing, fertilizer, beer, paints, and some steel.

I was especially interested to visit the largest cashew plant. Not highly mechanized, it depended on more than 2,000 workers, mostly women. In one huge room some 800 women at long benches cracked the nutshells with hammers. The room was filled with the sound of cracking shells, the hum of conversation, and background music coming through a loud speaker. The nuts were then sorted by hand and packed in large tins, also manufactured in the plant, for shipping. Ninety percent of the export was to the United States. The plant also extracted a fine oil from the shells for export.

Part of the grand plan was to hasten the organization of communal villages and producer cooperatives. The dream was that by the end of the

---

*The first was in 1962, the second in 1968.

1980s the bulk of the rural population would live in communal villages and work through co-ops or on state farms.

The plan, however, did not work the way it was hoped. Production fell by 50 percent over a two-year period. Trained personnel were insufficient. Machinery broke down and spare parts were lacking. The country also suffered from a balance-of-payments problem. Prices for Mozambican exports sank, while the cost of imported oil, steel, and trucks rose. The farm cooperatives did not attract mass support from the farmers, who preferred to work their own land. The incentive to communal work was lacking, especially when consumer goods were in such short supply. With more money available than goods to buy, prices rose and the black market prospered. People's Shops were defunct because of the lack of goods and poor management.

THE FOURTH CONGRESS

In this troubled atmosphere, FRELIMO held its fourth congress in 1983. When I arrived about three months later, its main decisions were explained to me. Reversing the policy of the third congress, FRELIMO was again setting off in a new direction. Big industries and state farms were deemphasized in favor of the private sector. Family farming, local industries, and private shops even in the communal villages were encouraged. It was tacitly recognized that family farmers produced most of the crops. Machel set out on a trip to Western Europe and later to the United States to seek aid, with some success.

Other considerations bolster my hope for the future of Mozambique. Despite the twists and turns in the fortunes of the country, FRELIMO has been remarkably stable. Divisive internal power struggles have not occurred. No purges have taken place. The assumption of power at independence did not lead to a round of executions of former collaborators and party dissidents, although there were punishments, and for three years pictures of "compromisers" (who had actively worked with the Portuguese during the struggle) were posted at work places. A series of meetings between hundreds of former collaborators and the president ended this phase of public humiliation in 1982.

My visit to a communal village named February Third, the date of Eduardo Mondlane's murder, was also encouraging. Nearly 300 of the 3,500 villagers, many of them women, constituted a welcoming committee. They sang beautifully as we gathered in the shade of a large mango tree. In the discussion that followed, one villager after another spoke about their life together. They emphasized the problems—lack of tractors and adequate food and water. There was no hesitation about speaking out in the presence of the FRELIMO officials accompanying us. This was a message not to foreign visitors but to their own government. I liked this freedom of expression.

On a visit to the Francisco Manyanga secondary school in Maputo, named for a FRELIMO hero, my son, Steven, a teacher, and I talked with a young woman math teacher from Eastern Europe, who had been in Mozambique for two years. She marveled at the freedom of speech and said she wished they had as much back in her home.

In a small restaurant in a town in Tete Province, I noticed the Portuguese woman proprietor talking worriedly with one of my FRELIMO companions. A few hours earler, an African patron had leaned back on the two hind legs of a fragile chair. When she had asked him to sit squarely lest the chair break, he had reacted furiously, using disparaging racial epithets. The woman was appealing to the official, whom she knew, for help. He assured her that FRELIMO was nonracial and she was within her rights to protect her chair; she was to let him know in case of further trouble.

Janet Mondlane told me that she thought Mozambique was the least racist country in the whole world. Although the great bulk of people are black African, everyone in the country is called a Mozambican, regardless of color or ancestry. The party and governmental leadership is racially well mixed. Martins, the first minister of health, was white; Marcelino dos Santos, a Coloured in South African parlance, was married to a white South African. Many leaders were of Asian or Afro-Asian extraction. My friend Sharfudine Khan, the FRELIMO representative in New York for so many years, had an Indian and African background. His wife, Norma, is a Christian Egyptian, while he himself is Muslim.

I was in Maputo on April 7, 1981, the Day of Mozambican Women. This annual holiday reminds the people of FRELIMO's dedication to the liberation of women. The celebration was capped off by a huge parade with dancing, singing, and speeches led by the women of the Organization of Mozambican Women.

Women are campaigning for complete equality. FRELIMO is breaking the traditional mold by discouraging polygamy and the old system of bride price, under which a man virtually paid for a wife who would then do his household work and bear his children. Some significant changes have occurred. More than a quarter of FRELIMO party members are women, although the party and the society are still male dominated. As of the middle 1980s there had been only one woman minister, Graça Machel, minister of education and wife of the president.

Some of the worst features of political favoritism are resisted in Mozambique. High government officials are not permitted to carry on business pursuits on the side to enrich themselves. There is, however, a formality to government life that has been inherited from the Portuguese. Those of high rank and aspirants to it are expected to wear suits and ties, unlike the informal dress in Tanzania, which I personally prefer. They also enjoy special privileges—front seats on planes; better facilities in hotels, restaurants, or hospitals; and the opportunity for family members to travel abroad for education and medical treatment. Generally, though, elitism is frowned on.

Mozambique is a one-party state, yet there is a lot of give and take in party politics. Elective positions in the local and national assemblies are hotly contested. In the 1978 elections, 2,200 candidates approved by the party were turned down by voters.

I regret some practices FRELIMO has adopted. Following the fourth congress, in 1983, public executions and floggings took place for economic crimes. Up to 1979 there was no death penalty and up to 1983 it was used only for treason. Since then I have read newspaper accounts of public execution by firing squad of a smuggler and also of a train engineer who sold off some of his cargo of sugar. The executions were discussed in hushed tones when I was in Mozambique a few months later.

At about the same time, the government enacted a dubious policy of shipping thousands of the unemployed, nonresident men floating around Maputo and other cities to the far northern provinces for a kind of forced labor. The program was intended to ease the tight economic situation in the cities by putting the jobless to useful work, but protests mounted and the program was soon dropped.

MOZAMBIQUE AND THE UNITED STATES

The relationship of Mozambique to the United States has grown increasingly pragmatic. In the early days of independence, the legacy of the U.S. alliance with Portugal soured any possibility for friendship. Mozambique was on the American black list. The U.S. consulate in Lourenço Marques was closed down. By congressional action no economic assistance was permitted. The United States was not even officially invited to the independence celebration, although Sen. Dick Clark and Rep. Charles Diggs were invited as individuals.

By the time of my second visit to Mozambique, in 1978, relations had improved. I talked several times with U.S. Ambassador Willard De Pree, who was informed about, and sympathetic to, Mozambique and was well received by Mozambican officials. Food was being shipped to Mozambique, although other aid was still prohibited. He told me there were only 54 Americans then in the country.

Andrew Young, U.S. ambassador to the UN, had gone to Maputo in 1977 for a UN conference. Machel had gone to the UN in 1978 and had met President Jimmy Carter. Machel said the time had come to "wipe the slate clean" between the two countries and start again.

Mozambique has followed a neutralist foreign policy. During the years of combat with Portugal, the Soviet Union and other Eastern European countries supplied most of FRELIMO's military equipment. Mozambique remained neutral, however, in the Sino-Soviet split. It signed a 20-year friendship treaty with the Soviet Union in 1977 but did not set up an embassy in Moscow until 1980. Excepting military help, technical aid has been more important in Mozambique's relations with Eastern Europe than has trade. Eastern European doctors, teachers, and technicians are in Mozambique in significant numbers. The Soviet Union has helped build

schools and offered liberal scholarships. More than a thousand Mozambicans were studying in Cuba on the Isle of Youth when I visited there in
1982. But only 15 percent of Mozambique's trade was with Eastern
Europe. The country is not a member of the socialist economic community. Furthermore, it resisted a Soviet effort to establish a naval base
there.

By spring 1981, the administration of Ronald Reagan had set a tone
distinguishing its African policy from Carter's. During my travels time
and again African leaders asked me: "What is Reagan trying to do?" "Is
the United States really going to choose to work with South Africa over the
rest of the continent?" Everyone I talked with was familiar with the
current debate in Congress on repealing the Clark Amendment, which had
disallowed U.S. aid to dissident movements in Angola. Was the CIA to be
reactivated in Angola? I detected not so much anger as incredulity about
the posture of the new administration.

My trip in 1981 coincided with the first trip of Chester Crocker to
southern Africa as the State Department's assistant secretary-designate for
Africa. Our paths crossed in Mozambique and Angola. From my conversations with officials, I learned that his discussions with them, particularly in Mozambique, had been tense. Only a few days before his
arrival, four U.S. embassy staff had been expelled for suspected CIA
connections. His discussion with Foreign Minister Chissano was strained
and ended abruptly and inconclusively. Later, in Angola, I asked a member of Crocker's delegation at our hotel how the trip was faring. He said,
"Fine, everywhere except Mozambique."

What Mozambique's new turn in economic policy since 1983 may mean
for future relations with the United States remains to be seen. In the early
1980s Mozambique had a favorable balance of trade with the United
States—some $28.5 million in exports and $20 million in imports. The
United States, which with Western Europe accounted for 80 percent of the
country's trade, was the chief customer for two main Mozambican exports—cashews and sugar. There was little private American investment,
principally Exxon and General Tire Co.

Crocker played a significant role in orchestrating the Nkomati Accord.
Thereafter, the U.S. government waived the ban on development aid to
Mozambique and approved a bilateral program. The United States authorized more food aid to Mozambique than to any other African country
during the drought of 1982–1983.

President Machel traveled to Western Europe in late 1983 in an attempt
to attract investment in Mozambique.* He went to the United States in
late 1985 and met with President Reagan. Future good U.S.-Mozambican
relations may depend less on events within Mozambique itself than on
events in South Africa.

---

*The tragic death of Machel October 19, 1986, in a suspicious plane crash in South Africa
and Chissano's accession to the presidency took place after this chapter was written.

CHAPTER TWENTY-ONE

Western Sahara:
Struggle in the Desert

U ntil the middle 1970s, Spanish Sahara (Western Sahara since 1976) had been little more than a place on the map to me. I had spent time in all the countries of North Africa and had inevitably touched the Sahara, but the small areas under Spanish control were a blank to me.

My experience of Western Sahara began in May 1979 in western Algeria, 20 miles from the desert town of Tindouf, about 1,200 miles west of Algiers. There the Popular Front for the Liberation of Saguia el Hamra and Rio de Oro (POLISARIO) maintained a reception center in close proximity to desert refugee camps where some 100,000 Sahrawi (Saharans) lived.* For a week I visited some of these camps. My most constant companions were an Algerian linguist named Farouk, who served as interpreter, and Ahmed Ali, a Saharan assigned by POLISARIO to accompany me. Although he spoke a little English, some French, and some Spanish, Ahmed was most comfortable in Arabic. A short man in his 20s, he was both a guerrilla and a mathematics teacher in a POLISARIO military school.

This trip and one in November in 1979 rank among the most fascinating I have had in more than 30 years of travel in Africa. This was true in part because of the desolation, beauty, expanse, and mystery of the desert setting. Also I felt that I was witnessing the establishment of a nation by a people displaced by war who were reconstructing a way of life uniquely their own. In addition, I had the opportunity to see something of POLISARIO organization in a contested zone in the desert.

BACKGROUND TO CONFLICT

During the 1950s and 1960s, there was no liberation struggle to attract my attention to the Spanish colonies. Spain, like Portugal, did not become a member of the UN until 1955, so even in the glass house on the East River Spain received virtually no attention.

As a UN member, Spain tried to avoid the attention focused on nonself-governing territories by claiming it had none. In 1958 Spain did as Portugal had done and made its colonies (the small enclave of Ifni, on Morocco's southwest coast, Rio Muni, and Spanish Sahara), which it had

*In the mid-1980s there were more than 150,000.

held since 1884, provinces of Spain. Only after the UN passed Resolution 1514 in 1960, on granting independence to colonial countries, and set up the Decolonization Committee to implement it, did the Spanish colonies become a matter of UN debate.

The focus of debate, not yet really heated, was on how to induce Spain to allow the people of Spanish Sahara to exercise their right of self-determination. All the most concerned countries—Spain, Morocco, Mauritania, and Algeria—agreed on a referendum under UN auspices. But Spain was not anxious to proceed rapidly for fear that it would lose control of the rich phosphate deposits just discovered in the desert and the lucrative fishing rights in the coastal waters. Morocco and Mauritania each assumed that, given a choice, Spanish Sahara would choose association with their country.

In the meantime, a new nationalism began to take root in Spanish Sahara. In the Zenila suburb of the capital, El Aaiún, then a town of about 29,000, a group of young anticolonialist Sahrawi who had studied abroad began to meet clandestinely. They organized a rally on June 17, 1970, at which a petition for reforms was presented to Spanish officials. When police were called in to disperse the demonstrating crowd of some 1,500, several protesters were killed. Hundreds were arrested in the aftermath. This Zenila Massacre spelled the demise of this group but spurred others to action.

POLISARIO was organized at an unpublicized gathering at the desert town of Bir Lehlu in Spanish Sahara May 10, 1973. Its charismatic leader was El Ouali Mustapha Sayed, a Sahrawi who had studied law in Rabat, Morocco, and with other young anticolonialist Sahrawis had begun the discussions that led to the Bir Lehlu meeting. The name of the new nationalist movement incorporated the names of the two parts of Spanish Sahara—Saguia el Hamra in the north and Rio de Oro in the south. The movement was committed to guerrilla warfare against Spanish rule, although by 1975 it may have included no more than 200 guerrillas.[*] El Ouali was elected secretary general.

UN debates on a referendum in Spanish Sahara might have proceeded quietly for some years had the April 1974 military coup not taken place in Portugal, Spain's neighbor. That caused new urgency to end the rule of Spain, Europe's last colonial power in Africa. In the fall of 1974, the UN made two critical decisions. One was to submit the case of Spanish Sahara to the ICJ to clarify its status. The other was to send a visiting UN mission to report on the situation in Spanish Sahara. The idea of a referendum was sidelined.

In its decision (late 1975) the ICJ found no evidence of ties between Spanish Sahara and either Morocco or Mauritania prior to Spain's occupation. The UN mission reported that "at every place visited, [it] became

---

[*]For a more detailed discussion of the formation of POLISARIO see Tony Hodges, *Western Sahara, The Roots of a Desert War* (Westport, Conn.: Lawrence Hill and Co., 1983), ch. 15.

evident to the Mission that there was an overwhelming consensus among Saharans within the territory in favor of independence and opposing integration with any neighboring country." POLISARIO "appeared as the dominant political force in the territory."[1]

In response, Morocco took direct action. The highly publicized Green March was organized (the holy color of Islam being green). Promoted by King Hassan II, this huge demonstration of 350,000 Moroccans marched south into Spanish Sahara. The march confused many opponents of colonialism because although it appeared to be an act of protest against Spanish rule, its purpose was quite different. The Green March sabotaged any plans for a referendum by occupying the territory. Spain called the act "a march of agression." Less publicized was the fact that as unarmed Moroccans marched into one part of Spanish Sahara, Moroccan troops were occupying other areas.

With General Francisco Franco on his death bed in Madrid, Spain had no desire to fight Morocco. The result, a success from Morocco's point of view, was a complete turn-around by Spain. Yielding to Moroccan pressure, it gave up its commitment to hold a referendum. In a tripartite agreement with Morocco and Mauritania, Spain turned over the northern part of the area with its phosphate deposits to Morocco and the southern part to Mauritania.

As Moroccan forces moved into Saguia el Hamra and Mauritanian troops took possession of Rio de Oro, they became the focus of POLISARIO action. The struggle for Spanish Sahara's self-determination took on dimensions that were to persist for many years. Spain's administration was due to end formally February 26, 1976. By that time Moroccan and Mauritanian troops had occupied all the major centers and new administrations were in place. The next day POLISARIO announced it had formed the Sahrawi Arab Democratic Republic (SADR).

THE SAHRAWI

The people of what is now Western Sahara are the descendants of Berbers and Arabs, with some mixture of black African blood. They speak a distinctive Arabic dialect called Hassaniya. A nomadic people, living in tribal units, in precolonial times they had regulated their affairs through councils called *djemaa*. Hassan II of Morocco, however, claimed that the people of Western Sahara were really Moroccans, and further, that POLISARIO was composed essentially of dissident Moroccans, Mauritanians, and Algerians under Algeria's control. I wanted to visit the country and see for myself. The opportunity came in 1979.

I had met Madjid Abdullah, POLISARIO's representative in New York, in 1978. The ACOA was invited to send a representative to the celebration of the third anniversary of the SADR on February 27, 1979. My colleague Richard Knight accepted and came back with a fascinating account of visits to refugee camps in Algeria and a brief foray into Western

Sahara. His report made me all the more eager to make the trip myself. I departed in May.

The desert reception center, near Tindouf, was a low, concrete building with a corrugated metal roof, over which the POLISARIO flag with its crescent and star was flying. The rooms had no furniture. Mattresses and blankets covered the concrete floor. Using the center as a base, Farouk, Ahmed Ali, and I visited several refugee camps.

I learned that most of the Sahrawis had streamed into the camps three years earlier, either in an act of solidarity with the POLISARIO-led resistance or to avoid being caught in military action when their towns were occupied by Moroccan troops. I could hardly believe the stories I heard about this mass migration. Whole communities—children, women with babies, old people—walked, sometimes for several hundred miles, to the area Algeria turned over to POLISARIO for their use. But the migration took its toll as the people tried to settle in what had been just flat, open desert. Food, clothing, water, and firewood had to be transported long miles over poor roads. The winter nights were very cold; tents and blankets were in short supply. In such conditions, disease ran rampant—polio, cholera, diphtheria, tetanus. Malnutrition was endemic. The UN High Commissioner for Refugees estimated that in 1976, 25 percent of the babies died before they were three months old. At first, international sources gave only limited help. Major aid came from the Algerian government and the Red Crescent, its counterpart of the Red Cross.

I was astounded by the efficient organization of the widely separated POLISARIO camps. Over the years I had been in many refugee settlements, large and small, for Angolans, Mozambicans, South Africans, Namibians, and Zimbabweans, but I had never seen such organization as at the POLISARIO camps. Perhaps it was because a large part of the Western Saharan people was there, so that there was no identity problem, or because the Sahrawi have a nomadic legacy and did not find it difficult to live in tents in the desert. Perhaps it was because the Algerian government came to their assistance. I believe, however, that a dominant reason why the refugee camps seemed more like settled communities than just gatherings of displaced persons was that the people were united in purpose and had a sense of nationhood under effective leadership.

I quickly discovered that the camps were divided into three large areas, called *wilayas*, or provinces, corresponding to the divisions of the country itself.* Each *wilaya* was divided into *dairas*, or districts, again corresponding to local areas inside Western Sahara, for a total of 23.

Each camp consisted usually of hundreds of tents strewn over the desert plain. A few goats, some privately and some communally owned, wandered around. The tents were much larger than the kind I have used when camping, perhaps 30 by 30 feet. They were strongly reinforced and anchored against the powerful desert winds. Inside, I was amazed at the

---

*By the mid-1980s there were four.

homey atmosphere created by tapestries on the walls and by rugs, mats, and pillows, making a floor over the sand. There were no chairs, tables, or beds. People sat on the rugs, propped up by the pillows, a position I found surprisingly comfortable.

The vast majority of the people in the camps were women, with many children and some old people. Most of the men were with POLISARIO inside Western Sahara or on duty elsewhere. The women wore the traditional long black gown with attached hood over the head but no veil. Sahrawi women, unlike many other North African Muslim women, do not cover their faces. Dark haired and dark eyed, they were striking to look at.

From my many conversations it was clear that virtually all the refugees were POLISARIO members. They were organized in 11-member cells. "Were they socialist?" I asked. The answer came back that there were many tendencies in POLISARIO, and their immediate task was to win independence. Then the people would decide. The Soviet Union did not recognize their SADR and even maintained a cordial trading relation with their adversary, Morocco.

There was no regularity to meals. Except for the tea drinking, which was ordinary hospitality, I would usually have nothing to eat all day. Finally, often late in the evening, just before we moved to another tent, almost miraculously food would appear—traditional couscous (a steamed grain) with goat meat. We ate out of a large communal dish. The food was delicious.

On one day's expedition we were up by 4:30 A.M. and off for a camp in the *wilaya* of Dakhla, some 125 miles and more than three hours away. At two check points in the desert, blue-uniformed POLISARIO military checked our papers in an entirely unthreatening manner. Twice our Toyota Land Cruiser stalled in the sand. I thought we might be stuck for the day, but the POLISARIO driver knew just what to do. In a moment the hood was up, the gas filter cleaned of dust and sand.

The town of Dakhla, for which the camp was named, was in the Rio de Oro division of Western Sahara, then occupied by Mauritania. The refugees in Dakhla camp had trekked hundreds of miles to reach Algeria. The terrain of the camp was flat and sandy with tents in every direction. A few animals roamed around. Part of the area was an oasis, looking almost like a Hollywood set, with date palm trees and a well from which people were drawing buckets of cool, clear water. Camels were tethered close by. They were community property, used for carrying loads and also as a source of protein. When we finally ate, at 2:00 P.M., sure enough, the stew had camel meat in it. The well water was used to irrigate a garden with melons, tomatoes, and other vegetables.

I spent several hours talking with the members of the camp council, composed entirely of women. As we sat in the shade of a tent, drinking tea from time to time, I learned that the work of the community was essentially done by five committees—health, education, food distribution, justice, and handicraft. One person from each tent was assigned to work with each committee. The education committee, for example, was responsible for teaching the younger children to read and write, using the Koran. The literacy rate was 85 to 95 percent.

In one large tent I met with 50 women who were responsible for justice. Their chief tasks were to handle marriage arrangements and divorce proceedings, although there were very few of the latter. There was virtually no stealing or individual violence. There wasn't much in the way of personal possessions to steal, and there was no place to go with any loot. Also, the sense of national purpose militated against ordinary crime.

The health committee had responsibility for the clinics and central hospital, a low building with 13 rooms, a kitchen, and a small refectory. No doctor was then available, but there were 18 nurses. The hospital was busy with mothers and newborn babies and with sick children, many with respiratory problems, accompanied by their mothers.

One fascinating evening was devoted to Western Saharan music and culture. We were ushered into an unusually large tent, where about a hundred people, mostly women, were gathered. Outside, the moon was almost full. Inside, kerosene lamps gave a soft light. In the center of the tent, eight women sat around a large drum. They sang traditional songs of welcome and POLISARIO freedom songs in the somewhat shrill North African style, punctuated by beating the drum. The music was interspersed with discussion of the role of women and how POLISARIO had revolutionized their position. I noted, however, that while most of the practical work of running the camps was done by women, the administrators were all men. The women were optimistic that their subservient role was changing.

One camp I visited gave special attention to children suffering from malnutrition. They were fed an enriched diet, which usually restored them to good health in a few months. I couldn't help but wonder whether the hordes of buzzing desert flies had anything to do with the spread of disease. They seemed to gather particularly on the heads of children too weak to brush them off, whose mothers had to do so for them. Yet miraculously at nightfall the flies disappeared.

I spent some time at the national school, called simply June 9, commemorating the date on which El Ouali was killed in battle. It had been in operation for only a little over two months when I arrived. There were about 1,500 students, almost half of them girls, but it would accommodate twice as many students when it was completed. The children ranged from 6 to 15, and their studies were designed to last six years. Emphasis was on reading, writing, geography, and math, with generous attention to the history and aims of POLISARIO.

I also visited a military school for POLISARIO guerrillas. It was called October 12, after the Day of National Unity established in 1975. The school, where my companion Ahmed Ali taught, was about a two-and-a-half-hour drive from the reception center. Our orientation discussion was held in an underground bunker. I visited classes in politics, math, and military theory and then went out in the open desert to watch maneuvers with live ammunition.

This visit was in contrast to my visits to peaceful refugee camps, where I rarely saw a weapon or a soldier. It was an introduction to the other side of the struggle of the Western Saharan people.

My overwhelming impression was that the camps were the Western Saharan nation in forced exile. I found it impossible to think of these people as just refugees. They were dependent on friendly countries and international organizations for food and clothing to be sure, but they were independent of outside control and had organized themselves according to their own way of life. Although the Moroccans and Mauritanians occupied 10 or 12 towns in the country, I felt the nation was here, united in its commitment to independence.

ACROSS THE DESERT WITH POLISARIO

After a week of visiting camps, on the eve of my scheduled departure, I was unexpectedly offered a new adventure. It was midnight, and I had just lain down on my blanket when Ahmed Ali came into the room. In his halting English he said, "George, we are leaving very soon to cross the desert to the Atlantic Ocean. Do you want to come?"

In my mind I began marshaling reasons for not going. An arduous trip across 400 miles of desert had not been part of my original plan. I had already used my allotted time and had appointments in Algiers and a UN conference in Geneva. "How long will the trip last?" I asked Ahmed. "At least a week," he replied. I ascertained that I would be joining a group of POLISARIO guerrillas driving in captured Spanish Santanas (similar to Land Rovers) to the ocean near Cape Bojador. We would go through areas where POLISARIO guerrillas and Moroccan troops were fighting. Did I want to risk that? It was one thing to visit refugee camps in Algeria and quite another to go into a war zone in the Western Sahara.

One of my companions of the past few days was José Martin Artajo, a free-lance Spanish journalist whose father had been foreign minister under Franco. While briefly in the foreign service in Libya, my companion had fallen in love with the desert. He had broken politically with his family and now called himself an anarchist. Anxious to take the trip and hoping he would be included, he spoke urgently, "George, you can't miss this opportunity. You may never have another chance to cross the desert. You will always regret it if you don't go."

I asked Farouk if he could go. He told me that he couldn't because if an Algerian was captured by Moroccans in the company of POLISARIO guerrillas, there would be an international scandal. Then he explained that if I went I would have to sign a waiver to indicate that I absolved the Algerian government of any responsibility in case of "accident." If nothing else brought home to me the seriousness of the decision I had to make, the waiver he showed me did.

After a few moments' inner turmoil, I signed. I wrote an explanatory letter to my wife, which Farouk would take back to Algiers, together with

José Artajo (left), Spanish journalist, and George Houser at POLISARIO headquarters near Tindouf, Algeria, 1979.

a cable message to Geneva and messages to Algiers. Then I lay down on my blanket for a little sleep.

It seemed only a few moments before I was awakened at 3:30 A.M., a half hour before departure. There were two Santanas, each with six occupants—nine armed POLISARIO combatants and three foreigners. Joining Artajo and me was an Italian metallurgist, Dominico Palumbo. Outside in the cold morning air I was glad for my lined windbreaker and the comfort of my *shesh,* or scarf, which I wrapped around my face, neck, and head in Arab fashion.

TO THE OCEAN

We boarded the Santanas and headed west in the darkness, toward the unmarked Western Saharan border. The vehicles had no roofs or windshields. Glass would have been a hazard both because it would have reflected the sun, making us more visible from planes, and because it could shatter. We sped along, the wind rushing in our faces. Headlights were on, but there was no road, just tracks on the sandy or stony surface.

Soon Ahmed told me we had entered his country and he felt free. A little farther on we stopped. A fire was built of well-dried desert scrub for making the traditional, heavily sugared tea. We rested on blankets spread on the ground, waiting for dawn, I assumed. My companions told me that I was the first American to take this journey all the way to the Atlantic.

Because of our somewhat zigzag course, the trip would cover about 1200 miles.

At sunrise, about 6:00 on Saturday, May 12, we drove on again. For eight hours we traversed sand and bare rock, up and down low hills. Occasionally we passed a clump of short trees or some grass with desert flowers in bloom. Once I saw a large lizard, like an iguana, which wriggled away at our approach. In the distance I spotted a large bird floating overhead. There was no other sign of life. Most of the time, the Santanas drove in tandem, and the unfortunate one in the rear was peppered with dust and sand thrown up by the one ahead.

As the day wore on, it became hot, and I shed my windbreaker but not the protective *shesh*. My hands began to burn, and I wished I had brought some light gloves. The drivers skillfully adjusted from high speed on flat, smooth surfaces to a crawl on bumpy terrain. On my map I tried to keep track of where we were. It always seemed to me that we were charting our own course like a ship at sea. But POLISARIO people know the desert.

About 2:00 P.M. we stopped in the relative shade of some thorny trees. Blankets were spread again, and a fire was built for making tea. We lay down to rest. Two guerrillas disappeared over a hill. I wondered if they were sentries but was told that the Moroccans would not venture five miles outside fortified towns. POLISARIO controlled the desert. I heard gun shots. Soon the two men returned carrying a rabbit. Tea was served in the small glasses that the Sahrawi seem always to carry with them. I felt a little rested but hot and dry. Water, carried in large drumlike barrels, was used sparingly. I was hungry, but apparently this was not the place or time for food.

Another hour of travel brought us to a camouflaged underground bunker, where we stopped again. Water was available and food was prepared—couscous and camel meat. After a short rest, we piled into the Santanas again and moved on west as the sun was sinking. About 10:30 some buildings appeared suddenly in the moonlight. There had been no signs or roads, just a town rising out of the desert. We had come to Tifariti.

It was 1:00 A.M. before I lay down on the sand in a blanket, too tired to ask any questions. In the morning I learned that the population of Tifariti might have been about 15,000 including Spanish troops and Sahrawi living in tents close by. The Moroccans had occupied the town in 1976. A two-year conflict ensued, off and on. A month and a half before we arrived, POLISARIO had captured the town. The signs of battle were everywhere—the small burnt-out school, discarded weapons, helmets, spent bullet casings. All the people were gone, leaving only a few forlorn dogs behind. The airstrip was no longer in use. In a large graveyard, mounds of rock and sand marked the places where bodies of Sahrawi civilians and Moroccan and POLISARIO combatants lay buried. We spent a good while exploring the area—the empty shops, the debris of the battlefield, the old administrative center with its abandoned tennis court, a captured GM truck, still in running shape.

Late in the morning, we pushed on west. On the way we stopped by a

POLISARIO guerrillas in the desert shade, Western Sahara, 1979.

mostly dry streambed, where I took a welcome bath in a pocket of leftover rainwater. In the late afternoon we reached the desert town of Amgala, now occupied only by a few POLISARIO sentries. I was impressed by the extensive defense network the Moroccans had constructed in the sides of the surrounding hills. The final battle for the town had ended only two weeks before we arrived. Fresh graves and the debris of combat gave evidence of the ferocity of the fighting. The roofs of virtually all the stone houses were crushed in. The one bright spot was an undamaged well with the coolest, clearest water I had yet tasted on this trip. We drank deeply before moving on.

It was midnight before we stopped in open desert, made a fire, and prepared food. I was glad for my extensive camping experience, for I had no trouble sleeping well on a blanket under the stars. Just before dawn I was awakened by a distant rifle shot. Immediately three of my POLISARIO companions sprang to their feet with their rifles ready. One of them shot tracer bullets into the air, quite visible in the semidarkness. Startled, I wondered if the Moroccans were coming. It was some moments before it was explained to me that the shots were POLISARIO signals. There was to be a rendezvous, but one vehicle had run into mechanical trouble. The first rifle shot had come from a POLISARIO comrade who had walked and run all night to get close enough for his signal to be heard. One of our Santanas went to the rescue with an extra wheel.

Soon seven POLISARIO vehicles had gathered, and we moved on a short distance to a concentration of thorn trees, which offered shade. Here we spent the day waiting for the disabled vehicle to be repaired. It gave me a chance to converse and observe the life of the desert guerrilla. With Ahmed's and Artajo's help, I talked with Mussa. He was reluctant to say much about himself. POLISARIO is what counts, he told me. Nevertheless, I ascertained that he came from El Aaiún and had joined POLISARIO at the beginning in 1973. He stated his concern about U.S. policy toward Western Sahara: "We want to be friends with the U.S." Others spoke out vehemently against U.S. policy of supplying arms to Morocco. Mussa lashed out at King Hassan. "He tells the Soviet Union that POLISARIO is composed of religious fanatics and reactionaries. Then he tells the U.S. that POLISARIO is Communist. How can a movement be Communist and Islamic at the same time?" Mussa asked. "It is a contradiction." He and others were concerned about U.S. elections (in 1980) and hoped there would be a change of policy. "We build our hopes on this."

As the day passed, it grew hot. A Santana brought water to fill up our tank. It looked like dish water and tasted of mud, yet my body was so parched that I drank it eagerly. Sometimes on the trip canned milk or a maize substance and sugar were mixed with the water in a large communal pan, which was passed around for everyone to drink. Occasionally the water had a gasoline taste from having been siphoned into a drum by a fuel hose. Eating was communal style too, with everyone dipping his fingers into one large pan. The question of sanitation never bothered me, and I had no stomach trouble at all.

During my week with the POLISARIO guerrillas I never saw a hint of conflict among them or a struggle to exert authority. It was difficult to tell who was in command. Each person had his task and did it—one cooked, one made tea, two or three would fetch wood, and some would hunt. They changed assignments from time to time. I noted a kind of hierarchy, but it was a matter of first among equals. When we stopped, Bashir assumed command, indicating where the vehicles should park so as to be hidden from the air. He rode in the front seat of the lead vehicle. Otherwise he seemed to be just "one of the boys." The POLISARIO are all Muslim and say their prayers regularly.

We were at this campsite for 15 hours, long after the crippled vehicle had been repaired. We were not far from Bu Craa, a Moroccan stronghold and site of the phosphate mines, from which we could make a nighttime dash to the sea. I shall never forget that ride. The waning moon rose about 11:00 P.M. and by 12 was high enough to give needed light. Four Santanas were in our party now. We moved across the moonlit desert in a southwesterly direction, the four Santanas side by side, headlights off, skimming over the flat, smooth sand at high speed. The beauty of it was overwhelming. We didn't stop for more than three hours. We must have been well beyond the Moroccan base, for fires were built for making tea, and sand-baked Sahara bread was passed around. Even the invitable crunch of sand in the bread didn't bother me.

I slept soundly for two hours. At about dawn, we started on. I felt the cool ocean breeze and could even smell the salt. Before we came within sight of the ocean, we came upon a wrecked American F-5 jet. The Moroccan pilot had parachuted to safety and was a prisoner of war. I photographed the American markings just in case evidence might be needed that U.S. military equipment was being used by Morocco in Western Sahara, contravening a U.S.-Moroccan agreement.

After more driving, finally we reached the Atlantic. What a thrill! I felt like an explorer who has just made a great discovery. No palm trees or any other growth lined the shore, unlike the coast farther south in tropical Africa. The sand of the desert melted into the sand of the beach.

We were some distance north of Cape Bojador. A disused lighthouse rose high above the shore. Two small, abandoned freighters were beached a mile apart below high-water mark. We clambered aboard one and amazingly found a lot of Spanish beer. Our Muslim companions drank nothing alcoholic, but we three foreigners quenched our thirst. I picked up a few stones and shells as souvenirs.

The Atlantic at this spot is very cold and sparklingly clean. We swam and bathed, and I washed my two shirts, which dried in minutes. We didn't tarry long, however. We had a long trip back.

THE RETURN TRIP

As we left the ocean and headed northeast, we crossed a narrow, paved road (the first I had seen since leaving Algiers), the main road from El Aaiún to Bir Enzaren in the south. The Moroccans didn't use it, for POLISARIO controlled the desert. A German-made truck wrecked by a land mine lay along the side. There was no risk of coming across Mauritanian troops because Mauritania wanted to get out of the war, and a cease-fire was in effect. In the south, POLISARIO militants traveled freely, despite the presence of about 8,000 Moroccan troops.

After many hours of driving, we came to a camouflaged bunker, where we ate the usual late night meal and stretched out to sleep. Up early, we sped north across the desert for three hours to within 20 miles of Semara, the second largest town in the country. Here we saw U.S.-made 75mm cannon, manned by POLISARIO, and I was told that a bombardment of Moroccan defenses was about to begin. Artajo, Palumbo, and I were presented with long Saharan gowns so that we could not be distinguished from our companions if planes gave chase. I had not asked for experience of combat, but there was no escape. In early afternoon, the hottest time of day, we clambered up a rocky hill to watch. We were told to lie low. The rocks were too hot for me to touch and for the camera and tape recorder with which I documented the scene. It was quite a feat to hold my equipment and stay below the brink of the hill.

Then the bombardment started. Through binoculars I watched six POLISARIO shells land about four miles away, marked by a puff of smoke, and then heard the delayed sound of the explosion. Moroccan troops were dug in there on the perimeter of the defense system of Semara, about 12 miles from the town. Only a few moments passed before answering fire came from the Moroccans. I decided this was not really a serious military exchange but just a way of saying, "We're still here."

Suddenly my POLISARIO companions told us to get out of there immediately; Moroccan planes might come. We ran down the hill, jumped into the Santanas, and raced at high speed about two miles to a growth of trees, where we hid in the shade. I was relieved that no planes came. After half an hour, I divested myself of the gown, and we proceeded. I was really glad when we came to a place where rainwater had collected to form a small pond. It was muddy, but I drank it and then, fully clothed, poured the cool water over my head and let it trickle down. We drove on, and in five minutes I was dry and just as thirsty as before.

We arrived at a base where several Santanas and more than the usual number of guerrillas had gathered. Trenches and camouflaged nooks in the rocks provided shelter. We did not stay the night but decided to make the dash back to the reception center in Algeria. We ate about midnight and set out in darkness. This was my second night in a row virtually without sleep. By this time, I was tired and couldn't fight off a cold. All night we drove, at times very fast and at other times cautiously over rough terrain. Between moments of sleep I fantasized about water, imagining leaning over a Rocky Mountain stream and drinking the cool, clear run-off from a glacier. It was a relief to reach the reception center at mid-morning and lie down on a mattress for a long sleep.

The next day a sand storm confined us to the building. This gave me a chance to catch up on notes and to talk. As Artajo and I summed up our experience, we agreed that the POLISARIO guerrillas were a remarkable people—hardy, friendly, companionable, hardworking, and efficient. They were not dilettantish but kept to a schedule. In the desert they slept from midnight to dawn, traveled, stopped in the heat of the day for a late lunch and rest, and then started off again in the evening. I heard no bickering, arguments, or angry voices. When meeting other POLISARIO guerrillas in the desert, they stopped, embraced, laughed, and said touchingly genuine farewells. I felt their sense of unity in a cause.

Since I had not shaved for almost two weeks, I had quite a beard. As a memento of this experience, I decided not to shave it all off until independence was achieved.

A SECOND TRIP

This memorable trip had a sequel later that year. I accepted the invitation of the Algerian government (as the only private U.S. citizen) to attend the November 1 celebration of the 25th anniversary of the beginning of their struggle against French domination. Still entranced by my desert trip in May, after several days in Algiers, I went to POLISARIO headquarters and made arrangements to fly to the reception center at Tindouf, again accompanied by Farouk. The main object of my trip was to visit Mahbes in Western Sahara.

The year 1979 was one of great advance for POLISARIO. Without knowing it, in May I had seen some of the fruits of the so-called Boumedienne Offensive, named for Houari Boumedienne, who as Algerian president for 13 years had aided the POLISARIO cause. The victories at Tifariti and Amgala testified to its effectiveness. POLISARIO had driven occupying Moroccan troops out of almost all the towns of Saguia el Hamra except for El Aaiún, Semara, and the phosphate mines at Bu Craa. Not until mid-October had the fortified town of Mahbes, the easternmost center in Western Sahara, been attacked.

In the opening pages of this book I have described something of the devastating scene I encountered at Mahbes, which had been a major Spanish stronghold before 1976. POLISARIO claimed that some 700 Moroccans were killed in this vicious battle. POLISARIO casualties (although I never obtained the figures) must have been considerable. Planes had bombed their positions. Ahmed Ali, who again was with me on this expedition, told me that the Moroccan commander had escaped to Morocco with about 40 tanks. POLISARIO had captured 450 tons of ammunition at Mahbes and taken 45 prisoners.

Later in the day we went to a spot in the desert where some of this captured matériel was stored. Here was more military equipment than I had ever seen—cannon, rifles, machine guns, and tanks, French, Austrian, and U.S.-made—in an area about the size of a football field.

Nearby, a straggly line of about 50 prisoners of war were standing at ease or sitting on the sand. Many had been captured at Mahbes. I talked with a captured air force captain who spoke good English. He had trained at Randolph Field in Texas. His plane, an American F-5, had been shot down about 11 months earlier near Semara, and he had parachuted to safety. He came from Meknes in Morocco, was married, and had a four-year-old daughter, whom he missed. I also talked with a lieutenant, who had commanded a tank and been captured April 11, 1979, in southern Morocco.

Although we were not in the presence of POLISARIO personnel, these prisoners gave fairly pro forma responses to my questions. They looked in good shape and said they were well treated. They said the war was a foolish one and they would like it to end so they could go home. I could not avoid a feeling of sympathy for them with the bleak future they faced.

OBSERVATIONS ON U.S. POLICY

The day ended in an unexpected way. Back at the reception center, the SADR minister of the interior, Mahfoud Ali Beiba, invited me to join him for a late dinner. With him was a member of the National Council and two older leaders at a refugee camp. We conversed as we sat on mats around a long, low banquet table at the center. The discussion began with Ali Beiba making a lengthy statement about their struggle and their concern for U.S. policy. I was surprised at his knowledge about the situation in the United

Moroccan prisoners of POLISARIO, Western Sahara, 1979.

States. He said that POLISARIO could not understand why at this particular time, when it had made a great leap forward, the United States had decided to give new, sophisticated weapons and equipment to Morocco. "Can this be called neutrality?" he asked. "Neutrality would be giving weapons to both sides or neither side in the conflict."

In 1978 Morocco had spent $900,000 hiring a public relations firm to lobby the U.S. government for six months. In late October 1979, the United States, in response to urgent requests from Hassan II, had agreed to supply aircraft, helicopter gunships, and armored personnel carriers to Morocco. It had provided $2.4 million worth of spare parts for fighter and transport planes and $3 million worth of aircraft ammunition.

The U.S. rationale was that strengthening Hassan would make POLISARIO realize that it could not win a military victory and thus render it open to a negotiated settlement. This was a strange interpretation of neutrality. There was real controversy within the Jimmy Carter administration between National Security Adviser Zbigniew Brzezinski and others such as Andrew Young and Donald McHenry at the U.S. Mission to the UN. Furthermore, Dick Clark, chairman of the Senate Subcommittee on Africa, and Stephen Solarz, chairman of the House Subcommittee, were pressing for a pullback in military support to Morocco.

Back in Algiers I made an appointment with the U.S. ambassador, Ulric Haynes, whom I had known for some years because of his long involvement with Africa. He was quite eager to talk because his news of POLISARIO came second or third hand. I asked if he had ever met with

POLISARIO. "Of course not", he replied. "You know we have instructions not to talk with POLISARIO. There is only one part of the government to which this stricture does not apply, the U.S. Mission to the U.N." U.S. embassy personnel at that time were not permitted to visit the refugee camps either.

Haynes and a few of his staff wanted to know what the chance for a political solution would be. Would POLISARIO make a deal if Mauritania made a separate peace and POLISARIO then occupied Rio de Oro? I said this obviously could not end the conflict because POLISARIO saw the whole country as its property. Mauritania and the SADR did make a separate peace in 1979, but the fighting with Morocco continued, as Moroccan troops occupied former Mauritanian centers.

Haynes put forth the principal fear of the U.S. government, that if Hassan compromised by reaching a settlement with POLISARIO, his government might fall. The United States then, would lose a staunch ally and possibly landing rights for U.S. planes. Further, if the United States did not back Hassan, it would make our government appear weak and indecisive. I pointed out that by backing Morocco, the United States was sabotaging a peaceful solution of the contoversy through a UN-sponsored referendum and was supporting an occupation that was just as imperialistic as Spain's.

THE STRUGGLE IN THE MID-1980s

As of this writing, there is still no end to the struggle in the Sahara. It is a war of attrition. The chances are that neither side can win an outright military victory. Morocco has in excess of 100,000 troops committed to the conflict at tremendous cost. Yet Hassan resists negotiating an end to the fighting. He refuses to allow a referendum, which he agreed to at an OAU meeting in 1981, probably because he fears he would lose.

As a defense against the constant incursions of POLISARIO guerrillas into southern Morocco and around Moroccan-occupied centers in Western Sahara, Morocco has constructed a nine-foot wall of sand and stone. It stretches about 1500 miles from the Algerian border to the Atlantic, giving some protection to El Aaiún, Semara, and the Bu Craa phosphate mines. This wall made it possible for the mines to be activated again in 1982, after six years of disuse. The wall has observation posts, American-supplied radar and electronic sensors, land mines, and barbed wire.

POLISARIO can breach the wall by making concerted attacks at considerable cost. Perhaps as many as 20,000 guerrillas pursue the conflict. In the south, outside the wall, which cuts off perhaps two thirds of Western Sahara, the guerrillas still have the run of the desert. They win significant victories from time to time, as for example, in 1981, when they drove the Moroccans out of Guelta Zemmer and Bir Enzaren.

In 1984, five years after a cease-fire, Mauritania officially recognized the

SADR. Recognition was given by 31 African states and altogether 63 countries by the end of 1985. The OAU accepted the SADR as a member in 1984. Morocco resigned in protest.

There is no lessening of Algeria's support for POLISARIO. As a guest at the 30th anniversary celebration of Algeria's struggle for independence (November 1, 1984), I talked briefly with President Chadli Benjedid in a reception line. I was asked by his aide not to take long, so as I shook hands, I simply congratulated him on Algeria's continued support for POLISARIO. To my surprise and embarrassment, as the aide watched me, he responded, with enthusiasm and at some length, that Algeria would always back up POLISARIO.

CHAPTER TWENTY-TWO

Zimbabwe: Winning Independence

After the 1974 military coup in Portugal, it was hoped that the independence of Mozambique and the detente between Zambia and South Africa would speed the process toward the independence of Zimbabwe. The detente was designed to neutralize South Africa's support of the Ian Smith government in Rhodesia so that negotiations could begin to reduce white minority control there. Furthermore, it was hoped that the detente atmosphere would help unite the liberation movements. Unfortunately, neither purpose was realized.

INTERNAL DISUNITY

The problem of unity was particularly vexing. The idea of setting up the African National Council (ANC) as an umbrella organization to unite ZANU, ZAPU, and later FROLIZI seemed to be an ideal solution. Under Bishop Abel Muzorewa, who was chosen president of the ANC in a ZAPU-ZANU compromise, it was thought that negotiations with Smith could proceed. But the struggle for power among the nationalists was overwhelming. According to the agreement of December 1974 in Lusaka, the ANC was to hold a congress in four months to choose its leaders. Joshua Nkomo of ZAPU was for it, but Muzorewa, Ndabaningi Sithole of ZANU, and James Chikerema of FROLIZI were unalterably opposed, so it was not held. Muzorewa and Sithole, whom I saw in Dar es Salaam in November 1975, told me that it would have been divisive. It was likely that Nkomo would have won the presidency.

Both Zambian president Kenneth Kaunda and Tanzanian president Julius Nyerere, the key African leaders involved in settling the Rhodesian conflict, tried to make the ANC formula work. The offices of ZAPU and ZANU in Dar es Salaam and Lusaka were closed. When I was in Dar in October 1975, I found the ZAPU office empty. On a trip to Lusaka, I had trouble finding George Silundika and Jason Moyo. A friend in the African National Congress of South Africa took me to the market near the old ZAPU office. In only a few moments Silundika appeared out of nowhere. The office might be closed, but ZAPU was still operating.

In the meantime, efforts were still proceeding to bring Ian Smith to the conference table. Just as Zambia and Tanzania pressured the nationalist groups to join the ANC, so South African prime minister John Vorster pressed Smith to open discussions with the nationalists. Vorster publicly announced that South African troops would be withdrawn from Rhodesia.

Preparatory discussions for substantive negotiations in Rhodesia were set in a neutral site, a railroad car on the bridge across the Zambezi River at Victoria Falls, between Rhodesia and Zambia. But the discussions collapsed almost before they started when Smith refused to guarantee immunity from arrest for nationalist leaders (such as Sithole, Moyo, and Chikerema, all of whom had illegally left Rhodesia) if they later attended the substantive negotiations inside Rhodesia. According to what Muzorewa told me, Smith purposely planned to scuttle the Victoria Falls discussions and was rude and haughty toward them. The nationalists agreed there was no basis for further meetings. The ANC never again served as a united front. Shortly afterward, Smith capped off the failed talks with the statement in Bulawayo: "We have never had a policy in Rhodesia to hand our country over to any black majority government and as far as I am concerned we never will have."[1]

The division in the ANC became permanent when Nkomo, still inside Rhodesia while Muzorewa and Sithole were outside, made known that he was calling a congress to elect a president in keeping with the Lusaka plan. A majority of the ANC leaders were inside Rhodesia and accepted Nkomo's plan. At once Muzorewa expelled Nkomo from the ANC. The way was clear for Nkomo to call a congress, whose 6,000 delegates unanimously chose him president. A few weeks later, Muzorewa's supporters held a rally in Salisbury at which more than 20,000 denounced Nkomo's move. By October 1975, there were two ANCs, one led by Muzorewa and the other by Nkomo.

There were serious strains in ZANU also. The division between Sithole and Robert Mugabe did not heal. Sithole was working through the ANC as he had agreed at the Lusaka meeting. Mugabe was critical of this agreement and of the Kaunda-Vorster detente. He firmly believed that only armed struggle led by ZANU would bring Smith to terms. Sithole told me in Dar es Salaam that he had little contact with Mugabe. "We have occasional correspondence, but not as much as I would like." Mugabe was just not involved in all the maneuvering for control of the ANC. His focus was entirely on ZANU and the struggle against Smith.

Two serious events nearly halted the struggle in Rhodesia for a year. One was the Nhari revolt, led by Thomas Nhari. In November 1974, a group of guerrillas fighting in northeastern Rhodesia, dissatisfied with the support they were receiving from the ZANU politicians and military leaders comfortably situated in Lusaka, kidnapped the wife and children of the head of the ZANU forces. They demanded the replacement of the entire military command and briefly took over ZANU's main base on the Zambia-Mozambique border. Some 60 ZANU militants died before the leaders of the revolt were executed.

The other event was the assassination of Herbert Chitepo, ZANU's chairman, by a bomb explosion as he started his car on the morning of March 18, 1975. As the only African barrister in Rhodesia, he had a busy practice in Salisbury in the 1950s and had then worked in Dar es Salaam. When ZAPU split in 1963, he sided with ZANU. At the first ZANU

Robert Mugabe, president of ZANU, in the ZANU office in Maputo, Mozambique, 1978.

congress, he was elected chairman under Sithole's presidency, responsible for overseeing external political and military work. His headquarters were in Lusaka, where I had frequently talked with him.

Who was responsible for Chitepo's death? The simple answer was agents of the Smith government, but they were not the only suspects. Many blacks with whom I talked put the blame on the power struggle among Shona subtribes within ZANU. This was also the conclusion reached by the International Commission of Inquiry set up by the Zambian government. Whoever committed the murder, the effect was to put the brakes on effective ZANU prosecution of the armed struggle for a year. Zambia imprisoned many ZANU leaders and detained about 1,500 ZANU guerrillas.

Despite the collapse of the Victoria Falls conference, Nkomo, the only major nationalist leader still inside Rhodesia, decided to make his own effort at talks with Smith. Smith was willing because in that way he could give the impression that something significant was happening without having to concede anything. He could stall for time. The 13 Nkomo-Smith discussions lasted for almost three months, ending in March 1976.

Nkomo's ZAPU colleagues Moyo and Silundika told me in Lusaka that there was no contradiction between negotiations and the continuing armed struggle. "Negotiations are a game. Both sides play at it. Smith is arming while talks take place and so are we." They pointed out that the United States and China were negotiating in Warsaw while they were fighting in Korea and Vietnam.

When the negotiations, unsurprisingly, broke off, Nkomo said Smith insisted on a transition period of 10 to 15 years before majority rule. Smith said Nkomo wanted an immediate transfer of power to an interim council headed by a British-appointed chairman with an equal number of government and ANC members. Driving home his point, he subsequently said on British television, "I don't believe in majority rule ever in Rhodesia— not in a thousand years."[2]

For foreign supporters of the liberation struggle, this was a frustrating period. Smith seemed to be getting away with his stalling tactics. The detente with South Africa had not brought him to the conference table. The ANC was split between Muzorewa and Nkomo. ZANU leadership had shifted from Sithole to Mugabe, who had established headquarters in Mozambique.

THE STRUGGLE INTERNATIONALIZED

If 1976 was marked by black nationalist disunity, it was also notable because the conflict became international. The intensification of fighting was partly responsible for this shift. Mozambique, independent since June 1975, provided a friendly base for a guerrilla organization. Within a few months, some 20,000 young nationalists escaped across the border to join guerrilla units for military training. From bases in Mozambique, infiltration into eastern Rhodesia increased.

On March 3, 1976, Mozambique closed its border with Rhodesia, thus cutting off Rhodesia's access to the Indian Ocean port of Beira, the use of the railroad, and the import of oil through the pipe line. The closing was expensive for Mozambique too. At the UN Security Council and in conversation with me, Joaquim Chissano, Mozambican foreign minister, estimated the annual loss of revenue from exports and imports and the compensation for Rhodesian use of facilities at about $150 million. In retaliation, Rhodesian forces invaded Mozambique in August and attacked a refugee camp at Nyadzonia in Tete Province. They slaughtered an estimated 1,000 people, almost all civilian refugees.

The surprising involvement of U.S. secretary of state Henry Kissinger also contributed to the internationalization of the conflict. After Angola won its independence with the support of Cuba and the Soviet Union, he traveled to Africa in April 1976 and in a speech in Lusaka gave notice of a new U.S. concern about southern Africa. The United States would give no support to the Smith government. He warned American citizens not to go to Rhodesia and urged those who were there to leave. He committed himself to work for repeal of the Byrd Amendment. He then began a dialogue with Nyerere and Kaunda to try to reduce the struggles in Rhodesia and Namibia. His two highly publicized meetings with South African prime minister John Vorster, in June and September, set the stage for a second round of discussions with Kaunda, Nyerere, Vorster, and Smith. Out of this shuttle diplomacy came the Kissinger proposals for a settlement of the Rhodesian conflict, calling for majority rule within two years. Under a multiracial interim government, with a black majority but with whites in the Ministries of Defense and Internal Security, sanctions would end and fighting would cease. Later Kissinger proposed an international fund of $2 billion to $3 billion to provide an incentive for Europeans to stay after independence or to help in their resettlement elsewhere.

This plan was not acceptable to the Zimbabwe nationalists. Nevertheless, with British and American urging, it was agreed that a conference would convene in Geneva in late October. Mugabe and Nkomo, presenting a united position, formed the Patriotic Front (PF), although ZANU and ZAPU maintained their separate organizations. Smith headed the Rhodesian delegation; Muzorewa, the ANC; and Sithole his splinter from ZANU.

The conference was stalemated for weeks on the issue of a date for independence and was suspended on December 14, when it was clear that no progress was being made. In general the lineup of forces after the conference continued right up to independence. The PF maintained a fragile unity of ZANU and ZAPU, Muzorewa headed the ANC, and Sithole, heading his own ZANU group, worked with Muzorewa but not with Mugabe.

THE ROAD TO LANCASTER HOUSE

Three years elapsed between the Geneva conference and an agreement at Lancaster House, London, that laid the foundation for the independence of Zimbabwe. During these years the nationalist movements grew in strength, the liberation war expanded, and Ian Smith tried one device after another to stave off the inevitable. Britain, the United States, and African leaders played important roles. I kept in touch through the UN, contacts in Washington, and several trips to Africa.

ZAPU IN ZAMBIA

By 1978 ZAPU and ZANU, in the PF, were applying pressures that made the Rhodesian issue of international concern. I was amazed at the size of ZAPU's exile organization in Lusaka, where I spent some time in August and September. Civil headquarters was Zimbabwe House, which now consisted of a complex of buildings in a large walled compound guarded by ZAPU troops. (Military headquarters were elsewhere.) Hundreds of people were engaged principally in work for the vast numbers of refugees (who called themselves Zimbabweans) pouring into the country. Medical and educational programs and work among youth and women were emphasized. I felt that I was not viewing a movement struggling for survival but a disciplined organization preparing itself for major resonsibility. The atmosphere was like that at FRELIMO headquarters in Dar es Salaam just before the transitional government took power in Mozambique.

In the ZAPU compound I ran into Edward Ndlovu, whom I had known for years. He told me there were about 45,000 refugees in Zambia then, compared to 20,000 the year before. Their number was increasing every day because of the intensification of the struggle in Rhodesia, the closing of rural schools, and overcrowding in cities, to which rural people fled for safety. The refugees were staying in large camps. The aim of the refugee program, Ndlovu explained, was to keep the people occupied and train them for work back home. They made clothing, grew vegetables, and raised poultry and pigs in an effort to be as self-reliant as possible. About 300 teachers, many of whom had fled with their students, were working in the educational programs.

At Zimbabwe House I also met Jane Ngwenya, who was now in charge of women's work. She told me about her brush with death a year and a half earlier. On a Saturday morning (January 22, 1977), she and two ZANU leaders, Dumiso Dabengwa and John Nkomo (no relation to Joshua Nkomo), had been in conference with Jason Moyo. Moyo had been given a small package addressed in the handwriting of a friend in Botswana. Ignoring regulations, he opened the package himself. It exploded, tearing out his stomach. The others were injured but not fatally, and Ngwenya had fully recovered. This bomb was unquestionably the work of the Rhodesian secret police.

During our conversation, Joshua Nkomo arrived. It was fascinating to watch the response to him. He was regarded not only as the organization's leader but as disciplinarian, chief, and father figure. He was called Mdala, or "old man," a term of respect in Ndebele. When he entered a room, people stood at attention. When young girls handed him anything, they curtsied or knelt down as a sign of respect. Nkomo expressed outrage to me about the controversy then going on in the World Council of Churches over its grant of $85,000 to the Patriotic Front. The Salvation Army was threatening to leave the WCC because funds were being given to "terrorists." Nkomo remarked that he would like to invite someone from the Salvation Army to visit PF refugee centers, particularly where infants, children, and old people were suffering. "This might have an effect on them," he said. "After all, $85,000 means only a little over $40,000 for each movement [ZAPU and ZANU] and this is nothing compared with the millions needed." Nevertheless he was grateful for what the WCC granted.

With Jane Ngwenya I visited a refugee settlement about 30 miles from Lusaka. Several small buildings served as crowded dormitories for 113 women with 115 babies, who averaged 5 to a room. I saw no beds, only mattresses and blankets on the floor. The director was a middle-aged woman who had spent time in prison for participating in a woman's protest action. There were two nurses, who had very little equipment. On the land around the buildings well-cultivated gardens were producing vegetables. I was told that better facilities would be available soon.

Later I went with Nkomo to visit the Girls' Victory Camp in the former headquarters of a Yugoslav company. I was surprised by its size—some 6,000 girls were living in new dormitories and tents, and another 5,000 were expected from Botswana. The camp was financed chiefly by the UN, although contributions also came from various countries and private organizations. Nkomo told me that the United States had given $1.5 million. Thirty cement block buildings were under construction for dormitories and classrooms. At the moment, classes were being conducted outdoors in any available shade. Everyone seemed to be busy. One large building was filled with men and women sewing clothes for the girls on machines donated by East Germany and the Soviet Union. I talked with the principal of the school program for both this camp and one for boys a few miles away. He had been a teacher in a school in Rhodesia that had marched across the border to join the ZAPU community in Botswana. The Smith government claimed they had been kidnapped by guerrillas. The principal laughed as he explained how in fact the whole student body of 400-odd had carefully organized their own escape.

Shortly before we left, Nkomo led me by the arm to a large athletic field ringed by several thousand girls. They started singing with an enthusiasm and natural harmony that thrilled me. The songs were of freedom, the struggle, and their desire to return home soon. "What shall we do with Muzorewa, with Sithole, with Chirau [one of the traditional chiefs working with Smith]?" one of the songs went. "We shall decide when we return home," was the response.

In Lusaka I visited Nkomo's home, provided by the Zambian government. He introduced me to a five-year-old child who had been picked up a few days earlier wandering on the Botswana side of the border. He didn't know where his parents were. The Botswana police asked him where he was going. He had heard about the Geneva conference and replied, "I'm walking to Geneva to join Nkomo." Nkomo picked up the lad and said, "He has arrived in Geneva."

ZANU IN MOZAMBIQUE

The central offices of ZANU's exile organization were in Maputo, capital of Mozambique. The Mozambican government gave ZANU office space in a former apartment building. As with ZAPU, I was amazed at the size and scope of the operation. Eddison Zvobgo, secretary for information and publicity, with whom I talked many times, had a staff of 39 but expected to triple it soon. I had the feeling that ZANU leaders were poised and ready to take governmental responsibility. My opinion was confirmed by another new arrival in Maputo, my friend Davis M'Gabe, who had been a key ZANU representative in the United States and was on a sabbatical from his teaching post at Staten Island Community College. "George, I had no idea of the size and the strength of the movement before I came here."

There were many more Zimbabwean refugees in Mozambique than in Zambia. ZANU was inundated by young men and women crossing the border and wanting to join the military. About 45,000 men and women were attached to the armed forces. Zvobgo said there were as many as 70,000 waiting for training in Mozambique and another 100,000 in Rhodesia. ZANU had facilities, however, to train only 5,000 every three months.

According to the UN representative, in 1978 there were 75,000 refugees in Mozambique in five camps. ZANU was sponsoring educational and medical programs among them. I had met ZANU's secretary for health, Dr. Herbert Ushewokunze, when he came to New York in early 1978 to raise funds for medical work among the refugees. The ACOA had coordinated his travel schedule and arranged for many meetings. For years he had run his own medical service in Bulawayo and helped recruit for ZANU. He had been in exile since 1976. When he heard I was in Muputo, he traveled the rough roads from one of the ZANU camps far to the north to meet me. He gave me vivid accounts of Rhodesian bombing raids on refugee centers. Twenty refugees, mostly women, had been killed in one raid. Another had lasted six hours but wounded only six people.

For a time Ushewokunze was the only doctor serving the camps. He moved from one to another with virtually no equipment or facilities and no anaesthetics for surgery. I was introduced to six young ZANU soldiers, all of whom had just received artificial legs from the International Red Cross. All but one had been injured by antipersonnel mines near the border.

My long-time friend Nathan Shamuyarira was in ZANU's Department of Education. The education program was directed not only toward the refugee camps, where eight schools operated with some 30,000 students and 700 teachers, but also toward an estimated 1 million people in the liberated areas inside Rhodesia. ZANU was even beginning to use some of the rural schools that the government had been forced to vacate.

By 1978 the stepped-up military campaign was having a marked effect on Rhodesia. Casualties on both sides were up dramatically. White emigration rose to almost 14,000 in 1977. Tourism dropped by about 75 percent in 1978 compared with 1972, when the serious fighting began.

About 30 missionaries were killed during the conflict. These atrocities, attributed by white Rhodesians to guerrillas, received much publicity. The Patriotic Front in turn claimed the murders were the work of special Rhodesian guerrilla units called the Selous Scouts, who posed as rebel forces. Some missionaries were known to be giving guerrillas food and clothing. By attacking these missionaries, the Selous Scouts could both teach them a lesson and score propaganda points against the ZANU and ZAPU forces. In fact, since most missionaries were in unprotected rural communities, if the guerrillas had wanted to kill them, few would have survived.

STRAINS WITHIN THE PATRIOTIC FRONT

Most of the fighting took place in eastern and northeastern Rhodesia, to which ZANU forces in Mozambique had relatively easy access. The activity of ZAPU forces based in Zambia was more limited, a sore point for ZAPU. Nkomo was agitated by an article that quoted me slightly out of context as saying that ZANU forces were doing most of the fighting. He had a coworker write a strong letter accusing me of no longer being a friend of the Rhodesian struggle. The next time we met, however, there seemed to be no rift in our relationship.

Although the Patriotic Front held together for three years, serious rivalry between ZAPU and ZANU persisted. The PF was in real jeopardy in August 1978 when Nkomo was holding secret talks with Ian Smith in Lusaka, unknown to Mugabe. According to the *Daily News* in Dar es Salaam, Nkomo denied any such meetings, but I talked with many people there who firmly believed they had taken place. Muzorewa and Sithole were enraged, presumably because they felt Smith was bypassing them. Nyerere was upset that Kaunda had allowed such meetings without telling other African leaders.

A few days later in Lusaka I learned that indeed Nkomo and Smith had met. According to Kaunda's press representative, who had been at the meeting, Smith's strategy was to have Nkomo return to Rhodesia to head a transitional government. Apparently, Smith rightly perceived that neither Muzorewa nor Sithole could control the guerrilla forces and end the fighting. Nkomo, he thought, could accomplish this, especially because of his alliance with Mugabe. Nkomo was interested in the proposal but could not follow up without Mugabe, who would not agree. The ZANU Central Committee met in Maputo and turned the plan down.

The episode strained relations between Mugabe and Nkomo. When I saw Mugabe in Maputo, he made it quite clear that he was upset by what he felt was a maneuver by Smith to break up the PF. Neither Nkomo nor Mugabe could afford to scuttle their PF alliance, certainly not Nkomo, who could not control the ZANU forces that were doing most of the fighting.

A NEW INTERNATIONAL INGREDIENT

International pressure, particularly by Britain and the United States, helped end the war in Rhodesia. Kissinger had laid the groundwork. The Jimmy Carter administration came into office in 1977 determined to act resolutely on southern African issues. Vice President Walter Mondale had a well-publicized meeting with Prime Minister Vorster in Vienna. Speaking bluntly, Mondale said, "If South Africa persists in its ideology, our paths will diverge and our policies come into conflict."

The Byrd Amendment was repealed by Congress in the third month of the new administration. Andrew Young played a key role in African policy in the early part of Carter's term and was supportive of efforts for African liberation. Shortly after he became U.S. ambassador to the UN, he let me know that Carter had asked him to provide leadership on African issues. He was happy about this assignment.

Young, whom I had first met when he was associated with Martin Luther King, was not a typical government operative. He was freewheeling. He understood the language of organizations that had causes and was at ease with representatives of the liberation movements in Africa, such as

Oliver Tambo, Sam Nujoma, Mugabe, or Nkomo. This facility stood him in good stead. Early in his UN term a resolution calling for sanctions against South Africa was introduced in the Security Council. Traditionally the United States had vetoed all such resolutions and probably would have done so again. In behind-the-scenes discussions Ambassador Leslie Harriman of Nigeria, chairman of the UN Special Committee Against Apartheid, succeeded in toning down the resolution, and Young was spared the embarrassment of voting negatively on an antiapartheid resolution. His effectiveness at the UN was enhanced by his deputy, Donald McHenry, who, like Young, was black and had diplomatic experience and deep knowledge on African issues.

Young worked with David Owen, British foreign minister under James Callaghan, to help lay the foundation for a Rhodesian settlement. Carrying on their own shuttle diplomacy with all the principals involved, they presented the so-called Anglo-American proposals. These included a new constitution for an independent Zimbabwe, a National Assembly to be elected by universal suffrage, a Bill of Rights to protect minorities, a Zimbabwe Development Fund of $1.5 billion, a six-months transition period under a British resident commissioner, a cease-fire, and the lifting of sanctions. The African reaction was that at least the proposals were a basis for negotiations. The Owen-Young team had separate meetings with Mugabe and Nkomo, representing the PF, on Malta and in Dar es Salaam to try to work out an agreement.

In the meantime, Ian Smith continued compounding the difficulties. During the height of the Owen-Young diplomacy, he called for elections in which his party, the Rhodesian Front, won all 50 seats reserved for whites. To placate black and international objectors, he eased discriminatory practices in some restaurants and allowed limited sports events between black and white schools. At the same time, he authorized air force attacks on Zambia. Shortly after I returned to New York from Zambia, the news came that the ZAPU Boys' Victory Camp, which I knew was not military, had been bombed. More than 200 were killed and hundreds wounded. A few days later, commandos raided Nkomo's house in Lusaka, which I had visited. The house was destroyed, but fortunately Nkomo was not there.

THE INTERNAL SETTLEMENT

Making a last desperate effort to establish the semblance of majority rule, Smith reached an agreement with Muzorewa and Sithole on a so-called Internal Settlement. It was so named to distinguish it from the international efforts for majority rule. It included a new constitution calling for elections in which blacks would participate; a black prime minister and a cabinet with a black majority would be chosen. Whites would maintain control of the police, army, civil service, and prison system. They also would have more than enough votes, including 28 reserved seats in the legislature, to block any constitutional changes. The PF rejected the settlement.

A resolution was introduced into the U.S. Congress calling for the United States to send impartial observers to monitor the elections, scheduled for April 1979. The ACOA interpreted this move as tacit recognition of the validity of the Internal Settlement and therefore joined with others to campaign against the resolution, which was defeated.

When Muzorewa's United African National Council (UANC, formerly the ANC) won a victory, and he became the first African prime minister of the country now called Zimbabwe-Rhodesia, the issue arose again. Should the United States lift sanctions? The ACOA argued that they should be maintained. The elections could not have been free with martial law in 90 percent of the country and military forces of the government and the Muzorewa and Sithole militia ranging the country pressing for votes. Furthermore, the PF had been banned. Under these circumstances the vote of the 64 percent of the electorate who cast ballots had to be questioned. President Carter vetoed the Senate's vote to lift sanctions.

It soon became apparent that Muzorewa could not end the war. The guerrillas did not accept him. No countries recognized his government. Muzorewa went to the United States to win support, but his sponsorship by the right-wing forces of Sen. Jesse Helms was surely not the way to win points with the Carter administration. Casualties were mounting. The guerrilla armies numbered close to 25,000. About 25,000 people were killed in the seven years of the war, which cost the Muzorewa government more than a $1 million a day.

LANCASTER HOUSE

A Commonwealth summit conference in Lusaka in August 1979 put final pressure on the British. To avoid a crisis, Prime Minister Margaret Thatcher and the new foreign minister, Lord Carrington, agreed to call a constitutional conference in London with all parties represented, which even Muzorewa, lacking international recognition and facing domestic crisis, had to accept.

Most people thought the Lancaster House conference, beginning in September, would probably not last more than two weeks. Six weeks later, when I was in London, it was still going on, although it was by no means clear that an agreement would emerge. There were touchy questions to deal with: How would the British government exercise and implement power during the interim period leading to new elections? Would the PF forces be integrated into the army, police, and civil service during this interim so that elections would be fair? Would a UN force be called upon to maintain order, since a cease-fire would otherwise be difficult to achieve?

It was encouraging to see that the PF had a united delegation. Both ZAPU and ZANU representatives with whom I talked (including Nkomo, Zvobgo, and Ushewokunze) were skeptical that a workable agreement could be reached, yet they did not want to be responsible for breaking up the conference. On the one hand, if no agreement was reached, they felt

Zimbabweans celebrating at the election, February 1980.

the Muzorewa government would be recognized and the fighting would go on, putting them back where they started. On the other hand, they were sure that if elections were fair, the PF would win an overwhelming victory. Zvobgo dogmatically stated that Muzorewa, caught between the white minority and the British and saddled with continuing a war against the PF, was losing influence.

Despite these perplexities, an agreement was thrashed out. A constitution providing for majority rule was accepted. The conditions for a cease-fire were set, and a date for elections was chosen. The next problem was how to put this agreement into operation.

THE MIRACLE OF ZIMBABWE

Elections under the Lancaster House agreement were to take place the last three days of February 1980. I felt that there was no place more important for me to be than in Rhodesia just beforehand. Provision had been made for both official and unofficial international observers to see that campaigning and the election were conducted fairly. I organized an unofficial delegation of Americans representing the ACOA, the Washington Office on Africa, the NAACP, and Trans Africa. Our team of five consisted of Ted Lockwood, director of the Washington Office; Tilden LeMelle, a professor at Hunter College; Cynthia Canady, a lawyer; Robert Edgar, a professor at Howard University; and me. Our friend Mike Shuster of

National Public Radio, although officially there as a journalist, was part of our group.

I had been a prohibited immigrant in Rhodesia ever since 1954. Could I get in now? I took the precaution of talking with Sir Anthony Parsons, the British ambassador to the UN, about my possible problem. He made inquiries and gave me an official letter saying that the interim governor's office in Salisbury had approved my entrance.

When our unofficial team arrived in Salisbury about two weeks before the election, the atmosphere was so tense, the intimidation so widespread, that it was easy to think the whole process would break down overnight. The main contenders were Muzorewa's United African National Council, Sithole's ZANU splinter, and the two parties of the PF. It was the choice of Mugabe's ZANU that the uneasy alliance in the PF forged for the Geneva conference did not hold for the elections.*

Our team was only a small part of a large number of foreign observers and journalists on hand. According to official statistics, there were 281 observers and 680 journalists in a country just a little smaller than California. By dividing our forces our group covered each of the eight provinces by car and plane, visited cities, Tribal Trust Lands, tea estates, European-owned farms, and protected villages. We attended mass political rallies, visited party offices, and talked with leaders and ordinary people.

For me the intimidation began when we arrived at Salisbury airport. I went through the immigration line with some nervous misgivings but seemingly with no trouble. As I was changing some American traveler's checks, however, the black immigration officer who had passed me through came running after me to say that his superior wanted to see me. With sinking heart I waited in an office for the white chief immigration officer, who bluntly told me I could not stay, that I was "prohibited." I then produced the letter given me by Parsons in New York. The officer scowled and angrily asked why I hadn't produced it in the first place. "I didn't expect any difficulty," I replied. After a telephone call to the governor's office, to my great relief, I was allowed in—until March 1.

The peace during the campaign period was obviously fragile. There was an uneasy truce among the four different Rhodesian and Zimbabwean armies on Rhodesian soil. On highways, signs read, "Warning to motorists: it is dangerous to travel this road after 3:00 P.M." Outside principal cities, road blocks manned by police and troops let cars with whites through with a nod but searched Africans and made them produce identification papers. One could not enter a hotel, bank, or public place without having bags and parcels scrupulously examined for weapons or explosives. In the Tribal Trust Lands there was curfew from sundown to sunrise. At the daily official press briefings, statistics gave evidence of violence. On February 19, for example, there were 14 "incidents," 11

---

*Because of the popularity of the PF, Nkomo campaigned in the name of the PF, not ZAPU. To maintain some aura of the alliance, Mugabe's party was called ZANU(PF), which also distinguished it from Sithole's splinter.

"contacts" (meaning actual exchange of armed fire), 8 deaths, and 12 violations of the cease-fire.

I dropped in on Zvobgo at the ZANU office, who informed me that his wife had just been arrested along with Richard Hove, a ZANU leader, for allegedly aiding a terrorist. They had gone to the rescue of a wounded ZANU member near Fort Victoria. They ultimately won their case.

I visited the Domboshawa area, a Tribal Trust Land, near Salisbury. A crowd was gathered around one of the houses, where a young man had been shot the night before as he came home about 7:00 P.M., after curfew. His bereaved mother took me inside to see his body lying under a white sheet.

I accompanied Nathan Shamuyarira to his hotel in the African township of Highfield. He told me the room had been ransacked by the police the night before. It was a mess. Suitcases had been emptied on the floor. Papers were strewn about. Many papers and Rhodesian $1,000 of ZANU money had been taken.

Several attempts were made on Mugabe's life. A hand grenade was thrown at his home but missed. A more serious attempt was made after he had addressed a mass rally at Fort Victoria. An explosion on the highway just missed his departing car, leaving a gaping hole in the road. The last two major ZANU rallies of the campaign were held without him because of the danger to his life.

Several times I found the street to the ZANU office in Salisbury cordoned off and blocked by police. It was on account of more bomb scares, which were becoming routine, but ZANU officials suspected it was police harassment. They frequently took a chance by staying at their desks rather than pouring onto the street.

Our group had a harrowing experience that brought home to us the prevalent atmosphere of intimidation. On a quiet Sunday we set out in two cars for the Chiota Tribal Trust Land, about 60 miles south of Salisbury in the company of four ZANU friends who had been campaigning for ZANU candidates. Our objective was to talk to whomever we could to ascertain their experience in the campaigning.

We turned off the paved highway onto a dirt road and headed toward the village of Mahusekwa. On the way we detoured to stop at the Furamera School run by Wesleyan Methodists. We talked with the headmaster and several initially cautious teachers. As they gained confidence they reported some of the coercive tactics used to stop people from attending ZANU meetings. We were just getting back to the main dirt road when a frightened, dissheveled African rushed up. We stopped and he began to tell us that down the road he had just been beaten by soldiers, who were coming this way. Before we could get his whole story, we saw a truck speeding along the road raising a cloud of dust in its wake. As it approached, the driver slammed on the brakes, and a dozen shouting black soldiers with guns aimed at us and nervous trigger fingers jumped off. They ordered us to get out of our cars. A sergeant shouted that no one should move or he would be shot. We stood still. I was not alone in thinking that this might be the end of the road for us. The soldiers were searching for "terrorists," and ZANU sympathizers were looked upon not only as terrorists but as Communists as well.

The sergeant then gave us crisp orders. LeMelle and Shuster and three of our ZANU companions were put in the back of the truck with the soldiers pointing guns at their heads. Cynthia Canady was put in one car with a ZANU driver and two soldiers. I was at the wheel in the other car with two soldiers in the back seat, their guns leveled at my neck. The sergeant barked, "Stay behind the truck. Do not go more than five miles an hour or you will be shot." I could clearly see Cynthia in the car in front and LeMelle and Shuster in the truck. We headed slowly down the road, I wondered where.

To cover my nervousness, I began to talk to my two soldiers, who had both gone to mission schools and spoke good English. I told them my name and why I was there. They told me where they came from and where they went to school. I could see that they gradually moved their guns away from the back of my head toward the open windows, which made me feel more comfortable. They began to warn me against terrorists. There was still a war on in their country, they said. There were 500 "terrorists" in the Chiota Tribal Trust Land and their job was to find them. They told me I was unsafe with the ZANU men and that if the soldiers had not "rescued" me and my companions, we would have been taken into the bush and shot. They called the ZANU guerrillas "gooks" who kill whites. That day, they said, they were looking for a terrorist known as Durban and thought one of our ZANU companions was he. They were silent when I protested that these were not guerrillas or "terrorists" but our friends.

Soon we arrived at the military base at Mahusekwa. Soldiers congregated at the gate cheered loudly, for they believed our soldiers had captured Durban. Inside the compound we four Americans were separated from our ZANU companions and interrogated briefly by white Rhodesian officers. Who were we? What were we doing with these men? How did we meet them?

Presently we were put in our cars again and taken several miles farther to Marandellas, regional headquarters of the Special Branch of the Police. Here a white Rhodesian officer asked whether we were victims of intimidation by the ZANU men. He told us we were foolish to have come with them and might have been killed. We in turn told him that the only intimidation we had suffered was from the government soldiers and from the Special Branch as we tried to carry out our assignment as foreign observers of the election. Our exchange was tense and unfriendly.

We were finally released from this four-hour ordeal with the warning that we had better get back to Salisbury before dark, since the roads were not safe at night. When we reached Salisbury, we telephoned back to Marandellas and learned that our ZANU friends had been released shortly after we were. When we met them later, they credited our presence with having saved them from being shot as terrorists with no one the wiser. Such incidents were common during the campaign.

The atmosphere was more relaxed in areas of ZAPU strength. LeMelle and I tried to attend a huge rally in the beautiful Motopos Hills area of southwestern Rhodesia. The spot for the rally was some distance off the main road. When a big rainstorm struck, we abandoned our car and tried to walk through muddy paths to the meeting place. I shall long remember the great sense of unity among the laughing, singing, shouting thousands, who, like us, were sloshing through rain and mud, never to reach the rally spot until after Nkomo, the main speaker, had come and gone in his helicopter.

The next day we attended a ZAPU rally at Gwelo. There must have been 20,000 Nkomo supporters on hand. Police were there too, but rather inconspicuously. It was a festive political occasion capped off by the appearance of Nkomo, who made a basic appeal for good will among all Zimbabweans and added a particular plea for whites not to leave the country.

Robert Mugabe was looked upon as the main threat by the media and most white Rhodesians. ZANU was seen as almost satanic and assuredly terrorist and Communist under his leadership. Bishop Muzorewa was the darling of the whites. Typical of articles in the daily *Herald*, was a front-page story of February 27, 1950, the day voting began, in which Muzorewa was quoted as saying, "Zimbabwe will be invaded by Russians if the election result goes against the wishes and design of the Communists." The bishop was pictured as religious, moderate, strongly anti-Communist, and a friend of the white man. By all odds, he had the best-financed campaign. He had six helicopters at his disposal. ZANU (PF) had none. In many full-page ads, he was usually pictured in his clerical vestments holding a scepter and a Bible. Mugabe was portrayed as anti-Chrisitan, Marxist, and a destroyer of churches.

The corridor talk among journalists was that probably no party would win an absolute majority of the 100 seats in Parliament. Smith already had won all the 20 seats reserved for whites. It was assumed that none of the African parties would win 51 seats out of the 80 reserved for Africans. So probably a coalition government would have to be formed, perhaps led by Nkomo joining with Muzorewa and leaving out Mugabe. Yet this was not the way Nkomo talked. He was disappointed that ZANU and ZAPU had not stuck together for the election. Yet during the campaign he and Mugabe were careful not to attack each other. I talked with Josiah Chinamano, vice president of ZAPU, who said, "We are not in a battle against ZANU. I don't say all is well, but bad feeling is a creation of the press." There was certainly some bad feeling between them, but it was kept under wraps during the campaign.

Racism among the whites was by no means dispelled by the prospect of a black majority government. It came up frequently in subtle ways. For example, before election day I had lunch at a country club on a white-owned tea estate in the eastern part of the country. I asked one middle-aged white woman how many people lived on the huge estate. She replied, "Twelve." I thought she had not understood my question, for I had seen hundreds of African workers whose homes were on the estate. So I asked how many workers there were. She then said: "Twenty-four hundred."

On the eve of the elections, no one knew what might happen. If a coalition government was formed against ZANU, would the 22,000 still-armed guerrillas stay in the 16 assembly points around the country where by terms of the cease-fire they were gathered? What about another 3,000 or more still ranging the countryside and the still more thought to be on call in Mozambique or Zambia? If Mugabe won, might there be a white coup backed by South African troops?

My visit to an assembly point called Romeo, a three-hour drive north-east of Salisbury, was a strange experience. Several hundred ZAPU guerrillas, with weapons and tattered uniforms, were there with a smaller force of white troops as part of an attempt to integrate the armed forces. The atmosphere was stiff. Only a few weeks earlier these units had been involved in fierce combat, but now they were beginning to go on joint patrols. While I was there, Nkomo with the white commander of the Rhodesian forces arrived by helicopter to pay a formal visit. A military assembly was called, the troops standing in neat rows. Nkomo spoke briefly, calling on the troops to be ready to accept the election and stressing the necessity of black and white living together in peace. Mugabe was making similar visits.

Very few people outside of some ZANU leaders foresaw the overwhelming victory that ZANU won. More than 93 percent of the potential voters went to the polls. In spite of the pervading air of intimidation, there was virtually no violence during the three days of balloting. Our group covered many polling stations in the Salisbury area and saw no infractions worth mentioning. People waited their turn in long lines and cast their ballots without interference.

The election results were astonishingly one-sided. After all the money spent on his behalf, Bishop Muzorowea won only three seats and 8 percent of the vote. ZAPU won 20 seats and ZANU 57, an absolute majority plus 6. The governor asked Mugabe to form a government.

What was to be expected from this leader of the "terrorists" who was now to be prime minister? He had been quoted in 1978 as having said, "What I want is for Mr. Smith to be taken before a people's court, judged, and I seriously hope shot by a firing squad." While the ZANU enthusiasts were dancing and singing in the streets, shocked white Rhodesians, were making plans to adjust the only way they knew how. According to the *London Sunday Times* (March 9, 1980), "Within hours, civil service resignations poured in, husbands phoned wives telling them to pack a bag and leave for South Africa, children had even been sent to school that morning carrying bags packed for flights in case early rumors of the results were true. Yet within 24 hours this panic rebounded with an equally unfounded optimism."

Most whites had had no exposure to Mugabe, for he had hardly ever been seen on television, heard on radio, or quoted in the press except as an object of negative propaganda by his white opponents. So when he spoke to the nation over radio and television as prime minister-elect, it had a momentous effect. Miraculously this speech changed the atmosphere of the country. He said, "Our theme is reconciliation. We want to ensure that there is a sense of security on the part of everybody, winners and losers. . . . Forgive others and forget, join hands in a new amity and together as Zimbabweans trample upon racialism, tribalism, and regionalism and work hard to reconstruct and rehabilitate our society." Mugabe made immediate moves to quell fears. He said he would take whites into his government and maintain his alliance with Nkomo by including ZAPU leaders in his cabinet. He told the business community there would be no early nationalization. He promised civil servants that pensions and property rights would be respected. Foreign policy toward South Africa would be one of coexistence but by no means acceptance of apartheid. After all the bitter years of a violent struggle, he set the tone for a new era.

PROSPECTS FOR THE FUTURE

The independence of Zimbabwe in April 1980 marked a milestone in southern Africa. The minority government, in control for 92 years, was finally overthrown. The new government took on its responsibilities with enthusiasm, and the response was equally enthusiastic. I could feel it in New York. Mugabe was warmly welcomed at the UN. Of all the receptions the ACOA sponsored for African leaders, none was more thrilling than the one for the new prime minister of Zimbabwe. Zimbabweans who had been working or studying in the United States made plans to go home to help build a new country, even though the move often involved personal and financial complications.

With independence the exodus of whites increased. One to two thousand people a month streamed out of Zimbabwe. It was estimated that a hard core of 100,000 whites (out of some 280,000) would stay on. The attitude of many was, "I'll stay as long as it pays." On the whole, those who stayed lived as comfortably as they did before independence. On one of my visits I asked the white desk clerk of my small hotel how everything was going. She replied, "I'm just waiting to get out of here." Then, unsure of my sympathies, she quickly added, "I'm no racist, though." Other whites were very supportive of the government. A new group of whites sympathetic to the government were attracted to Zimbabwe for jobs in teaching, government, technology, and development schemes, a trend that augurs well for the future.

Some changes came quickly. When a new city council was elected for Salisbury, the name of the city was changed to Harare, after Neharawa, the Shona chief at the time of the Pioneer Column in 1888. Names of other cities were changed to their originals such as Gwelo to Gweru, Fort Victoria to Masvingo, Umtali to Mutare. And street names were changed—in Harare, Jameson Avenue became Samora Machel Avenue and

Kingsway was changed to Julius Nyerere Avenue. The statue of Cecil Rhodes on the main thoroughfare was toppled.

More fundamental changes came too. Within a year after independence the number of students entering secondary school rose from 18 percent to 83 percent. Free medical care became available for everyone with an income of less than Zimbabwe $235 a month. A national minimum wage was set in commerce, industry, and mining.

There were dissatisfactions, too, however. Land reform proceeded slowly. In the first three years the plan called for 162,000 people who needed land to be resettled on unused or underused land acquired by the government, but only a little more than 20,000 had actually been resettled. Some 5,500 white farmers still owned 39 percent of the land. Multinational corporations, although paying a 50 percent tax on profits, were still exercising a powerful influence.

Perhaps the most serious problem was the continuing political and tribal conflict. Dissidents in Matabeleland, once loyal to Nkomo's ZAPU, had hidden arms, presumably to initiate antigovernment attacks. Some people in government circles thought Nkomo was involved. He emphatically denied it, and I believed him; armed revolt was not his style. He was a politician, not the architect of a violent coup. It seemed rather that he could not control the dissidents, some of whom were disgruntled former ZAPU guerrillas and some common criminals. The government responded to the threat of violence by taking emergency military action in which thousands of innocent people suffered, especially in Matabeleland, presumably for harboring dissidents. I know from my visits in the Bulawayo area that many people feared traveling into the rural areas where government troops might apprehend them.

The conflict strained Mugabe's coalition government. Nkomo was dismissed from his ministerial post. Feeling in danger of arrest, he secretly escaped from the country in disguise and went to London. He told me in Harare only a few weeks before he fled, "I suppose there has to be an unsettled period after independence, but does it have to be like this?" Other ZAPU leaders had moments of disillusionment. One asked, in a dispirited tone, "Is this what we fought for?"

My own feeling about Zimbabwe is optimistic. The progress in education and health care is heartening. The economy has recovered with the end of the crippling drought. Critical voices, white and black, sensible and nonsensical, can speak out. Even Ian Smith was for several years still in Parliament, although he was hardly a friend of the black government. The transition to independence is never easy, but the future of Zimbabwe looks promising.

CHAPTER TWENTY-THREE

South Africa and Namibia: The Final Conflict

S outh Africa has not basically changed in the 35-odd years I have been concerned with it. Organizations and individuals resisting apartheid are still being banned. Since the Sharpeville Massacre of 1960, 3.5 million blacks have been forcibly relocated out of urban areas by the government. Political prisoners and executions are still, per capita, the most numerous in the world. Torture is routinely used by the police. The vast majority of the people, the Africans, still cannot vote. What were in the 1950s called "native reserves" have been renamed "Bantustans," then "homelands"; a few are even known by some as "nations" and have a pseudo-independence. But a separate status for the mass of people, most of whom live in ignominious poverty, still persists.

From my vantage point outside South Africa I have watched the course of the struggle. I experienced the brief wave of optimism that swept southern Africa after the FRELIMO government was formed in Mozambique. I listened skeptically as South African prime minister John Vorster wished it well, pledged that he would work for peace and development in an African context, and hinted at unexpected change within South Africa in six months. Reality returned, however, when SASO, the BPC, and the Black Allied Workers' Union announced they were holding a public rally in celebration of FRELIMO's victory and the government banned the rally and arrested the leaders.

THE SOWETO UPRISING AND AFTER

The excitement aroused by the Soweto uprising of June 16, 1976, was comparable only to that surrounding the Sharpeville Massacre of 1960. Unlike Sharpeville, the uprising in the sprawling Soweto Township outside Johannesburg was led by young students, not older liberation organizations. The Soweto Students' Representative Council (SSRC) was the only organized group openly mentioned. The demonstration of some 10,000 students protesting the 1955 requirement that Afrikaans be a language of instruction in the schools may have arisen out of their identification with the pervasive black consciousness movement.

For several weeks the students had been actively protesting and boycotting subjects such as mathematics and science taught in Afrikaans. Their protest culminated in a march the morning of the 16th with students

345

singing forbidden songs of the banned African National Congress (ANC) and giving the black power salute. They were stopped by armed police, who used tear gas and, when the marchers did not disperse, fired shots. Twelve-year-old Hector Peterson was killed immediately; he is now revered as the first martyr of Soweto.

The demonstration spread and erupted into rioting. Bantu administration offices were burned; hundreds of white students at the University of Witwatersrand, joined by black students at the University of Zululand and the African University of the North, marched in protest. A thousand protesters ranged the streets in Alexandra Township. Within two weeks there were 1,300 arrests. According to government statistics, nearly 500 had been killed; unofficial estimates put the figure at more than 1,000.

One of the colorful leaders to emerge was 19-year-old Tsietse Mashimini, president of the SSRC. He came to public attention (generally anonymity was important to avoid reprisals) when a clandestine interview with him in Johannesburg, arranged by a British television crew, was aired in London. He became a wanted fugutive for whom a reward was offered, but he successfully eluded the police and finally escaped to London. At my invitation he came to New York, where the ACOA held a press conference for him. Like most youthful leaders, Mashimini was disarmingly frank and unsophisticated. "I didn't even become a revolutionary until I came out," he said. "I have only just learned about things like capitalism and Marxism and communism, and I still don't know much about them. They're just a bunch of 'isms'."

The SSRC achieved a significant degree of control in Soweto. At its insistence, state beer halls were closed for a time. The state-controlled Urban Bantu Council, including the chairman, David Thebahali, who was threatened with having his house burned down, all resigned. Some time later Thebahali came on a U.S. government-sponsored visit to the United States and stopped at my office. He did not impress me by rationalizing that he was working with the apartheid government to weaken it from within. He told me that government officials had convinced him that reforms in housing and education would come and that "shouting for political freedom has done absolutely nothing to improve the things that really matter to the people."

The government cracked down after Soweto in reaction to the continued student protests and the boycotting of classes and exams by 300,000 students. Especially devastating was the arrest of the young leader Stephen Biko in August 1977 and his murder in prison 28 days later. The shock at learning the details of the torture and beatings he suffered before he died was compounded by a sense of outrage that at the inquest the legally untrained chief magistrate in Pretoria found that the police bore no responsibility in Biko's death. "To me it was just another death," Marthinus Prins said. It was grotesquely callous for him to add that with the case over he was looking foward to relaxing and doing some fishing, as if the ordeal had been his.[1]

Almost eight years later (July 5, 1975), a medical panel ruled that the two doctors who allowed the police to transport Biko by van, naked, manacled, and suffering from brain damage, 800 miles from Port Elizabeth to Pretoria, were guilty only of "improper conduct." One doctor was reprimanded and the other suspended from practice for three months.

Biko's death was a terrible loss. I felt that what he quietly said about black consciousness was important not only for blacks but also for white people like myself to hear. So often whites who try to identify with blacks in the struggle for justice develop a kind of martyr complex or tend to think of themselves as especially annointed leaders. It is a good antidote to such a false sense of importance to be told that blacks must be in the vanguard and whites in supporting roles.

The government crackdown was reminiscent of the treason arrests of 1956 and the post-Sharpeville period. In September 1977 the government suppressed all opposition. Eighteen organizations were banned, 2 major black newspapers were shut down, and some 60 black (and a few white) leaders were arrested.*

Many young leaders of the black consciousness movement fled South Africa in the aftermath of Soweto. Some wanted to join the ANC and the PAC outside, through which they could receive military training or go overseas to study. Others wanted to establish a firm external base for the various organizations identified with the black consciousness movement, notably the BPC.

In Gaberone, the capital of Botswana, in 1978 I met many of these activists. Botswana was the easiest refuge to reach and Gaberone was hardly 12 miles from the border. This small town reflected South African influence. The major radio programs, the food in the hotels and restaurants, and the goods in the shops all came from South Africa. As one who had made a point of personally boycotting South African goods, I was confronted with an impossible situation.

Botswana's proximity to South Africa often resulted in tension. The day I arrived in Gaberone a crisis was unfolding. Students had been denied permission to hold a demonstration, and police had used tear gas to disperse a gathering of protesters. Several arrests were made. In retaliation the students had burned some of the surrounding veld. The crisis had arisen because the government had put on trial several soldiers who had killed two South Africans and a Briton apprehended near the Rhodesian border while engaged in suspicious activities, presumably for the Ian Smith government. The students were protesting the trial, which they felt came about only because of South African pressure on Botswana.

Botswana was a haven for nationalist refugees from its troubled neighbors, particularly Rhodesia and Namibia. Camps were set up aided by the UN and international church agencies through the Botswana Christian

---

*Among the organizations banned were the BPC, SASO, SSRC, Christian Institute of South Africa, and Union of Black Journalists. Well-known individuals detained or banned included Percy Qoboza, editor of *The World*, the largest black newspaper; Donald Woods, white editor of the *East London Daily Dispatch;* Beyers Naudé, white director of the Christian Institute; and Dr. Ntatho Motlana, chairman of Soweto's Committee of Ten.

Council. The roughly 2,000 South African refugees, mostly political, were less numerous than the others. The ANC representative in Gaberone said about 50 people a month came through the ANC, most of them in transit. They were fed and housed in three buildings as they waited to move on. I visited with some who had been involved in the Soweto demonstrations and had left to avoid arrest and to study abroad.

These young escapees were new to exile politics. Some of them hoped the BPC could receive enough financial aid to become a viable force in exile. They respected the older ANC and PAC as history but no longer looked to them for leadership. They were convinced that they themselves represented the new freedom fighters in the struggle against apartheid. I thought they were quite unrealistic about their prospects for political survival removed from their base inside South Africa. The ANC, especially, with its prestige and respected leadership, was already effectively tapping governmental and nongovernmental support for the antiapartheid cause internationally. It would be difficult for anyone else to break in.

I talked with Joe Matthews, who was no longer with the ANC but was in private law practice in Botswana. He was afraid the ANC was losing touch with the day-to-day life of the people in the country and was spending too much time, energy, and money in just keeping the external apparatus going. More conservative now, he was critical of the campaign to stop investments in South Africa, but he cushioned his remarks by saying that the campaign wasn't the key to bringing internal change in South Africa. I didn't disagree, for few proponents of divestiture believed it would end apartheid. Rather, we believed it was a way for outsiders to highlight the role of business in strengthening the apartheid regime.

Matthews asked me if I remembered the police lieutenant who had interrogated me when we were picked up near Port Elizabeth in 1954. How could I forget him! Matthews told me he had telephoned this official recently in connection with a law case and that he had risen high in the South African police system. The official had asked Matthews whatever happened to that white guy he had picked up years ago. Matthews had responded, "He's still at it."

OUTSIDE REACTIONS

The Soweto uprising and the subsequent government crackdown spurred a crescendo of activity outside the country. The UN General Assembly and Security Council spent hours debating the issue. Western countries would not accept overall sanctions, but the arms embargo was strengthened.

Especially important at the UN was the watch dog body set up in 1963 and later known as the Special Committee Against Apartheid. It was a low-level committee composed mostly of African, Asian, and Latin American countries (no permanent Security Council members), so it did not automatically carry much influence. It could, however, be freewheeling, and behind the scenes it engineered many UN resolutions and strategies. It served as a rallying point for nongovernmental organizations internationally and helped many of them. Through the ACOA I appeared many times at its hearings.

The success of the Special Committee was largely due to the behind-the-scenes work of its chief of staff, Enuga S. Reddy. An Indian, he had studied at New York University and had become a researcher at the UN in 1949. He tackled the initially nonprestigious job with imagination and energy and made the Special Committee into one of the most active bodies in the UN. Its staff increased from 5 to 35, and its budget grew to about $3 million. Another $5 million was raised for victims of apartheid and for scholarships for black South Africans.

I was among those who hoped that the post-Soweto Jimmy Carter administration would mean a more vigorous policy in opposing South Africa. Andrew Young at the UN told me that the government would take some new initiatives. He traveled to Maputo, Mozambique, to participate in a UN Conference in Solidarity With the People of Zimbabwe and Namibia. There he spoke of a "new interest in Africa" and alluded to policies that would "represent something of a revolution in the consciousness of the American people."

The United States donated $500,000 to the UN Education and Training Programs for Southern Africa, repealed the Byrd Amendment, and changed the Zimbabwe Development Fund so that it would be used for development projects rather than for encouraging whites to stay. When Biko was killed and protest organizations were banned, the United States backed a strengthened UN arms embargo against South Africa.

The most troublesome aspect of U.S. policy on South Africa for me was its emphasis on the centrality of the business community in encouraging change. In a speech to business leaders in Johannesburg, Young said, "I've come to think of the business community as . . . being the key to the hope . . . for South Africans to live together as brothers. . . ." He used the analogy of the civil rights struggle in the United States as relevant for South Africa; he said that Martin Luther King had told the people of the Southland that "their economic system could not run without the support of black Americans." He specifically told how he and King had organized a committee of 100 business leaders in Birmingham, Alabama, which negotiated "the end of apartheid in Birmingham in spite of the fact that on the books of law it was still illegal to desegregate anything." In private conversation Young reiterated these same points to me.

I felt that this approach gave business leaders the impression that not only should they continue their profitable pursuits undisturbed but they could also be consoled by thinking that in so doing they were a force for change. I felt that the U.S. civil rights struggle was not essentially revolutionary. It was aimed more narrowly against discrimination and segregation, not at basic political and economic control. It could not be a model for South Africa, where the white minority rightly perceived that their privileged way of life was at stake. I felt that the outlawing of the pass laws, the recognition of black trade union rights, and the achievement of a universal franchise would condemn the old system. A philosophy that saw remedial reforms in business practices as the means of bringing about basic change seemed to me a delusion. Internal conflict would inevitably lead to international strife in which the United States would back up a white government with whose preservation it was concerned. For by the 1980s the United States was South Africa's chief trading partner, supplying 19 percent of South Africa's imports and buying 15 percent of its exports, and U.S. investments had mushroomed to more than $14 billion.* Furthermore, American investment was substantially concentrated in critical areas of the South African economy—manufacturing and energy-related enterprises.

I did not believe that the Sullivan principles, which stressed reforms in the workplace of American-owned businesses, would make fundamental changes in the injustices of the system. The advocacy of greater equality in the workplace would have virtually no effect on apartheid in the larger comunity—separate housing, black homelands, and lack of voting rights. Moreover, how could the Sullivan principles have much effect when only 1 percent of South African workers were employed in American-dominated industries?

The ACOA initiated campaigns in coalition with other organizations to implement a divestiture strategy. We organized the Campaign to Oppose Bank Loans to South Africa (COBLSA), directed by Prexy Nesbitt of our staff. It involved 48 cooperating organizations. We concentrated on urging state and local governments to divest themselves of investments in banks or corporations heavily involved in South Africa.

The ACOA's research work on divestiture was ably headed by Jennifer Davis. Dumisani Kumalo, a founder of the Union of Black Journalists in South Africa, who had fled police harassment there, made speeches and organized efforts around the country. His outgoing personality and his experience as a black South African made him an effective speaker.

Divestiture campaigns on college campuses began to reach significant proportions after the Soweto uprising and the murder of Biko. Students at Hampshire College in Massachusetts occupied the administration building in April 1977, demanding divestiture, and they won. Other student groups rallied to the cause, and the ACOA was besieged with requests for information on the economic ties between the United States and South Africa.

ACOA staff members were frequently asked to speak on college campuses. I was invited to participate in a conference at Northwestern University in May 1981. A generous honorarium was offered, which, like everything I received for writing or speaking, would have helped the ACOA's budget. My plans were aborted, however, when a faculty-student protest

---

*In June 1983 U.S. banks were loaning $3.8 billion to South Africa; corporate investments totaled $2.6 billion; and American individual stockholders owned $8 billion in shares listed on the Johannesburg stock exchange.

was organized by my old friend Dennis Brutus, professor of English. Protesters called on the invited speakers to boycott the conference because they felt it was a way of circumventing a face-to-face confrontation on the issue of Northwestern's $80 million investment in U.S. companies doing business in South Africa. They promised to picket all sessions of the conference. I knew I would not be able to cross a picket line of those I considered to be allies in the divestiture campaign. Consequently I and several other speakers withdrew.

ACOA efforts to combat apartheid were not turned exclusively to economic investments. We were also concerned with South African participation in sports events. When the Davis Cup tennis match between South Africa and the United States was at Vanderbilt University in Nashville in 1978, the ACOA joined a coalition of organizations to protest South Africa's participation. The NAACP was prominently involved, as was Franklin Williams, president of the Phelps Stokes Fund, but the chief leader was Richard Lapchick, a teacher at Virginia Wesleyan University in Norfolk and a specialist in the relation of sports to society. The demonstration outside the gymnasium and the publicity given the protest had their effect. Only about 1,100 attended the match in the gym, which would seat 9,600. As a result, Lapchick received considerable public attention and suffered the consequences. Late one night in his university office he was physically assaulted by two white men, who, after beating him unconscious, carved "niger" (sic) on his stomach. They were never apprehended.*

Three years later we again worked with Lapchick in a campaign against the U.S. appearance of the South African Rugby team. We forced the cancellation of scheduled matches in New York, Chicago, and Rochester. At the one public game that was held, in Albany, the demonstrators outnumbered the spectators 10 to 1.

FROM PROTEST TO INSURRECTION

The campaign against apartheid and white minority domination changed both quantitively and qualitatively inside South Africa in the early 1980s. Prime Minister Vorster left office in 1978 in the aftermath of the so-called Muldergate scandal, in which an estimated $100 million had been spent on projects backed by Vorster and Cornelius Mulder, minister of information, to counter the growing international isolation of South Africa. P.W. Botha, minister of defence, became prime minister. Sounding like a reformist, he told the South African people they would have to adapt to new realities or die. Then he initiated some highly touted reforms such as eliminating laws

---

*The full story of the racism of the police is grim reading in Lapchick's book *Broken Promises, Racism in American Sports* (1984.)

forbidding interracial marriages, giving black trade unions certain rights of collective bargaining, ending the reservation of certain jobs for whites, lifting the ban on multiracial political parties, and establishing black community councils with some responsibility for administration in black townships.

About this time, in 1980, Ronald Reagan was elected U.S. President. The Reagan policy of "constructive engagement," a phrase coined by Chester Crocker, the assistant secretary of state for Africa, was a disheartening innovation to most of Africa. Reagan called South Africa a "friendly country" in a television interview with Walter Cronkite. Crocker said in a speech that the United States "seeks to build a more constructive relationship with South Africa, one based on shared interests, persuasion, and improved communication."[2] In a private memo to Secretary of State Alexander Haig, he said, "We can work to end South Africa's polecat status in the world."

This shift in policy led to many new government actions. Additional honorary South African consulates were opened across the United States. The way was cleared for enriched uranium to be exported to South Africa. Restrictions against shipping some types of U.S. goods for police and military use were relaxed. South African naval officers were trained with the U.S. Coast Guard. Between 1981 and 1983 the United States did not vote favorably on even one of the 38 UN resolutions concerning apartheid.

The Reagan administration responded enthusiastically to Botha's reforms. Secretary of State George Shultz announced, "There has been more change in South Africa in the last four years than in the previous thirty." U.S. enthusiasm was hardly dampened by the brutality of the Botha government's attempt to dismantle the Crossroads shantytown near Cape Town. Nor was it cooled by the destabilization efforts of South Africa in backing the MNR in Mozambique and UNITA in Angola nor by the intransigence of the Botha government in forestalling UN-sponsored elections in Namibia. My former ACOA colleague Richard Leonard argues in his book *South Africa at War* (1983) that South Africa is already at war, having a defense force that has grown from half a million to more than a million during the Botha years.

Ironically it was a major "reform" instituted by Botha that opened the floodgates to a new, hitherto unequaled level of protest. Botha initiated a new constitution in 1984, under which he became president and two houses were added to Parliament for Indians and for Coloureds. The Coloured and Indian voters were displeased, however, as was clear when 80 percent boycotted elections, and the Africans, who were more than 70 percent of the population, were left out.

Some 600 organizations came together to oppose the new constitution and set up the most formidable legal opposition yet seen, the United Democratic Front (UDF). A continual series of protests began. Eight hundred thousand students boycotted their classrooms; a two-day general strike was organized in Johannesburg; a confrontation between police and people erupted in the Crossroads shantytown; 19 were killed as the police tried to break up a Cape funeral procession on the 25th anniversary of the Sharpeville Massacre; UDF leaders were arrested and banned. More than a thousand people were killed in a little more than a year.

New South African personalities were thrust into prominence: Bishop Desmond Tutu, who won the Nobel Peace Prize in 1984; the Rev. Allan Boesak, a founder of the UDF and president of the World Alliance of Reformed Churches; and the Rev. Beyers Naudé, the founder of the banned Christian Institute and general secretary of the South African Council of Churches. Anyone who watched televison or read newspapers became acquainted with the imprisoned nationalist Nelson Mandela.

One of the most remarkable developments of this period was the resurgence of the ANC. Although banned for more than 25 years, its mention forbidden in the media or in public speech, it achieved a new level of popularity partly as a result of its continued campaign of sabotage. The ANC is credited with 150 armed attacks between 1977 and 1982. Most daring were a series of attacks on plants for the conversion of coal to oil in the Johannesburg area in June 1980. Damage was estimated at $7.3 million. In 1983 the nature of the attacks began to change when the explosion of a car bomb outside the South African Airforce and Military Intelligence offices in Pretoria killed 18 people and wounded 190, including some Africans. Although these attacks were not expected to overthrow the government, they spoke eloquently for the presence of the ANC.

The ANC also had the advantage of being identified with Mandela, who gained in stature through his years of incarceration. Winnie Mandela, his wife, became a headline personality in her own right.

The opposition inside South Africa inspired renewed activity internationally on a much larger scale and with sustained pressure. U.S. action escalated. Initiated by the black lobby organization TransAfrica, the Free South Africa movement caught the imagination of U.S. opponents of apartheid. Beginning on Thanksgiving Day 1984, with arrests at the South African embassy in Washington, thousands of Americans volunteered for arrest at South African consulates throughout the country. Many were prominent citizens—members of Congress; stars of films and television; church, labor, and civil rights leaders. Being arrested became the thing to do. Even the police and judges usually cooperated with the protest. When I was arrested in a group outside the South African consulate in New York, charges were dropped in court and the judge made sympathetic remarks.

Other campaigns intensified too. The divestiture effort gathered great momentum. Even Chase Manhattan Bank, against which we had campaigned for so long, announced it was ending loans to South Africa in 1985. Since the start of the divestiture campaign, 17 states, 60 cities, and 9 countries had ended their South African investment to the tune of $5 billion. Eighty-five colleges and universities had partially or totally done so for a total of more than $500 million.

The pressure of events in South Africa and the United States, especially in Congress, made the Reagan administration listen. To forestall stiffer measures in Congress, in September 1985 Reagan banned the sale of

computers to the South African government, barred most loans, proposed a ban on the import of Krugerrands, and prohibited most exports of nuclear technology. A year later, sanctions became law over his veto. The fact is, however, that by the mid-1980s neither the deepening insurrection in South Africa nor the mounting international protest had been sufficient to shake the apartheid regime into making fundamental change.

THE CONTINUING STRUGGLE IN NAMIBIA

SWAPO of the 1980s was a far cry from the fledgling organization I had first encountered more than 20 years earlier. Now it had a well-run office near the UN with a permanent staff headed by Theo Ben Gurirab. Other offices, almost embassies, were in Dar es Salaam, Lusaka, London, and Luanda. An army of several thousand carried on a guerrilla conflict against a South African army in Namibia more than 10 times its size. SWAPO president Sam Nujoma was received almost like a head of state as he traveled around Africa.

Many leaders I had known since their student days had developed an impressive assurance and maturity. Our relationship had, of course, changed. In Lusaka I dined at a restaurant with Hage Geingob, who directed the UN-sponsored Namibia Institute, and Hidipo Hamutenya, who was on the teaching staff. Both had studied in the United States. As we ended our pleasant evening of discussion and reminiscing, I reached for the bill, expecting to pay as in the past, but Geingob beat me to it. He laughed as he said, "No, George. Things are not as they used to be. You are our guest this time." I knew that at the institute the SWAPO staff members gave 50 percent of their modest salary to the organization; I appreciated Geingob's gesture.

The UN Institute for Namibia was a major project with which SWAPO

Sam Nujoma, president of SWAPO, at the celebration of the 10th anniversary of Zambian independence, Lusaka, Zambia, October 1974.

was closely related. By the early 1980s more than 400 young Namibians were taking a three-year course there to prepare for practical leadership in an independent country. The institute, which opened in 1976, was the brain child of Sean MacBride, UN commissioner for Namibia in New York. It was one of the better examples of UN aid to the former mandated territory.

The institute eventually had a staff of more than 60 from 15 different countries and a budget of about $4 million a year. The students were introduced to law, economics, history and political science, education, and agriculture. In 1983 about 90 percent of them were women, compared to 40 percent in 1981. Most of the young men were in Angola preparing for, or actually in, combat with South African forces. Four students with whom I talked on my 1983 trip were all in their third year. They expected to have a brief practical internship with the Yugoslav government and then be assigned to Angola, where 65 of the last graduating class of 80 were serving.

Another of SWAPO's major responsibilities was running refugee centers, chiefly in Zambia and Angola. In 1981 with my friend Irving Wolfe, I visited the largest one, in Kwanza Sul district of Angola, some 200 miles south of Luanda. The trip took us about four hours of a hair-raising ride with some SWAPO friends in two Mercedes, tearing along a narrow road, sometimes at 100 miles an hour.

Although the center, founded in 1978, was 1,000 miles north of the

Hage Geingob, director of the UN Institute for Namibia, at the institute,
Lusaka, Zambia, 1978.

Namibian border, the danger of South African attack was by no means
absent. Many of the refugees were survivors of the South African air and
land attack in 1978 on a similar refugee camp at Kassinga, about 150 miles
north of the border, in Angola, where more than 800 were killed, including children, and more than 400 wounded.

The Kwanza Sul camp, like Kassinga, had nothing military about it.
Here we were seeing the rank and file of SWAPO people, comrades in
resisting South African control of their country. The settlement, scattered
widely under huge trees on a high plateau in a coffee-growing area, was
delightfully cool. The majority of the 50,000 people, most of them young,
were living in tents. Large numbers continued to arrive from the south
every day. They were assigned to a particular sector of the camp depending
on whether they were mothers with babies, farmers or workers, or persons
receiving help at the health and education units.

I was impressed to see how the people adjusted to a rather difficult life.
There were 10,000 students, age 7 to 18, in the school program, super-
vised by 100 teachers, some of whom I had met before. One familiar-
looking young man greeted me by name. He was an Angolan agricultural
specialist assigned by the government to work in this area. He reminded
me that the ACOA had given him emergency aid 18 years earlier, which he
had never forgotten. How grateful I was for his expression of thanks!

The head doctor, with whom I had corresponded, was Namibian. Our
Africa Fund had sent medicines and supplies over the years. There were 3
other doctors, from Finland and Sweden, 14 nurses, and 70 student

nurses, dealing with such tropical diseases as malaria and intestinal problems.

The spirit of the people was inspiring. We arrived on the 21st anniversary of the founding of SWAPO, and the evening was given over to some of the most beautiful singing in natural harmony that I have ever heard. They sang SWAPO freedom songs, in which they expressed a longing to return home, condemned the evil of apartheid, praised their leader, Sam Nujoma, and committed themselves to continue the struggle until victory was won.

SOUTH AFRICA'S INTRANSIGENCE IN NAMIBIA

Nothing illustrates South Africa's determination to resist change more clearly than its continued efforts to frustrate Namibia's independence. When the independence of Angola and Mozambique was not quickly followed by Namibian independence, as many had hoped, the struggle became more bitter and intense. The United States during the Henry Kissinger years feared that leaders with Soviet sympathies would become more prominent, and this fear had activated a new level of U.S. involvement. Yet it seemed absurd to attribute Moscow alignment to SWAPO, which had earlier had good relations with the FNLA and later with UNITA. When South Africa first invaded Angola in 1975, I well remember how a SWAPO leader in Dar es Salaam told me that all cooperation with UNITA would end.

In 1976 the United States supported the UN Security Council in adopting Resolution 385 condemning South Africa's illegal occupation of Namibia, its growing military domination, and its oppressive rule and calling for elections under UN supervision and control leading to independence. South Africa, however, had embarked on its two-track policy, sponsoring moves to set up and control a de facto internal government based on apartheid but at the same time never saying absolutely no to the UN so that it could be acceptable to the international community. Its chief problem was that SWAPO's mass following would make the first objective difficult and the second impossible. Therefore, South Africa's more limited goal was to establish a credible internal government but at any cost to keep SWAPO out of power.

In 1975 South Africa had sponsored the Turnhalle Conference in Windhoek in an old gymnasium (*Turnhalle* in German). Delegates came from the 11 ethnic groups in Namibia, including whites. SWAPO, of course, did not participate both on principle and because no nonethnic political body could be represented. The delegates agreed to set up 11 separate regions and a National Assembly chosen by tribal association. They perpetuated themselves as a political coalition called the Democratic Turnhalle Alliance (DTA). In elections in December 1978, the DTA won 41 out of 50 seats, and the new legislature was transformed into a National Assembly. Real power was in the hands of South Africa's appointed administrator general, who could veto any measures or intervene at any time. The UN rejected the elections, as, of course, did SWAPO.

The UN had tried to forestall this development in 1977 through negotiation. The United States and the four other Western states on the Security Council, as a "contact group," held separate meetings with South Africa and SWAPO to thrash out an acceptable arrangement. The council revamped Resolution 385 into Resolution 435, calling now for UN-supervised elections, phased withdrawal of all but 1,500 South African troops confined to two bases, and formation of a UN Transitional Assistance Group (UNTAG) to police observance of the agreement. A special representative of the UN secretary general would administer the UN part of the responsibility.

Both South Africa and SWAPO had accepted Resolution 435, but South Africa never agreed to its implementation. It objected first to the monitoring role of the UN, then to the size of the UN force, and again to the UN's lack of impartiality, and then to the location of SWAPO bases and of South African forces in a demilitarized zone. In 1983 it dissolved the four-year-old National Assembly and assumed direct control of Namibia through its administrator general.

Obviously it would take more than UN resolutions for South Africa to agree to relinquish its control, for it was clear that in a UN-supervised election, SWAPO would win. Time and again the United States, Britain, and France vetoed international sanctions by the UN. Although SWAPO carried on a low-level guerrilla war against South African forces in Namibia, it was no match for its powerful adversary.

Discussions in Geneva under UN auspices in 1981 broke down when South Africa questioned the UN's impartiality. A conference hosted by Kenneth Kaunda in Lusaka in 1984 likewise ended quickly with no agreement. South Africa's final stall against implementing Resolution 435 was its refusal to withdraw its troops from Namibia until Cuban troops left Angola. But how could Cuban troops leave when South Africa was arming the UNITA military force bent on overthrowing the MPLA government? To make matters worse, the United States was giving aid to UNITA as well.

In the meantime the terrorism of the South African Defence Force, especially in northern Namibia, went on. I had some inkling of its methods through Bill Anderson, a young white South African draftee, who deserted from the army because he not only opposed South Africa domination of Namibia but was also appalled by its methods of torture. He came to public attention when his testimony about torture appeared in the *Manchester Guardian* in September 1976. In visits to the ACOA office, he also described it to me. He had heard the screams of Namibian suspects being tortured at a camp while a throng of soldiers looked on—electric shock on genitals, the head forcibly held in a pail full of water, kickings and beatings. His battalion had scoured the countryside to bring in any male over the age of puberty. For several weeks some 1,000 men and boys were tortured, of whom 40 were finally charged with terrorist offences.

Andimba Toivo ja-Toivo, secretary general of SWAPO, after his release from prison in 1984.

I gained another perspective on the conflict when I met Andimba Toivo ja Toivo after his sudden release from an unfinished 20-year prison term in March 1984. As I talked with him in New York, I could not overcome the feeling that I was meeting a legend. I had seen pictures of him in the 1960s but I would not have recognized him. Not only was he 20 years older, but he had lost hair, grown a full beard, and gained weight. His handshake was firm and his smile friendly. He gave the impression of strength. After serving 16 years in a maximum-security prison, he resisted the idea of sudden release. He wanted to know why he, and not all the other political prisoners, was being released. He did not wish to desert his comrades who were still behind bars. It took great persuasion from his family and fellow prisoners to convince him to return to Namibia. I had the feeling that he was still uneasy about his decision. The South African authorities probably released Toivo in the hope that he might challenge Nujoma as leader of SWAPO and thus cause a split. If so, the hope was in vain. Toivo certainly made it plain to me that he accepted Nujoma's leadership and was a loyal and committed nationalist. He felt he could do his part as secretary general of SWAPO.

CHAPTER TWENTY-FOUR

"You've Got to Take the Long View"

On a trip to Zimbabwe in 1983, I spent a stimulating three days with Garfield Todd, then a senator in Parliament. My son Steve and I drove with him from Harare to his home some 150 miles southwest near Zvishavani (formerly Shabani), where we enjoyed his hospitality and conversation. After just three years of independence, Zimbabwe was facing difficulties. A crippling drought had damaged crops. Corn was being imported, instead of, as in normal years, exported. Todd, like many other farmers, had had to slaughter a lot of the cattle on his ranch because there wasn't enough grass for them to feed on.

Furthermore, the antigovernment violence in Matabeleland, followed by an excessive reaction from government troops, strained the coalition government. Todd was deeply disappointed in the breakdown of the Patriotic Front, for he had always been close to Joshua Nkomo. Although he felt positive about advances in education and health care, the problems faced by the new country seemed overwhelming. When I asked him where Zimbabwe was going, he responded thoughtfully, "You've got to take the long view," and he looked confidently to the future.

I liked Todd's response and I have tried to adopt such a long view myself as I look at the African continent from the vantage point of the many years I have spent following, and sometimes being a part of, events there. It is not easy to be objective. Nor is it possible to avoid genuine dismay over many developments in the newly independent countries.

SOME SOBERING REALITIES

One must face immediate and depressing realities in Africa. The continent has 29 of the 34 poorest countries in the world. Per capita income is about $365 a year, the lowest in the world for one continent. Before independence, Africa produced most of its own food, but now almost all countries are net importers. Furthermore, the trend is not too hopeful. Africa's population has increased something over 3 percent a year, twice the rate of the rest of the world. In the 1950s the population was a little over 200 million. It now approaches half a billion.

Natural circumstances make rapid development in many countries next to impossible. Often economic advancement depends on only one or two resources. When the world price of copper went down, Zambia, for example, was faced with catastrophe because 80 percent of its export earnings were tied to copper. Ghana's economy was severely affected when the price of cocoa fell; while income from exports dropped dramatically, consumer prices increased 70 percent.

Leaders have sometimes used bad judgment. For example, Kwame Nkrumah was undoubtedly the greatest figure in the rise of nationalism in modern Africa, yet he made early administrative mistakes in Ghana. Millions were spent on nonessential new construction—a conference center, a super highway that ran only a few miles, a new state house. Foreign exchange reserves dropped from a surplus of almost $500 million at independence to a debt of more than $1 billion in 1964.

The continent as a whole was burdened with a $78 billion debt in the mid-1980s, far above the amount brought in by exports, and the deficits will doubtless continue to soar. Agricultural production is likely to continue to decline. The ecological system, especially the advance of the Sahara, is likely to deteriorate further. Population is likely to continue its phenomenal growth.

Economic problems are compounded by problems of political instability. In the 30 years since Ghana's independence there have been more than 70 coups in Africa. Only three African leaders have voluntarily given up office. Refugees in Africa number close to half the world's 9 million. General health statistics are not too good. Infant mortality is about 137 for every 1,000 births, the highest in the world, with an average of one and a third doctors for every 10,000 people. Life expectancy is only 49 years. Although education has advanced, some two thirds of the people are still illiterate.

Statistics, of course, are only impersonal figures. More emotionally disturbing are the images of poverty, disease, and hunger I have seen in many parts of Africa. Deeply troubling to me personally have been individual acts of violence against leaders I have known and worked with. I think of the murder of Sylvanus Olympio in a military coup shortly after he became president of Togo, or the assassination of Tom Mboya in downtown Nairobi in an act inspired by tribal conflict, or the slow death of Diallo Telli (the first ambassador of the Republic of Guinea to the UN and the first secretary general of the OAU) by neglect and starvation in a prison in Sékou Touré's Guinea. The death of these men and others like them are tragic in quite a different sense from the martyrdom of Amilcar Cabral, Eduardo Mondlane, Patrice Lumumba, Jason Moyo, and many others, who were killed in the line of duty in the liberation struggle.

I followed with horror the mass killings wrought by Idi Amin in Uganda, some of whose victims I had known. And the genocide in Burundi, when some 200,000 Hutus were killed by the ruling Tutsis in perhaps the worst outbreak of demonic tribalism in recent times in Africa.

The problems have outweighed the simple successes in the early years of transition to independence. Some people in Africa have developed a kind of cynicism, when dreams of an uncomplicated independence of peace and plenty have been dashed. Others have adopted an attitude of objective noninvolvement, like that of a detached specialist who is fascinated by what is happening but has no sense that it is a part of his own life experience. I reject this attitude for myself. I still feel like a partisan in the struggle for justice and equality in Africa, even if I am removed from day-to-day events.

A PERSPECTIVE

By taking the long view of Africa, looking at its past and its future, as well as its present, I try to put developments in some perspective.

It must be recognized that the long period of foreign occupation from which Africa is just emerging has contributed heavily to its present problems. The colonial powers were devoted to serving their own best interests. They were not essentially seeking progress for the people of the lands they controlled. Whatever advances were made were quite incidental.

For example, the European scramble for Africa confused an already complex situation of 2,000 ethnic groups, most of them speaking their own languages, by dividing individual groups by artificial political boundaries. Transportation and communication systems were set up to suit European political and economic interests rather than African ones. Furthermore, the colonizers, who benefited from a one-crop economy, did not try to broaden the economic base of their colonies or give the people skills that would allow them alternative occupations to subsistence farming. The peoples of the more than 50, mostly small, states of modern Africa have had to gain technical and political experience in the midst of struggle.

Finally, colonialism was accompanied by racism. To be sure, not all regions of the continent have suffered equally from it. Racism has generally been most severe in areas settled by a relatively large number of whites, notably South Africa and Southern Rhodesia. But even in areas with an enlightened colonial policy, a benevolent paternalism was the best that the system could produce.

Africa has suffered also from natural calamities, particularly drought. The highly publicized famines of the last few years are testimony to the devastation wrought by natural forces.

To recognize these conditions is not to overlook the responsibility of the people and leaders in some countries for corruption or for excesses in the struggle for power. For example, it is sad that in a country as potentially rich as Zaire, per capita income is only $127 a year, and 50 percent of the budget goes to service a $5 billion debt. Yet its ruler, Mobutu Sese Seko, is reputed to be one of the wealthiest men in the world.

When I was briefly hitchhiking in Dar es Salaam in the early 1980s, I was picked up by a young Briton. This was a trying time for Tanzania, when gasoline was $5.00 a gallon, people formed long lines to fill small receptacles with very costly fuel to burn in their homes, and the government was spending 60 percent of its foreign exchange for oil. The country also was suffering from years of drought. The East African Community

(Tanzania, Uganda, and Kenya) was breaking up, and Tanzania had borrowed money to end Uganda's aggression. Nyerere's plan for self-reliance and a non-Marxist, African socialism wasn't working as it had been hoped. My driver, who had been in the country for only a short time, commented, "Independence was a mistake. These people don't know how to run anything." This was the attitude of many skeptics.

Africans generally take a different view. Tom Mboya put it straightforwardly in a speech he made at the AAPC in 1958: "Civilized or not civilized, ignorant or illiterate, rich or poor, we the African states deserve a government of our own choice. Let us make our own mistakes, but let us take comfort that they are our own mistakes."

I do not believe that colonialism is the embodiment of all evil. And it is quite obvious that independence will not lead immediately to stability, peace, and plenty. Nevertheless, I strongly believe that without banishing colonialism, tackling the long-term problems would be an impossibility. This period of the anticolonial struggle has been a prerequisite for African development. I also believe that if the struggle had not achieved independence in most countries, Africa would be engulfed by expanding guerrilla warfare, from which no creative solutions could emerge. With independence, at least attention can be focused on the right issues.

In taking the long view there are some heartening facts to bear in mind. It is amazing to me that despite the history of the slave trade, the decades of colonial domination, and in some countries the years of guerrilla conflict, there has been no campaign in independent Africa against the white presence. There is no antiwhite persecution. More whites are on the continent now than during the colonial era. Even in Zimbabwe, where the struggle for independence was most bitter and was most clearly in terms of a black-white confrontation, the white presence has stabilized, and the wholesale exodus has halted. There are twice as many British in Kenya as at the time of independence. The French in Africa are five times more numerous than before 1960. (This may be a questionable boon, since many of them are in the Ivory Coast, where they almost monopolize the civil service and have significant control in trade and investment.)

Even in South Africa, where the struggle against white domination promises to be the cruelest and most protracted, the military head of the ANC expresses the fear that the young people inside the country will stop listening to the ANC's nonracialism and seek only revenge.

Another heartening fact, given the way in which the modern map of Africa was drawn by the European powers, is that on the whole the independent countries have accepted the boundaries they have inherited from the colonial era. This principle was adopted at the second OAU conference in 1964 with only Somalia and Morocco in opposition. The conflict between Somalia and Ethiopia in the Ogaden, the war between Libya and Chad, and the struggle in Western Sahara are among the few exceptions. Tribal conflict has not been wiped out; yet considering the multiplicity of ethnic groups, languages, and traditions among the African peoples, the efforts to minimize conflict have been outstanding. There have been tragedies such as Burundi and Rwanda. Yet there are the remarkable examples of the 120 ethnic groups in Tanzania living in harmony, and the peace between the peoples of Nigeria following their civil war.

The efforts to wipe out illiteracy have a long way to go. Yet in a country as poor as Tanzania the literacy rate has risen from about 20 percent to 80 percent since independence. In Zimbabwe, in the first five years of independence, school enrollment rose from 800,000 to 2.7 million.

An important asset for the distant future is Africa's supply of untapped resources, the largest in the world, although they are not evenly distributed. They include oil, gold, diamonds, water power, cobalt, phosphates, and coal.

Perhaps there is no more encouraging development than the intensification of the struggle to uproot apartheid in South Africa, because until that is accomplished, Africa's progress will be crippled. Despite sanctions, which most African states support, virtually all of them trade with South Africa. Despite South Africa's policy of destabilizing its neighbors (especially Angola and Mozambique), two thirds of their foreign trade is with South Africa. Nothing indicates more clearly South Africa's economic power. Through the Southern Africa Development Coordination Conference (SADCC), nine states have joined forces to limit their dependence on South Africa. But it takes time to construct the roads and railroads that by-pass South Africa by going through Angola, Mozambique, and Tanzania, and they must be maintained. South Africa's destabilization efforts frustrate these procedures. Nothing major can be done without the successful resolution of the struggle within South Africa itself.

Obviously ending that struggle will not be easy. A people such as the Afrikaners, who perceive their power and privilege being challenged, do not give up gracefully. Ian Smith and his white supporters in Rhodesia fought stubbornly, and in the final 13 years of the conflict, 25,000 lives were lost. That struggle was a skirmish compared to the probable devastation and destruction to come in South Africa. Africa's travail cannot all be laid at the doorstep of South Africa, of course; but the problems of the southern African states will be eased immensely when the struggle against apartheid is no longer necessary.

The Afrikaner government hasn't really started to fight yet. It has not had to because the whites have not really begun to suffer. I believe, however, that events will force the government to make changes. Serious urban violence has not yet spread to the white community, but unless the conflict is diffused, such violence will spread, as it did in Algeria. The black trade union movement has only begun to show evidence of its potential. Protest actions, spontaneous and planned, legal and extralegal, can be expected to increase. Sabotage is bound to become more commonplace as black demand for citizenship rights becomes even more urgent. The white exodus from South Africa, so far only a trickle, will become a torrent as violence increases.

When the white government feels desperate enough, it will think of countless options to stave off granting citizenship to all the people. It could propose an array of reforms such as a fourth House of Parliament for Africans but without real power; a National Convention excluding the ANC but including elements forswearing all violence; relinquishing control of Namibia. It might be willing to participate in international conferences on solutions to the South African conflict. It might even propose partitioning the country to allow for a "white homeland" reduced in size but well endowed. Or it might begin promoting black collaborators who emphasize tribal allegiance. If Gatsha Buthelezi does not allow himself to be so used, the white government will find others who will. It will still resist granting citizenship rights that could put an African nationalist government in power. But change there will be. "No one can stop the rain."

In the meantime, those outside will take serious action toward South Africa only as events inside compel them to do so. International economic pressure in the form of sanctions and divestiture will not by themselves bring down the apartheid system and its government. What they will do is give the South African government the unmistakable message that the people of the world will no longer support the injustice of apartheid and help force the white government to recognize the necessity of change.

ANTIDOTE TO CYNICISM

Any tendency I might have toward cynicism is tempered by the memory of the innumerable acts of African generosity and goodwill that I have experienced over the years. For example, during our 1980 trip to observe the Zimbabwe elections, when our car was stuck in deep mud in a rural area, some nearby villagers helped us pull it out. Then they brought a pan full of deliciously ripe mangos, which we ate together with great enjoyment, the sweet juice dripping off our faces and hands. One of the Zimbabweans remarked with a laugh, "This is African communism. We share what we have."

Or I recall the pain I suffered on my 1962 hiking expedition with rebels in Angola when I stubbed my toe hard on a rock hidden in the tall grass. I thought my toe was broken. That night in camp it was painfully swollen, and the next morning it was no better, but we had to move on. For a while I hobbled slowly, trying to keep up. Then one of my Angolan companions, not much larger than I was, insisted on carrying me on his back. I demurred, but he persisted. So for a short time I rode piggy-back. I think he would have carried me all day, but I could not stand the idea, so I hobbled on, footsore but strengthened by his act of solidarity.

Garfield Todd told me about one of his prison experiences during the Ian Smith days. He was segregated from the African prisoners and allowed only a half hour of exercise a day, which he had to take alone. His cell door had only a small peephole. One day as the Africans were exercising in the yard outside, he heard a voice through the peephole, "Are you all right, sir?" "Yes, I'm all right,: he replied. Then several black fingers were thrust through the hole. Todd grasped them in a moment of shared fellowship. He never knew who the African was, but he could not forget this act of friendship.

Perhaps some will say I am being sentimental. A few acts of human kindness do not mean that the problems of Africa are going to disappear. That is true, but such actions are an antidote to cynicism and strengthen one's faith in the future.

As I look back on the years of struggle and change in Africa from the 1950s into the 1980s, I have the overwhelming realization that I have been greatly privileged to have lived through this era. The period of the 1950s and early 1960s was certainly the honeymoon phase of the struggle for freedom, the time of greatest unity and uncomplicated enthusiasm. Everything seemed possible. Many people believed that freedom would come soon and a much better day would dawn.

That things weren't all that simple soon became clear. Should one therefore conclude that it was better for Africa to be on the threshold of freedom than to cross into that difficult status where countries have to take a large share of responsibility for their own mistakes? I do not think so. Every period of history has its significance. We should be grateful for high moments of unity and optimism no matter what may follow.

Should one embrace a cynicism and look with scorn on a continent wracked by poverty, famine, and strife? I do not believe so. "You've got to take the long view." Who knows what the situation may be a hundred years from now?

A phrase that was popular especially during the liberation struggle in Mozambique is both good politics and good theology: *a luta continua* ("the struggle continues"). The struggle for a better person, a better life, a better country, and a better world never ends. Perhaps the moment of greatest freedom is found as we engage in the struggle to achieve it. And that moment is always with us.

Notes

CHAPTER 2

1. Daniel Malan, quoted in South African Press Association dispatch, 30 January 1952.
2. Flag Boshielo, quoted in National Action Committee for the Defiance Campaign, Bulletin No. 2, July 1952.
3. Ibid.
4. Charles E. Allen to Fosdick, 6 November 1952.
5. Albert J. Lutuli, *Let My People Go* (London: Collins, 1962), Appendix.

CHAPTER 3

1. John Gunther, *Inside Africa* (New York: Harper & Brothers, 1953).

CHAPTER 5

1. *New York Times Magazine,* 18 December 1960.
2. Richard M. Nixon, quoted in *New York Times,* 7 April 1957.

CHAPTER 7

1. Jackie Robinson, weekly column in *New York Post,* 11 September 1959.

CHAPTER 8

1. John Wesley Jones to Houser, 2 November 1956.
2. Laurent Schwartz, quoted in *Le Monde,* 20 March 1958.
3. *Le Monde,* 20 March 1958.
4. Charles de Gaulle, quoted in *A Savage War of Peace* by Alistair Horne (New York: Penguin Books, 1979).

CHAPTER 9

1. Winston Churchill, quoted in *Kenneth Kaunda of Zambia* by Fergus Mac-Pherson (New York: Oxford University Press, 1974), 16.
2. Sir Roy Welensky, quoted in ibid., 114.
3. Joshuo Nkomo, written in 1959, in *Africa South,* quoted in *Crisis in Rhodesia* by Nathan Shamuyarira (London: Trinity Press, 1965), 50.
4. Hastings K. Banda, quoted in *Kenneth Kaunda of Zambia* by Fergus MacPherson (New York: Oxford University Press, 1974), 267.
5. Kenneth Kaunda, quoted in ibid., 60.
6. Welensky, quoted in ibid., 59.
7. Godfrey Huggins, quoted in ibid., 52.

8. George Loft to Houser, 17 March 1959.
9. Philip Stoddard to Houser, 10 November 1959.
10. Ibid.
11. Banda, quoted in *Time*, 5 January 1959, 34.
12. Kaunda, quoted in *Kenneth Kaunda of Zambia* by Fergus MacPherson (New York: Oxford University Press, 1974), 296.
13. John Gaunt, quoted in ibid., 300.
14. Kaunda, Houser's notes of May 1960 press conference.

CHAPTER 11

1. Anthony Sampson, *The Treason Cage* (London: Heinemann, 1958), 38.
2. Albert J. Lutuli, quoted in "Treason in South Africa," by George Houser, *Christian Century*, 6 March 1957.
3. Erwin Griswold, statement at ACOA conference, New York, 30 September 1958.
4. Ibid.
5. Griswold, article in *London Times*, 25 September 1958.
6. Griswold's notes to Houser, 14 August 1958.
7. Sampson, *The Treason Cage*, 5.
8. Lutuli, *Let My People Go* (London: Collins, 1962), 172.
9. Humphrey Tyler, article in *Africa Today*, May 1960.
10. Patrick Duncan, article in *Africa Today*, April 1960.
11. Ibid.
12. Ambrose Reeves, quoted in *The International Impact of the South African Struggle for Liberation* by George M. Houser (New York: UN Centre Against Apartheid, 1982).

CHAPTER 12

1. Moise Tshombe, quoted from an official government report on the conference.
2. Patrice Lumumba, ibid.
3. Thomas Kanza, *Conflict in the Congo* (Harmondsworth, Middlesex, England: Penguin Books, 1972), 84.
4. Lumumba, quoted in ibid., 161.
5. Kanza, *Conflict in the Congo*, 119.
6. Madeleine G. Kalb, *The Congo Cables* (New York: Macmillan Publishing Co., 1982), 233.
7. Ad in the *New York Times*, 14 December 1961. It called for U.S. recognition of Tshombe as the legitimate spokesman for Katanga.
8. Humphrey to Houser, 6 April 1962.
9. David Martin to Houser, undated, sent January 1963.

CHAPTER 13

1. A.J. Venter, *The Terror Fighters* (Cape Town: Purnell and Sons, 1969).
2. Arthur M. Schlesinger, Jr., *A Thousand Days: John Kennedy in the White House* (Boston: Houghton-Mifflin Co., 1965), 562.
3. Fulton Lewis, Jr., *New York Mirror*, 19 August 1961.

4. Gilchrist to Houser, August 1962.
5. Venter, *The Terror Fighters*, 84.
6. *Johannesburg Star*, 25 July 1970.
7. Gilchrist to Houser, 25 August 1964.
8. Venter, *The Terror Fighters*, 29.
9. Douglas Wheeler, "The Portuguese Army in Angola," *Journal of Modern African Studies*, 1969, 425–439.
10. UN Document A/109/L, 842, 20, February 1973, "Angola," working paper of the Secretariat for Decolonization Committee.
11. Reported in August 1972 in *Angola in Arms*, an MPLA publication.
12. The source of this information was *Angola 1966–67*, issued by the Friederich Ebert Foundation in Bonn.

CHAPTER 14

1. Mondlane later wrote of this in detail in his book *The Struggle for Independence* (Harmondsworth, England: Penguin Books Ltd., 1969).
2. 10 December 1969.

CHAPTER 15

1. House Committee on Foreign Affairs, Subcommittee on Africa, Hearings, 26 February 1970.
2. Ibid.
3. Amilcar Cabral, quoted in *Armed Struggle in Africa*, by Gerard Chaliand (New York: Monthly Review Press, 1969), 50.
4. Cabral, quoted in United Nations, *The United Nations and Southern Africa*, Bulletin No. 11, August 1972.
5. Cabral, Subcommittee on Africa, Hearings.

CHAPTER 16

1. Joshua Nkomo, quoted in *Crisis in Rhodesia* by Nathan Shamuyarira (London: Trinity Press, 1965), 77.
2. Paul Moorcraft, *A Short Thousand Years* (Salisbury, Rhodesia: Galaxie Press, 1980).
3. Ian Smith, quoted in *Rhodesia to Zimbabwe: A Chronology* (New York: Africa Fund, 1976).
4. *New York Times*, 27 January 1972.
5. 12 December 1966.

CHAPTER 17

1. *London Daily Express*, 1 July 1968.
2. Jannie de Wet, quoted in *Namibia* by Colin Winter (Grand Rapids, Mich.: Wiliam B. Eerdmans Publishing Co., 1977), 117.
3. Ibid., 130.

CHAPTER 18

1. 8 August 1962.
2. 14 November 1964.

3. Quoted in *Steve Biko, Black Consciousness in South Africa,* ed. Millard Arnold (New York: Random House, 1978), introduction.

4. Donald Woods, *Biko* (New York: Vintage Press, 1979).

5. *New York Post,* 12 December 1965.

CHAPTER 19

1. Quoted by Richard Tholin in "Angola: Confrontation or Cooperation," *Christian Century,* 13 May 1981.

2. James Brooke, "Angola's Economic Problems," *New York Times,* 31 January 1986.

CHAPTER 21

1. United Nations, Official records of the General Assembly, 30th Session, ch. 3, sec. B, para. 202, 11.

CHAPTER 22

1. *New York Times,* 3 December 1977.

CHAPTER 23

1. Ian Smith, quoted in *Rhodesia to Zimbabwe: A Chronology* (New York: Africa Fund, 1976).

2. Ibid.

Index

AAPC (All African People's Conference), 68, 69–75 passim, 77, 79, 86, 89, 91, 96, 103, 108, 136, 137, 151, 164, 199, 363; at Accra, African commonwealth, 74, 128; nonalignment, 73; nonviolence, 73, 74; at Tunis, Algerian war for independence, 74; Belgian Congo independence, 75; and Holden Roberto, 80; protest against French atomic tests, 75

AAPSO (Afro-Asian People's Solidarity Organization), 71, 72, 73

ABAKO (Association pour la Sauvegarde de la Culture et des Intérêts des Bakongo), 136, 137, 151

Abbas, Ferhat, 93

Abdullah, Madjid, 311

Accra, 26, 27, 29, 69, 72, 78, 79, 86, 151, 247

ACOA (American Committee on Africa), 61, 99; and Algerian Struggle, 91–98 passim; and Angola, 152, 160–62, 173, 290–92; beginning, 63–66; and Black Power, 265–67; and Central African Federation, 99, 100, 105; and CIA, 170–73, 189, 292; and Congo crisis, 146, 147; and Declaration of Conscience, 146, 147; and Guinea-Bissau and PAIGC, 205, 212; and Holden Roberto, 79; and Mozambique and FRELIMO, 148, 187, 190, 299; and South Africa, 257, 264, 267–68, 346, 350–51; and Southern Rhodesia and Zimbabwe, 231, 232, 235, 242, 333, 336, 337, 343; and South West Africa and Namibia, 112, 248, 251, 252, 255, 358; and Tom Mboya, 81–86 passim; and treason trial, 117, 120, 123; and Western Sahara, 311

Action Group, 33, 34

Adamafio, Tawiah, 28

Addis Ababa, 164, 165, 254, 258

Adesola, B.F., 34

Ad Hoc Committee for the Development of an Independent South West Africa, 244

Adoula, Cyrille, 135, 146, 147, 159, 163, 164, 168, 188

AEMO (African Elected Members Organization), 84

AFL-CIO, 72, 83, 128

Africa Bureau (London), 81, 108, 111, 129

Africa Defense and Aid Fund, 85, 127

Africa Freedom Day, 86, 98, 100, 105, 108, 127, 152, 269

Africa Fund, 194, 278, 356

Africa Today, 64, 66, 86–87, 125, 270, 272

African-American Institute, 72

African-American Students Foundation, 88, 89

African Heritage Studies Association, 267

African Studies Association, 266

African University of the North, 346

Africanists, 125, 126

Afrikaans language, 11, 245, 345

Afrikaners, 10, 11, 49, 110, 273, 364

AFSAR (Americans for South African Resistance), 12, 16, 17, 19, 20, 21

Air Transport Agreement, 276

Ait Ahmed, Hocine, 93, 94, 95, 98

Aldeamentos, 170, 185, 194, 195, 299

Algeria, 2, 60, 70, 91–98, 127, 156, 159, 163, 164, 169, 183, 184, 190, 206, 207, 211, 224; and Western Sahara, 309–15 passim, 321, 322, 324, 325

Algiers, 94, 190, 303, 309, 315, 316, 320, 321

Ali, Ahmed, 309, 312, 314, 315, 316, 319, 322

Ali, Muhammad, 275, 277n

ALIAZO (Alliance des Ressortissants de Zombo), 80, 159n

All African Trade Union Federation, 75, 89

ALN (Armée de Liberation Nationale), 94

ralization Service (Sponono case), 276; Marshall aid, 36; Mission to UN, 17, 269; and Mozambique, 189, 307–8; National Security Study Memorandum (39), 234, 269. Policy toward Africa: Carter, 349–50; Eisenhower, 268; Kennedy, 268–69; Nixon, 269; Reagan, 352; summary, 268–69. Portugal, assistance to, 197; and Scott, Michael, 111; Senate Foreign Relations Committee (Subcommittee on Africa), 87, 95, 267, 291; and South Africa: aircraft carrier visitation, 277; economic investment in, 270; satellite tracking stations, 277; Sharpeville massacre, 127; South African Airways, 276–77; and Southern Rhodesia, 229; Byrd Amendment, 234–35; sanctions, 229, 332, 334–35, 336; and South West Africa (Namibia), 252, 253–54, 357–58; State Department, 17, 268: advisory Council on African Affairs, 268, 269; Bureau of African Affairs, 60, 160, 268; Supreme Court, 244; and Tambo visa, 129; and UNITA, 358; and Western Sahara, 319, 320, 322–25
United Steelworkers, 83
Unity Movement, 56
University Christian Movement, 270
University of Natal Medical School, 262
University of South Africa, 103, 231
University of Witwatersrand, 126, 179, 346
Unlawful Organizations Act (Southern Rhodesia), 223
UPA (União das Populações de Angola), 76, 79, 80, 150–51, 152, 172; peasant revolt, 153, 155–59, 161
UPC (Union des Populations Camerounaises) 35, 36
UPNA (União das Populaçoẽs do Norte de Angola), 76, 77, 79
Urban League, 68, 69, 261
U.S. Olympic Committee, 275
Ushewokunze, Herbert, 333, 336
USSR (Soviet Union), 60, 71, 75, 134; and Angola, 284, 288, 290, 292, 294, 329; and Congo crisis, 140–46 passim, 175, 189, 190, 207, 215,

219, 232, 259, 268; and Mozambique, 307–8; and Soviet-Chinese cold war, 188, 307, 332, 357; and Western Sahara, 313, 319

Valentim, Jorge, 285
Van Riebeck Day, 11
Venter, A.J., 154, 165, 168, 249
Verwoerd, Henrik, 65, 260
Victoria Falls Conference, 327, 328
Vieira, João Bernardo (Nino), 205, 206, 215
Vorster, John (B. Johannes), 198, 232, 240, 246, 254, 274, 289, 326, 329, 334, 345, 351

Waldheim, Kurt, 254
Walvis Bay, 254
Ward, Harry, 6
Washington Office on Africa, 235
Weischoff, Heinrich, 145
Weiss, Peter, 63, 64, 74, 140, 251, 267
Welensky, Roy, 101
Western Powers, 141, 148–49, 168, 188, 209, 212, 215, 348
Western Sahara, 2, 280, 309–25, 363. *See also* Spanish Sahara
Whipping Post Law, 19
Whistlefield Farm, 238
Whitehead, Edgar, 102, 223
Whyte, Quintin, 18
Wilaya, 312, 313
Wilkins, Roy, 87, 266n
Williams, Franklin, 351
Williams, G. Mennen, 144, 145, 268
Wilson, Harold, 228, 229, 233
Windhoek, 113–16 passim, 245, 246, 254, 357
Winter, Colin, 254, 255
Woods, Donald, 262, 347n
World Alliance of Reformed Churches, 353
World Council of Churches, 261, 331
World Federation of Trade Unions, 89
World Lutheran Federation, 241
World War II, 221, 243
Worthy, Bill, 12

Ya Otto, John, 250, 254
Yazid, M'Hammed, 92, 94, 95, 98
Yoruba, 32, 33, 34